More praise for David Siegel's books

I have my own web design company, and everything was going along just fine until I read your book. It changed my life!!!!

  – Bob R

I am a web designer, like you, who builds third generation sites. I use a lot of your tips and, because of your book and your sites, I have won various awards. I am looking forward to your new book.

  – Nick G

I've sent a number of potential clients off to read *Creating Killer Web Sites,* so they would be better educated when they were ready to hire a designer. Showing examples of good design in my copy of the book has helped many clients appreciate the necessity of working with a multi-talented design firm. Siegel's books are timeless because he talks about the issues we face as designers.

  – Eric P

I have bought your book (it's now out in German). Then I read it. The only thing I have to mention: Please more!!!!

  – Ralph W

I am a young graphic designer in Iceland, working at an advertising agency, and my job for the next months will be to make web sites for our customers. Finding your pages was a vital thing for me before I start putting something on the www. I am hoping that my work will improve the quality and design of the www and as yours, encourage others to think about what they are doing.

  – Anna K

I bought your book ye[...] amount of the informa[...] I'm building for my bu[...]

  – KE

I used to whip a poor-to-fair web page out in about an hour. Now, thanks to you, I spend about 20 hours on each page. Then I trash it and start over. I should have a site ready for your perusal in about ten years or so.

  – Jim H

Your tips have changed my life. Though my home page may never make the High Five, my work is a thousand-fold improved by my having read and absorbed this great resource you've provided to all writers and designers in our emerging community. As my partners and I go on making web pages, we will continue to pass along the concepts you have freely given. I am sure we will not be alone.

  – Jeffrey Z

Your book truly left me speechless. I am so glad to see a complete shift in web design philosophy.

  – Matthew H

I like your book a great deal. So does my boss. After reading my copy, she went out and bought her own. It has helped me refine my work.

  – John M

I enjoyed your book, *Creating Killer Web Sites,* and refer to it constantly in my work as a graphic designer for new media. Thanks so much for your creative insights and willingness to share your knowledge and expertise with others in the field.

  – Elizabeth G

secrets of successful web sites

secrets of

successful
web sites

PROJECT

MANAGEMENT

ON THE

WORLD WIDE

WEB

Hayden
Books

David Siegel

SECRETS OF SUCCESSFUL WEB SITES

Trademark Acknowledgments
All terms mentioned in this book that are known to be trademarks or services marks have been appropriately capitalized. Hayden Books cannot attest to the accuracy of this information. Use of a term in this book should not be regarded as affecting the validity of any trademark or service mark.

Library of Congress Catalog Number: 97-72148
ISBN: 1-56830-382-3

Printed in the United States of America
1   2   3   4   5   6   7   8   9   0

HAYDEN BOOKS

The staff of Hayden Books is committed to bringing you the best computer books. What our readers think of Hayden is important to our ability to serve our customers. If you have any comments, no matter how great or how small, we'd appreciate your taking the time to send us a note.

You can reach Hayden Books at the following:
Hayden Books
201 West 103rd Street
Indianapolis, IN 46290
317-581-3833

Email addresses
America Online: Hayden Bks
Internet: hayden@hayden.com
Visit the Hayden Books Web site at http:// www.hayden.com

President:	*Richard Swadley*
Associate Publisher:	*John Pierce*
Publishing Manager:	*Laurie Petrycki*
Managing Editor:	*Lisa Wilson*
Product Marketing Manager:	*Kim Margolius*
Development Editors:	*Robyn Holtzman,*
	Steve Mulder
Publishing Coordinator:	*Karen Williams*
Manufacturing Coordintor:	*Brook Farling*
Production Team:	*Trina Brown*
Indexer:	*Joe Long*

Table of Contents

Part I

Part II

ACKNOWLEDGMENTS

This book was a big project, and perhaps a typical one. Many people contributed enthusiastically to this book, which really came together in the last few weeks before the deadline. We first owe thanks to all the people in companies around the world who contributed tips, stories, and images, and especially to the people who took the time to be interviewed for the case studies in Part I.

The core team of this book deserves my deepest thanks: Amy Wilkins and Joe Silva stuck with it when the going got tough, and they pulled rabbits out of hats to keep things on schedule. Amy is really the co-author of this book – she interviewed over 30 sets of people and wrote the 15 chapters of Part I, getting all parties' approval and writing the interesting, page-turning stories. Joe put the book together, dealing patiently with changes, last-minute additions, and countless system crashes. His quality standards are reflected in the design and execution of every page. If we had taken more of our own advice, perhaps he wouldn't have had to spend so many nights sleeping on my floor. Thank you Joe and Amy.

The volunteers were fantastic. Kathy Lester provided the statistics you see in the graphs and charts. Her eagerness and thoroughness were a big boost. Tammy Dunaye was instrumental in assembling the Astro Cabs material, both here and on the book site.

Project manager Brian Bouldrey and illustrator Geoff Gladden came in and battened down the hatches when things were flying about. Brian's keen eye and willingness to go the distance kept us on track, while his sense of humor kept us from taking ourselves too seriously. Geoff dug in and cranked out almost every graphic in the book, often when I needed him to draw it first so I could change it later. Editor Louise Galindo held me to a higher level of quality. Wow. Thanks for cutting out all those one-word sentences. David D. Cullinan produced many of the infographics, while Jennifer H. Wolf proofed the text with an expert eye. Betsy Vobach helped with research. Amy board-proofed the entire book and caught all the misteaks. Purvi Shah designed the brilliant cover and contributed to several chapters. Philippe Augy did illustrations for Chapter 8. Doug Millison contributed branding and editorial content. Christina Cheney and Gino Lee developed much of the methodology and contributed to almost every chapter.

Several people worked hard to review the manuscript. Kirsteen Barton, Mary Tesluk, Todd Landfried, Carol Porter, and Chris Dunlap all read the "confused, unstructured" drafts and helped straighten me out.

The people at Hayden are fearless and wonderful to work with. Special thanks go to our publisher, John Pierce, who believes in us even when we're late. Robyn Holtzman, our development editor, stood steadfast during the storms of manuscripts, and Steve Mulder paved the way for a smooth landing. The rest of the development and marketing team deserves thanks for their energy and trust.

The case studies could not have been produced without the tireless assistance of our contacts at the web-development companies. They scheduled interviews, provided assets, coordinated contact with their clients, organized photo shoots, and kept track of all our miscellaneous requests. Special thanks go to Julie Beeler of Second Story, Jay Wolff at Big Hand, Dalin Clark at The Designory, David Burden at Margeotes | Fertitta + Partners, Ramona d'Viola and David Burk at Clear Ink, Patrice Paul at Headland Digital Media, Olivia Ongpin at fabric8, Andrew Sather and Bernie DeChant at Adjacency, Scott Rosenberg at Salon, Stefan Fieldings-Isaacs at Art & Science, Larry Asher at Worker Bees and Marla Katz at Brazil Design Group, Lizi Obolensky and Anders Brownworth at Evantide Graphical, Matt Owens at methodfive, Anita Corona at Ikonic, Christina Cheney at Studio Verso, Emlyn Christenberry, Yancey Hall, and Laura Miller at National Geographic, and Ellen Pack at Women's Wire.

I would like to thank our friends at Adobe Systems, especially George Jardine, who provided us with the software to produce this book. Thanks also to the many project managers and web developers in San Francisco who participated in our surveys, meetings, and requests for information.

I add a special thank-you to Kathryn Polk, whose willingness to speak out resulted in Amy Wilkins coming to work for Verso Editions. Amy is a godsend. Finally, I want to thank the people at Studio Verso, not only for their help and contributions but also for their support of this book. With their encouragement and insight, we were able to give the developer community our hard-won secrets. I thank them for making this book possible.

CREDITS

Development Editor:	Robyn Holtzman, Steve Mulder
Case Studies Writer:	Amy Wilkins
Copy Editors:	Brian Bouldrey, Louise Galindo
Proofreaders:	Amy Wilkins, Jennifer H. Wolf
Readers:	Kirsteen Barton, Christina Cheney, Chris Dunlap, Todd Landfried, Carol Porter, Mary Tesluk
Researchers:	Tammy Dunaye, Katherine Lester, Elizabeth W. Vobach
Project Manager:	Brian Bouldrey
Layout/design:	Joe Silva
Cover Design:	Purvi Shah
Illustrators:	Philippe Augy, David D. Cullinan, Geoff Gladden
Book Site Team:	Joe Silva, Amy Wilkins

"We aim above the mark to hit the mark."

– Ralph Waldo Emerson

To be part of a web-development team is to be
on the cutting edge of a new work paradigm,
one that mingles fluidity and community
with the construction of something vast, something complex,
something we can never see in its entirety –
yet something people around the world will explore
the moment we turn it on.

This book is dedicated to the people who stick with it,
who take the challenge of building web sites seriously
and pursue perfection in the middle of the night.

Introduction

INTRODUCTION

All around the world, people are going to meetings, sitting down with people they've never met — people who have been working together for months, not years — trying to figure out what to do about their web site. They know they must put together a team to make their site or make it better, while pleasing upper management and the webmasters, brandmasters, and contentmasters who must make it all happen. Above all, they must please the visitors who come to the site. And they must do all of this in less than three months.

This book is about web-based project management — if you're not doing it now, you will be soon. Although the book focuses on the process of web development, both from the client's and the contractor's point of view, much of it applies to projects of any kind. If you have a distributed team of people working on a project, or a client more than a block away, you will want to consider using the Web to run your project. This book will show you how.

While it's mostly written for contractors, I hope what I've written proves more than useful to clients. I want clients to peek into our world, so they can see what contractors go through to build their sites. I want designers to read it for the client stories, to see what a web-development project is like from the other side of the contract.

Contracting in cyberspace is not too different from contracting in almost any other field. This book is not meant to replace the excellent literature on project management or starting your own business. It is meant to show how contracting in cyberspace differs from other kinds of contracting. While the foundations of design methodology are universal, the details as we implement them on the Web make all the difference.

ABOUT THE BOOK

This book is divided into two parts: there are 15 case studies in Part I and 11 chapters on methodology in Part II. It begins with the case studies, because the real world of site design consists of people solving hard problems, occasionally throwing the rulebook out the window. I hope you'll get to know the people who made these sites, because they are more than construction workers. They are multi-talented entrepreneurs who became addicted to surfing and found their passion in making web sites.

The second part is my way of documenting the processes we at Studio Verso have developed for designing sites, while adding a number of other points of view from others in the field. I hope to provide a kind of road map – or at least a start – to getting your project done right the first time and on good terms with the rest of the team.

This is the story of hundreds of people who take these issues – our issues – seriously. And in these pages you can share with them the heartaches and the triumphs of planning, building, and launching some of the world's best web sites.

THE BOOK SITE

The *book site* is **www.secretsites.com.** It contains legal documents, templates, a bookstore, and other resources mentioned herein. It is a free resource available to all. Please visit the site for more tips, updates, and to participate in a live email discussion of online project-management issues.

Part I

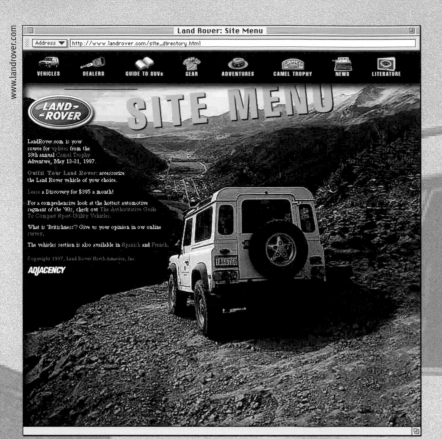

Purpose of the site

Land Rover recognized the Web as an opportunity to promote its brand, to provide consumers with vehicle and dealer information, and to provide an online presence that equaled or eclipsed more heavily funded, highly competitive automotive sites.

The players

Andrew Sather,
Creative Director

Bernie DeChant,
Art Director

Anton Prastowo,
Production Manager

Carlo Calica,
Technical Director

How the developer was chosen

Adjacency created a demo site to accompany their proposal. Land Rover recognized that Adjacency already seemed to understand the product's marketing position and realized Adjacency was a company of Land Rover aficionados.

Launch date

April 8, 1996

"Hmm," said Land Rover North America merchandising director Chris Marchand.

Then silence.

This young, smart web-development company has a well-developed process, from pursuing the business of brands it likes to delivering creative, innovative, professional web sites.

IT WASN'T quite the enthusiastic response Andrew Sather, creative director and CEO at Adjacency, had anticipated. This was the first creative review for the Land Rover site, and it wasn't even face-to-face – Andrew had to narrate the presentation over the phone. Talking even more rapidly than usual, he described what made their design complement Land Rover's marketing campaign. Adjacency had faithfully recreated the classic British look of the brochures, he explained; the script initial caps visually reinforced the current marketing message that Land Rover embodied good taste. After all, Andrew believed Land Rover's primary concern was that

Adjacency not cheapen the brand with this site.

On the other end of the line, Chris searched for a way to respond diplomatically. There was a reason he'd chosen this group of 20-something designers based in Madison, Wisconsin, to create the Land Rover site, and it wasn't because they could

This brochure promotes the elegant, classic side of Land Rover.

dutifully adapt Land Rover's existing print aesthetic to the Web. But how could he tell Andrew he'd missed the mark? After a moment, Chris said, "I think you need to take more creative freedom. Think more about the rugged, off-road side of Land Rover. Think about a younger audience, one who wants to do things, to get out there." He paused for Andrew's reaction.

"Totally!" agreed Andrew, far from hurt. He'd wanted all along to create a more rugged design. Andrew now felt his team had been authorized to create a site about "guts, fun, adventure, off-road driving – challenging one's mettle." To him, that's what Land Rover was about. Everyone at Adjacency was pleased with the new direction, even though it meant they had to create a new design from scratch.

Enthusiasm gets clients

Andrew likes Land Rovers. A lot. He doesn't understand how anyone could *not* like Land Rovers. He explains, "They're neat. They're cool. There was one in the Louvre." Since

Adjacency wants to create web sites for products it likes – the best brands on the planet.

he and his coworkers liked the brand, Andrew decided to pursue the business – Adjacency's philosophy is to design sites for the products they love. But they doubted enthusiasm alone would convince the prestigious automobile manufacturer to contract a web site out to five designers and programmers in their early twenties in Madison, Wisconsin. They had to prove they could do it. So they scanned photos from brochures and made a demo Land Rover web site.

They had good timing. Land Rover's marketing department had been thinking tentatively about doing a site but hadn't yet gotten around to talking to any web developers when they received Adjacency's proposal. Chris was impressed that they'd spent the time putting the demo together before getting the business, and also noticed that they seemed to understand the product and marketing position. "In the traditional marketing applications that I deal with, be it brochures or showroom point of sale, there always seems to be a learning curve when dealing with other companies, and Adjacency didn't seem to have it. We soon found out upon speaking with Andrew that they were Land Rover enthusiasts, that they loved the product so much they had learned about it prior to getting in contact with us," says Chris.

Chris was interested enough to invite Andrew to Land Rover's offices

in Lanham, Maryland, to make a presentation. In a meeting with a few people in an office, Andrew showed them the online demo and other sites they had done, but more important, he demonstrated a love for their product and an understanding of their business. He described his ideas for the site and how it would stand apart from the competition. "He showed us some of the differences in a sense of the traditional web site and what he would like Land Rover to do. And how we could differentiate our site from others," says Chris.

> "You need to determine the goals of the site: what are you trying to do? What information are you trying to promote? Whom are you addressing, and how do you think they'll interact with a web site? How do you *want* them to interact with the web site?"
>
> **– Andrew Sather**

Chris, just 31 himself, liked the idea of hiring this young company to do the site. "I felt it was important not to have the site designed by a traditional ad agency and to get someone who was a little different. I don't want a design by 40-year-olds for 40-somethings, I'd rather have a design by 20-somethings for everybody." In this meeting, Chris emphasized to Andrew that the site had to represent and uphold the brand, saying, "We want a really good site. We want it user-friendly, and we want it to represent Land Rover."

Two weeks later, Chris made his decision, and he and Andrew worked out a proposal, including a schedule. However, some of Land Rover's executives didn't understand the Web as a marketing medium and were

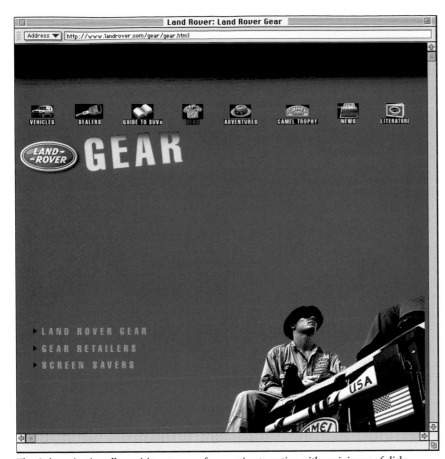

The site's navigation allows visitors to move from section to section with a minimum of clicks.

worked on the other sites ("We never emulate. We always improve upon," says Andrew) and which sites they felt were boring or simply didn't understand the medium.

Studying Land Rover's branding materials and marketing strategy helped Adjacency understand the Land Rover audience. "You learn so much in the phase where you're researching and distilling the brand that you really know who's using the products. And if your web company is worth its weight in whatever the cliché is, you're going to know who's using the Web, and you're going to be able to see pretty easily where those two groups overlap," says Andrew. Many of the people who work at Land Rover fit into the typical Land Rover buyer profile, which helped Adjacency get a sense of the real people behind the marketing statistics. Andrew describes them as "younger-to-middle-aged professionals who are techno-savvy, have fun on the weekends, and really, really like their Land Rovers!"

Adjacency came up with a navigation scheme with no frames, just section icons across the top of the page. Once in the section, users must go back to the main section page before entering another section. Andrew describes the site navigation: "The ultimate goal is to limit the number of superfluous screens between the user and the information they desire. We also try to let people know how deep they are in the site. We encourage them to return to the main menu page for that section. We want to debrief people on their way out of a section, reinforce that

reluctant to sign off on the project. "We had to coach them as to why we needed to do the site, why we thought it was cost effective to do a web site, and the importance to the brand," says Chris. One convincing point was that the Land Rover web site would put the company on equal footing with the much larger budgeted Jeeps and Toyotas of automotive sites. "While our advertising budget will never approach theirs, that doesn't matter as much on the Web. The most popular sites have become that way through word-of-mouth, not an advertising budget. This point definitely persuaded our CFO to sign off on the project," says Chris. Land Rover signed and Adjacency got to work.

Web sites that dominate

Andrew and Bernie DeChant, Adjacency's art director, threw themselves into the new project with gusto. They'd requested all of Land Rover's collateral and branding materials and spent time researching past marketing campaigns and the positioning of the product.

Andrew's strategic philosophy behind making web sites is deceptively simple. "Ultimately a web site is like any other product. You need to compete for customers. Therefore, you need to create a web site that totally eclipses the competition." And since the competition was on-line or would be online, Adjacency researched the auto industry sites thoroughly. They delivered an auto-motive-site report to Land Rover, listing the features that they felt

"The vehicles themselves are all the inspiration you need."
From left: Discovery, Defender 90.

architecture, and let them know where they are. We sometimes have a tendency to be a very weak, nervous species, and we often require reinforcement and benchmarks."

Rugged. Gutsy. Grrr.

Andrew half-jokingly insists they used a method-acting approach to come up with the new Land Rover site. "If I were a Land Rover web site, what would I look like? What would I say?" They used rugged earthtones, big all-caps headers that run like tire-treads across the page, and photos of the vehicles in action, rather than in the showroom. "The vehicles themselves are all the inspiration you need," says Andrew. "Look at them! Have you seen a Defender 90 or a Discovery? They're big, they're tough, they're brilliant." His enthusiasm for their design sometimes transcends language. "They're ... grrr," he growls in a exaggerated, affected approximation of a British accent. When Chris saw the final, rugged design, he knew they'd nailed it.

For creative reviews, they laid out the site-menu page and the first page under each icon, and Chris approved the layout based on that. "And then they went and did the formatting of all the information under each heading and I was okay with that. I did some minor reformatting from a text standpoint," says Chris. He liked the creative work and didn't have many modifications.

But Andrew's main technical production epiphany (which he claims happened during the "plodding" or "festering" stage) was using self-adjusting full-bleed images. When he presented the look to Land Rover for approval, he had no idea how they were going to do it, only that it was the look he wanted. "In other words, we had rather brashly committed to solving a production problem that at the time was an impossibility," says Andrew. Fortunately, Adjacency found a solution. By making the whole page a table, they were able to align images so that they always appeared in the corner of the browser window, even if the user adjusted the window size. At the time of the site's launch, a Range Rover appeared to be driving up a mountainside in the corner of the screen. While making this design trick work challenged Adjacency, since different browsers reacted to it in different ways, seeing the innovative design on the site was reward enough. "Grrr," says Andrew, satisfied.

Killer Java applets, kick-ass trips, and Land Rovers sold

Andrew insists the production and launch aspects of the Land Rover site don't make a good story – he prefers to talk about Land Rover's commitment to post-launch site development.

Making the self-adjusting full-bleed images work in different browsers challenged Adjacency's production staff.

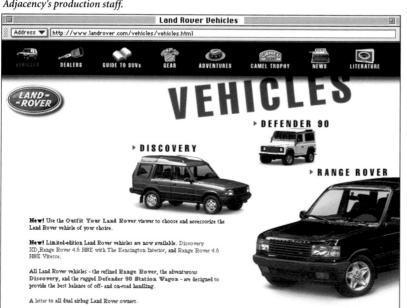

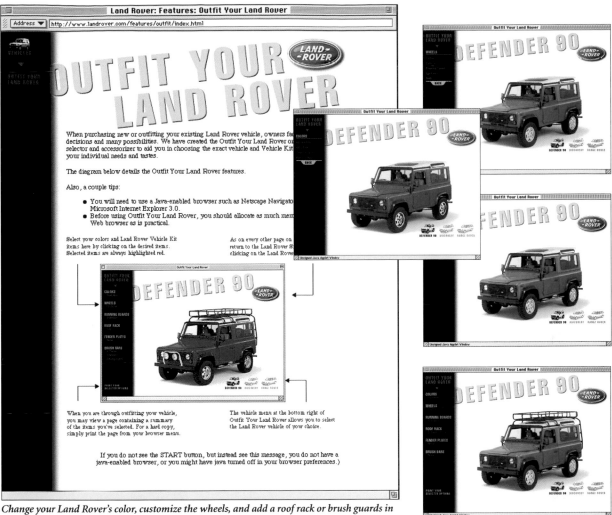

When purchasing new or outfitting your existing Land Rover vehicle, owners face decisions and many possibilities. We have created the Outfit Your Land Rover on selector and accessorizer to aid you in choosing the exact vehicle and Vehicle Kit your individual needs and tastes.

The diagram below details the Outfit Your Land Rover features.

Also, a couple tips:

- You will need to use a Java-enabled browser such as Netscape Navigato Microsoft Internet Explorer 3.0.
- Before using Outfit Your Land Rover, you should allocate as much mem Web browser as is practical.

Select your colors and Land Rover Vehicle Kit items here by clicking on the desired items. Selected items are always highlighted red.

As on every other page on return to the Land Rover S clicking on the Land Rover

When you are through outfitting your vehicle, you may view a page containing a summary of the items you've selected. For a hard copy, simply print the page from your browser menu.

The vehicle menu at the bottom right of Outfit Your Land Rover allows you to select the Land Rover vehicle of your choice.

If you do not see the START button, but instead see this message, you do not have a java-enabled browser, or you might have java turned off in your browser preferences.)

Change your Land Rover's color, customize the wheels, and add a roof rack or brush guards in this JavaScripted section of the site.

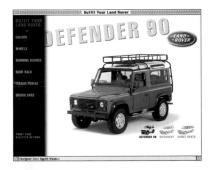

And Land Rover is committed. Unlike many clients, who after launch don't want to pay for more development, Chris Marchand believes fervently that Land Rover can't be complacent when it comes to putting new content on line. "Creating new and different items should be rule number one in web-site management," he says.

After launch, Adjacency developed a JavaScripted section of the site called Outfit Your Land Rover, which allows users to select a car, color it, and accessorize it from rims to rails on the fly, just by clicking the mouse. Land Rovers have vehicle-kit items, or accessories, as well as lots of colors. Andrew says, "All of those things

combined let you experiment with an insane number of combinations. So we had to create an engine that would allow you to select from all those options without selecting vehicle-kit items that overlapped or contradicted each other." Land Rover delivered three vehicles to Adjacency to photograph, complete with a Land Rover employee to affix and remove kit items.

While they were working on the applet, Andrew remembers reading an article in *Forbes* by Mac evangelist Guy Kawasaki hyping the BMW site, praising its use of CGI scripts to select cars' colors and accessories – users click submit, and the script sends a new page with the custom BMW. Adjacency realized then how much more sophisticated their design and execution of the concept was. "I thought, 'Wow, I guess Outfit Your Land Rover is pretty revolutionary,'"

Andrew and Bernie found plenty of photo opportunities on their six-day off-road trip.

says Andrew. "Outfit Your Land Rover is a pretty remarkable WYSIWYG version of that whole customize-your-vehicle idea."

Land Rover's and Adjacency's commitment to creating new site content also resulted in a chance for Andrew and Bernie to get off-road driving time in the vehicles they love. Chris was in charge of an owner trip Land Rover was putting on, where Land Rover owners drive with professional instructors through some of America's most beautiful and challenging off-road scenery. Chris thought this would be a good opportunity to get Adjacency more involved with the product by getting them actual drive time and to reaffirm the enthusiasm they have for the product. It would also be a great

opportunity to get spectacular images of the Land Rovers following the Great Divide on the site. "It's almost a Land Rover tradition in a sense of getting our vendors involved with the product. It reduces the learning curve, and the enthusiasm you can't put a price on," says Chris. Andrew and Bernie got to spend six days on the trip with six vehicles, Land Rover owners, and professional drivers. When they recall the trip, they interrupt each other enthusiastically.

Andrew describes the trip as just

one more of the personal sacrifices he's willingly made for the company he founded. "The worst part was staying at the four- and five-star hotels every night. It was rough."

Bernie adds, "And the night we had to camp out …"

"Oh, that was horrible!"

"And the heated tent …" adds Bernie.

Besides chafing under the hardships of roughing it, Andrew and Bernie took extensive photographs and videos, which they used to update imagery on the site, create

an online trip log, and develop a free, down-loadable screensaver for the site's Gear section.

Success stories have furthered Chris' resolve to keep the site fresh and constantly evolving. Since the site's debut, Land Rover, initially reluctant to put up a site, found that their owners and the online community intersect. Land Rover owners are more likely to be wired and more likely to have personal computers and subscribe to an online service than the owners of virtually any other brand. And of those Land Rover owners who are online, nearly half of them used the web site to determine which model they were going to buy and research their purchase.

But a more important success story goes beyond marketing reports – it demonstrates that the site is truly

influencing buyers. While working on a project at another client's company, Andrew heard from one of the client's employees whose parents bought a Land Rover Discovery after learning about it on Land Rover's web site. According to the employee, his

Downloadable screen savers provide fans with a slide show of Land Rover action shots.

A full-service new media design firm, **Adjacency, Inc.** conceptualizes, strategizes, designs, produces, hosts, maintains, and grows high-profile, award-winning web sites for some of the best-known brands on the planet. Adjacency's work for clients like Land Rover, Specialized bikes, Rollerblade, Patagonia, PowerBar, Lufthansa, Motorola and NeXT/Apple Computer has won them publicity and awards from Fast Company, *Web Week, Advertising Age, Brand Week, USA Today,* CNET, TV.com, Yahoo!, and David Siegel's High Five, as well as inclusion in *Print Magazine's* and *Graphis* magazine's respective upcoming design annuals.

Founded just two years ago in a basement in Madison, Wisconsin, by 23-year-old graphic design, creative writing, and art-history student Andrew Sather, Adjacency won its first accounts – Patagonia (Ventura, CA) and Specialized (Morgan Hill, CA) – in 1995. In early 1997, Andrew and the three other principles moved the entire company to San Francisco and set up shop at the foot of sunny Potrero Hill. Today, Adjacency consists of 17 people – designers, programmers, marketing strategists, production artists, and content developers. The average age at Adjacency is 23. Most people commute to work on Specialized bikes, Rollerblades, and decal-plastered skateboards. Adjacency is living proof that a diverse group of super-talented, passionate American 20-somethings with a handful of computers, big dreams, and un-slacker-like work ethics can take on the big guys ... and take over the world.

2020 17th St., San Francisco, CA 94103-5130 415-487-4520 www.adj.com

parents had never really considered buying a Land Rover until they saw the site. No one in their immediate group of friends and neighbors owned one. They had no idea the company made any vehicle other than the larger, more expensive Range Rover. Once they got a sense of the brand through the site, they went to the dealer and shortly

thereafter purchased their Land Rover.

If people are buying Land Rover products because of the site, it has met – perhaps exceeded – expectations. As the president of Land Rover said, "Our web site does as fine a job representing our brand as anything we have done."

As Andrew would say, "Grrr."

"Guts, fun, adventure, off-road driving, challenging one's mettle" – the site shows the rugged side of Land Rover.

How the developer was chosen

Worker Bees already handled Pyramid's advertising account and proposed the web site idea to the client.

The players

Larry Asher
Marla Katz
Ben Myers
Derrick Chasan

Launch date

January 17, 1996

Six months into the project, and they were still making revisions. Revisions to revisions.

Focus

what you will learn

How the quest for a perfect site (plus difficulties working with other contractors) kept this site from launching for months

LARRY ASHER of ad agency Worker Bees and Marla Katz of Brazil Design Group had been working on the Pyramid Breweries site since April, and now it was November. After months of revisions, Larry was starting to feel less than receptive to the client's suggestions.

Larry, Pyramid's PR representative Ben Myers, and vice president of marketing Derrick Chasan went down the weekly list, reviewing changes made and new content. These meetings usually stretched to three or four hours due to the level of detail of each review.

Well into the third hour of one meeting, as Larry was jotting down client revisions as fast as he could

write, the discussion bogged down over the particular shade of red Larry and Marla were proposing for a button bar (that was ultimately never used). Larry remembers hearing the words, "Can't you guys do any better than that?" Then something snapped.

Although he'd never walked out of a client meeting before, Larry had had enough. He walked out of the room, leaving Ben and Derrick holding their review checklists, wondering just what had gone wrong.

Getting the bid

As part of his ad agency, Worker Bees, creative director Larry Asher met regularly with Pyramid on

25

Worker Bees recommends knowing the answers to these questions before beginning work on a web site:

Goals and Requirements

1. What are the primary goals of the site?
   (to sell? inform? engage? inquire? visits?)

2. Who are the primary and secondary audiences?
   (describe interests, needs, skills)

3. Audience capabilities (browser, speed, savvy)?

4. Will site attract different audiences? Who?
   What areas are of interest to each?

5. What's the number one take-away
   (key message to convey content)?

6. Existing content or new?

7. What existing images are available?

8. Do we need to capture user data?
   What do we need to know? Why?

9. What new technologies will be used?
   What, specifically, and why?

10. What information will change?
    How often and how extensively?

Tone and Personality

11. What's the product position?
    (Include client's personality vs. competitors)

12. Describe product as if a person
    (serious? weird? young? reliable?).

13. What areas benefit from updating? Who?
    What areas are of interest to each?

14. Strengths and weaknesses (compare to competition)

15. When does the site need to be complete?

16. Who will approve our work? What actions require approval?

17. Who will host and maintain site?

18. How long is the site intended to last?

19. What is the budget?

20. What are the plans to promote the site?
    Who is responsible for this activity?

---

advertising projects. He'd recently run across some demographics that convinced him microbrew drinkers could be targeted through the Web – web users were in the same age, income, and interest areas. Larry started bringing up the Web in the client meetings. "Have you seen RedHook's site?" he'd ask George Hancock, Pyramid's president and CEO. "You could easily do better than that." Week after week, he tried a new angle, but when Pyramid didn't seem interested, he let the subject drop.

After a few months passed, he tried again. "You know," he said, "I bet it's been two whole months since I said the word 'Internet.'" George had a surprise for Larry. Not only had he been thinking about doing a web site, he'd signed a contract with the Speakeasy Internet Café, a new hosting service, to do a site. Worker Bees wasn't going to get to do the site after all.

Pyramid had just built a new brew pub in Seattle. One way to add value to the bars and pubs that sold its beer might be to have a computer hooked up to the Internet in the foyer of the brew pub. A web site could identify the bars and pubs where customers could purchase Pyramid products. Speakeasy had happened to make a pitch to Pyramid at a convenient time, and George signed.

Larry wasn't giving up the project that easily, feeling he could still be involved in the design. George, no surfer himself, hadn't seen Speakeasy's design work. Larry printed out some sample pages, saying, "Their expertise seems to be in the technical aspects of the Web, not design, copywriting, and marketing communications. You can decide what's preferable. They play with the medium

Meet real brewmasters speaking with RealAudio.

instead of persuade with the medium." George agreed that the design should reflect Worker Bees' marketing expertise, so he gave Larry the go-ahead to do a feasibility document. Speakeasy would still be involved as a host and would help with CGI scripts and HTML.

The honeymoon

Larry and his Worker Bees partner, Ann Rhodes, felt it would make a lot of sense to bring in a designer with serious web experience, so they invited Marla Katz of the Brazil Design Group to head up the art direction and web development for the site. Together Larry and Marla worked on the feasibility study, providing concept, a schematic (or architecture), and creative for approval, along with a budget. They came up with a written page describing the angle, which was how to bring the human side into web interaction.

Out on the patio of the Pyramid Brew pub, Larry and Marla presented their concept. The site used the metaphor of the newly opened Seattle facility: the pub, the brewery, the loading dock, the office, and even the restrooms. Beer drinking was a social act, but web surfing was not – this site would have sociability. They

wanted to humanize the site with illustrations of people, RealAudio of people speaking, a chat area of people talking, a pub cam of people drinking, and more. Larry had done some branding work for Pyramid recently and knew Pyramid wanted to position themselves as a cutting-edge, alternative, hip, human company. Larry and Marla had mastered the details of what would make this site special and were prepared to sell their thoroughly researched idea to George.

Marla and Larry like George a lot, describing him as a true hands-off manager. While he has experience in the computer industry as a systems

analyst, at the time he didn't have much first-hand experience with the Web and expected Larry and Marla to bring in a great project without much client involvement. Says Larry, "You're all caught up in the details and the fine points of how you're going to execute something and he's like, 'Yes. Well. Fine. Go on.' He expects you to bring in a great finished product, and he's not going to hand-hold it. Ultimately, these are the best clients."

George approved the creative and the schematic, but there was some negotiating over the budget. They'd already gone far beyond the idea of listing the bars that served Pyramid.

No pub is complete without the conversation.

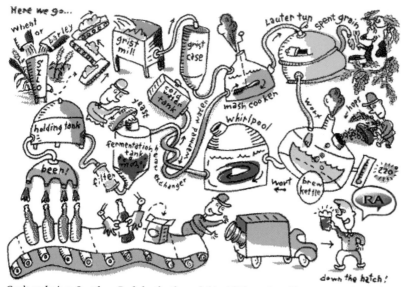

Can't make it to Seattle or Berkeley for the real thing? Take a virtual brewery tour instead.

Ben had other things to do for Pyramid besides write this copy – a lot of other things. He became so busy that the site copy had to take low priority. Ironically, one of the things on hold the longest was the reason George had agreed to do the site in the first place: the list of bars and restaurants serving microbrews. Ben was relying on the salesforce to supply the data, and they never did. The upshot was that throughout the site, little pieces were missing. The whole project didn't drag to a halt, but at the same time, there was no closure. No section was completely done – every section had holes in it.

George wasn't willing to devote huge amounts of marketing dollars to a project that might not generate any return. The suggested CU-SeeMe feature and pub cam had to be cut.

But they had the go-ahead to proceed, and started by storyboarding the site. Once that was approved, Larry started copywriting, and Marla did some sample screens by drawing roughs, scanning them, putting them together in Photoshop, and fooling around with different looks. They bounced ideas off each other, enjoying working together as a team. But soon other people would join the project, and with more people, more complications to the project.

Adding a content provider

When Pyramid hired Ben Myers in April to do public relations, he brought a lot of copywriting skills to the table. He also knew a lot about beer. It made sense to use Ben's in-house skills as a way of saving money, rather than paying Larry to write the copy. Larry was concerned at the prospect of bringing in another

writer, worried the tone and voice of the copy might not be consistent.

Ben Myers is a personable, charming guy. He enjoys his work, he enjoys writing, and he enjoys beer. A natural choice to write everything relating to beer care and beer product knowledge, he wrote copy for the virtual brewery tour, food tips, the first part of the short story contest, and the 22 beer backgrounders. As he turned in assignments, it soon became apparent that Ben, like any good writer, could adopt the tone Larry had set. The problem was getting the copy.

Every short-story (or case-study) writer feels like this at some point.

Working with another contractor

While getting copy could be frustrating, it was nothing compared with what Marla was going through trying

Pyramid prepares food with panache.

to get the Speakeasy Internet Café to appreciate the importance of layout and design. While Marla did the majority of HTML, Speakeasy was to fill in on revisions to the code, as well as any CGI programming. She would post her pages to a file on their server, and they would move them to the real site.

This relationship of designer and programmer required a lot of back-and-forth. But Speakeasy was a start-up. For the first month, they were in the process of building their café, and sawdust was flying around the workstations. But then that hectic period ended, and there was no improvement. They were new at dealing with agencies. The programmer was unreachable by phone, wouldn't answer email, or when he did, would respond with, "I don't understand." Marla repeatedly requested that he call her if he had a question, but he never would. Communication nearly ground to a halt.

The two groups were approaching the project from vastly different perspectives. Speakeasy provided simple web-design services and had satisfied customers. They'd never dealt with the level of detailed marketing, copywriting, and design issues with which Marla was concerned. She wanted to make certain items in HTML tables line up. She wanted to control how copy would break. She wanted to add leading to paragraphs. Speakeasy couldn't understand why she was so "difficult," since their other clients were happy. Marla found that phrases like "flush left" and "leading" didn't mean anything to them, and had to make her requests in more technical terms, saying "align left" instead of "left justify" or "insert a <P> tag" instead of "add leading."

Marla was also concerned about Speakeasy's method of meeting deadlines. As check-in meetings with Pyramid became weekly, Marla and Larry would sit up until midnight the night before, reviewing the work on the site to make sure it was done to spec. But it was hard to check work that hadn't been done and wouldn't get done until they walked into the

meeting the next day, or to check work that was being done while they were in the meeting. They'd have to keep hitting reload.

Describing the problem to Pyramid was like explaining something in a foreign language, because they needed to understand the technical nuances to understand the complaint. Finally, Larry and Marla requested Pyramid to tell Speakeasy to be more responsive. But that request was too nebulous to be enforced. Marla says, "We were an indirect client, but we weren't a client. We were just somebody bugging them. We weren't paying their bills." Says Larry, "It's a really inefficient way of getting work done."

Revisions to revisions (reprise)

In September, Pyramid hired a new vice president of marketing, Derrick Chasan. Unlike George, Derrick has a hands-on management style. The team began meeting weekly, for three- or four-hour stretches at a time. Every page of the site was reviewed, and there would be changes to every page.

The lack of closure to sections of the site dragged the meetings out. Since no page was really finished, they'd have to review every page for the status of the minor tweaks requested last week. Meeting notes show that most of the proceedings were simply check-ins. For example,

Marla worked closely with Speakeasy to get the dart game working correctly.

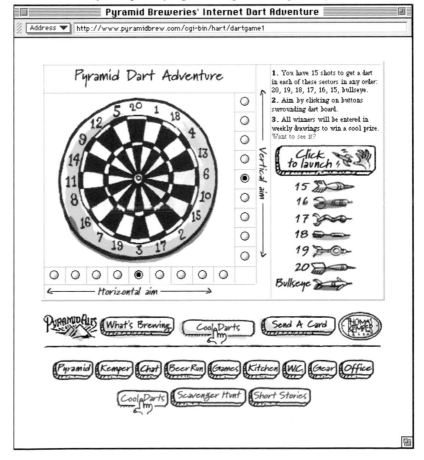

Illustrations were closely reviewed and tweaked until they were just right.

notes from November read: "Web site doorway: Revised illustration direction approved. Proceed with final illustration. Splash page: Basic look of the illustration color approved. Make dart board, glasses, tabs, and shirts more prominent and proceed with final illustration." And from December: "Animation needs to be sped up by dropping size and colors. Marla will investigate options, taking care not to minimize how inviting the central illustration needs to be." It was all standard stuff.

The trouble was, these meetings had been going on for months. And this level of detailed tweak was happening to everything. Larry remembers the brew kettle illustrations going through round after round. "They were approved, and then they weren't approved, and first the Pyramid one was on the left, then the Pyramid one was in the center, and then the Pyramid one was on the left again – now put this logo in, now take this logo off, now make it the logo color, now make it black and white." Pyramid didn't understand how much time and detail work was involved in making changes to graphics or HTML code. For example, changing the color or size of a graphic was sometimes so problematic that they'd have to rescan the illustration. By trying to be accommodating, Larry and Marla found themselves doing detail-intensive work over and over again.

Tension built. By the time Larry walked out of the client meeting, he'd been frustrated for weeks. "I'm not prone to bursts of anger," he says. "Rather than expressing my growing dissatisfaction, I was probably saving it all up. I think this was the first signal they had of, 'Oh, are we doing something wrong?'"

Ben admits that micromanagement was a problem. "It got down to the point where we were looking at things like colors, and why can't the colors for this bar be the Pyramid colors and the colors for this bar be the Thomas Kemper colors." Because there was no hard deadline (as in a print campaign when things go to production and can no longer be changed), they found it hard to stop making changes. "The Web's so mutable that it was easy to keep revising, expanding the focus, or messing with the alignment of things. Did it ultimately result in a better product? Probably. But it took seven months."

After that incident, there was a period of walking on eggshells, but the content didn't change. While the client would preface remarks with, "I don't know if I should be saying this, but," they were still saying them and still micromanaging. Eventually, this management style would result in Worker Bees resigning the account – not just Web work, but their advertising account as well.

Launch

After seven months of building the site, it was finally going to launch the next day at 5PM. Pyramid was having a launch party at the Speakeasy Café. There even would be TV cameras from local news stations.

Marla and Larry combed through the site, reviewing items on a checklist they'd given Speakeasy to complete. A GIF headline hadn't been placed. Links to the RealAudio files weren't working. A missing image here, a typo there, a wrong button bar, image mapping not working…four pages of items. And they weren't done. They stayed up,

Marla remembers sitting in the gallery of the School of Visual Concepts, where both Larry and Marla teach. They were collaborating on what they wanted for a look. It just happened that the school's illustrators were having their exhibit at the time. So they'd point at illustration styles, trying to find the look they wanted. "Well, see how that one over there's sort of informal and whimsical and see how this one's too formal." One illustrator's work, posted over Marla's shoulder, looked perfect. His name was Mark Widmer, and although they'd never heard of him, they asked him to bid on it.

They asked a few others as well. One illustrator they liked a lot had a full page piece published in the *New Yorker* the week they were thinking of hiring him, thus shooting well out of their budget range. They needed an illustrator who would be ultra reasonable. And Mark Widmer, because he'd only had his commercial practice going for less than a year, was pleased to get the work. He was negotiable.

Larry says, "I can think of situations working with illustrators where you're doing a garden-implements ad, so we want to draw a shovel, a hoe, a rake, and a bale of peat moss. So that's four illustrations at $200 a piece. Then, maybe somewhere along the way you decide you need a spot drawing of garden gloves, too. With the vast majority of illustrators, that's another $200. Mark's approach was different. He put his energy into coming up with ideas for the site, not the bookkeeping details. He'd say, "Here's your rake, your shovel, and your hoe, and I did ten others because I thought these might be fun. Let's do a wheelbarrow."

Marla interrupts, "He would do a rough concept. He would brainstorm with me or with Larry and come up with ideas, and he'd go, 'Cool, I'll try that.' He'd come up with his own, and whoever's was best, won."

The illustrator didn't just execute ideas. Mark was part of the concept process. Adding another smart, creative brain to the process made for a much better site.

Mark Widmer's illustration style gave the Pyramid site a distinctive look.

While ultimately a successful project, the Pyramid site was a learning experience for those involved. Larry Asher of Worker Bees offers the following take-aways to be learned from his experience:

1. Get as much detailed input up front as you can. The worst thing is to find out midway through a project that you're going to have to come up with content you thought the client was providing – especially when you've made no provision in your estimate for this extra work.

2. Treat web-site development the same way software publishers treat their products – that is, completely finish version 1.0 before moving on to 1.1. With the Pyramid site, the revisions "pyramided," so we were spending more time revising prior revisions than finishing the basic content. Complete your site from top to bottom before going to work on the revisions.

3. Don't get into a situation where you have no leverage over suppliers. If you're going to expect work out of programmers, make sure you're the one writing their checks. And, if your client is going to supply the copy, realize that you'll have very little to say about enforcing their adherence to deadlines and copy style – they are, after all, the client.

4. Create as much of the site as possible on paper before committing to HTML. Especially with today's advanced WYSIWYG web authoring programs, there's a temptation to start posting pages to a trial site long before client buy-offs are solid. For some reason, it's easier to get clients to commit when ideas are expressed as paper layouts and manuscripts of body copy. If you make the process of getting pages up on the Web look too easy, clients feel they can change things, since that must be easy, too.

and stayed up, hoping things would get done.

Marla remembers, "And we didn't hear back from them at all that night when we sent them our list. We were both tearing our hair out worrying, 'Are they going to do it?' It was very nerve racking."

It didn't get done until 4PM the next day, one hour before the press arrived. Finally, everyone could relax, have a pint, and enjoy their work. The client was delighted with the project. Ben says, "The site reflects the image and philosophy of the company. We've positioned ourselves as a cutting-edge, alter-native, hip, human company, and we were able to carry that through thematically in the site. Very few people achieve that level of integration."

The site quickly garnered awards and attention. It has been honored by the High Five, ProjectCool, MSN Site of the Day, Luckman 5-Star, NetGuide Live, and RealAudio. More important, the number of visitors to the site has been growing steadily since launch. Larry and Marla succeeded in creating a place as comfortable as a brew pub where people can hang out, be sociable, and play a game or two.

While the project had its frustrating moments, both Pyramid and Larry and Marla regard it as hugely successful. Larry emphasizes that despite the walkout, Pyramid was one of his favorite clients. Marla enjoyed the chance to create something fun and collaborate with Larry. They are all proud of the final product. After seven months of intensive labor, a new site was born. And it was a beauty.

Speakeasy continues to host the site and is responsible for minor maintenance work. Ben Myers supervised the site and wrote copy for two subsequent site "face-lifts" since launch. Marla Katz continues to provide occasional design work for the site. The relationship they've built has lasted beyond the initial site build – Larry, Marla, and Ben still share a pint now and then.

Worker Bees was one of the first creative groups in the Pacific Northwest to use email, FTP, faxes, cell phones, and telepathy to make the "virtual agency" concept work successfully. Head Drone Larry Asher and Queen Bee Ann Rhodes were formerly creative director and senior art director (respectively) for the celebrated Borders, Perrin & Norrander advertising agency out of Portland and Seattle. In addition to their mainstay of ad work for clients like AT&T Wireless, Sierra On-Line, Shurgard Storage Centers, and Washington state's Blue Shield health plan, Worker Bees has also created web sites for ad clients, as well as The School of Visual Concepts (www.svcseattle.com), a computer graphics, web design, advertising, and graphic-design school Larry co-owns. Ann and Larry no longer do ad and web work for Pyramid Breweries, Inc., but continue to wistfully quaff their former client's product.

2935 71st Ave. SE, Mercer Island, WA 98040 206-930-3417

Brazil Design Group was founded in 1994 by partners John Beezer and Marla Katz. Both had previously worked in Seattle ad agencies before joining forces in 1992 to form Beezer-Katz Advertising, winning many awards for their work. Beezer-Katz began using online technology to market themselves worldwide by using the Internet, and over the next two years sold ad campaigns to clients in markets from the East Coast to the Far East. Impressed by the results of this early foray into online commerce, Beezer-Katz Advertising transformed itself into the Brazil Design Group – naming themselves after the movie, not the country. Their first site, for Capons Chicken, was among the first successful transaction-based sites on the Web. In 1995, Brazil worked with Progressive Networks to launch RealAudio, developing the product's brand identity and designing their web site. John is the founder and manager of Seattle's first web-based grocery delivery service, and Marla serves as creative director at Progressive Networks.

Brazil Design is located in Seattle, WA.
206-323-2350 www.brazildg.com

Marla Katz, Larry Asher.

HIV | InSite

Address: http://hivinsite.ucsf.edu/get?&Mlval=insite_home_submit&tier1_open=2091.2002&tier1_oids=%270000%2e0000%27%2c%2

HIV nSite
Gateway to AIDS Knowledge

Help
Search
Home
AIDS

Medical
AIDS Knowledge Base
Trials Search
Anti-HIV Drug DB
AIDSLINE
Glossary
Tx Guidelines
Case Studies
Clinical Facts
Medications
Newsletters
Links

Prevention
FAQs
Basic HIV Info
Safer Sex Info
Fact Sheets
Newsletters On-line
People at Risk?
Best of Science
Epidemiology
Federal Guidelines
Developing Programs
Evaluating Programs
Funding Programs
Instruments
Prevention Models
Grassroots Programs
Get Involved!
Web AIDS Net
Prevention Links

Social Issues

Resources

US Map

Key Topics

Feedback/Survey

A project of the University of California, San Francisco AIDS Research Institute, the University of California, San Francisco AIDS Program at San Francisco General Hospital, the Center for AIDS Prevention Studies, and the Henry J. Kaiser Family Foundation.

What's New About This Site ...
- New Draft Federal Guidelines for Use of Antiretroviral Agents in Adults and Adolescents Released June 19, 1997.
- Women of Color and HIV/AIDS Policy
- ¿Se Pueden Adaptar los Programmas de Prevención del VIH?
- Medical Advice for Persons Who Inject Illicit Drugs
- Antiretroviral Update: Once a Day Dosing of ddI Also, a May, 1997 Review of antiretroviral therapy by Steven Deeks, MD.
- When the condom breaks: Post Exposure Prophylaxis (PEP) *in Key Topics*
- Physician-Hastened Death: Advisory Guidelines for the San Francisco Bay Area
- The Benefits Game : Solving the Puzzle of Insurance & Government Benefits for People with HIV (from Legal services)
- KS virus (HHV8) by Don Ganem, Tuberculosis (TB), HIV Antibody Testing Methodology: New chapters from the 1997 AIDS Knowledge Base

Today's News

Medical Information
The latest findings in clinical research. Expert clinical information from comprehensive textbooks, discussions and case studies. Listings of clinical trials to meet individual needs.
- **AIDS Knowledge Base**
- **Trials Search**
- **Antiretroviral Drug Database**
- **AIDSLINE**
- **Glossary of HIV-Related Medical Terms**
- **Treatment Guidelines**
- **Case Studies**
- **Clinical Fact Sheets**
- **Access to Medications**
- **Newsletters, Journals and Publications**
- **Links to Other Useful Medical Resources**

Prevention and Education
Information on what works and what doesn't for preventing HIV infection, effective programs for different populations, background on who's at risk for infection and where the epidemic is going.

Social Issues
Materials related to AIDS and society, with information on policy and legislation, legal services and current topics in the news.

Community and Research Resources
Databases, lists, and links for people needing more facts or looking for additional resources. U.S. and World Statistics from the CDC.

US Map
State-by-state information about HIV/AIDS: statistics, government programs, hotlines and other resources.

Key Topics
Comprehensive information on key HIV and AIDS topic areas. A compilation of news, articles, opinion pieces, documents, abstracts, bibliographies, contacts and links.

Purpose of the site

HIV In Site provides up-to-date articles and research on AIDS and HIV, from medical and prevention topics to social issues and resources.

How the developer was chosen

The university selected Art & Science after having begun the project with another developer, but found themselves unhappy with the other developer's process model.

Launch date

February 20, 1997

Chapter 3

www.hivinsite.ucsf.edu

When the client couldn't be motivated to make decisions, this not-for-profit job ran seven weeks late

Something mysterious was going on at Art & Science's database subcontractor, Web Factory.

Focus

what you will learn

How Art & Science built an effective content-management system and front end for this enormous database-driven research site.

The university declined the chance to participate in this case study.

Every time Stefan Fieldings-Isaacs or anyone else from Art & Science tried to call them to check in, someone new would answer the phone, and their contact never seemed to be available. Art & Science was starting to worry. They'd just spent months developing the front end for an enormous university AIDS research site – the templates were done, the university liked the look and feel – and now they were waiting for Web Factory to finish building the back-end database for the site.

Finally, one of A&S' staffers found out through the grapevine that Web Factory had folded – their staff had all been quietly quitting to form their own firm. Stefan faced the prospect of telling his client that their database wasn't being built at all, and the already late project would launch even later ... unless he could think of an alternative. Quickly.

Getting it rolling

The HIV In Site project was to be a true research site, with university professors, researchers, and scientists all contributing content to the site. The web developer's job was to create a user interface and content-management system so the huge number of AIDS-related publications could be entered, stored, and retrieved online. In May 1996, A&S had a company meeting to decide

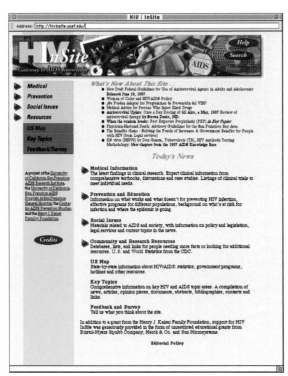

The site's home page promotes the latest and most important information.

whether to undertake the huge nonprofit job for the University of California, San Francisco. The staff was enthused – it seemed like a good cause, so they decided to give it a shot.

When the fall semester started, the project began in earnest. A&S kicked off what they call the Discovery Phase of the project with a meeting to discuss features of other AIDS-information sites, determine the audience, and discuss the university's goals for the site. While reviewing other research sites, many of which were developed and maintained by clinicians and technicians, A&S pointed out how a better designed user interface would have made the sites easier to use. The other sites provided *complete* information, but didn't make it easy for users to find *specific* information. The university committee saw that ease of use

should be top priority. Stefan explains, "My philosophy is that good information design and good information architecture brings to the fore things that are most interesting to the user, anticipates what the user needs, and provides those things first."

To anticipate what the user needs, one must first know the user. Although corporations' demographic studies of their customers help them target their marketing, a research site has a more diverse audience, spanning age, education level, and purpose. A 15-year-old might need information for a school paper, an infected visitor might seek the results of the latest experiments, and a medical professional might search for a particular academic paper. With this wide audience, the site would have to be organized in a manner meaningful to everyone. It would mean throwing out some of the names for sections the university community used in favor of more global, commonly used terms.

The breadth of the audience limited A&S' ability to take advantage of the latest browser features – the site had to be accessible to just about everyone. Stefan says, "The university had a laundry list of things we couldn't use: separate pop-up windows, JavaScript, ActiveX, Java, frames – just an absolute host of things." They couldn't even disregard text-only Lynx users. Although they represent

only 2% of the online population, they represent a disproportionately large part of the research community.

Ultimately, the university wanted this site to be the best information site on AIDS in the world. They felt their site should reflect their position as a leading research institution and present a good face for the university.

The content-management system

A&S' task was to build a multifunctional content-management system to allow the university to input and organize the database's content. They had to include an expiration mechanism to delete out-of-date information. They had to build a standardized content entry form for moving text from the source format to the database. Finally, they had to structure the site and decide how to categorize the content. The system needed several layers of access. While volunteers could add content

Each heading contains a number of topics, which the visitor can display without leaving the current page.

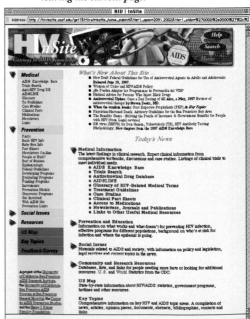

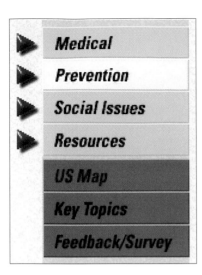

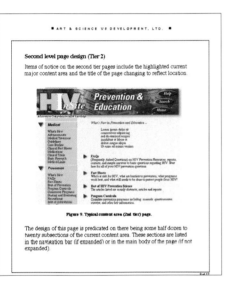

Second level page design (Tier 2)

Items of notice on the second tier pages include the highlighted current major content area and the title of the page changing to reflect location.

Figure 9. Typical content area (2nd tier) page.

The design of this page is predicated on there being some half dozen to twenty subsections of the current content area. These sections are listed in the navigation bar (if expanded) or in the main body of the page (if not expanded).

to the database, editors could assign value to a piece of information. Something important would rise to the top of a page, even if it was not the latest thing posted. In yet another layer of access, site administrators could move documents from section to section if necessary.

The navigation was critical. It had to allow visitors to explore the site without getting lost in the vast amount of information that would grow every day as volunteers added more and more. Stefan keeps a notebook he calls, "Solutions Without Problems" – navigational

ideas he's come up with that don't yet have a site to go with them. One of these, an expand-in-place model borrowed from the Mac interface, seemed perfect for the site. Visitors could click on the arrow for a list of the section's content areas. This solution didn't require JavaScript or

Top left: The site's navigation borrows from the Macintosh interface – click on an arrow to see what's in each section. Bottom left: Art & Science creates explanations of the design to give the client. Above: These essential buttons reside in what Stefan calls the most important real estate on the page – the upper right-hand corner.

ActiveX and provided the visitor with a list of what was in each section. A&S wrote an architectural document for them, explaining the objectives of the navigation. By early October, five weeks into the project, the university approved it.

Focus on form

Stefan prefers to present design to clients in stages: first form, then type, then color. He feels strongly that once color is involved, the discussion stops being about the design. "I've found in this sort of work that color decisions separate people. They fight over them: 'I hate that color, I love that color.' They will fight over the color when it's relatively unimportant compared to the user interface."

A&S printed their designs for the interface in gray scale and didn't show colors until the team agreed on a form. Then A&S could say, "Now that we've got this interface, here are three different versions in different colors. Which one do you like the best?"

A&S also focuses the client on form by using low-resolution graphics in their printouts. "We made sure when we gave them art that everything was fuzzy. We did that on purpose. We made sure they couldn't distinguish the typeface," says Stefan. The main idea was getting the form, with the bar across the top and the expandable navigation, approved. After that, type treatments weren't an issue.

A&S presented round after round of palettes. Stefan says they showed the logo and buttons over and over in different shades. The university had already prescribed that they didn't wanted red, due to the red ribbon campaign, or green, because it was too bilious. Finally, everyone agreed on the blue and yellow combination.

Slipping deadlines

U.S. Vice President Al Gore was available in late December to open the finished site as part of his support for AIDS research. A&S hoped that this narrow window of opportunity would motivate the committee to finish the project. Unfortunately, the project ran into a number of delays that would eventually cause the team to miss Al Gore's window.

First, decision making on every issue bogged down in politics and argument, since it was decision by committee, not by an individual. Stefan compares the situation to a corporation, where people have responsibilities and generally the

Stefan is aware that budget is a big question with clients, but he encourages them to think of the question in a different way. He says, "How much does a car cost? Are we talking about an Edsel or a Rolls Royce? The same thing is true when they ask how long it will take to build. Is it a coach-built car, or something coming off a production line?" He thinks clients should focus instead on developing the scope of their project, so he can make accurate estimates and timelines. "A better question is, 'How long will this overall process take? How long will our dialogue take before we reach a point where we can say go ahead?'"

Stefan creates a detailed estimate from the project plan. From each resource (e.g. human hours doing coding), he can predict a cost. If they know it will take 40 hours of HTML time to produce a section, they can estimate that cost. The detailed estimate is an attempt to show the client exactly why the site costs what it does, item by item. He admits, "Sometimes they want to nickel-and-dime you to death and pull line items out. I think we're getting better at explaining it's a totality, it's a holistic undertaking. It'd be kind of hard to pull out some line items without affecting something else.

"We knew it was going to be a very big job right from the start, and we used project-management tools right from the start. But when your client doesn't really care about dates and meeting goals for those dates and cannot be motivated by outside concerns, then those dates are of limited utility. In actuality, the number of hours we spent was fairly close to the number of hours we budgeted. On the other hand, the time expanse over which we had budgeted it was much shorter."

politics don't extend to every decision. "Some decisions are of course political, but they argued over every decision tooth and nail." A&S tried to stay out of the fray as much as possible, encouraging the team to make decisions and offering choices. In a corporate site, A&S would charge for late decisions and missed deadlines, but they couldn't with the pro bono site.

A&S was doing the site for cost, not for profit. To some members of the committee, this still seemed like a lot of money. The university team was used to working with staff, not with outside consultants – they

expected Stefan's group to be on call and make as many changes as they wanted. They found it hard to accept that while this was a big project, they had a limited number of revisions that were reasonable.

Second, as the project matured, more people became interested and came to meetings. They wanted to revisit decisions made earlier without them. "Ideally, you would have everybody involved from day one in the design process, so nobody would pop up 12 weeks later and say, 'I don't like this color.' We had a little bit of that, but at the same time the administrator was able to put her

foot down and say, 'Look, you know, you've all been invited to all these meetings, and if you chose to blow them off earlier, you don't have the right to complain about it now.' But those are hard things to enforce, and we wasted quite a few weeks on administrative and political discussions. Or they wasted them, rather, internally. I'm not sure it could have been done any better in a university environment," says Stefan.

As late as December, decisions were still being made about the design. A&S' job had been to build templates. One contains the navigation, header bar, and user interface A&S had so carefully designed. The other is a "heavy-text" template, which, to conserve space for text, has no navigation elements. The university felt that with long documents, they should eliminate the margin to allow more text to fit on each page. Stefan was dead set against the heavy-text template, feeling that PDFs should be used for such long documents. "I thought we'd have varying page representations when people came in. Sometimes they're going to see the proper design, and other times they're going to just see this very odd bar across the top of the page."

Third, Sun Microsystems had promised to donate a SPARC Ultra II to host the database. Unfortunately, Sun couldn't deliver it until the second week of November, and the university didn't get it configured properly until the second week of January. A&S wasn't allowed to build the site on the target machine and would have to troubleshoot once the site moved to the new server.

They didn't make Al Gore's window of opportunity. Stefan says, "Everything got pushed back. It impacted our production schedule pretty seriously to run over seven or eight weeks. You have a finite number of human resources, and they could be working on a for-profit job." Then, of course, there was the little problem of the missing database.

Going live

Fortunately for A&S and the project, Web Factory had a parent company. A&S approached them with the uncompleted contract, asking them to finish the work. The parent company agreed and contracted a new company – the one Web Factory's ex-employees had started. The same people who began building the database would finish it.

Says Stefan, "There were all kinds of discontinuities and difficulties in the coding. These people really hadn't given a damn, because they knew they were going to be leaving this firm shortly. So a lot of it was clean up. We told them, 'This is the code you wrote, so you can't tell us this is somebody else's problem. It's your problem – you have to fix it.'" The schedule, already behind, didn't suffer from this new problem, because Sun still hadn't delivered the computer. It took some time for Sun and the university to coordinate on configuring the hardware and software correctly, buying A&S some time to finish the database. In the end, the subcontractor finished the database and did an excellent job.

A&S wanted to test the system before going live. To meet the new launch date, they decided to let university volunteers load the content before the content-management system was finished. It wasn't ideal, but A&S wanted to get the site launched. "We could have the site done and working really well with no content, or we could take a risk and load the content at the same time as we were finishing the implementation of the site," says Stefan.

For the most part, the launch went smoothly. The site worked with no major problems, even though they launched without having their site and database running off the SPARC Ultra II, but on an older machine that was also performing other tasks. Finally, they put the site and Illustra database on their new Ultra II, considerably speeding up the site's performance. A&S also spent time training the volunteers to use the content-management system.

The people at Art & Science are proud of the product of their months of effort. Although the HIV In Site project took months to plan and months more to build, the end product is a site and database that will be of use to researchers, academics, those infected, and everyone else searching for more information on the virus for years to come. They've built a research tool and built it to last.

Art & Science was founded late in 1993 to offer professional technical writing services to high-tech clients in the Silicon Valley area. In 1994, the firm transitioned to doing creative and engineering work on the infant World Wide Web. Microsoft was sleeping, Netscape had not yet been formed, and server push was state-of-the-art. Stefan Fielding-Isaacs and creative partner Steve Rapport were aggressive in their marketing, signing up-and-coming Joe Boxer as their first major client. The site (www.joeboxer.com) was released in spring of 1995 and has won every major award on the Web, including a bronze Clio in the Interactive Media category. The partners split after the completion of the first big site, and Stefan went on to grow the business into an industry leader. Art & Science W³ Development, Ltd. was incorporated in 1996, and numbers among its clients Disney, the Gap, Sun Microsystems, Silicon Graphics, Mercedes-Benz, and NTT.

615 Third St., San Francisco, CA 94107 415-974-1067 www.artandscience.com

ART & SCIENCE	
Stefan Fielding-Isaacs	*Creative Director and Information Architect*
Brian Moseley	*Perl scripting and database*
Junryo Watanabe	*HTML/QA*
SUBCONTRACTORS	
Sean Brennan	*Artist*
Jeff Wisdom	*Artist*
Anne McMillan	*Contract Project Manager*
Fort Point Partners (née Web Factory)	*Contract Database Programming*

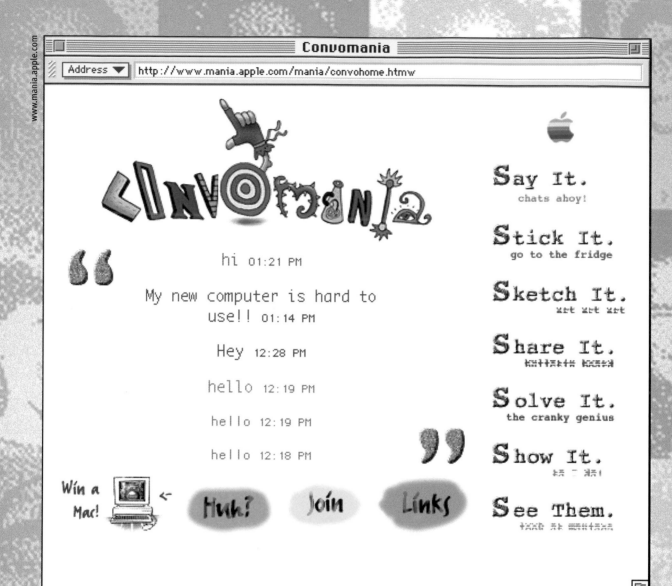

Purpose of the site

Convomania provides a community for sick and disabled children to express themselves.

The players

Alan Brightman
Peter Green
David Burk
Steve Nelson
Dan Livingston
Ramona d'Viola

How the developer was chosen

Clear Ink responded to an RFP with some design mockups. Apple's WDSG felt Clear Ink would be willing both to lead the design and to take chances with it.

Launch date

January 8, 1997

So you're in the hospital and it's your birthday and you've got surgery tomorrow and your stomach still hurts from the operation before.

Focus

what you will learn

How good project management and teamwork saw this project through numerous iterations and revisions

YOU'RE BORED AND LONELY, but it's past visiting hours, plus your friends are avoiding you because you're sick again and they don't know how to deal. You want to talk to people who *do* know how to deal. Without any violins or saccharine after-taste, please. Or, worst of all, a long download.

When you're a kid with clear sarcoma of the kidney, systemic lupus, or leukemia, you face challenges most people around you don't understand. When you're a company trying to build a site for these kids, you've *got* to understand. You need to get inside their heads, listen to what they want, and be willing to rebuild when they say something isn't

working, even if you think it is. Apple's Worldwide Disability Solutions Group (WDSG) knew they had to get a lot of feedback to make sure the site they wanted to build was right for their users. So before going live, they debuted a pilot Convomania site to a small group of kids and asked for their feedback.

Called Outposters, these 45 kids, recruited from places like the Ronald McDonald house and children's hospitals, served as an advisory panel. With Apple-supplied Macs and Internet connections, they logged on to the site from home every day, put the site through a rigorous test drive, and made lots of suggestions. They thought all the graphics made the

Address ▼ http://tesla.clearink.com/~dan/mania/cafesicko/cafe.html

Cafe Sicko

Café Sicko is in the artsy, chic part of town
where the tourists never go.

But don't worry. We checked you
out. You're okay.

Double half
skinny half
decaf latte
with
nutmeg?

CUMULO

Half price if you've
pierced something.

Speak your thoughts at Open Mike Night!

Watched over by the café's owner, Cumulo, tonight's the
night to speak your thoughts in any form you want: poems,
stories, and illustrations. You know the rules. Break them.
On the other hand, Robert Frost, a famous poet, once said
writing poetry without rhyme was like "playing tennis
without a net." You decide.

Open
Mike

Look through the "Watching the
Walls" Art Gallery. Cumulo is
always on the lookout for new
talent. Do you have a painting
decrying the anguish of man
against the cosmos? A drawing of
a Martian riding a T-Rex?
Whatever.

Message
Board

Amie!
Meet U
in the
Torches

Leave notes
for your
buddies!
Writing a
play and
need some
help? Post
it here. And
WHAT?!

Watching
the Walls

You haven't sprayed the graffiti wall yet? Jeez.
Just don't let Cumulo catch you...

Home | Open Mike | Watching the Walls | Message Board

*Dan's prototype design was a little dark in color and humor for Convomania, but it
demonstrated the creative potential that won Clear Ink the account.*

Clear Ink of Walnut Creek, California. Would they be interested in talking about redesigning a site that enabled sick and disabled kids to express themselves?

Getting the job

No, thought David Burk, president of Clear Ink, when he got the RFP. They were just too busy. But designer and illustrator Dan Livingston liked the idea from the start, grabbed a pad of sketch paper, and drew up a few dozen ideas. Since Dan was excited about it, Clear Ink decided to take a chance and mock up some prototype pages for a presentation in response to the RFP.

> ## "As far as how the site looked – they were not into that at all."
>
> – Dan Livingston

Based on the reactions of the kids to the pilot, Apple figured these kids didn't want an overly cheery, Barney-esque approach to their site. Dan's prototype site was dark, both in colors and humor. With a post-nuclear, radioactive feel, fluorescent graphics glowed out of the black background in a fluid, mysterious structure. A green hypo injected a coffee cup while a magenta, goatéed host Cumulo of Café Sicko loomed overhead. Café Sicko hosted Open Mike Night, where kids could post their poetry, illustrations, and thoughts. The white HTML instructions told visitors, "You know the rules. Break them."

Alan and Peter liked the potential they saw in Clear Ink. They were looking for a contractor that wasn't looking for a lot of artistic direction

site take too long to download and cluttered it. The activity areas that encouraged kids to draw, collaborate on a play, and write were too workbook-like. They didn't want to open another program, do the work, and then come back to their browser — the activity had to take place within the page. Long explanations of how the site worked

bogged it down. They didn't want to read a page of instructions, they wanted to go chat.

From this feedback, Alan Brightman and Peter Green of WDSG realized the pilot site needed an overhaul before going live at Macworld in January – three months away. So they sent an RFP to one of Apple's preferred web-design groups, and had a feeling they could partner with Clear Ink. Says Peter, "We wanted a group who could bring a lot to the table. It's rare to find a group that would say to us, 'You guys are wrong.'" However, the look was not what they had in mind. Peter says, "We wanted a stripped down design, minimalist, so kids could get on with the business of Convomania – the bulletin boards and chats."

Steve went back to the office and played with some ideas. If they wanted a stripped-down design, then maybe the site should be mostly black-and-white, and the kids could add the color – literally. Their chats, their statements, and their illustrations would show up in colored text, taking center stage on the screen. Illustration would still take advantage of Dan's humor and style but on a white background. He came back with three sketch sites with different

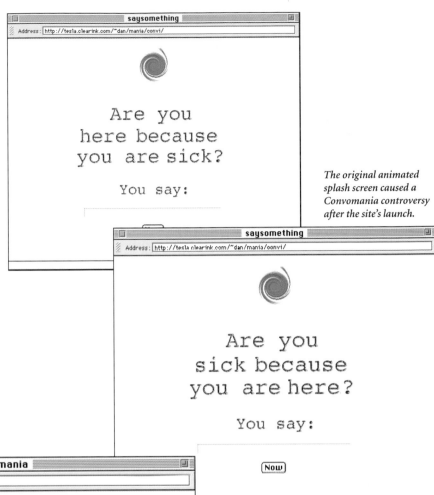

The original animated splash screen caused a Convomania controversy after the site's launch.

Even the splash screen encourages Convomaniacs to participate in the site.

layout and ideas, but all with the same structure and kid-first focus.

When Steve presented this round of ideas, Alan and Peter knew it was right. Kids would be invited to say how they felt on the splash page and then would see their comment in colored text on the home page. Right away, they'd be participating, and they'd also know how many other kids were there, giving them a sense of the Convomania community. They liked the brighter look of Dan's illustrations. And the overall design just seemed right – for now. The real test would come when the Convomaniacs would get a chance to test drive the site.

The gateway page to the chat area doesn't overwhelm kids with instructions but provides them if needed.

it came to reviewing a specific illustration or animation, he said he would know it was right when he saw it. Says Dan, "It's hard to work with somebody who says, 'It just doesn't feel right, or it's not quite there.'" He jokes, "I mean, if they don't like my work the first time I do it … "

While Alan and Peter had wanted a group that was willing to try lots of different directions, the danger of I'll-know-it-when-I-see-it creative direction is that the web developer may have to go through iteration after iteration, hoping to hit upon the magic concept, and possibly falling behind schedule in the process. To avoid these potential pitfalls, Clear Ink did what a good creative group does – they hired a project manager to interface with the client.

It just feels right – creative direction

At an early brainstorming meeting with both teams, Clear Ink learned Alan's ways of communicating his vision for the site. He wasn't describing a look, but how he'd feel when he saw the pages. David Burk describes Alan as the real driving force behind Apple's disability project. He says, "Those descrip-

tions of those feelings were probably much more detailed than a sketch of a site or telling us to put which pixels where."

The Clear Ink team talks about Alan with a lot of affection and respect but admits he wasn't the ideal client when it came to creative direction. He talked in global terms, as in, "The goal of this site is to make kids express themselves." But then when

Account management

Ramona d'Viola joined the Clear Ink team part way through the Convomania project, claiming that's when she "stepped in and started slapping people around." It was up to her to make sure they stayed on track. This site was to debut at Macworld, and funding from Apple depended on making a showing there. This client wanted to be involved in the day-to-day progress

"How about a spinning mouth?" Ramona's suggestion became this animated GIF on the Say It page.

of the site, and Ramona kept everyone up to date on approaching deadlines and approvals to be made.

Every week, Ramona would negotiate with Dan and decide what needed to be done that week – for example, illustrating the Say It page, the Convomania chat area. Dan would then focus on illustration and put up a web page showing three different looks for a concept. When he was finished, Ramona would send Peter an email saying that for the site to stay on track, she needed him to look at the page, give preliminary feedback by a certain date, and make a final decision by another date.

"I sent literally thousands of emails to Peter Green," says Ramona. "And he was really good about sending me detailed emails back. Then, if we needed to, we'd talk on the phone to clarify things. We'd talk for an hour, and I'd take notes on all the things Peter had ideas about."

Every time Ramona and Peter would talk, she would write a set of notes that would condense all the ideas of the day and send it back to him, just so they'd be on the same page before she'd pass things along to Dan. Peter would correct, modify, or verify the plan and send it back.

Since they had so much phone and email contact, the Clear Ink and WDSG teams rarely met face to face. Therefore, Clear Ink was careful to keep WDSG up to date. David says one of Clear Ink's philosophies is that they want clients to know how hard they're working on the project, and in a weekly status report meeting, they're accountable for what's happened. He says, "I think clients' experience with many vendors is that

they sell the client and then don't do anything. The face-to-face meeting was really a checking in – this is where we are, this is the work that's been done, what do you want to see next week, this is the direction we're going."

Ramona made sure deadlines were met by allowing iteration and back-and-forth until a certain date. After that date, she'd warn, they were going with what they had. Technical issues required a lot of discussion

Alan really liked the feeling of anarchy in the Convomania logo.

of what could go on a Mac server, what had to be on a UNIX server, and how much programming Clear Ink should do.

One usual source of tension between clients and contractors – getting assets – wasn't present here, allowing the teams to focus on creative and technical solutions. Ramona says, "They were really, really good about deliverables." Since their funding was tied to the Macworld debut, no one at WDSG wanted to hold up progress. "When I'd ask Peter for things, he'd have it within a day."

Teamwork

Because Ramona kept track of what was approved and what hadn't yet hit the mark, she worked closely with Dan, not only on the schedule but also on creative solutions. (As Dan puts it, "She has the design background – mine's in marine zoology.") For the Say It section (the Convomania chat area), Dan came up with two gigantic, flapping lips. Peter told Ramona he thought it was too cliché, too literal, and that Dan should come up with an illustration that was not as obvious as a mouth, but "still obviously some talking thing." But Dan was out of ideas.

Ramona had been thinking about the idea, too, though, and suggested, "How about a spinning mouth?" Dan went with it, animating a face with four mouths going around the head. Says Ramona, "It was one of those things where it took Dan a couple of tries to do it, but when we showed it to Peter, his response was, 'Dead on. Perfect.'"

About a month into the design, Peter mentioned that they really liked the logo and wanted to make sure it was used throughout the site, not just on the home page. The trouble was, the logo is large and unwieldy in the clean, spare design of Convomania. Ramona and Dan wrestled with the problem until hitting upon the solution – separating the hand from the logo. They could put a different hand in each section. Dan drew up a fist with a spiked "anarchy" glove, and Alan immediately loved it. Says Ramona, "Alan has a big wide anarchy streak in him."

The Clear Ink and Apple teams were relying on gut feel for what was

David Burk was approaching his 35th birthday when he got approached by a product manager at Apple to do some web work. This product manager had seen David's and designer Jon Stevens' work on their company's web site. The site had been for the AG Group, an Apple developer. David explained to the manager that the AG Group was a product company, not a web developer. But the question inspired some soul searching. On July 15th, the day after his birthday, David announced to the AG Group that he wanted to do web development. Jon Stevens, Carla Hansmeyer, and Steve Nelson filled out the staff.

Their first move was into offices across the hall, where a radio station and school of broadcasting were the tenants. Even though they had leased the space, the station was slow in finding new space and had a lot of heavy equipment. So, they spent many months sharing the space mock "studios," and they'd hear the students doing their demo tapes over and over and over. But one of first big clients, Adia Personnel (Adecco) found the whole arrangement charming and decided to sign up.

Now Clear Ink is leasing half the building. They've grown from three to four, then four to eight, then eight to 13, then 13 to 20 in one year. Says David, "What's remained consistent is the great pleasure we have working with each other (we laugh a lot and very hard) and a focus on serving the clients. It's really in the culture – work hard, play hard."

2540 Camino Diablo, Suite 203, Walnut Creek, CA 94596 510-937-2100
www.clearink.com

Steve Nelson	*Creative Director*
David Burk, Ramona d'Viola	*Account Management*
Dan Livingston	*Project Management*
Roanne Hindin	*HTML Programmer*

around, it made the last days challenging. Not to mention painful.

But of course launch meant the site was going to meet its worst potential critics – the kids. And again, they didn't absolutely love everything about it. They thought the graffiti wall was too slow and that it didn't work the way you'd think it would. They didn't like that you needed different software to use the chat function. They thought it was too difficult to have to download the software and then go to another area. They wanted the site to be more integrated.

It was all fixable. What was important is that they *did* like the look and the attitude. All those iterations – Alan waving his arms around, Ramona and Dan brainstorming on spinning mouths – had resulted in the right "gut feel."

Ramona remembers, "Dan and I were invited to Macworld for the Convomania party. And we got to meet some of the kids in the initial group, Brisy and Beau. We got to see some videos of some of these kids, and these are some very brave people. You feel like a team, like part of a family."

Convomaintenance

Part of the vision of the Convomania site is that it is a living site. Kids aren't going to find community there if its pages are stagnant. Immediately after launch, Clear Ink submitted an Ongoing Development Proposal listing maintenance duties, immediate changes to be made, new additions to the site, and how much time per week this maintenance would take.

Opening the site up to Convomaniacs had resulted in new feedback. The Convomaniacs weren't satisfied

working and what wasn't – but they had to be sure this "gut feel" was what the kids wanted. The kids reviewed the designs and gave their input to Peter, who summarized their concerns and passed them along to Clear Ink. Although the prototype site had been taken down, there was still a regularly scheduled chat session among the Outposters and other Convomaniacs. Steve, Dan, and Ramona hung out through the

chats to get a sense of what was and wasn't important to the kids.

Launching for Macworld

The weekend before the launch, Dan decided to burn off some stress and go snowboarding.

The accident wasn't serious.

All that was broken was his finger. But for someone who spends the day typing, drawing, and moving a mouse with the graffiti wall. The graffiti wall had been a headache from its conception. It was a cool idea, but it wasn't right yet. Under the heading, "Spray It," kids could type in their remarks, send them, and see them appear in colored type on the wall graphic. Unfortunately, a Mac server wouldn't let them place the text at angles other than vertical and horizontal – not without a whole lot of programming. That part of the site had to run off a UNIX platform, even though Apple wanted the whole site to be hosted on a Mac server. Also, the kids had complained that the section just didn't work as they expected. It still wasn't quite right.

The Convomaniacs hadn't liked the splash page, either. The original text had asked, "Are you here because you are sick?" and animated to "Are you sick because you are here?" The text generated controversy – some kids hated it, and some defended it. At first Peter liked that it was causing a stir. "It's not bland, it's not boring. It's not like the violins start playing once you come to Convomania." He also feels it's mostly the younger

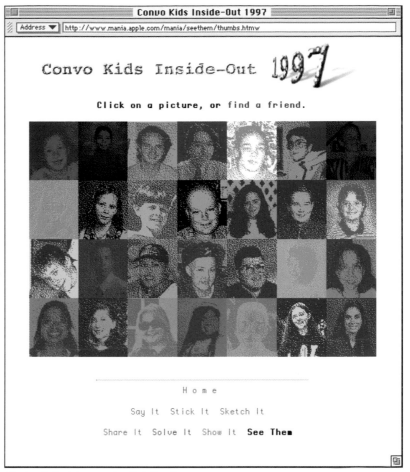

Having their pictures on the site helps give Convomaniacs a sense of ownership.

The Genius down the Well, an adult Convomaniac, helps kids solve their questions about life, being sick, and anything else they want to know.

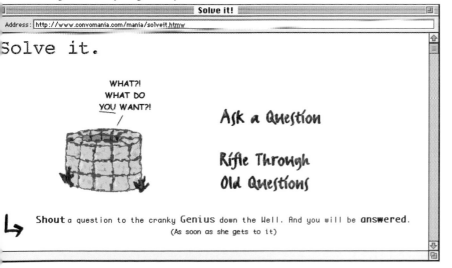

kids who don't like the bolder aspect of the text. But over time, more kids complained, and they decided to change it. Now the splash page features quotes from Convomaniacs.

This proposal suggested Clear Ink be responsible for ongoing tasks like developing short term and long term direction for the site, proposing timelines for execution, and monitoring and recommending new technologies. Weekly brainstorming sessions would keep the site fresh and also provide a forum to respond to "user issues," the constant feedback provided by Convomaniacs.

The proposal also suggested ideas for expanding the site into new activity areas, such as "Stick It," a JavaScript-based magnetic poetry

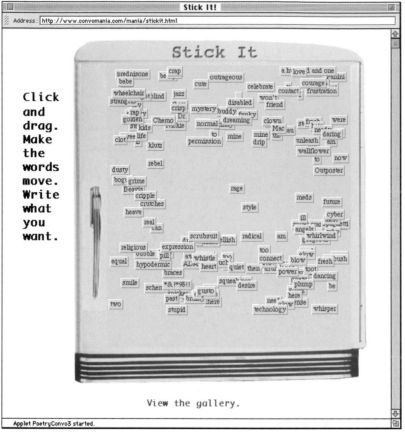

Stick It uses JavaScript to let kids express themselves in refrigerator art.

Convomania's home page lists the comments of the latest kids to log on.

area, and training a 16-year-old Webmaster, Jacob, to maintain the Show It pages of the site. Jacob belongs to the thespian group Ta-Da, which works with Convomania to bring theater and performance opportunities to disabled kids. The community of Convomania now extends even to maintaining the pages. Other redesigned elements include moving the kids' comments to center stage, crowding the buttons for the sections to the far right. And past chat transcripts are available to read, if you want to hear what kids have to say about their doctors or the future.

Success

If success is measured in terms of a continuing relationship between client and contractor, then Convomania is a hit. Beyond the Convomaintenance already administered, weekly brainstorming sessions continue to generate site-improving ideas. The team is functioning.

Success is measured in terms of participation. This site is all about quality interaction. The site is successful because it has accomplished its mission – to provide a place for kids to express themselves. This online community discusses what to do when friends don't know how to treat you when you're sick and gives advice on dealing with evil nurses and mean sisters. Says Peter, "The yardstick we're using is seeing active participation on the message boards, chats – we'll know by activity in general if we're on the right track or not."

Peter was surprised to find that Convomania's audience seems to be older kids. They found that it's hard to create a site for expression for younger kids, as expression mostly deals with words, and "younger kids just don't type that well." He also feels the younger kids, in the 9-11 age range, are more into the technology aspect of the Web than focusing on a chat or writing project. Convomania may end up being two sites – or even three or four, as the parents of Convomaniacs have expressed an interest in an online support group – and there may be a place online for doctors and professionals who interact with Convomaniacs.

Right now, though, the site is working, and the kids are using it. As the logo says, "It's a place where it's okay to be not okay." It's a place where kids can be straightforward: being sick sucks, you're right. Now, go chat.

In 1985, Apple created the industry's first Worldwide Disability Solutions Group (WDSG) with the goal of making computer technology that meets the special needs of disabled children and adults. WDSG works with product development teams to ensure that every Macintosh meets or exceeds basic accessibility requirements. They work with developers of add-on accessibility products. WDSG also works with marketing and communications divisions to make sure that, as a company, Apple remembers the estimated 800-million individuals who comprise the worldwide disabled community. Other projects besides Convomania include Creating the Alliance for Technology Access, which helps teach people with disabilities about technology, and Convening Coup de Tech, a meeting for rehabilitation professionals from around the world to discuss technology applications in their work.

For more information on WDSG, visit www.apple.com/disability or call 800-600-7808 (VOX) or 800-755-0601 (TTY).

"My day was so cool – I got tickets to Metallica!!!"
-- Mike, age 17

"I want the cansor to go away now."
-- "Nickie", age 6

"Hospital food tastes like mush!"
-- "Cowboy", age 10

"My big pet iguana Vern says, 'Hi!'"
-- Rosemary, age 9

"I think I'm in love!"
-- "Julie", age 16

Salon Magazine

Address ▼ | http://www.salonmagazine.com/

TABLE TALK   COLUMNISTS   21ST   TASTE   WANDERLUST   GAMES   COMICS   CONTACT US   ARCHIVES

SALON MAGAZINE

One tough mother

FIVE WAYS "ROSEANNE" KICKED NETWORK TV'S BUTT INTO THE NEXT CENTURY

EARLIER
TWILIGHT OF THE GOATS: MAILER, ROTH AND BELLOW

MONDAY, MAY 19, 1997

CARVILLE High-priced elephant dung: The GOP's foreign money scandal

NEWS Christianity's "third force": Holy-rolling race mixers

MEDIA Don't drive on me: Mini-van moms unite to fight NYT trend story!

BOOKS Mailer's "Gospel": Jesus by a TKO

MUSIC GBV's "Mag Earwig!" hits bull's eye

TV "Better than bare breasts: National Geographic's "Volcano!"

X-WORD Double Double Meanings

SALON IS HIRING

WHY WOMEN WHO END THEIR MARRIAGES DO SO WELL.
by ASHTON APPLEWHITE

Pack your bags.
We're sending you to Europe!
Enter the SALON Wanderlust "Off to Europe" Sweepstakes

DETAIL OF ILLUSTRATION BY CHARLIE POWELL

Salon 21st | Can We Talk: Personal encounters with talking bots By Tracy Quan
Salon Wanderlust | Open-mike philosophizing in Paris cafes By David Downie

EARLIER IN SALON

FRIDAY, MAY 16, 1997

Twilight of the Goats By D. T. Max
They're old and in the way, but Mailer, Roth and Bellow won't leave the barnyard! (05/16/97)

"Night Falls on Manhattan" By Robin Dougherty
Despite a fresh star in Andy Garcia and some powerful moments, Sidney Lumet's latest police corruption drama walks the same old beat (05/16/97)

Sound Salvation By Sarah Vowell
Southern culture on the skids: Oxford American's Southern music issue needs more grits, less gravy (05/16/97)

The Listress By Amy Wallace
Famous Last Words (05/16/97)

Newsreal: Baiting the Bear By Jonathan Broder
Will the U.S.-backed push by NATO into central Europe start a new Cold War? (05/16/97)

Media Circus: $600,000 an episode, and worth every penny By Joyce Millman
"Seinfeld's" characters aren't yuppies -- they're babies. Long may they drool (05/16/97)

Sneak Peeks By Elizabeth Judd
Virginia Woolf: Not just a suicidal aesthete (05/16/97)

Sharps & Flats By Ezra Gale
Brand New Heavies' retro-funk (05/16/97)

Blue Glow By Joyce Millman
"Busted on the Job"; "The Odyssey" (05/16/97)

The Hero Santon By Don Asmussen (05/16/97)

MAY 15 - MAY 13, 1997

Purpose of the site

To provide a top-notch, professional-quality, online magazine of books, arts, and ideas.

The players

Mignon Khargie
Andrew Ross
David Talbot
Scott Rosenberg
Dan Shafer
Elizabeth Kairys

Launch date

November 20, 1995

The office is cubicle-land. If you stand up, you can see the occasional head bob up, Muppet-like.

But the people toiling within the labyrinth are far from isolated.

Art director Mignon Khargie has been working on the new travel section for days. She lets out a wail:

"I hate Wanderlust!"

Focus

What you will learn

Maintaining excellent site content day after day requires a talented staff, teamwork, and a supportive working environment. Find out how Salon developed their system for success.

INSTANTLY, heads bob up over the partitions. "What?" "Who?" "You can't hate it yet!" "It hasn't even launched yet!" Mignon has set off an outburst. Some don't bother to stand up; they just yell through the cubical walls. This lively newsroom environment forced Salon to move from their original office, a corner in a quiet architecture firm, to their current space in San Francisco's China Basin building at the south end of Multimedia Gulch.

In an earlier time, the clatter of typewriters would have added to the dull roar of the newsroom. Now, quieter keyboards seem to provide more opportunity for vocal chatter.

"Deng Xiaopeng died!" managing editor Andrew Ross shouts. By the time he weaves through the maze to get to the design department, they've already headed over to the photo service to get Deng's picture, stepping over someone lying on his back in the aisle assembling a keyboard tray with a drill.

The secret of Salon's success appears to be a combination of talent, teamwork, and a supportive working environment. While running a daily online magazine requires organization, running a Salon-quality online magazine requires a dedicated, talented staff who work closely together in the pursuit of excellence.

Chapter 5

www.salon1999.com

Talent

Or, why the staff of the *San Francisco Examiner* left *en masse* for the online world.

When the staff of the *San Francisco Examiner* went on strike in November 1994, they knew non-striking management would use the newspaper's web site to continue to publish the news. A group of the striking reporters decided they should publish their own paper on the Web. One of them had an account with an ISP that offered them server space. The strike started on a Tuesday, and the San Francisco Free Press site was up by Thursday.

You can still see the site at www.ccnet.com/SF_Free_Press with its patriotic red-and-blue logo. The home page consists of links to each day's news. While rudimentary in architecture and design, the "picket lines in cyberspace" story attracted a lot of attention from the media. When the strike ended after 11 days, the Free Press site ended, too. But the reporters going back to the print world now had a taste of publishing online.

Back at the paper, post-strike morale was low. The enthusiastic owner of the *Examiner*, William Randolph Hearst III, left the paper almost immediately, disheartening many of the staff he'd hired. They felt that management wasn't behind the paper and that it was beginning to deteriorate. Staffers and managers were thinking about possible careers changes. Among them was the editor of the style section, David Talbot.

Salon's new travel section, Wanderlust.

David had always wanted to start a magazine, but the costs of starting a print publication were prohibitive. He didn't know a whole lot about the Web, but he knew it was going to be big. What if he started up his magazine online? It might be more feasible financially, and he already knew a lot of talent – talent dissatisfied with their present jobs.

David got out his Rolodex full of numbers acquired through his years as a newspaper editor and started gathering information. Along the way, he connected with Apple's Richard Gingras, who was running Apple's online development efforts. Richard liked David's idea a lot – so much that he gave him enough money to develop a prototype and hire some key people.

David went back to the *Examiner* and convinced designer Mignon Khargie and news editor Andrew Ross, as well as Ikonic's David Zweig, to form Salon's initial staff. With discounted computers from Apple, the four of them hunkered down in some rented space in the corner of an architecture firm to come up with some demo pages.

Picket lines in cyberspace.

Design talent

Mignon remembers sitting in David's office at the *Examiner* when the topic of the Web came up. She mentioned she'd been experimenting with web design. She recalls, "He said, 'Hmm.' A few days later I found out what he meant." An engaging woman who laughs easily and often, Mignon began working on Salon's design on August 14, 1995, having left her job the weekend before. Mignon quickly learned HTML and web-design tricks. (She remembers clearly the day she figured out how to make a white background.) She says, "It came together more smoothly than I thought it would. It helped that everyone was in there from time to time. We had great editorial input."

Mignon says David helped the design process by clearly stating his vision of Salon's design. Rejecting the notion that because the magazine was on the Web, it had to be cluttered with bright neon colors, he brought

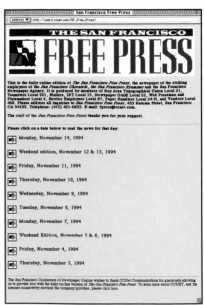

Mignon a stack of Art Deco books. The illustration style, with its fields of flat color and bold shapes, compressed well for web pages. Mignon's own illustration style easily adapted to the Art Deco look, as did her friend Zach Trenholm's. Zach's work is most apparent in the caricatures throughout the site. The staff feels that just as the writing has a voice on the site, so the illustrations express an intimate, personal voice.

One of Salon's basic design decisions was to increase their font size. In Salon's 1996 Cool Site of the Year Awards Profile, Andrew Ross (whose method of teambuilding between design and editorial consists of bringing the designers treats, like potato chips) describes designing for an audience older than what he calls the "café generation" – "If you look real

appreciate the same sort of thing." To this day, Salon gets email from readers of all ages thanking them for making the text more readable (readers who are probably unaware that they could adjust the default font size through their browsers).

The prototype site was interesting enough to Borders Books and Music that they agreed to sponsor the book-review section. As soon as the financing came through in October, Scott Rosenberg (theater critic, movie critic, and digital-culture columnist), Laura Miller (a freelance writer), Gary Kamiya (book editor, movie critic, and media columnist), and Joyce Millman (a TV critic) all left the *Examiner* and formed Salon. The first issue would launch three weeks later.

Technical talent

Scott Rosenberg discovered that having written a column called "Digital Culture" is not necessarily good experience for taking over the tech support role in a brand-new company. While he had been involved with the Free Press site and had also launched his own site, Kludge, it didn't exactly make him an expert. But without a technical person on staff, somebody had to do it.

Scott helped configure others' computers to have email and reach the Web. He successfully solved a problem at launch when a firewall at Apple wouldn't let them upload to their site – the problem was that their ISP randomly assigned

IP addresses, and the Apple server didn't recognize them. But he ran into trouble after launch when Salon's conferencing area, Table Talk, experienced continual problems.

Scott's delight for language, writing, and expression is obvious from even a brief conversation. He is

Wide fields of flat color are perfect for web graphics. David rejected the notion that web design had to use neon colors.

devoted to Table Talk and the idea that the Salon community can express their views. However, there wasn't a whole lot of Mac-server conferencing software to choose from in November 1995. They'd had some programmers set up some software called Tango that allowed the web server to talk to Butler, the database. Tango was a quick fix that frequently broke.

Scott also wanted a mailing list to be set up so that they could send out email announcing new Salon features. He says their biggest mistake was not having a mailing list set up when they launched – they couldn't get the software to work. He feels strongly that people were visiting the site who would have signed up to receive the newsletter had there been a place to do it. A few weeks after launch, they were named Cool Site of the Day, which gave them a big spike in traffic – and lost mailing list

Having produced his own site made Scott Rosenberg the resident technical expert.

close, despite the Retin-A and the Minoxydol, I'm not a member of that generation. My eyes are failing just a little bit, so I needed slightly larger type on the screen ... [We thought] there were like-minded people who'd

From news coverage and media commentary to movie and book reviews, Salon's "daily clicks" sections both entertain and provoke its readers.

candidates. They needed a technical director.

Author of more than 40 books on computers and technology, Dan Shafer was welcomed into the Salon team not as a writer, but as their technical guru. Dan Shafer's first priority was to get rid of Tango and implement Web Crossing, a product developed by a friend of his, Tim Lundeen.* The best part about Web Crossing was that Tim was willing to tailor the software to Salon's needs. Salon wanted more control over the pages than Web Crossing originally provided, like layout and how the posts were displayed. Web Crossing used a Usenet-style, tree-like posting system, but Salon preferred a linear system, so users could just scroll over others' comments. "In our experience," says Scott, "the latter works better if your goal is to build something of a community ... the other model is better if people are exchanging information, like if they had a problem with some software." Tim reconfigured the software to accommodate the request. "When we tell him the conferencing system really needs 'X,' he says, 'Oh, good idea, I'll incorpo-

*Shafer resigned from the Salon team at the beginning of April, 1997, to continue his own consulting and writing work.

rate that.' It's much healthier." It wasn't expensive to customize the software, as Tim was happy to have the feedback and incorporated it into version 2.0. Working with the Salon team paid off – Salon was the first major site to use the software, and now the New York Times site and other prominent sites use it, too.

TEAMWORK

Going daily

Salon published its first issue on November 20, 1995. Every two weeks, they put out another issue, packed with stories. From the beginning, Salon planned to go weekly, and within a month or two of launch, they knew that changing the content even weekly would be too slow. It would have to be daily to build the kind of repeat, core community they were looking for. But in March, they didn't have the resources to support a daily. They could, however, support a weekly magazine with daily elements.

By the April 22nd issue, Salon had gone weekly, as well as adding three "daily clicks" sections – the Newsreal, Media Circus, and Sneak Peeks (reviews) sections. Says Scott, "The traffic on those daily sections was intense from the beginning and drove our numbers up. People would bookmark those pages, knowing every day there'd be a new story. The more new stuff you're putting up, the more your loyal reader will come back."

The daily/weekly hybrid was the first step towards going daily; it also demonstrated the new level of organization and coordination required to go daily. All summer, as traffic increased, staffers talked about what would be needed to go daily and when they would be ready.

Duking it out: determining the content

Both the editors and designers refer constantly to the teamwork between the two groups when it comes to determining the content. Elizabeth Kairys, who was hired as a designer immediately after Salon's launch, tells a story of receiving a caricature of Rupert Murdoch from Zach. The story, entitled "Chairman Murdoch's Little Red Bucks," was about Murdoch's new Chinese-language web site. But when Elizabeth showed the illustration to Scott and David, they felt it didn't say "Mao" right away. "It was a great caricature of Rupert Murdoch," says Scott. "If you knew what Rupert Murdoch looks like, you could see it. But you couldn't see the joke, which was that we were dressing him as Mao." So Elizabeth sent the illustration back to Zach and asked him to put a Communist cap on Rupert.

During weekly editorial meetings on Monday, which last anywhere from an hour and a half to three hours, editors discuss the week's upcoming stories and bring up story proposals. These meetings sometimes get heated as other editors think of possible problems with story ideas and argue their case. Editors use their mission statement to help them select story ideas. An online magazine of books,

At the same time, there were other things to coordinate like transitions in the business staff and the arrival of a new publisher, Michael O'Donnell. The staff wanted Michael to be familiar with Salon before changing it. Once he arrived, they began two months of serious planning.

As in any good site design, the staff spent the most time on structure. They asked questions like. "If you change the feature every day, where do you put yesterday's feature so people continue to notice it?" They also needed to determine what needed to be on the home page and what would go in the navigation bar at the top. Advertisers wanted the ad to show on a 14-inch monitor. They decided to put headlines in HTML, although if users have changed the default settings on their browser, the page might look different than the designers intend. But this is less problematic than doing the headlines as GIFS – last minute changes take a lot longer to fix if a designer has to recreate the headline in Photoshop.

Salon: Editorial Statement

Address ▼ http://www.salonmagazine.com/archives/welcome/editorial.html

SALON | ARTICLES BY SUBJECT ▪ ARTICLES BY DATE ▪ TABLE TALK

What is Salon?

SALON is an interactive magazine of books, arts and ideas. Inside Salon you'll find not only authors, artists and thinkers, but a kinetic community of readers and kindred spirits eager to thrash out cultural issues.

We are inspired by the creative potential of the Internet, but unlike many other Web sites, Salon is not a techno-cult. As refugees from the atrophying world of newspapers and magazines, our primary allegiance is to written communication, to the power of the word. We think of digital technology as an exciting means to an end, but not the end itself.

American journalism has become a pitiful giant, ensnarled by commercial formulas and political tribalisms. Where once its voice shook mountains, it now squeaks cautiously and banally. The Net allows publishers to burst these bonds, to howl again.

It's the duty of writers to speak with a "terrible honesty," in the words of Raymond Chandler. This is the term historian Ann Douglas used to define the ethos of New York in the 1920s, where the high and low, black and white, male and female all came together in jazzy union to create an original American culture. Salon is dedicated to this same fearless creativity.

Cultural ferment was once the province of Greenwich Village bars, Left Bank cafes and North Beach bookstores. But Salon will free these smoky discussions from time and space. Readers from all over the world can drop by at their convenience, and when they do they will always find well-known writers, artists, musicians, filmmakers and multimedia designers as well as other savvy, opinionated readers. We provide the room. The drinks are on you.

Salon stands for a "militant centrism," to use journalist Jim Sleeper's term. In this angry, entropic age, the very idea that Americans share a common ground has become a radical notion. The Internet, which breaks down the distinctions between readers and writers, is the most democratic medium in history. Salon hopes to employ this electronic forum to advance the cause of civic discourse. We believe that communication in the '90s can be more than the ugly cacophony of talk radio. By using technology to bring forth what Walt Whitman called the "varied carols" of our nation, we hope, like that great prophet of democracy, to hear all America singing.

A final note on Salon conversations. We request that you use your real name when participating in a discussion. This makes for a responsible exchange.

We also make a plea for common courtesy. Slander and boorishness don't encourage an enlightening meeting of the minds.

And now, meet your hosts, the staff of Salon.

--The Editors

SALON | ARTICLES BY SUBJECT ▪ ARTICLES BY DATE ▪ TABLE TALK

arts, and ideas, Salon is not an online magazine about being online. The editors feel there is plenty of information about the next beta release of a hot desktop publishing program elsewhere on the Web.

The Salon stance against techno-cultism makes editors walk a fine line when writing about digital culture, between over-explaining and assuming their readers already know. They use each other as points of reference. Scott tells a story about an editorial meeting where he introduced a story idea. **"One of our contributing writers was here who was not a tech devotee. And I was saying, 'There's this idea that search engines don't work anymore.' To me it was an old idea, one that I thought I'd write about anyway because it's still interesting. She piped up, 'Really?** Search engines don't work? What do you mean?' That kind of thing reminds me that it's very easy to fall into a trap of staying too far ahead of the curve, not remembering that a lot of people are still getting used to the idea of email."

The Salon buzz: The working environment

Part of the energy of Salon is that no one is allowed to burn out by doing the same task day after day. The designers have set up their schedule to share responsibility for the cover story or stories. Designers who work on the cover and accompanying

stories for that day usually work on nothing else. Elizabeth describes a non-cover day for her: "I had Sarah's column to do, and I took on the daily clicks because Karen was doing the cover, and Mignon was doing Wanderlust. We knew what the music review was, so I got the art, scanned the art, and set up that page. For the Media Circus section, I ran over and got a photo of Mia Farrow and put wings on her and a halo. It's a lot of back and forth." The new copyeditor – Gary Kaufman, hired when they went daily – helps by writing on the white board what stories are due that day.

Scott describes an editor's day broken into chunks of editing, research, and working with writers – unless he's writing a piece, in which case he spends his day writing. Generally he spends time reading and reviewing story ideas and proposals, surfing, or reading things like *Mac Week* to keep up with the tech world. He edits as needed. "There's a lot of daily stuff, and a lot of that's sort of cooperative, whoever's available to edit. I edited a book review because it needed to be moved."

Working hours are generally sane. When Salon was bimonthly and they were putting out big issues, the Friday before launch was always a late night for

everyone. And when they went daily, they were launching the issue at 9AM – leaving the window open for late nights. But now, the new issue of Salon goes live at 6PM. By putting a cap on the working day, the Salon team prevents burnout.

Business plan/success

The Salon staff is full of ideas for expansion of their site. One of these, Salon 21st, had always been an idea the staff had batted around. It was a good department name for technology writing. Only recently has Salon 21st actually developed as its own subsite with its own mission.

They found that any time they ran a story about digital culture or the effect of technology in people's lives, these stories were immensely popular. Targeting intelligent readers who were interested in technology but weren't tech-heads, Salon's approach found a home in the 21st

Salon 21st gets technical –
www.salonmagazine.com/21st

pages. Although definitely part of the Salon site, it has its own look and its own URL. They hope that by making it easy for readers to get to 21st, they can serve both those readers only interested in technology and those readers who arrive via the home page.

Once the Salon 21st pages went live, the business staff went to work finding a sponsor. On other sections, the staff plans to reverse this order, first finding a sponsor, then launching the section. They're still experimenting to find what works best.

Salon's conversation area sometimes heats up as readers debate the day's issues.

The Salon community seems to be functioning as intended. The Rupert Murdoch story on his collaboration with *The People's Daily* set off some controversy in Table Talk as a guy who worked for an ISP in Beijing promptly posted his own views,

David Talbot	*Editor and CEO*
Michael O'Donnell	*Publisher and President*
Mignon Khargie	*Design Director*
Andrew Ross	*Managing Editor*
Gary Kamiya	*Executive Editor*
Darlene Townsend	*Associate Publisher*
Laura Miller	*Senior Editor*
Scott Rosenberg	*Senior Editor, Technology*
Joyce Millman	*Senior Editor, Television and Music*
Don George	*Wanderlust Editor*
Marc Wernick	*Vice President, Marketing and Business Development*
Dwight Garner	*Book Editor*
Elizabeth Kairys	*Art Director*
Steve Michel	*Webmaster*
Gary Kaufman	*Copy Chief*
Mary Elizabeth Williams	*Table Talk Host*
Cynthia Joyce	*Music Editor*
Bonni Hamilton	*Manager, Publicity and Promotions*
Karen Templer	*Associate Art Director*
Patrick Corcoran	*Interface Director*
Alexander Hughes	*Circulation Director*
Lori Leibovich	*Assistant Editor*
Suzette Lalime	*Administrative Assistant*
Jenn Shreve	*Editorial Assistant*

CONTRIBUTING STAFF

David Futrelle	*Contributing Writer*
Andrew Leonard	*Contributing Writer*
Carol Lloyd	*Contributing Writer*
Dan Shafer	*Contributing Writer*
Zach Trenholm	*Caricaturist*

SEE THE WELL WRITTEN, ENTERTAINING BIOGRAPHIES OF THE ENTIRE STAFF ON THE SALON SITE.

which were that the Chinese government was succeeding and that Western media doesn't report it correctly. The writer was on hand to respond to the posts. New sections like "Wanderlust," now launched, continue to attract attention from loyal and new Salon fans. Other sections, including "Mothers Who Think," are on the way.

As Salon expands, a priority is to maintain the close, dedicated working atmosphere. Their challenge is to preserve the spirit as they grow. Says Scott, "Everyone's excited. We're all working really hard, but we're work-ing on things we're excited to be doing. David sets a warm atmosphere. We get heated some times at edit meetings, but other than that, everyone gets along great."

Mignon agrees. "We can go into meetings with ideas of our own and be listened to. You can tell David anything and he'll listen. If it's a great idea, he'll consider it."

A talented, dedicated team. A challenging, spirited working environment. And finally, a consistently excellent site. Take a look at it. Daily.

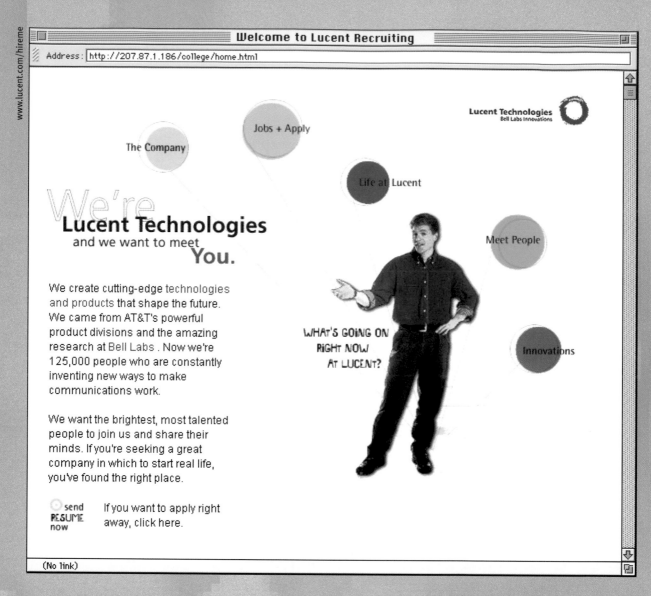

Welcome to Lucent Recruiting

Address: http://207.87.1.186/college/home.html

The Company

Jobs + Apply

Life at Lucent

Lucent Technologies
Bell Labs Innovations

We're

Lucent Technologies
and we want to meet **You.**

Meet People

We create cutting-edge technologies and products that shape the future. We came from AT&T's powerful product divisions and the amazing research at Bell Labs . Now we're 125,000 people who are constantly inventing new ways to make communications work.

We want the brightest, most talented people to join us and share their minds. If you're seeking a great company in which to start real life, you've found the right place.

WHAT'S GOING ON RIGHT NOW AT LUCENT?

Innovations

send **RESUME** now   If you want to apply right away, click here.

(No link)

Purpose of the site

Lucent built this section of their site to recruit college students and collect their resumes online.

How the developer was chosen

Lucent selected Verso based on its response to an RFP and an introductory meeting.

Launch date
March 12, 1997

Database launch date
April 23, 1997

In just four weeks, Verso had managed to meet Lucent Technologies' need for a college-recruitment section for their web site.

Focus
what you will learn

Verso's designers modified their process and found a streamlined approach to get this site launched in just four weeks.

THE SITE WAS READY. Verso had finalized the design, written the copy, dropped in the pictures from the photo shoot, and tested the code. It was already March, and students were ready to apply for Lucent jobs online, using the handy automated recruiting system where they could submit resumes to a database. Unfortunately, the database wasn't ready.

Producer Christina Cheney had been trying throughout the project to coordinate with Lucent's database contractor, so their two groups could work as a team to build the Lucent site, but she had found them unresponsive to email and phone contact. Now the deadline loomed, and they weren't going to make it. Verso was frustrated because they'd done their part – they wanted to get the site up. And Lucent *had* to get the site up so that it could begin hiring students.

Lucent team leader Chad Theule proposed a temporary solution. They should launch the site without the automated submission form and back-end database. Students could email or mail their resumes for a while, until the database was ready. This meant going back through the site and eliminating the many references to the automated recruitment system – an extensive task. But since they'd managed to build this site in just four weeks, the last thing Verso wanted to see was a late launch.

Four weeks to meet requirements

On February 4, 1997, Verso met with the Lucent recruiting team in Morristown, New Jersey to discuss the scope of the project and the client's needs and expectations for the site. Lucent needed to hire students – 800 of them. By adding a college-recruitment section, code-named "Team 800," to their existing web site, they hoped to fill job positions and significantly reduce the time it takes to hire new employees. Since Lucent hoped to acquire these new campus hires by the beginning of summer, the site had to launch in early March.

The Team 800 site was part of three intermingled human resources projects. The four-week goal was to get Team 800 online and taking resumes – Verso would have to work closely with the company building the database handling the resumes to develop an appealing and functional user interface for the automated recruitment form. Verso was also to do a quick redesign of the existing Market Hire section of the Lucent site, which handles their market and executive recruiting and hiring. The pages had been designed by another firm but weren't currently online, because Lucent hadn't been happy with the design. After these two sites went live, Verso would work on expanding and refining the Market Hire section and would revisit the Team 800 site to improve and change things they hadn't been able to do in the quick, four-week build.

In this kick-off meeting, Verso learned about Lucent's existing methods of hiring, how they hoped the web site would streamline their methods, about Lucent's campus recruiting process, and about Lucent as a company. Another goal of the site was to provide assistance for Lucent's campus recruiters who visit schools. The web site had to provide a level of functionality and ease of use that would encourage the recruiters to use it as another tool for filling their open job positions.

The site had to excite the student and persuade them to apply. It had to anticipate the students' questions and needs. The architecture had to be open to allow for new promotions and additions to the site. The meeting concluded with creating a wish list for the site, with the clients suggesting the site sell Lucent to the candidate, provide good resources students can use (like information on housing), and feature a job hotlist.

The Verso team flew back to San Francisco with a lot of work in front of them. There would be no real strategy phase, as design would have to begin immediately. Verso's designers would be drafting the creative brief as they went. Says Christina, "We did a very brief strategy, which would allow us to continue and go forward. Usually we do a goals and requirements document and extensive question-naires – we didn't have time to do any of that."

The design direction

Chad strongly recommended that the site be fun. Since it was aimed at college students, he hoped the Team 800 section of the Lucent site could be technically exciting. While taking

The site had to provide all-around information to the student – not just life at Lucent, but life in New Jersey.

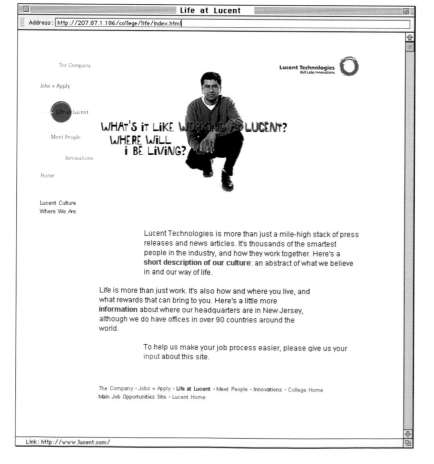

So do they.

The designers surrounded themselves with magazine images aimed at the same target audience.

his recommendation into account, Verso wanted to make sure their design would be the best direction to serve the students. They also wanted to present an accurate version of Lucent – Verso felt a responsibility to the students not to overdo selling Lucent as the ideal place to work.

The compressed strategy phase left little time for a creative brief, so Verso's design team – Gino Lee, creative director; Mary Tesluk, senior designer; and Purvi Shah, designer – had to get the basic design direction right the first time. It was the first time the three of them had collaborated on a project, and they applied a new creative strategy to expedite the process. They knew that as the project progressed, they would have less and less time for meetings and design reviews. There was no time to go back and forth on creative direction. Gino and Mary worked on the copy, while Purvi focused on the

design, and they decided to circulate their finished ideas constantly to keep everyone in the loop, so that they were all moving forward together.

The team's first step was to create storyboards of sample students. One student might be a geek but might envision himself as a well-dressed business-person having high-level discussions with intelligent colleagues. Another student might be more together but uncertain about the future. "We came up with four different scenarios," says Purvi. "We asked ourselves, 'Who are these students and what do they want?' Because visually we didn't have anything." They worked on the tone of the copy at the same time, working together to brainstorm buzzwords and ideas. Once they agreed on a direction, they hired a copywriter, but unfortunately his copy wasn't quite what the team was looking for. Since they had no time for iterations, Gino and Mary decided to write the copy themselves.

To add to the idea pool, the three researched the magazines aimed at that audience, the web sites they surfed, and recruitment web sites from competitors like Hewlett-Packard, Microsoft, Intel, SGI, and others. Some approaches seemed

more successful than others, while other sites seemed boring or too aggressive. Verso wanted to sell Lucent to the students with a more direct message. Students wouldn't believe copy saying over and over again that Lucent was great. What they might believe was actual Lucent staff saying, "What I'm working on here at Lucent is great." Verso focused on Lucent's high-profile accomplishments, like their having invented C++, UNIX, fiber optics, the FAX machine, and more. They knew these projects would be the aspect to sell – students would want to be a part of this innovation.

Gino, Mary, and Purvi decided to work on creating design languages for Lucent to review, coming up with five different approaches. Not

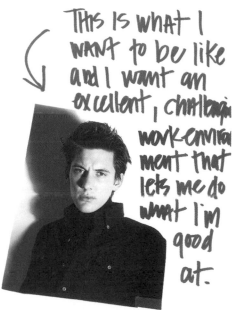

THIS IS WHAT I WANT to be like and I want an excellent, challenging work-environment that lets me do what I'm good at.

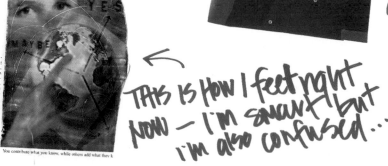

THIS IS HOW I feel right NOW – I'm smart but I'm also confused...

Storyboards helped the designers characterize different types of students.

finished designs, these were visual studies with different tones, type-faces, color schemes, and images creating different looks and feels. "Our goal was to not let Lucent perceive these as the final design, because if they did, we were in trouble," says Purvi.

Presenting the visual studies

In a Valentine's Day conference call between Verso in San Francisco and Lucent staff in New Jersey, Iowa, and San Diego, Verso presented the visual studies online. Verso identified three areas in which the client should consider the designs: appropriate tone, palatability within Lucent corporate ID standards, and overall attractiveness of concept. They emphasized that reviewers should

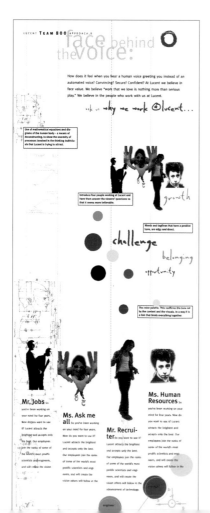

The visual studies presented different approaches to the client, not finished designs.

place themselves in the role of college seniors and graduates and judge the work from that standpoint.

Verso presented five studies on-line: Lab, the Face Behind the Voice, Want To Do, Montage, and Get Noticed. Each approach contained explanatory text about how the design enhanced the theme. Of the approaches, Face/Voice was most successful. The client felt others were too serious or were about the student's life, not the student's future

at Lucent. Face/Voice, while taking a similar approach by addressing students' questions, was about the people who worked at Lucent. Purvi says, "The client liked the tone, they liked the playfulness, they liked the colors. They liked the intelligence."

Purvi thinks showing the client the visual studies demonstrated to the client that Verso knew what it was doing. "They got to know who we were and what our strength was. This was important, so they would trust us. We didn't have much time, so we really wanted them to say go and do whatever you want to."

The next step: prototypes & balloons

Now Verso had to streamline the visual study into some actual prototypes using the language and creative feel from the Face Behind the Voice. They wanted to keep the colors and the playful, dynamic approach.

Purvi wanted to incorporate the balloons she'd used in that study to show the color palette. While she hadn't intended the balloons to do anything more than show the palette, she and the other designers liked the way the balloons looked. Purvi felt the need for a design element to guide the students to the resumé submission page and thought the balloons could serve this function. They could act as the navigation and add a playful element to the pages.

The balloons used to show the palette in the visual studies became the finished site's navigation.

By February 20, six days after they'd presented the visual studies, Verso was ready to present four refined prototypes to the client. This time, they included splash screens to set the tone and build anticipation. They pared down the use of people from many per page to one to save on download time. They had streamlined the copy tone and asked Lucent to review it as well.

Besides the client review, Verso had assembled a focus group of students to review the design. Verso used personal contacts at Stanford to assemble the focus group, asking them, "How do you approach finding a job? What do you want to see – photographs of people or illustrations? Do you want to know what it's like to live there? Do you want to know what you're going to be working on day-to-day?"

The students emphasized that they wanted to be treated like adults. They were making a very important decision. They wanted accurate,

The prototype design review included different splash screens to set the tone and mood of the site.

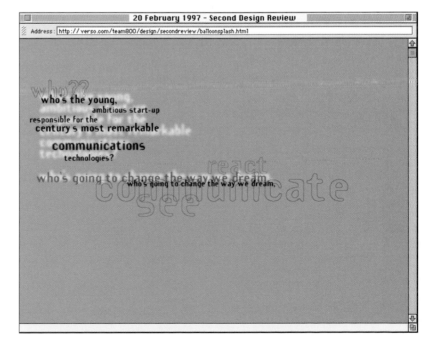

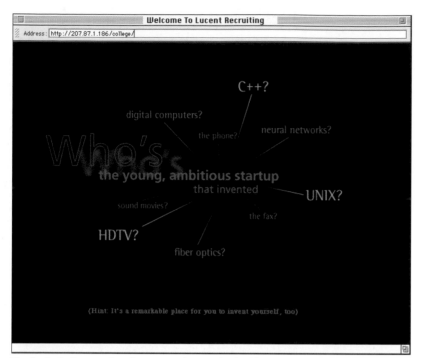

Welcome To Lucent Recruiting

Address: http://207.87.1.186/college/

C++?

digital computers?

the phone?   neural networks?

Who's
the young, ambitious startup
that invented   UNIX?

sound movies?

HDTV?   the fax?

fiber optics?

(Hint: It's a remarkable place for you to invent yourself, too)

The final splash screen doesn't use Lucent's name but builds anticipation and sells Lucent's successful projects.

reliable information presented in a positive and upbeat tone. They wanted to know what was happening in the company and why it was a good place to work.

By February 27, Verso had a final design direction ready for Lucent to review. Lucent made some specific suggestions, but overall, they were enthusiastic about the design. Verso scheduled a photo shoot with models and began production.

Contractor trouble

While Verso's designers developed a final design direction, Christina had been working with the database-development company and Todd Fahrner, Verso's design technologist, to determine the parameters for the user interface. Verso's goal was to incorporate the resumé-submission form seamlessly into their design of the rest of the site. Unfortunately,

the database was falling behind schedule.

Verso had hoped to work with the database company as a team, but throughout the process, they had been frustrated by slow responses. Christina says the database company was slow to get Verso feedback about how the user interface should interact with the database and was often unresponsive to email queries. Frustrated, since Verso's side of the project was on time, Christina made sure that Chad knew what the holdup was. Instead of reporting the results of communication with the database company to Chad, she suggested they have conference calls, so he could hear for himself why the database was late.

Chad suggested they launch the site without the page where students could submit their resumes to the database. Since the copy throughout the site had referred to the online submission process, this was no simple solution. Copy had to be streamlined throughout the site to suggest students mail or email their resumes instead.

While the site was essentially ready to launch, one technical problem was plaguing Verso – they could not get the rollovers to work in Internet Explorer. The secondary navigation used balloons to show the visitor where he was in the site. Rollovers changed the white balloons to different colors. It was a whizzy, client-pleasing feature with one problem – the JavaScript did not work in Internet Explorer 3.0. Christina brought in an ActiveX consultant to fix the problem, expecting a simple solution. Says Christina, "There was a lot of wasted time and effort on our part learning there was a bug in the ActiveX controls for IE 3.0." Verso tried using Flash instead, but it didn't

Studio Verso

Studio Verso (www.verso.com) is a high-end design and production firm in San Francisco. Verso makes web sites for demanding clients whose success is tied to the quality of their online presence. A one-stop consulting agency for strategy, advertising, architecture, design, and engineering, Verso combines the client-focused process of a professional, multidisciplined agency with the insights and knowledge derived from making web sites exclusively. Clients include Lucent Technologies, The RREEF Funds, NetObjects' Fusion, Sony, Doug Menuez, and GTSI.

512 Second St. #100, San Francisco, CA 94103 415.278.9900

work either – to this day, the balloons are static on the IE version of the site, but it doesn't affect their functionality.

Implementation & launch

The site, sans database, launched March 12. Immediately, students logged on and began sending their resumés. The college recruitment and Market Hire sites logged more than 15,000 user sessions in the first month, and more than 4,000 resumés were submitted in that first month. It's still too early to tell how many of those students submitting resumés to the site were hired. The database was finally ready in April, and the automatic recruiting system went live on April 23 – more than a month after their target of early March.

Verso is proud of their accomplishment with the Lucent site. As Christina says, "We knew what we needed to do. We parachuted in like paratroopers and got it all done." Purvi feels using the storyboard and visual studies was extremely valuable in the design and hopes to continue to incorporate this step in future sites. Most important, Verso accomplished their goal of making a successful web site under an exceptionally tight deadline. As Chad says, "Given all the inadvertent, unforeseen hurdles they faced, Verso was still able to pull it off."

LUCENT TECHNOLOGIES	
Chad Theule	Project Team Leader
Steve Miranda	Director - Strategy, Planning, Diversity, Human Resources
STUDIO VERSO	
Gino Lee	Creative Director
Christina Cheney	Producer
Purvi Shah	Concept Designer
Mary Tesluk	Design Director
Todd Fahrner	Design Technologist
David D. Cullinan	Production Manager
Jennifer H. Wolf	Production

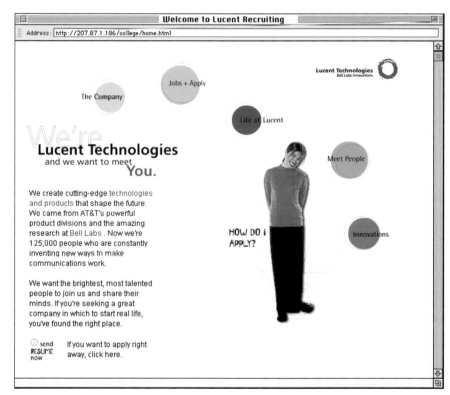

The final site's approach worked – more than 4,000 resumés were submitted in the first month.

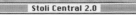

THIS SITE IS INTENDED FOR AUDIENCES OF LEGAL DRINKING AGE ONLY

www.stoli.com

Stoli Central 2.0

Address | http://www.stoli.com/

Stoli Central 2.0

Welcome to Stoli® Central 2.0™. That's pronounced, "stoh-lee-sen-trul-two-point-oh." Allow us to explain. In the early months of 1995, we launched Stoli Central. It had no numbers attached to its name, just plain old Stoli Central. You all seemed to like us a bunch, and we liked you too.

But things have changed a bit since our anniversary, and we were forced to have a little work done. A nip here, a tuck there, six new flavored vodkas, blah, blah, blah. So, we went back to the electronic drawing board, donned our cyber thinking caps, and brainstormed (virtually, of course). The result is what we call our own little Russian revolution.

So what's new? Nothing much, what's new with you? But seriously, folks. There's almost too much to mention, but we will.

Freedom of Flavor

How does a new section devoted entirely to flavored vodkas grab you? Freedom of Flavor, aptly named, will enlighten you on the most spectacular new taste sensations to hit the vodka scene: Kafya, Razberi, Persik, Zinamon, Strasberi and Vanil. We've even renovated the ever-popular STOLI NOTE ™ (148K) so you can spread the word to all your loved ones that Stoli Central 2.0 is here. If you're running one of those newfangled browsers like Netscape 3.0 or Internet Explorer 3.0, take a trip to our Java-enhanced version. For all you old-school users, classic Stoli Note still exists in its original form. But that's not all. Act now, and play our brand new game, Stoli Says (82K), absolutely free.

Freedom of Expression

If you're like us, you're into the classics after all, Stolichnaya® is the classic vodka, and Stoli Central is now a classic Web site. And we believe in keeping the classics alive. So that's what we've done. In Freedom of Expression, you can visit all the great games and pages we had on the old Stoli Central. Test your skills at the Stoli Cipher, or spend some time expressing yourself at the new Stoli Palette. If you hate games, don't worry, there are plenty of other blasts from the past to explore. And if you're looking for information on Stolichnaya-sponsored cultural events, you'll find them here.

Freedom of Vodka

What kind of vodka person would we be if we didn't devote an entire section to the good stuff? Well, we did. In Freedom of Vodka, you can learn everything there is to know about Stolichnaya, and all of our other premium spirits of the World. Sample our favorite cocktails in Spending of the House. Nothing cures what ails you here. Then try your luck the Bartender to find your own drink. If you think you can do better, introduce yourself to the Bartender. Here that you've determined what kind of libation imbiber you are, all you have to do is find a place to drink it. No problem, steppin' out will do it for you. And if you'd like to send a gift of vodka to a friend, you've come to the right section. And you must be of legal drinking age, it's so easy to order by clicking here.

This site is best viewed with Netscape Navigator 3.0 or Microsoft Internet Explorer 3.0. Earlier versions of either browser will limit your experience.

Please read this Legal Disclaimer before entering.

Stoli Central produced and designed by Margeotes | Fertitta + Partners and CyberSight.

Freedom of Flavor | Freedom of Expression | Freedom of Vodka | Help

Stolichnaya® Vodka, Product of Russia, 40% and 50% alc./vol., 100% grain neutral spirits.
© 1997 Carillon Importers, Ltd., Teaneck, NJ.

Purpose of the site
The upcoming launch of six new flavored vodkas was a perfect opportunity to redesign this marketing driven site.

How the contractor was chosen
M | F+P handles Carillon Importers' print and TV advertising accounts. M | F+P's interactive division created the original Stolichnaya site that launched in April, 1995, and proposed the redesign to accompany the launch of a new Stoli product.

The players
Patricia Barroll
Arnie Arlow
Bob Manni
Blake Robin

Redesign launch date
January 2, 1997

Chapter 7

www.stoli.com

When Margeotes | Fertitta and Partners planned a redesign for the successful Stoli site, they placed as much emphasis on managing the client's expectations as they did on strategy and design

This launch was a big deal.

Six new flavored vodkas, from vanilla and peach to strawberry and coffee, would hit the stores in a few more months.

Focus

what you will learn

M | F+P's ad-agency model emphasizes managing clients' expectations and integrating the web site with the existing marketing campaign.

Carillon Importers' ad agency, M | F+P, planned a huge advertising campaign to get the message out about the new Stolichnaya vodkas – print, billboards, TV spots. Everyone would soon have parties serving authentic Russian vodka, according to the plan. Authentic, flavored Russian vodka.

M | F+P's Digital Media division knew the marketing strategy overlooked one important element – the web site. And they wanted to do more than simply add some pages about the flavored vodkas – they wanted to "flavorize" the whole site in a redesign. Producer Blake Robin and account executive Bob Manni worked together to come up with a redesign proposal. The proposal would include a two-year comprehensive look at the future of the Web and the Stoli site's place on it.

While no one can say for sure where the Web will be in two years, it is typical M | F+P style to give the client a long-range plan. As Blake says, "Our fundamental mission statement emphasizes managing expectations and servicing the client. We want the client to know what they're getting and be happy with it from the top." In the meeting with Carillon's decisionmakers – Michel Roux, president and CEO; Patricia Barroll, vice president of marketing communications; and Ernie Capria, senior vice president of marketing –

Blake pointed out different trends on the Web and summarized what the competition was doing. He and Bob proposed a new design that would emphasize the flavors, yet hopefully remain true to the spirit of in the original design. They even presented a look for the site with a suggested new navigation to Carillon.

Although she felt the Stoli site worked well with the old design, Patricia Barroll was open to M|F+P's presentation. "We kept getting cited

as a wonderful example of a commercial web site and of how to integrate your print advertising. But the M|F+P team is the web expert, not us. We take what they say into consideration." Carillon's concerns were the same as they had been for the original design: make the site user-friendly, give the brand lots of visibility without making it seem like an advertisement, and get the user to hang out and spend time at the site. In addition, they were to make the

flavors prominent and keep the site consistent with the advertising. Knowing when to adhere to elements in the campaign and when to deviate required understanding of the strategy behind the current campaign. And there's no more flavorful talker to describe it than M|F+P's creative director, Arnie Arlow.

The campaign strategy

If you get him talking, Arnie Arlow will tell you the Soviet Bloc fell just to make his life easier selling a Russian product. In a conversation full of free-association and humorous observations, Arnie occasionally brings himself back to the subject at hand. He says, "Our entire strategy, whether print or Web or anything else, has to do with re-establishing the authenticity of Russian vodka. If I had 12 people in a room and I said to

M|F+P expanded on the existing advertising slogan Freedom of Vodka™, adding Freedom of Expression and Freedom of Flavor as names for the main sections of the site.

them, 'I'm going to give you something and you tell me the country it's associated with,' and said 'vodka,' I think 12 out of 12 would say Russia."

To create this authenticity, the print campaign used Russian artists, who submitted gorgeous canvasses of Russian Neo-Constructivist art – in the Soviet style immediately following the Revolution of 1917. Says Arnie, "We have made every effort to ensure that every person who does any of the graphics for Stolichnaya is Russian." Furthermore, the slogans appearing with the art emphasize freedom. As Arnie explains, Russia did become free, communism was over, and Freedom of Vodka™ meant freedom of choice, or at least the freedom to choose Stoli.

The choice of message and execution are very important, because this message must be enforced consistently over a long period of time. "The world is not really waiting for your ad. I don't see people lining up outside my window waiting for my new, wonderful expression. In advertising, the more consistent you are for a longer period of time, the more you'll be heard," says Arnie. The site had to be consistent, too, although Arnie and the Digital Media team knew it would differ from the print campaign in a few important ways.

While the site would use the ad campaign's Russian art and M | F+P would use the campaign's copywriters, the key difference was Carillon's directive to get the user to spend as much time on the site as possible. A print ad just conveys a message. A web site has to entertain. "In print, you can expect somebody to be with your image maybe two and a half seconds, if that," says Arnie. "On the Web, we can get someone to spend hours on our site, playing, doing, experimenting, exploring, having fun. It's just miraculous." The site had to have games and interactive features

Russian artists paint large, striking canvasses in post-1917-revolution, Soviet style for Stolichnaya's advertising campaign.

to get users to hang out. It would also need a lot more copy than the print ads.

The web-site strategy

M | F+P usually begins a site design with a four-to-six-week strategic development phase, in which they work on translating a client's existing ad strategy into a web strategy. To convince Carillon a redesign was necessary, however, they'd compressed the strategy phase and the next step, creative development, to show them a suggested look and feel in their proposal. While giving the overall two-year plan, Blake and Bob had shown color Quark printouts to Carillon that focused on the new navigation.

The old site had just three sections, and the new one would have four with the addition of the flavors. But the navigation needed to be simpler. They felt customers should be able to navigate between sections from any page in the site and suggested a section toolbar for every page. Since Carillon was concerned about less technologically adept customers, Blake and Bob didn't propose frames. They showed the top-level site structure at that first meeting. Blake says, "Because we were starting in the creative development stage, we wanted it to look as much like a prototype as possible. What gets approved at that stage is what we build. We want the client to know what they're getting so nobody says in the middle of production, 'Wait, we never approved that.'" So when M | F+P got the go-ahead for the redesign, they already had approval on the overall look-and-feel as well.

Now the creative team could go to work on the copy and adapting the art to the site. M | F+P's copywriters enjoyed the chance to use their skills, creating an "Ask the Bartender" section, where users could request a drink that made them feel a certain way from a number of options. But on the flavor pages, they outdid themselves. Each page begins with an excerpt from a famous Russian novel, like *Anna Karenina* or *Crime and Punishment* – an excerpt mentioning the featured flavor. It added

Strawberries are a part of Russian life – at least, according to Leo Tolstoy.

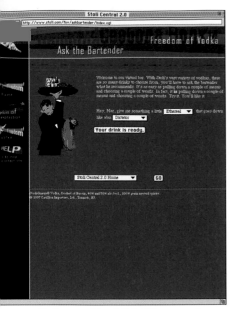

Feeling capricious? Crisp? Dangerous?
Ask the bartender for a recommendation.

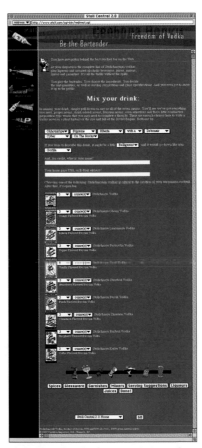

"In the Strategic Development Phase, we translate an existing ad strategy into a web strategy. It's the Discovery Phase: asking questions about what are we doing and why are we doing it. That usually lasts four to six weeks.

"In the Creative Development Phase, we translate strategy into executions. Specific deliverables include content structure, flow chart of every page broken out by section, the navigation, and comps of the look and feel. Comps usually include the home page and first page in each section.

"Since everything's been approved at this point, the Production Phase usually goes smoothly ... in an ideal world."

Blake Robin, producer, Margeotes | Fertitta and Partners

Blake Robin on Phases

authenticity and a certain intelligence to the site. "We could have said, 'Vanilla is a new vodka, and Russians know vanilla," says Arnie, obviously proud of the copy. "But this is turning up the soil a little bit."

Managing client expectations

While Blake made sure things ran smoothly at M | F+P, Bob Manni scheduled periodic client-review meetings. Bob is the group account executive for Carillon accounts, coordinating all interaction on Stolichnaya advertising or web production. Patricia says, "We have creative review meetings with M | F+P constantly and incorporate the site into that. They'd come out and show us bits and pieces of the site, and we'd approve it."

Bob says that normally the agency sends monthly or 60-day updates to the client, based on the amount of activity happening on the site. They also have quarterly overview meetings to review the past months'

activity and discuss future projects. During the redesign, reviews went weekly. Bob says they didn't give updates on the status of the project as a whole in these meetings but used them instead to feed pieces of creative to the client for approval. They had given the client a debut date – January 2, 1997 – and assured them it would happen, rather than worrying them with specific trouble spots.

Another facet of M | F+P's creative reviews is their attention to detail and quality. They want to be sure that when the client sees a piece of creative, it is exactly how they hope it will look on the site. Says Blake, "It doesn't go to the client until everyone's made their comments and proofed it, and everything is as we think it should be." Their in-house approval process has several steps. From the creative group, work is trafficked to account management, who routes it for legal review. Once legal has signed off, the work gets client approval, goes back to the traffic department, and goes to

Choose a vodka, choose your mixers, and name your creation – we liked Aunt Olga's Peach Minsk with a Smooth Lenin Libation.

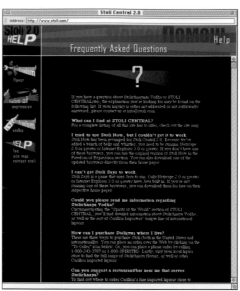

Posting an FAQ page reduced the volume of customer email to the site.

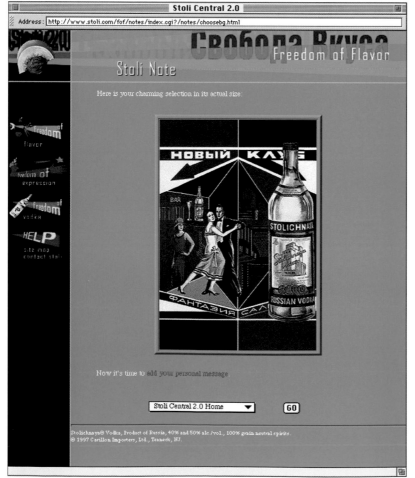

With their gorgeous neo-Constructivist artwork, Stoli Notes have been a consistently popular feature on the site.

production. Account executive David Burden says, "It can be hard when your production company's on the West Coast, your client's in New Jersey, and your lawyers are in Connecticut. A two-day timetable to get something routed and approved is pretty tight."

The emphasis is on keeping the client involved, but also making sure the client sees only the best possible work. "We do that without sacrificing interesting and innovative work," says Blake, who used to work at a production house where client expectations were not so carefully managed. "There's no reason why the work needs to suffer just because the client is in the loop."

As creative got approved, M | F+P would pipeline material to Cyber-Sight, a production company in Portland, Oregon. M | F+P hooked up with CyberSight in late 1994 and used them to produce the first Stoli site. Their main recommendation to M | F+P was to use frames to reduce the download time and produce a true cross-navigability between sections. Once convinced, M | F+P presented some numbers to the client, showing how many of Stoli's current users used frames-enabled browsers, and what percentage of the web population in general did. Carillon went with CyberSight and M | F+P's recommendation.

Blake says that once things are in production, generally things go smoothly as far as managing the client's expectations. "Once the project is in this phase, it doesn't require much approval from the client, aside from seeing the specific copywriting and page executions up front and towards the end." Although CyberSight admits that the refinements and beta testing phases were a crunch for time at their end, the site debuted on schedule the day after New Year's. The teams celebrated with a little Stoli Strasberi.

Success

The launch of the new flavors, aggressive banner advertising, and the redesign of the site combined to significantly increase traffic to the site. M | F+P keeps careful tabs on the site's effectiveness, using both quantitative (visits-per-week, home page views, banner click-through, number of drink-recipe submissions) and qualitative (email submissions, press, reciprocal link opportunities) analysis.

Carillon was happy to see a significant decrease in email submissions following the posting of a FAQ list. Customers are encouraged to check the list before sending email inquiries. Consumers get their questions answered, Carillon provides more information about their products, and the agency significantly decreased the number of hours required to answer email inquiries.

M | F+P continues to look forward in its plans for the site, both in practical applications and in a more fanciful fashion. Says Arnie, "It's so amazing to me what we're doing right now, and I know it's the tip of the iceberg. Before long we'll be using the Web to send our laundry out, watch movies, order food, watch TV, and maybe read our books. It'll really be the lifeblood into homes." While the Stoli site can't take care of your laundry, it can tell you how to serve Stolichnaya Pertsovka – in a Pepper Manhattan, perhaps. *Na Zdorovia!* Cheers!

Founded in 1973, this New York-based agency provides advertising services to clients like Benckiser Consumer Products, Campbell Soup Company, Carillon Importers Ltd., Coty Inc., and Friendly Ice Cream Corporation, among others. The digital media division, founded in 1994, creates integrated web sites, online advertising, and CD ROMs, with clients like Benckiser North America, Carillon Importers Ltd., Coty Inc., Sotheby's Inc., and Standard & Poor's.

411 Lafayette St., New York, NY 10003 212-979-6600 www.margeotes.com

Bob Manni	*Group Account Director*
Jim Nikola	*Account Supervisor*
David Burden	*Account Executive*
Tatiana Robinson	*Account Coordinator*
Paula Brooks	*Managing Partner Media Services*
Anne Censullo	*Associate Media Director*
Greg Brozenske	*Assistant Media Director*
Arnie Arlow	*Partner/Creative Director*
Dana Wallace	*Art Director*
Michael Rovner	*Copywriter*
Janice Salicrup	*Art Director*
Craig Deitch	*Copywriter*
Damian Fraticelli	*Copywriter*
Blake Robin	*Director of Digital Media*
Marla Stutman	*Account Manager, Digital Media*
Maya Valentin	*Webmaster/Interactive Art Director*
Terry Savarese	*Print Production Manager*
Laura Rosenblatt	*Traffic Director*
Joshua Young	*Traffic Coordinator*

From left, front row: Paula Brooks, David Burden, Bob Manni; middle row: Joshua Young, Marla Stutman; back row: Jim Nikola, Greg Brozenske, Blake Robin, Maya Valentin, Tatiana Robinson, Terry Savarese, Laura Rosenblatt.

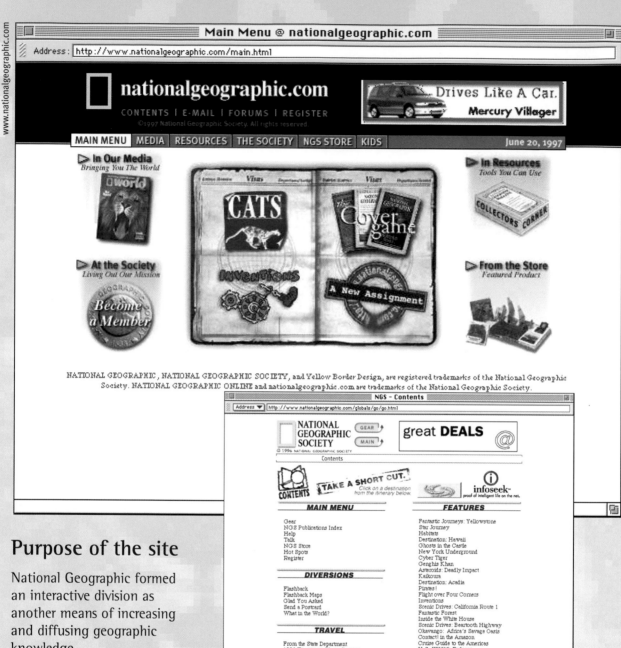

Purpose of the site

National Geographic formed an interactive division as another means of increasing and diffusing geographic knowledge.

Launch date

June 20, 1996

Featured modules

Kaikoura
Inventions
Pirates
Dinosaur Eggs
Okavango

Please see the credits for each module on the National Geographic web site.

FROM PIRATES, GHOSTS, AND MUMMIES TO WHALES, INVENTIONS, AND RAFTING TRIPS, THE NATIONAL GEOGRAPHIC SITE RAISES THE BAR FOR QUALITY CONTENT

Back in the 1960s, the National Geographic Society decided to use television as a means of achieving their mission – to increase and diffuse geographic knowledge.

what you will learn

How National Geographic uses web development firms from around the country to create features for this content-rich site

www.nationalgeographic.com

BANKING ON TELEVISION turned out to be a fine idea. National Geographic Television programs have consistently educated and entertained viewers and continue to win award after award. In early 1995, the board made a similar decision about another new medium – the World Wide Web. The new division, National Geographic Interactive (NGI), formed in June, 1995, with its own accounting, business, editorial, and technical staff, to build a web site (and to produce other multimedia projects, like CD ROMs).

The new division's first task was to translate the content expertise of the Society to the Web. Mark Holmes, new editor-in-chief of NGI, came up with the idea of content "modules," or features, for the web site. Previously an art director at the yellow-border magazine, he felt that every story they did was as in-depth as a college course, and that the site should follow the content-heavy model. With modules, the site content could have in-depth and experiential content, and each module could be developed independently of the others.

NGI knew it didn't have the technical or multimedia expertise it needed, or even the personnel, to come up with frequently changing modules. Even a web-production house wouldn't be able to handle the workload of four new modules a month. In November,

Five games, five levels. NGI suggested kids should go from invention game to game linearly, and between levels, there should be some sort of animation as a reward. The games and artwork for the site would come from the "Superfun" insert in *World*, National Geographic's magazine for children. NGI's producer for the module, along with Big Hand, thought carefully about the structure and the reward system. How would they lead kids from game to game? What was the incentive?

The cover of the "Superfun" insert featured a complex machine, a professor, and in the corner riding a bike to power the machine, a monkey. Once NGI's producer for this module, the creative teams at Big Hand and their partner, Circumstance Design, saw this artwork, they had an inspired idea – finishing each game would make more parts of the Rube Goldberg-like machine work. As further reward, kids would get a token after each game that they could use in the machine, reinforcing the idea that they were powering it up. Kids would click on the token, the monkey would stuff it in the slot, and some of the machine would work. They'd have to finish all five games to see what the machine actually did.

The cover of the "Superfun" insert.

As kids complete each game, more and more parts of the machine animate.

1995, Mark Holmes and Business Lead Chris Ward hit the road on a nation-wide tour of Web and multimedia developers. These groups had to be willing to work with NGI closely to meet the high standards of editorial and design quality. After their tour, they had about six design groups they wanted to work with, four for their launch.

Magnet Interactive designed an overall look and architecture for the site, which launched on June 20, 1996, with content modules by other developers. Over time, the module-development process has become more streamlined. Web developers who work with NGI agree – both the challenge and reward of working with NGI is the client's commitment to excellence. They are an involved, knowledgeable group, ready to do their share of the work.

Selecting a web developer

NGI typically begins the module-building process by meeting with the story teams from the magazines (in addition to the yellow-border magazine, NGI works with *Traveler* and *World* magazines) and TV divisions. They develop content in such a way that the divisions cross-promote, but don't duplicate, each other. Says Mark, "You don't want people coming to the web site to kick around stuff they've already learned in the magazine." Mark feels the web site will attract a new audience to the Society. "If you think the site is really cool, you should see what this magazine has been doing for 109 years," he says. NGI is trying to become a more integral part of the other divisions' story teams out covering these fields and collecting assets, with an eye to their use on the Web.

Once NGI's Online Planning Council approves a module idea, Mark assigns a producer to create a storyboard and decide on the creative direction for the module. This producer will pick a three- or four-person team to work with her to flesh out the editorial angle and direction, to take a

Creating perfect web sites

Second Story

Julie Beeler *Brad Johnson*

Brad Johnson and Julie Beeler of Second Story appreciate NGI's rigorous testing, as it helps them create better sites and also saves them testing on their end. Julie says, "We get a detailed list if something isn't here or there. We test everything for Windows 95, Macintosh, and both IE and Netscape to alleviate any major problems. But there will be little things that come up. The QA person proofs the entire site and says when the site can go live."

Getting the contract

Big Hand

Each web developer decides how much work is enough to win the contract. Jay Wolff, creative director at Big Hand, outlines the strengths and weaknesses of the storyboard and works with NGI's producer to improve it. He says, "We write a full proposal. In the beginning of projects, we always outline what we call 'guiding lights.' We identify the clients' objectives for the user experience, their objectives to leverage their content, and their objectives to entice advertisers." Once it gets the contract, Big Hand uses these guiding lights as a resource to begin developing the site in earnest.

BIG HAND™

preliminary stab at determining what kind of assets are available, and brainstorm on how to make the content specific to the Web. After thoroughly researching the idea and making a first pass at gathering content, they put together a storyboard with a suggested site structure and navigation. Before this storyboard goes to any web developers, it must be approved in-house by producers, art directors, creative directors, and financial and technology people. The producer sends the approved storyboard out to site developers, asking for proposals.

NGI might send the storyboard to three developers or just one. The team selects the group whose approach they like best. Sometimes they don't use the group's approach for that particular module but might pick up the developer for another upcoming project. The developers are expected to add their expertise to the process and take the initial idea to the next level. Mark says, "Each time the bar gets raised, because they're pinging back and forth between our editorial folks and the multimedia teams. So that, by the time we see the final storyboard, we're pretty excited about where it's headed."

When the developer is notified that they're doing the project, things are already in motion at NGI's end. They know what the launch date will be, because their sales force, PR people, and quality-assurance and research group organize their schedules around that date. Dates are usually anchored around the other entities' publication dates. If this launch date isn't feasible to the developer, the only choice for them is to tell NGI the deadline isn't possible, given the scope, or suggest cutting the project to fit. Once they have the contract, most developers thoroughly plan the site's execution to make sure it's feasible. They submit a final architecture to NGI, outlining all of the content areas. NGI puts an in-house writer and researcher to work, and it takes between two and four weeks to get final content back from them.

Quality assurance & testing

As a new division, NGI wasn't sure what their editorial process would be. Modeling it after the magazine would be too slow (the magazine has an 18-month production period). "We haven't had the luxury that most of the other entities around here have – we didn't have an editorial process that we could work from. We had to basically start with absolutely nothing, make no assumptions, and go forward," says Mark. For example, they quickly learned that trying to fact check after the site was mostly done was too expensive. "We have to compensate for that on the front end and try to do as much of that work before we get into development as possible."

There are few "night-before launch" stories with these groups – at least not the night before it goes live to the world. Developers submit a site two weeks before the launch date, and the NGI staff checks it to make sure every link works, that there are no typos, that it works in all the browsers NG supports. Besides making certain that every detail is correct, NGI tests the sites thoroughly with focus groups. For NGI kids' sites, three school systems in the Detroit metropolitan area act as beta testers. "We send them the initial concepts for something, and then we begin to send them the screens as they come through development and let them hit the module on our staging servers before we take it live. We're always soliciting their input into what it is that we're doing," says Mark.

Larry Lux, Vice President of NGI, says he never resents "those pesky customers," but instead tries to listen to their feedback with an eye toward improvement. "We have a group of people, Mark especially, who are constantly saying, 'No matter how good it is, we can do it better.' So we are always looking for some little thing we can do, some tweak or some change that'll make this more interesting or easier to navigate. That's something that pervades this whole place."

"Okavango" Refocusing the concept

Matt Owens, creative director at methodfive (formerly Myriad Agency), remembers modifying the metaphor for a module about little-known animals of the African delta. NGI presented methodfive with a selection of concepts, all revolving around the food chain. Matt says, "The producer came to us with a loose concept called 'Café Okavango.' After reviewing the idea, I felt the direction was problematic logistically." He suggested using a tracking/safari metaphor to layer over the food-chain metaphor, making for a strong experiential module.

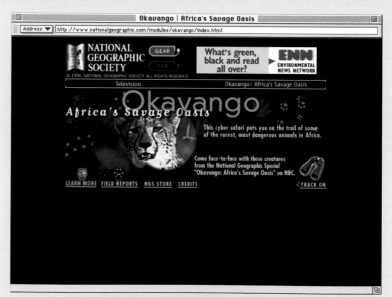

Pay attention to the tracks – there's a quiz at the end of this module!

For the "Pirates" debut, NGI proposed a five-day staged roll-out of the site. Each day new information would become available. While working out the logistics, Big Hand discovered some problems with the idea. For instance, if a kid missed the first day, what would happen? Would they be able to get several days' worth of information at once, and would that cheapen it for the kid who'd been coming every day? NGI prefers not to use recognition software because it feels it worries parents. Big Hand and NGI discussed the problem at length, but as Jay says, "We finally said there's no more time to discuss this and solve this

Kids learn about famous pirates, ships, and booty in this high-seas-adventure module.

problem. We won't have a site at all if we don't go forward." Mark agreed they needed to drop the roll-out aspect and focus on meeting the launch date.

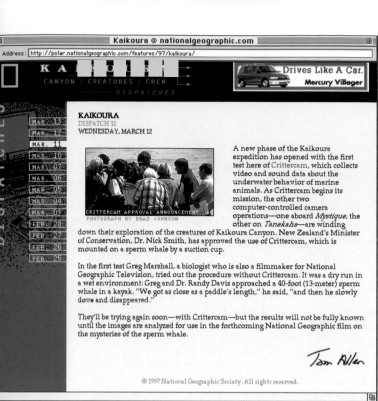

Drives Like A Car.
Mercury Villager

KAIKOURA
DISPATCH 12
WEDNESDAY, MARCH 12

CRITTERCAM APPROVAL ANNOUNCEMENT
PHOTOGRAPH BY BRAD JOHNSON

A new phase of the Kaikoura expedition has opened with the first test here of Crittercam, which collects video and sound data about the underwater behavior of marine animals. As Crittercam begins its mission, the other two computer-controlled camera operations—one aboard *Mystique*, the other on *Tanekaha*—are winding down their exploration of the creatures of Kaikoura Canyon. New Zealand's Minister of Conservation, Dr. Nick Smith, has approved the use of Crittercam, which is mounted on a sperm whale by a suction cup.

In the first test Greg Marshall, a biologist who is also a filmmaker for National Geographic Television, tried out the procedure without Crittercam. It was a dry run in a wet environment: Greg and Dr. Randy Davis approached a 40-foot (13-meter) sperm whale in a kayak. "We got as close as a paddle's length," he said, "and then he slowly dove and disappeared."

They'll be trying again soon—with Crittercam—but the results will not be fully known until the images are analyzed for use in the forthcoming National Geographic film on the mysteries of the sperm whale.

Tom Allen

Cameras mounted via suction cup? This dispatch introduces the Crittercam.

Second Story (formerly Brad Johnson Presents) creates an online skeletal version of the site's architecture using dummy copy and graphics to demonstrate the navigation. They send a site map to their producer at NGI for a reference. The producer clicks through the skeletal site and then discusses it with Brad and his partner, Julie Beeler. Brad and Julie find the skeletal site helps the whole team figure out if there's any missing content and if the architecture makes sense. For "Dinosaur Eggs," they had illustrations of three eggs on one screen, and on the next they had three scientists' perspectives on how to determine the egg's contents. They had photos for two of the scientists, but not the third. Brad says, "We didn't see that in the beginning. But now that we had it scoped out, we all saw there had to be symmetry."

Scoping out the content

Kaikoura

When you've got six days to construct your site before you fly to New Zealand, you don't have a lot of time to pack. Due to internal complications at NGI, Brad and Julie at Second Story hadn't known until the last minute that Brad would be leaving to make an on-site web site about a joint expedition between National Geographic and the Smithsonian, searching for the giant squid. They had known it was a possibility, however, and fortunately had planned some structure.

Brad and Julie came up with a structure based on a previous module they'd designed, "The River Wild." In "The River Wild," the viewer goes through a daily journal, and different elements of the site are reachable from different days' entries. They figured with each new dispatch, they could build out more content, based on what they found down there. Besides the live dispatches, the site would have explanatory content, such as what the expedition's mission was and the scientists' backgrounds. They would divide the content into three areas: The Canyon, or geography aspect of the module; The Creature, or more about the giant squid; and The Crew, or the people and equipment. But they hadn't actually built anything yet.

Brad would be working with writer Tom Allen to create assets for the site, but he and Julie needed to build a place to put this content. In the six days before Brad flew to Kaikoura, he and Julie made a skeletal site into which they could plug the content as it got built. It was text-based, with HTML links showing how the navigation would work, where the menu would be, and how the frames would function. They finished it two days before Brad left and sent it to their producer to be approved. Once it was approved, Brad was already in New Zealand generating content on the fly. Julie worked with Brad from their Berkeley, California, office to get the site ready for debut with the first live dispatch. NGI rushed it through the research department, and it went live five days later.

Working in the field

Brad was supposed to work on the National Geographic boat, right alongside the crew. But when he arrived in New Zealand and saw the boat, he realized there was no way this was feasible. While one person on the boat showed Brad how he'd used bungee cords to strap down his computer equipment, Brad, with his laptop, Macintosh 8500, and 17-inch monitor, wanted to be on land. Plus, he says, the boat was "really

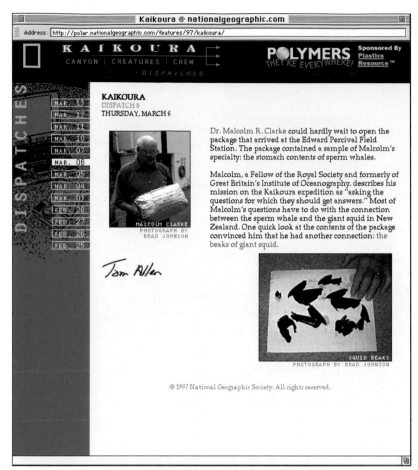

KAIKOURA
CANYON | CREATURES | CREW
DISPATCHES

POLYMERS
THEY'RE EVERYWHERE!
Sponsored By
Plastics Resource™

DISPATCHES

MAR. 13
MAR. 12
MAR. 11
MAR. 10
MAR. 07
MAR. 06
MAR. 05
MAR. 04
MAR. 03
FEB. 28
FEB. 27
FEB. 26
FEB. 25

KAIKOURA
DISPATCH 8
THURSDAY, MARCH 6

Dr. Malcolm R. Clarke could hardly wait to open the package that arrived at the Edward Percival Field Station. The package contained a sample of Malcolm's specialty: the stomach contents of sperm whales.

Malcolm, a Fellow of the Royal Society and formerly of Great Britain's Institute of Oceanography, describes his mission on the Kaikoura expedition as "asking the questions for which they should get answers." Most of Malcolm's questions have to do with the connection between the sperm whale and the giant squid in New Zealand. One quick look at the contents of the package convinced him that he had another connection: the beaks of giant squid.

MALCOLM CLARKE
PHOTOGRAPH BY BRAD JOHNSON

Tom Allen

SQUID BEAKS
PHOTOGRAPH BY BRAD JOHNSON

Brad had never photographed squid beaks before.

a rocker." He set up shop in a lab that looked like an eighth-grade science classroom, with its big sinks for oceanographic studies. In the next rooms, groups of scientists from MIT and Cornell worked on various projects.

Brad found being on land had another advantage – he and writer Tom Allen could keep track of both teams' progress. The Smithsonian and NG teams each had their own boats and also were using different approaches in their searches for the squid. The Smithsonian team's approach was more scientific, while NG was more journalistic, with a staff of photographers and a writer. If Brad had been on the NG boat as planned, he wouldn't have had any idea what was going on with the Smithsonian team. And then the site wouldn't be an accurate representation of the expedition as a whole.

At first, some members of both teams were reluctant to give Brad

Jay and his team began designing what they call "key frames." These are the main screens in the site and are used to get sign-off on the design from the producer. Key frames might be shown as sketches, laid out on paper, or sometimes mounted on boards. Jay says, "Those serve as the graphic bible." Once the producer approves the sketches, they produce final screens. They get color output, mount them on boards, and Fed Ex them to National Geographic.

Jay admits it would be easy to post the pages on a password-protected part of the server for approval but prefers the "boards in hand" approach for presentations to the client. "There are always technical problems on the other end that you can't control, like 'My monitor wasn't big enough; I kept getting cut off because my ISP broke down.'" Once the boards are approved and they have more of the design com-

pleted, they make a working model of the site in Photoshop and Director that represents the flow and the navigation of the site.

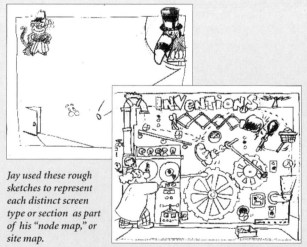

Jay used these rough sketches to represent each distinct screen type or section as part of his "node map," or site map.

"Inventions"

Hiding the Internet

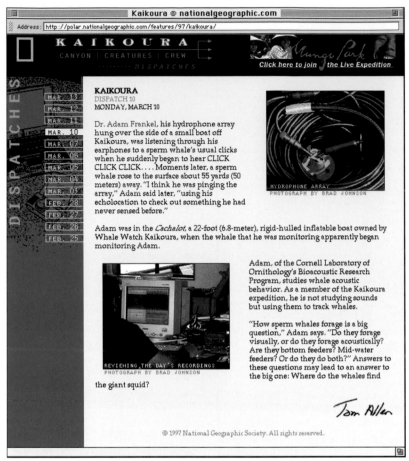

Address: http://polar.nationalgeographic.com/features/97/kaikoura/

KAIKOURA
CANYON | CREATURES | CREW

DISPATCHES

Click here to join the Live Expedition

DISPATCHES

MAR. 13
MAR. 12
MAR. 11
MAR. 10
MAR. 07
MAR. 05
MAR. 04
MAR. 03
FEB. 28
FEB. 27
FEB. 26
FEB. 25

KAIKOURA
DISPATCH 10
MONDAY, MARCH 10

Dr. Adam Frankel, his hydrophone array hung over the side of a small boat off Kaikoura, was listening through his earphones to a sperm whale's usual clicks when he suddenly began to hear CLICK CLICK CLICK.... Moments later, a sperm whale rose to the surface about 55 yards (50 meters) away. "I think he was pinging the array," Adam said later, "using his echolocation to check out something he had never sensed before."

Adam was in the *Cachalot*, a 22-foot (6.8-meter), rigid-hulled inflatable boat owned by Whale Watch Kaikoura, when the whale that he was monitoring apparently began monitoring Adam.

HYDROPHONE ARRAY
PHOTOGRAPH BY BRAD JOHNSON

Adam, of the Cornell Laboratory of Ornithology's Bioacoustic Research Program, studies whale acoustic behavior. As a member of the Kaikoura expedition, he is not studying sounds but using them to track whales.

"How sperm whales forage is a big question," Adam says. "Do they forage visually, or do they forage acoustically? Are they bottom feeders? Mid-water feeders? Or do they do both?" Answers to these questions may lead to an answer to the big one: Where do the whales find the giant squid?

REVIEWING THE DAY'S RECORDINGS
PHOTOGRAPH BY BRAD JOHNSON

Tom Allen

Brad and Tom made an effort to profile all the members of the expedition.

assets for the site. They weren't familiar with the Web and weren't taking the site seriously. Plus, the scope of the site had been decided beforehand, so that it wouldn't "scoop" the magazine or television program, and the team members had to consider if their assets could be used on the site. They would say of each photograph, "I don't know if you can use that," or, "You better get that approved."

That was before they saw the site. Brad showed them the sections that pertained to their work. After it went live, they could use the Internet access at the hotel to see new additions, and they became very excited about it. Seeing the site convinced them that Brad's focus was on the behind-the-scenes, not what they were gathering for their magazine or television pieces. "People were borrowing my digital cameras, and they were shooting a lot of digital video down there. They were bringing this stuff to me non-stop," says Brad. "I couldn't go and gather content because I was overwhelmed with the amount of media brought to me." The site became the hub for the expedition as both teams used it to post material – and to find out what was happening on the other boat.

Live dispatches from the field

When Brad and Julie did their first module, "The River Wild," the structure and content had been predetermined. On their next module, "Dinosaur Eggs," they recommended changing the content to go along with the structure they proposed. But on "Kaikoura," Brad had a more editorial role, working closely with Tom Allen, the writer on the module, to decide what content to put up and in what format. On one day, they would introduce and describe the Rope Cam, and on another they would add boat descriptions.

While Brad usually had the next few days' worth of content planned, he and Tom would change plans if the teams found something unusual. News came that they'd found three dead beached whales on the coast of New Zealand. Members of the team flew to photograph them and came back with the digital photography that night.

At first Brad thought he would save the footage, since he already had other material ready to post. But then news came that there were five more dead whales in a different part of New Zealand. While he was invited to go see them, he elected to stay and do the production for the dispatch about the first beaching. He was afraid that the footage of the second beaching would outshine the news of the first, and he felt both were important. So the first beaching ran as one dispatch and the second the next day. "We had to do something light-hearted the day after that," he says.

Brad regrets not having been able to leave the lab more for in-the-field photography and content gathering. He didn't have any production staff and needed help with cleaning up digital photos, pre-production, digitizing video, making QTVRs, and creating graphics. Julie says, "One person could take the files, digitize them, clean them up, and hand them off to the next person, who would put the site together. And then there had to be someone at the home base, because getting the site dispatches routed through and making sure they went live was a lot of work."

Brad worked late, comparing it to going hiking when you think you see the top of the mountain, but when you make it there, you realize there's still another summit. "There was so much happening. I wanted to introduce all these personalities, but I never really had time when these whales would come in, or these neat pictures of eels. It was only supposed to be a dispatch every few days, but we made it every day. It would have been unfair if some people got profiled and others didn't, because no one would know they were there."

Streamlined QA

For both Brad and Julie and NGI, the review processes had to be streamlined. Brad and Julie generally like to take time to make sure every detail is perfect on their sites. Says Julie, "We made the edits and two minutes later, the page was online. I could never really sit and breathe and look at it. Of course, I tested all the functionality and made sure everything worked. But usually we give ourselves a good solid week of testing and refining. If something's off by one pixel, we go in and fix it."

The production speed and amount of material challenged National Geographic's QA and Research process as well. To expedite each day's dispatch and not hold it up in QA and Research, they chose to put a disclaimer on the site, "In order to post these dispatches promptly, we have

curtailed the in-depth research customary at National Geographic." During the first week Brad was in Kaikoura, the QA and Research department went over his illustrations carefully with Julie, asking if diagrams were drawn to scale or if a piece of equipment had been detailed correctly. Although they realized after the first week that Brad was working alongside the people who would normally approve such illustrations, a National Geographic researcher helped QA the site content throughout the module's development.

In the end, the breadth and scope of Kaikoura ranged far beyond the 13 dispatches, even including a "since the expedition" update. For Brad and

Julie, building the live, in-the-field site was an incredible opportunity. Brad says, "As a kid, National Geographic was always the best. That brand stands for the best. To do something for them, to me it's an honor. You put it up and you have no excuses – it just has to be the best."

NGI hopes to create more modules like "Kaikoura." Mark Holmes says this module was a fairly radical departure for the division, a departure he's comfortable making. "To my knowledge, it's the first time we ever sent a multimedia person in the field to develop an entire module on the fly – from developing content to writing code. That, to me, is new-media journalism at its best."

"Whirling chopped-up fish" – Tom's writing has a flair for spotlighting the unusual.

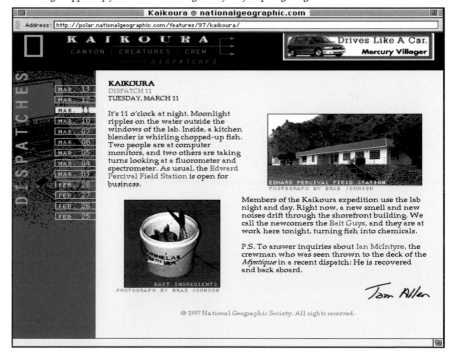

Big Hand, Inc.

Established in 1990, with studios in Dallas and San Francisco, Big Hand, Inc. (www.bighand.com) produces award-winning interactive programs to both entertain consumers and help corporate marketers promote products and services. With an extensive portfolio of CD ROM, Internet, interactive TV, and enhanced-CD products, Big Hand, Inc. has worked with a variety of partners, including Time Warner, Twentieth Century Fox, Capital Records, Mattel, National Geographic, GTE, Coca Cola, and General Motors.

**2140 Commerce St., Dallas, TX 75201
214-744-2888**

Second Story

Established in 1994 as Brad Johnson Presents, Second Story (www.secondstory.com) creates interactive experiences delivered on the Web and through disk-based media. Principals Brad Johnson and Julie Beeler work with teams of artists, writers, illustrators, and programmers to produce an inventive blend of technology and storytelling on topics ranging from adventure travel, architecture, and natural history to corporate merchandising and promotions.

239 NW 13th Ave. #215, Portland, Oregon 97209 503.827.7155

"Inventions"
Re-illustrating the problem

Sometimes putting art supplied by NG on the Web presents permissions problems, depending on the contract NG has with the artist. While they had the artwork from the "Super Fun" insert, Jay decided to have an in-house illustrator redraw all the characters. "We redrew it because we needed it in our particular format, it needed to be clean to compress well, and it was easier to actually re-illustrate stuff and match the style." NG negotiated the rights, and the module gave the original artist, Jim Carson, credit for the characters and this illustration style. That solution worked out for Carson's illustrations, but some drawings of old patents they wanted to use were a more complicated story.

NGI wanted to use drawings of old patents they had in house. Unfortunately, using them was going to require getting permission from not one, but many different publishers. It was going to take too long – it was already October and the site would launch in December. "We ended up re-illustrating all of those from a different perspective, or with a different functionality or focus in the illustration. We ended up using only three scans of original artwork in the whole site," says Jay. Having a team of illustrators in-house cuts costs because they don't pay by the illustration but by the hour.

Jay thinks one of the advantages of working with NG is their huge library of images and other assets. "But until multimedia is mature if not old, there will be limitations on how we reuse the art. We've never found a situation where we don't have to consider all of the original contracts. We never had a situation where we haven't had to consider all of the images separately."

Big Hand used an in-house illustrator to redraw the illustrations to make them work better on the Web.

"Inventions"
An eye for troubleshooting

To save on download time, Big Hand came up with the idea that the five games in this module could share assets. Jay says, "Same audio, same basic cast members – all the illustrations and movements of the professor and all the other characters were pretty much the same. We had different children in each game, but basically there were a lot of the same assets." The first game would require some downloading, but then each additional game would ideally just require downloading a little more code and some text, like the questions and answers in each game.

Unfortunately, at the time Shockwave wouldn't let two or more movies share the same assets. This was a big disappointment to the team, but they found a different solution: the main page, with the animated machine serving as a menu, would set up the user for all five games. So kids wouldn't have to wait for all five games to download,

it would automatically preload the games, letting kids play one game while the other four downloaded in the background.

And the problem with the machine was its size – 192K. When your audience is kids in schools, you can't expect them to spend that much time downloading. To solve that problem and still allow the managed downloading, the team came up with a longer, "staged" introduction to the main page. The professor enters a dark room – only his eyes are visible. He explains that he is a brilliant professor working for National Geographic, but he just can't find the lights. His speech bubbles give instructions for the site – meanwhile, the main page is loading. Jay says, "The original concept didn't include the guy walking around in the dark, obviously." They found a creative solution when technical limits required their plan be modified.

Formerly Myriad Agency, methodfive (www.methodfive.com) is a top-tier provider of Internet development and production services. They create elegant and innovative solutions to a wide range of Internet design, technology, and marketing challenges. methodfive offers exceptional performance and a history of fruitful, long-term relationships with a growing list of distinguished and discriminating clients.

632 Broadway, 10th Floor, New York, NY 10012 212-253-7488

methodfive

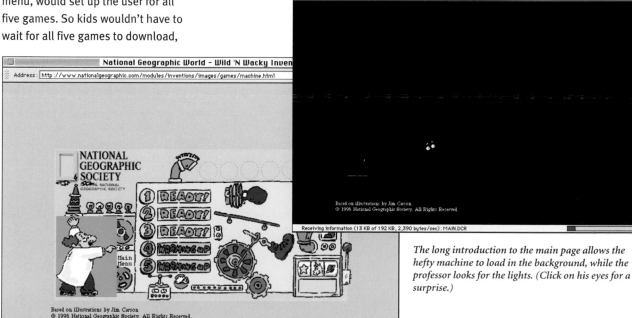

The long introduction to the main page allows the hefty machine to load in the background, while the professor looks for the lights. (Click on his eyes for a surprise.)

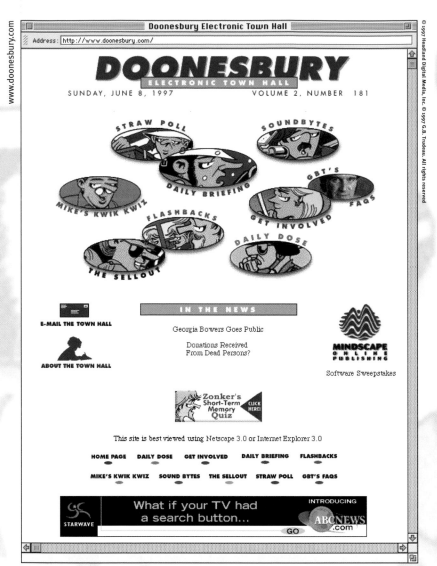

Purpose of the site

The Doonesbury Electronic Town Hall serves as an interactive online community, where visitors catch up on the news, participate in polls, read the strip, and post their opinions.

The players

Liz Armstrong
Charles Willi
Mark Nieker
Garry Trudeau
David Stanford

How the developer was chosen

In early 1995, Headland (then Mindscape) produced three Doonesbury CDs. Headland then approached the Doonesbury Group (a company that handles Doonesbury licensing) with the Doonesbury web site idea. Headland then mocked up some screens and showed them to Garry Trudeau, who gave them the go-ahead to proceed.

Launch date

December 1995

Redesign launch date

February 2, 1997

WHAT BEGAN AS MINOR FACELIFT TO THE DOONESBURY SITE SOON BALLOONED INTO A FULL-FLEDGED REDESIGN

Any web-site producer would love to hear that Garry Trudeau would be printing her site's URL in his popular comic strip, "Doonesbury."

Chapter 9

www.doonesbury.com

Focus

what you will learn

How Headland used effective project management to cope with this rapidly expanding project

EVEN BETTER, it would be running in the high-pro file Sunday edition of more than 1400 newspapers nationwide. There was just one problem – the site's redesign was scheduled to go live that Monday – one day too late to catch all those Sunday-comics readers.

That Thursday before the redesign's launch, Liz Armstrong, producer of Headland Digital Media's "Doonesbury Electronic Town Hall" site, had been working on her check-list of things to do, trying to organize the hundreds of details that needed attention before the Monday launch. Scripting for the online trivia quiz wasn't ready. The Flashbacks section, where visitors would be able to look up Doonesbury cartoons from years past, wasn't finished. Lots of pages still needed to be marked up in HTML. Plus, she was still waiting for some last-minute copy.

Liz called Garry Trudeau's assis-tant, David Stanford, to check in on the missing copy, but David had more on his mind. "By the way," he said, "on Sunday, there's gonna be a strip referencing the web site. Garry would really like it if the new site could be live for it." Garry creates the strip weeks in advance to fit his syndica-tion schedules – at the time, both he and Headland thought the new site would be online when the strip got published. But the scope of the redesign had expanded, pushing the launch date back – one day too late.

Liz remembers thinking, "There's no way we can do this." But at the same time, she knew the opportunity for exposure was too good to miss. She walked down the hall to the office of Brian O'Donnell, Headland's HTML manager, and sat down. "You're going to hate me," she told him, "but guess what I just found out?" The two of them looked at the to-do list and realized they were in for some late, late nights.

Schedule #1:
The November 5 debut

What began as a minor facelift to the Doonesbury site quickly mushroomed into a much bigger project. The Doonesbury Electronic Town Hall had maintained a political slant ever since its debut in December 1995, focusing on the 1996 U.S. presidential elections. A Straw Poll took a prominent place on the front page, which also included a News Brief and other

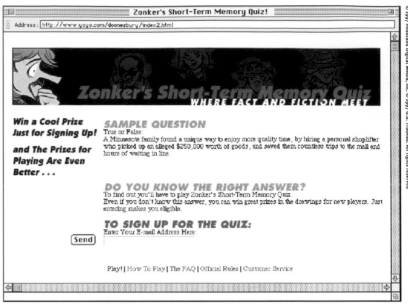

Zonker's short term memory quiz tests your knowledge of pop culture.

election tidbits. Four chat halls – The Site, The Strip, The Campaign, and Hot Buttons – provided a popular forum for visitors to the site.

By late September 1996, the team at Headland realized that when the election was over, the site could take on a new focus: less campaign oriented and more about the

Doonesbury strip, politics, and pop culture in general. Mark Nieker, Headland's president, and Charles Willi of Workshop 4, designer of the original site, thought the new focus could be achieved by redoing the front page to reflect the shift in emphasis and by adding two features. One of these features would be "Mike's Kwik Kwiz," a trivia quiz named in honor of a Doonesbury character, which would feature fresh questions daily. Also, because users often sent email intended for Garry Trudeau to the site, Mark and Charles suggested a section called GBT's FAQS, in which Garry would answer selected questions online. They also wanted to update the banners that headed the existing pages, giving each a new look. After getting the go-ahead from Garry on the facelift ideas, Mark turned the project over to Liz to work out the details as producer of the project.

Soon after the work began, the team realized that this quick fix wouldn't be adequate. Liz consulted the site's original producer, Nancy

The original design focused on politics and the upcoming presidential election.

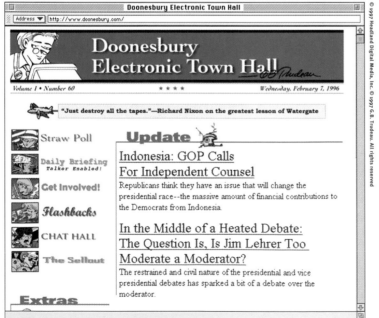

SECRETS OF SUCCESSFUL WEB SITES

Siadek, to develop a schedule outlining what needed to be done by whom and when in order to meet a planned November 5 launch. Liz and Nancy worked with Charles on the new home page and mocked up the trivia and FAQ pages, while the Headland team worked on the scripts and put the pages together. But once they saw samples, the team realized the facelift ideas didn't mesh with the old site as well as they'd hoped. When Garry saw the new home page combined with the only slightly modified design of the existing site, he didn't think it was working, and Charles agreed. Charles and Garry

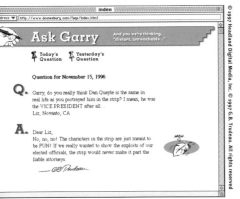

The old banners just didn't work with the new design, as shown in this roughed out version of GBT's FAQs.

got along well. They had established a trusting relationship in their work on the initial site design. Says Charles, "He felt comfortable with me working on his creation, his material. He knew I would stay true to the sensibilities of Doonesbury."

Once Charles explained his design dilemma to Headland, the team felt they might as well take the opportunity to revisit some of the technology in place on the site. Mark explains, "So you have a house, and you need to add rooms to the house. Once you start decorating a couple of rooms, you start thinking you want to redo

the whole place." Suddenly, adding on two features and redoing the home page had become a full-fledged re-design. Liz tossed the old schedule in the trash and prepared to start over.

Schedule #2:
The January 2 debut

With the new, much bigger project, Liz knew that they were never going to meet the original launch target of election day, November 5, 1996. A more realistic date would be January 2, 1997 – a new site for the new year. She sat down with a calendar and mapped out the process.

One of her challenges was coordinating the schedules of team members who were not only out-of-house, but out-of-state. Headland's offices are located in Novato, California, just north of San Francisco. Garry is based in New York, and Charles lives in Seattle, Washington, so Liz had to keep track of art being generated, produced, and approved on two different coasts. She coordinated three-way phone calls with Charles and Garry to go over designs and missing items.

Having produced Doonesbury-collection CDs meant Headland already had all the assets it needed to create the Flashbacks page in house.

She also had to build enough time into the schedule for Garry to write copy and review content. Garry and his assistant David not only had a ton of other commitments but were also responsible for providing original content to the site, including 200 trivia questions, miscellaneous feature text, and illustrations.

Meanwhile, the project was expanding even more. Given the opportunity to review the site technology, the team at Headland decided to update the Doonesbury Town Hall with more advanced features. They enhanced the

Garry wrote more than 200 trivia questions for the Kwik Kwiz.

Flashbacks section, giving users access to more than 26 years of archived Doonesbury strips, where previously only those strips from presidential-election years had been available. Garry suggested adding rollovers to the home page – when visitors rolled over each Doonesbury character, a dialogue balloon would pop up, telling what was new in that

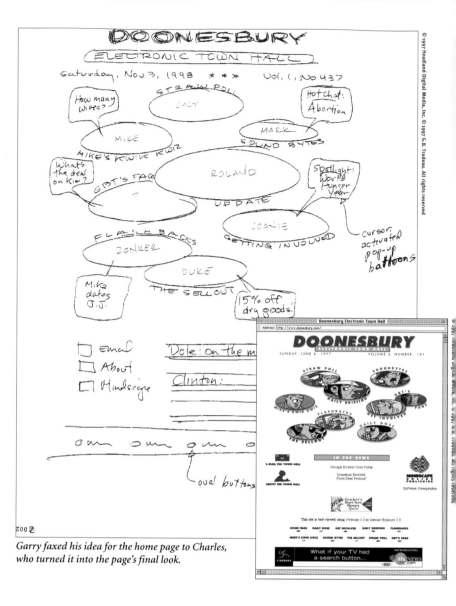

Garry faxed his idea for the home page to Charles, who turned it into the page's final look.

Headland Digital Media, the digital publishing arm of Pearson, PLC, and formerly the online division of consumer-software company Mindscape, Inc., creates, publishes, and distributes branded Internet programming that integrates themes and content from Pearson, PLC, publishing companies, and third-party content partners, as well as from self-developed original concepts. The company has successfully introduced more than a dozen digital publications and programs in key market segments such as sports, contemporary community, and turn-based and action gaming.

88 Rowland Way, Novato, CA 94945; 415-898-1999
www.headland-media.com

section. The Headland staff worked to build them with minimal download time.

Headland also wanted to update the user ID scheme by replacing it with cookies. On the old site, viewers

> ## "Project management here means a lot of time on the phone."
> ### – Nancy Siadek

were given an ID number, and this number tracked their progress through the site. If they went to the store, their shopping-basket contents could be tracked, even if the viewer left and returned later. Cookies would simplify it by loading the information to the user's computer invisibly. They could also be used to keep track of a user's cumulative score at the trivia game.

Liz made a timeline for some of these things, but new ideas cropped up and additional changes jeopardized the schedule. The trivia game and the FAQs needed to be redone to reflect the new design, and Garry had to try to find a way to fit writing new copy, trivia questions, and other

time-consuming tasks into his packed schedule. Plus, the main thrust of production was happening in late November and December. People began taking scheduled vacations, including Garry and his staff. As Charles says, "From my experience, that's not the most productive time of the year for large groups of people working on integrated projects." Because they wanted this redesign to be not just adequate, but great, the team decided to push the schedule back to incorporate everything they wanted to add. They needed another month to do it right.

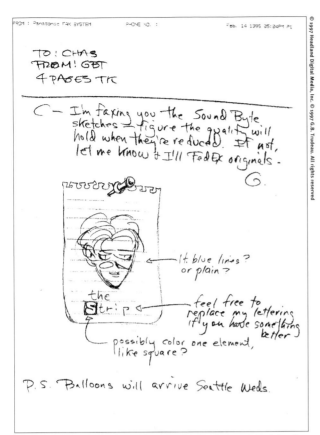

Garry preferred to work by fax, sending both rough and final sketches to Charles to scan, clean up, color, and put up on the site.

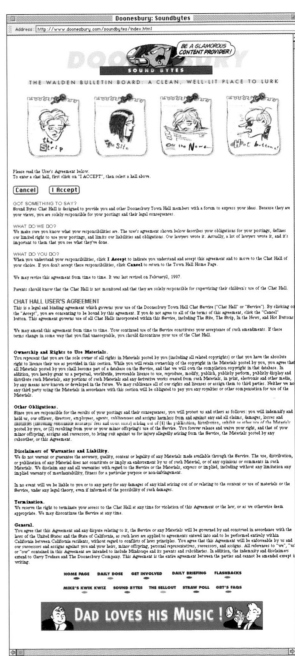

Schedule #3:
The February 3 debut

Because the launch date had been pushed back, the Headland team decided to add yet another feature: the Daily Dose. One thing about the site had consistently troubled Doonesbury fans: although archived strips were available in the Flashbacks section, there was no link to the current day's strip. Due to distribution agreements, Headland couldn't get permission to run that day's strip on the site. But they could link to the online comic sections of daily newspapers that carried the strip. This would involve still more planning and execution time in the redesign, but the team figured the visitor satisfaction would be well worth it.

Besides adding the Daily Dose, Headland spent the month of January finalizing the content and art and doing the final production work like coding and scripting. Liz's checklist was surrounded by other hastily jotted reminders outlining all the little things left to do. The launch date was approaching rapidly. And then Liz called David to check in on missing copy, and February 3 became February 2.

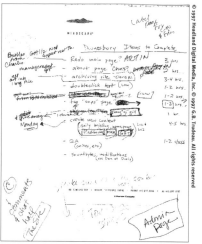

Liz's checklist helped her keep track of all the details.

Unable to get permission to run that day's strip on the site, Headland linked to daily newspapers' comic sections.

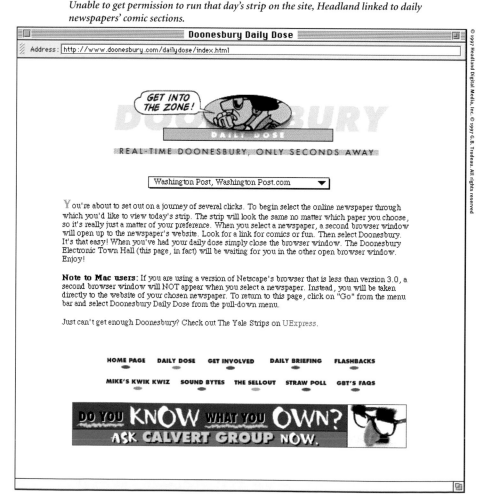

Launch: February 2

The weekend of the launch, Headland staff worked until four and five a.m. to get things done. Liz says it was like writing a college term paper the night before it was due. "Everyone drank so much coffee and lived off Cheetos and got it done. That's part of what makes it fun, in a sick kind of way – the fact that you can stay up all night, get something done, and see it live the next morning."

When the Sunday paper came out, the new site was live, running with no major problems. The team couldn't include the site's Sellout section (where users can purchase Doonesbury products online) due to scripting problems. There was a half hour when users couldn't access the site, because it was being moved from the staging server to the main server. Liz also received user email saying the home page took too long to download. Headland took it down and put up a front page without rollover bubbles until they could put up a fine-tuned, speedier home page, complete with rollovers, a few weeks later.

Headland intends to maintain the site as a forum for the Doonesbury community and will add new topics to keep firing up discussions. The developers also hope to grow that community by syndicating parts of the site. Mark Nieker explains, "We take some part of our site, or create a new bit of programming tied to our site, and we offer that to somebody who wants to be able to say, 'Hey look, we've got Doonesbury over here, too.'" Headland has been syndicating content for more than a year and anticipates expanding in this arena.

Meanwhile, the redesign wasn't lost on the vocal fans of the site. Liz said their reaction was very positive – even more so once the few bugs were worked out. *PC Magazine* agreed, naming the Doonesbury destination as one of their top-100 web sites. As Garry wrote about the chat hall, "It's a clean, well-lit place to lurk." The team has succeeded in building a community on the Web, with active regulars and frequent drop-ins engaging in lively discussions. Activity on the site has increased since the debut of the redesign. Doonesbury aficionados finally have a place where they can

Garry Trudeau.

Garry Trudeau	
David Stanford	
Mark Nieker	President, Headland Digital Media
Charles Willi	Principal, Workshop 4
Nancy Siadek	Senior Producer, Headland Digital Media
Elizabeth Armstrong	Associate Producer, Headland Digital Media
Elizabeth d'Errico	Associate Producer, Headland Digital Mediad
Anna Wyckoff	Associate Producer, Headland Digital Media
Kerri Atwood	Art Production Manager, Headland Digital Media
Brian O'Donnell	HTML Manager, Headland Digital Media
Cezzane Hendricks	Art Production Assistant, Headland Digital Media

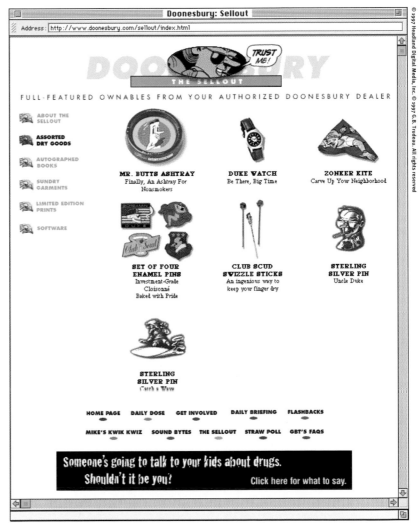

Creator royalties from The Sellout benefit the charities listed on the Get Involved page.

ask everything from why a certain character disappeared for eight years to whether Garry is Canadian (he's not). Just as the strip has done for more than 26 years, The Doonesbury Electronic Town Hall entertains and provokes its readers – and does it very, very well.

fabric8

Address: http://www.fabric8.com/

june 97

fabric 8

shop   pop   drop

where independent style
is the fashion . . .

no trends here. just a building ground for well-made,
unique items from san francisco's underground. feel free
to shop, check out a bit of sf style, and get the low-down on
fabric8. oh, and please join our mailing list -- we'll be
adding more soon. enjoy!

Purpose of the site

An online marketplace, fabric8
provides artisans a place to
showcase their handcrafted
wares

The players

Olivia Ongpin
Antony Quintal

Launch date

October 1995

WHEN YOUR CLIENT'S A CORPORATION, YOU START WITH THE MARKETING PLAN.
WHEN YOUR CLIENT'S AN ARTIST, YOU START WITH THE ART.

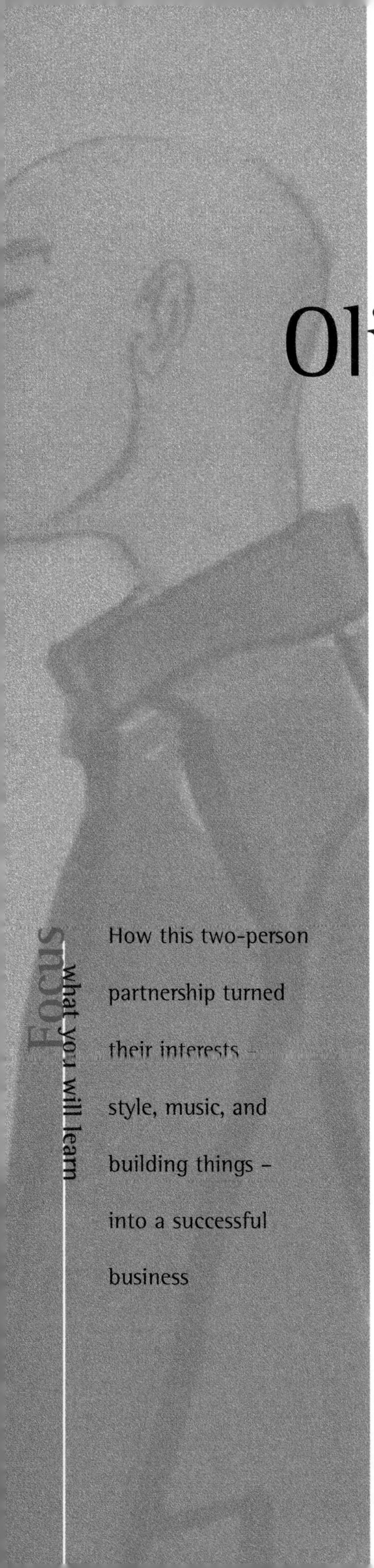

Olivia Ongpin loves two things: independent fashion and independent music.

Chapter 10

www.fabric8.com

Focus

what you will learn

How this two-person partnership turned their interests – style, music, and building things – into a successful business

HER BUSINESS PARTNER, the equally stylish Antony Quintal, likes architecture – building things. When they combined their talents to build a business online, it only made sense to build a web site that showcased the work of their favorite designers, artisans, and artists who created the individual style they both loved.

Back in 1993, while still working in the magazine industry, Olivia had met Sui Generis clothing designer Nancy Eastep. Olivia frequented San Francisco's Taber Alley Market, where independent clothing designers gathered to sell their clothes. She bought a piece from Nancy, and over time, bought more and more of Nancy's clothes and got to know her better. Olivia started to feel like a walking advertisement for Sui Generis – people would ask where she got what she was wearing, and she'd refer them to Nancy.

When Olivia and Antony started to brainstorm ideas for building a business online, Nancy's work seemed like an obvious starting point. Olivia had enjoyed helping Nancy sell clothes by recommending people to her, but maybe by promoting her on the Web, she could help Nancy more – and Nancy would be helping her by investing in Olivia's new business. Olivia suggested to Nancy that a web site would help her reach a worldwide retail market and enable her to communicate with wholesale buyers.

Naturally, Nancy wanted to know how her customers would be able to try on the clothes. Olivia and Antony had to figure out a way to make an online fitting room. Like a catalog, the site could rely on people's measurements to guide the sizing. But they could also use detailed illustrations to show people exactly just how to measure themselves, while CGI forms converted the measurements to sizes. Olivia and Antony watched Nancy measure someone and modified the method so people at home alone in front of their computers could do it. "Surprisingly, it worked," says Antony. "We're fitting people from across the ocean."

When the first order came in, Olivia and Antony gave the measurements to Nancy. She looked at them with her practiced eye and realized his sleeve length seemed a little long. Olivia trusted Nancy but was

Olivia and Antony modified Nancy's tailoring techniques so a person at home alone could measure himself.

concerned: "I was thinking this guy was going to send it back and say the sleeves are two inches too short, and then we'd have to go through this entire process again." But when the customer received his shirt with Nancy's adjustments, it fit perfectly. "She just knew it," marvels Olivia. "Even with different size bodies, she knows how things will fit."

They were taking orders, reaching new customers, and selling the product. With the addition of more pages about other artisans, fabric8 would soon become a marketplace where artisans could gather to sell their wares – not just to the locals, but worldwide.

Traditional, online trade

Olivia's initial idea for using her creative energy on the Web had been to create an online encyclopedia of independent style and culture, called check-it.com. Antony wanted to make a business on the Web. He feels the "grail" of the Web is finding a way to make it pay for itself. As a civil engineer, he was interested in

"building" an online commerce space. Though still in their 20's, both had relevant experience – Olivia's editorial publishing background and Antony's business and technology background would be the right combination of skills to make check-it.com happen.

What they liked most about their business idea was the chance to bring crafted products to the Web. They wanted to work with artisans and artists who craft, not manufacture, their products. Comparing the idea to traditional economies of the past, where merchants would travel to markets to sell their handcrafted wares, the site would act as the market. "As opposed to selling to a small village, however, you would have the entire world," explains Antony.

The Web's interactivity was perfect for the custom-made idea. Customers could special order their items, specifying a custom fit or design element. They'd feel like they had helped design the item. Olivia says that in the store, "You can't say, 'I don't really like this kind of pocket.

Noted ringologist Jigowat's home page.

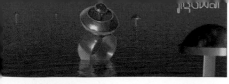

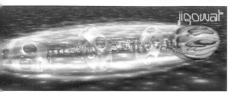

Different species of rings live in different habitats.

Can I have a different kind of pocket? Can I have it in this material?' This kind of flexibility works for people who aren't into what everybody else has, who would rather say they helped design something."

The first iteration of the Sui Generis site went live in September 1995. By February, they had already redesigned it, making it a more representative catalog. They put up an Independent Style Merchants (ism) site, showcasing the work of a collective of San Francisco designers. Their next client demonstrated how very important an artist's environment is to the work.

A new species of site

Jewelry designer Jigowat thinks of his rings as his creatures. He really likes insects, mushrooms, bugs, techno music, and outer space. His favorite artist is Hieronymus Bosch, known for his intricate, complicated triptych paintings. Olivia and Antony wanted to capture the personality behind the product – learning everything about what makes Jigowat tick and presenting his rings in that context.

Olivia and Antony learned everything they could about Hieronymus Bosch, studied his triptych *The Garden of Earthly Delights,* and read books about insects. "All this stuff is part of their soup. That's what I like to see; I like to see what they really love," says Antony.

"We wanted him to educate us on who he is and his design philosophy, so that would permeate even more in his site," interrupts Olivia. For the first few weeks, Antony and Olivia digested information and wondered how they were going to blend such diverse influences into one look for the Jigowat site – a look that still featured the rings. Finally they hit on it – they would showcase the rings as species.

All the biology books referred to insects by their Latin names, and since Jigowat referred to his creations as living things, it was natural for Olivia and Antony to rename the rings by genus and species. Genus *Celestia* encompasses the star species, *Bolta* the bolts, and *Spikus* the spikes. The pages present the rings in their habitats, along with background information. "We named the rings ourselves, and now that's how he refers to them," says Antony. "It's pretty cool to see that our process is now part of his process."

Antony and Olivia used vrml to show off the rings. Jigowat's rings are modular. The tops unscrew from the base, so the wearer can put a new ring on the same base. vrml allowed the customer to rotate the ring to fully examine all aspects, from the shine of the base to the patterns of the stone. The site also converts customers' finger size from millimeters around to ring size, and transfers this size directly to the order form.

A site by any other name

After having put up its first sites, check-it.com received an email from a company with the Check It trademark, politely informing them they had to give up the domain name. Surprised, Antony and Olivia went to the library, researched trademark law, and found there were seven different companies in different classes in the u.s. with variations of Check It as their trademark. The company that had contacted them owned the international trademark.

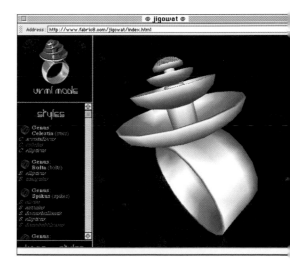

The Spikus oliviae *ring may have been named for one of fabric8's founders. Top: See every aspect of the ring in VRML. Bottom:* Spikus oliviae *in its habitat.*

More than just fashion, fabric8 is about style, from hip music to hot shopping buys.

Olivia and Antony had been thinking they should change the name anyway, suspecting it was a little too slangy. They were worried that in a few years people wouldn't know what "check-it" meant and that the term would be outdated. Now they had to come up with a different name for the site. Olivia looked through rhyming dictionaries for a name that would convey just the right attitude. Olivia and Antony discovered there was a lot more behind naming your business than just getting the domain name from Internic. Once they agreed on fabric8, they applied to trademark it. Says Olivia, "The whole time we were rushing so no one else would get the name, and then – "

Antony finishes her thought. "The government, the bureaucracy, and the system move so much more slowly than the speed we have to move with the Internet." Six months later, they still hadn't heard whether they had the trademark.

Using your network

fabric8 was more than the sum of its parts, a conglomeration of cool designers' sites. It was also about culture, music, style. It had attitude, light-hearted humor, and a sense of place – Olivia and Antony combined photos taken on an ism shoot in Golden Gate Park with whimsical text to add style to the site. Antony explains their focus on San Francisco as part of exporting the local economy worldwide. They wanted to start with what they knew – both Olivia and Antony have lived in San Francisco for years – and build their business from there.

They called their friends to help them – Olivia's background in magazines had given her a network of writers and designers who were eager to get their work on the Web. She says, "I thought of people I knew who were witty and said, 'You're going to help me write this copy.'" Their friends were eager to use their skills on the Internet.

Project managing friends requires a delicate balance between being casual and meeting deadlines. Olivia says sometimes she calls friends and asks, "Hey, you want to go out tonight? Great, before you do that, do you want to come over and design something for me?" She says it can become awkward when she is trying to meet deadlines, telling her friends she needs something right away. "We're all helping each other out and pushing each other to our potential."

Sometimes, the network of friends wasn't enough to solve problems. Antony came up with a JavaScript order form. He liked that it used JavaScript because it would perform all the calculations on the client-side, making the ordering process extremely fast. But the script had one fatal flaw. "It allowed you to order everything you wanted and calculated the price. Then you went to the page where you paid ... if you decided you didn't want one item anymore, you could delete it. The bug was that when you recalled the script, it would do it incorrectly. It would crash the browser."

JavaScript had only come out a month or two before, and lots of bugs had yet to be ironed out. After asking various other people in the field for help and still not finding a solution, Antony found out from the person who created JavaScript that there wasn't a solution for this bug yet. Antony had to devise a work-around where, if an item was deleted, the

Photos from the ism shoot in Golden Gate Park bring a touch of San Francisco to the site.

The English and Japanese versions of the Sui Generis site.

script would call a different script, and the new script would regenerate the entire order. It wasn't as fast, but it didn't crash.

Tapping the Japanese market

While many sites speak of tapping customers worldwide, fabric8 has found customers in Japan – and these customers are buying. Olivia and Antony figure part of the appeal is that similar products are much more expensive in Japan. To the Japanese, these custom-made clothes, jewelry, and art must seem cheap. Realizing that Japan was a potentially huge market, fabric8 hired a Japanese translator, Yoko Fujisake, to make a Japanese version of the entire site. Antony says, "Neither of us speaks Japanese. I studied it for two years, but that's just enough to know that I don't know Japanese." He says translating fabric8 is challenging because, "A big part of web design is knowing how an image fits with particular words. It's really difficult for us not to know the connotations of the language."

They plan to find someone who can specialize in that area of the site to handle the Japanese transactions, including email. They hope this person can also manage the nuances of language and connotations so often translated poorly. "We're still trying to formulate how one would market a site to the Japanese market. We're on Yahoo! Japan, and it's generating a fair amount of hits, but not as much as I had hoped. It could

be that in Japan things are a lot more expensive – apparently it costs around $700 just to get an Internet connection."

So far, similar numbers of Japanese visitors frequent each version of the site, but those who order online tend to order from the English site. Antony and Olivia can't explain why. They're still honing the Japanese version of the site. They want to capitalize on the rapidly growing Japanese online market but are aware they still have a lot to learn to do it right.

The evolution of fabric8

Olivia and Antony have learned a lot about making web sites for artists. They've moved away from the computer in the initial phase, preferring to sketch out their ideas by hand. Since they're working with artists, they try to involve the artist in the initial design work. They installed huge 4' by 8' white boards in their office so they can work directly with the artist, drawing ideas. Says Antony, "We're realizing more and more the value of the hand. Small designers are in love with their creation. It's really intimate for them. I think they have to be part of the design process, they have to feel they made the site – through our hands."

Olivia feels she and Antony have gained confidence and skill at adapting artists' styles to the Web. She feels they've learned to ask the right questions and absorb the right influences. Another challenge has been working with the different personalities. Some artists prefer to make changes up until the last minute, and others will get the projects done ahead of schedule. She tries to adapt the project schedule to the personality.

They're also proud of the way their site gives an opportunity to artists to work in another medium. For example, Norm Maxwell's Revolution had to showcase his ideologies as well as his illustrations and paintings. His rich, vibrant artwork packs a punch on its own, but communicating the ideas behind the art is Norm's true interest. Having previously worked in only two-dimensional media of painting and illustration, Norm was excited to use the animation of the Web to take his art to the next level.

Animation was the perfect solution to a problem that had been plaguing Norm – his logo. Written in a street graffiti style, some people had trouble reading it. He'd have to show them the R, the E, etc. Animation allowed him to morph his logo from the graffiti to a plain font, block caps reading "Revolution." Says Antony, "It does the explaining he had to do in the past. He really wanted to use his logo, that fiery sharp logo from the streets, but at the same time he wanted to communicate."

Olivia and Antony have built their online marketplace. As the site says, fabric8 makes global communication possible for artists and artisans. "An independent designer no longer has to rely on appealing to a majority in a limited geographical space to succeed ... we achieve success by appealing to a minority all over the world."

fabric8 (www.fabric8.com) specializes in style-related web commerce. They work with independent companies to develop a community of distinctive web sites. For more information, please contact Olivia Ongpin.

PO Box 420794, San Francisco, CA 94142 415.487.9702 ooo@fabric8.com

Top (from left): Adam Whelan, Antony Quintal, Olivia Ongpin, Nancy Eastep, and Norm Maxwell relax on a San Francisco rooftop. Middle and bottom: GIF *animation makes the Revolution logo's lettering more clear.*

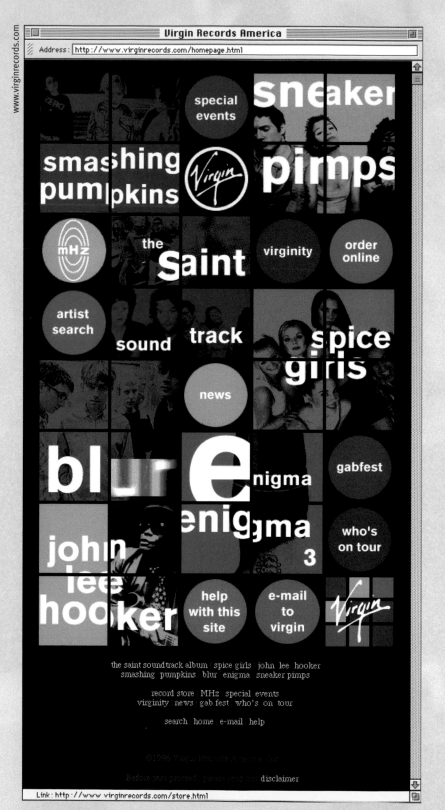

Purpose of the site

Virgin Records America wanted to promote new and existing artists and their music online.

The players

Cynthia Sexton
Tom Dolan

How the developer was chosen

Virgin interviewed several web developers but was most impressed with Ikonic's well established process model.

Launch date

September 3, 1996

With less than ten minutes to show time, the computer was still crashing when it tried to run ActiveX audio.

Chapter 11

Focus

what you will learn

How Ikonic adapted its process to fit the needs of a client who wanted to help design the site

From left: Bill Gates, Cynthia Sexton, and Robert May celebrate at the Internet Explorer 3.0 launch.

IKONIC'S PRODUCER kept trying to bring up Virgin Records' new web site, which would showcase Microsoft's Internet Explorer 3.0 to the assembled crowd. With minutes to go, Ikonic's technicians found the problem – and the news wasn't good. Nine hundred miles away, the Internet service provider's RealAudio server had gone down, and, unfortunately, their administrators had gone home. Ikonic's network technicians frantically grabbed patch cords, trying to re-route the site to Ikonic's San Francisco servers before Bill Gates finished his speech.

On the other side of the curtain at San Francisco's Yerba Buena Center,

Gates was telling the huge crowd how IE 3.0 was going to revolutionize the Internet. As soon as he finished, the curtain would lift, and Gates would walk over to the computers and show off IE's new features on the Virgin site and 12 others. Ikonic *had* to get the site up before Gates raised the curtain.

As Gates swung into his finale, Ikonic's producer reported that some,

"Ikonic's business is not building web sites. We build businesses on the Web; businesses that set and meet goals. So we start from a place that says, who are your current customers and why do they buy your product or service? What are your business goals: Share of market? Of customers? Your target margin contribution and time to break even? We assess the strategic goals for the brand, where the brand wants to go. Then, we work together with our client to develop a business and marketing plan to achieve these goals using the Web. After a dozen years, we've got a pretty good understanding of what's realistic in this business."

"At the end of the day, our mission is to partner with our clients in developing a profitable new line of business – for them. In a sense, we're building a car together. We agree up front: the car we build is going to go, say, 75 miles per hour and will get 25 miles to the gallon. When we're done, we jump in together and take a test drive. When we see the speed and mileage we wanted, it's a great feeling. But our job's not done until we've written a detailed owner's manual, so our client has the knowledge they need to drive it for years. We don't try to lock our clients into expensive maintenance agreements. We want to empower them to run their own business and enjoy the return on their investment. For example, a key part of our work for Virgin was to deliver detailed documentation on how to maintain and update the site, how to compress RealAudio files, and so on. Now Tom and Cynthia have an asset they control, and they're very happy."

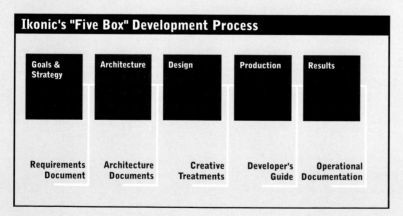

Ikonic's "Five Box" Development Process

Goals & Strategy	Architecture	Design	Production	Results
Requirements Document	Architecture Documents	Creative Treatments	Developer's Guide	Operational Documentation

Ikonic's "Five Box" process model illustrates the deliverables they give to the client at the end of each phase. The operational documentation gives the client enough technical information to run the site, expand it consistently, and re-create sections if necessary.

but not all, of the site had been transferred to Ikonic's server. Meanwhile, the ISP's server had come back up. Ikonic had to make some fast decisions without losing their cool. Did they want to use the ISP's server? Would *any* of the ActiveX controls work if the site were split between machines?

There was a burst of applause from the other side of the curtain, and it started to go up. And Bill Gates turned to walk over to the computers, ready to show off what his browser could do to the world.

Process gets clients

Beverly Hills, four months earlier. Atlantic had a web site. MCA had a web site. Even Sub Pop promoted its artists online. As the eager web developers making pitches argued, only Virgin Records America didn't have a web site. For a company in the entertainment business, that just wasn't cool.

Unfortunately, the "cool" sites in early 1996 all seemed to have some wacky metaphor running through them. Virgin wanted something more slick, more sophisticated, with the nightclub feel of a rock magazine or music video. The company was well aware that they were one of the last record companies to put up a site. But Virgin didn't want to jump on the web bandwagon prematurely and launch a site without first having established clear goals. They also wanted to hire a developer with a strong technical and administrative background, because although Virgin had plenty of creative talent and assets, they needed web-development expertise.

While Virgin Records America's parent company, Britain's Virgin

Music Group, Ltd., already had a Web site (www.vmg.co.uk), the American group in Beverly Hills wanted their site to show off their different roster of artists and make use of RealAudio. One of these champions of an American site was artistic director Tom Dolan, who worked on artists' packaging and other in-house design projects. Tom looked at other music-label sites and found most had no music on them, while others felt like a corporate brochure. He and his supervisor, Cynthia Sexton, knew this was the wrong direction for Virgin. They knew their site had to be about the music, because people didn't care about the label.

Virgin and Ikonic first met through an informal dinner with Cynthia, her husband Tim Sexton, and their friend

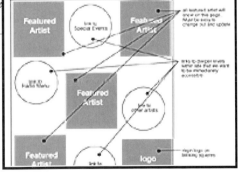

The evolution of a home page, from rough sketches to the final look (upper right).

Robin Raj, one of Ikonic's creative directors. Cynthia mentioned that she'd been interviewing web-design teams but felt they lacked administrative abilities. As Robin discussed Ikonic's development process, she was impressed by their track record, their administrative and technical strengths, and their in-house creative team, which she felt would complement Virgin's creative talent.

Tom Dolan and Cynthia then met with Ikonic more formally to review their process and abilities. "Once I met with Ikonic's CEO, Robert May, and others at Ikonic, I knew they were the right fit. Robert had experience in the music industry. I could trust his team would work *with* us," Cynthia says. After this meeting, Ikonic and Virgin took the next step: Ikonic told Virgin to set aside two days, hang out in the conference room, be prepared to surf, and think about what you'd like on your web site.

Prioritizing the shopping list

In musical terms, it was a jam session. In web terms, it was typical working hours – two 12-hour days. Sequestered in a conference room, the Virgin and Ikonic team members could sneak out for dinner but then would get right back to work.

The team quickly began discussing what they did and didn't like. Ikonic

works with clients to fine tune their goals with a business- and customer-centered perspective. Virgin knew they wanted to provide real content – music, raw demos, sound bites, and information a fan couldn't get anywhere else. What they didn't

want was for the site to be a vanity piece, with a huge Virgin Records America logo on every page.

The Ikonic team brought large white boards to write down what VIrgin wanted on their site, from must-haves to wild ideas. After the group had generated around 70 items, the Ikonic team asked the hard questions: which of these do you need? Which would be nice to have? What could be held off for later? Sometimes painfully, the ideas got filtered into categories. From there they determined the mission statement, defined the budget, and even began planning the site architecture. When the two-day meeting session was over, both teams were very tired of being in the conference room, but they also had a good idea of what the site would be. Ikonic's job was to estimate a price for it.

According to the statement of work the Ikonic team then submitted, building a site with all the features Virgin wanted – like extensive Real-Audio streams and multiple-page spreads on certain artists – would cost more than Virgin's allotted amount. One way to save would be to engage other companies to partner in the development of this cutting-edge site. Ikonic already had a working relationship with Microsoft and Macromedia and was experienced at working with multiple development groups. Microsoft was working on ActiveX. Maybe they would create some of the plug-ins in return for

proceed. But almost immediately, the plan had to be modified.

Modifying procedures

An experienced music-industry designer, Tom Dolan had strong ideas about what he wanted the look to be, and he knew just the designer for the job. He felt D. Thom Bissett knew Virgin's artists and understood his aesthetic. Ikonic's design department added Thom to the team, working with him remotely to establish a look that fit Tom Dolan's vision.

Ikonic approaches look and feel as two distinct aspects of site design.

magazine approach. One artist would be featured, with coverlines promoting six or seven other artists in type across the main photo. There would be three of these home pages so that they could feature more artists, and when a viewer reloaded, she would see a different page. Ikonic suggested that the magazine metaphor might limit the site's modularity. After all, the site had to be easily updateable.

Thom developed the current grid-based look and fine-tuned the typography, animations, and palette with Tom. Though he hadn't intended it, people immediately thought it looked

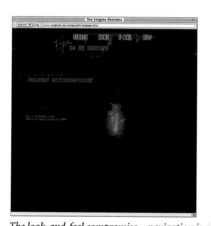

The look-and-feel compromise – navigation is always at the top, but its look varies.

exposure. Macromedia might be convinced to promote their Shock-wave Audio, which was also soon to debut. Cynthia arranged bartering relationships with the other companies. In addition, working with Macromedia might also serve as a bargaining chip with RealAudio for better prices. Virgin's in-house creative team was another resource. They could DeBabelize, cut up graphics, and work in conjunction with Ikonic's in-house design team.

It seemed like a good plan. Ikonic and Virgin modified the statement of work and signed a letter of intent to

"Feel" is the information architecture and the experience the user has, encompassing such items as toolbars and navigation. The "look" comes later. Once you've decided what's on the toolbar and where it goes, now you get to decide what color it is. Ikonic had assigned the look to Tom and Thom, but their user-interface designer would guide them in creating the feel.

The main design concern was how to make the site modular, so that it could be easily updated by one person once the site was launched. Tom Dolan initially came up with a

like a video wall at a night-club – exactly the association he had wanted. It solved the problem of spotlighting a few artists, but not too many, so the promoted acts wouldn't be lost in a long list. The modular design would also be easy to manage and update.

Now each of Virgin's more than 70 artists needed their own pages built. Some of them would be getting mini-sites, with extra articles and information. Others (those artists who hadn't released anything lately) would be represented on a template page. Ikonic recommended that all of the artists' pages should have common functionality – with navigation bars and tools all in the same place, the user wouldn't feel lost. On the other hand, Tom felt each sub-site didn't have to have the "search, home, and email" buttons in the same order or in the same corner of the page. Virgin and Ikonic found a solution that pleased them both – navigation is always at the top of the page, but the look varies.

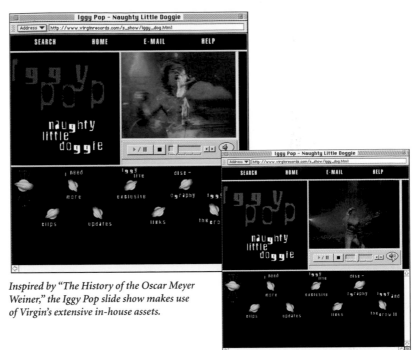

Inspired by "The History of the Oscar Meyer Weiner," the Iggy Pop slide show makes use of Virgin's extensive in-house assets.

Teamwork

Tom Dolan had no idea how to carve up a design to make it work on the Web. He'd send Ikonic a 320x480 Photoshop file of what he'd like a page to look like. Then he'd get feedback from the programmers as to what he could and couldn't do, and why.

Some nights Tom would call up and say he had an idea for the John Lee Hooker feature. He'd send the artwork, and Ikonic would test it. Then Ikonic and Virgin would have a conference call and say, 'Well, this works, Tom, but you can't have this overlay image." It was an education process.

Since the client was doing part of the development work, the team saved approval time. Virgin Records America's employees are empowered

to make decisions. If an image didn't work, in five minutes it'd be gone. Tom was creating and approving the site simultaneously.

At Ikonic, the core team soon found their roles blurring. On most projects the roles had been clearly defined: production art, art direction, developer, HTML, producer. Here everyone was working very closely together. Even Ikonic's receptionist contributed content – having recently returned from a trip to England, she'd seen *Trainspotting* before its release in America and had noticed how prominent Iggy Pop's music was in the film. She wrote a review to appear in the Iggy Pop pages before

American critics had even seen it.

One result of the creative atmosphere was the slide shows, which coordinate images and music in a video-like presentation. Halfway through the project, Ikonic was looking at the RealAudio site with its own slide show, called "The History of the Oscar Meyer Weiner." Virgin loved the idea, too. So Ikonic mocked up a slide show and showed it to Tom. Ikonic attributes the creative atmosphere to Virgin's flexible attitude. They weren't trying to micromanage the team, just to be part of it.

Iggy Pop's section included a review of Trainspotting, *a slide show, and other exclusive content.*

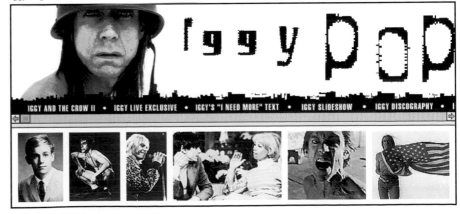

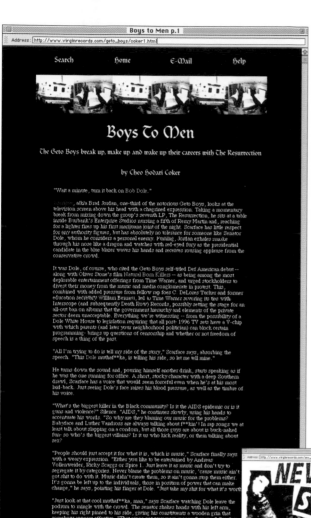

Some artists' sections, like those of the Geto Boys and Sex Pistols, included harder-to-find content, while others, like the Geraldine Fibbers, have template pages.

Getting the assets

While the inter-company team was functioning smoothly, Tom was having some trouble acquiring assets for the site. Every artist would at least have template pages with clips, photos, bios, and links to fan sites. He had creative autonomy but needed approval from the artists and their managers if he created new content for them. While the artists were receptive to approving the new content, it would simply take too long for each artist to have an approval round. The only way to get the site to debut on time was to use pre-approved content for the majority of the artists.

"With somebody like the Geraldine Fibbers, who got a single-page treatment, we took the path of least resistance and went straight to our publicity department to get a pre-approved bio and pre-approved image. There are downloadable clips, tour information, and links to fan sites," says Tom.

For other artists, Virgin sought harder-to-find content. For the Geto Boys, Tom got permission to use an article originally published in *Rap Pages* magazine by one of the country's most respected rap writers, Cheo Hodari Coker. The arrival of an electronic press kit for the Sex Pistols, including concert footage from the late '70s punk scene in London and interviews with the band about their getting back together, enhanced the Pistols' pages with material fans might not see anywhere else.

Technical challenges

The team wanted an interface for the RealAudio streams that was more exciting than the usual text links. Tom made one of his frequent visits to San Francisco one weekend, and the team met at the North End Café. Tom had already decided he wanted a retro vibe for the sound section, and he had a name – Megahertz. Everyone had ideas. Wouldn't it be neat if it were kind of Brazil-ly and it had a big oscillator? Ikonic left with a handful of napkin drawings.

Ikonic brought the napkin to Macromedia. Macromedia had agreed to build an interface for the audio to show off their Shockwave audio. However, Virgin didn't want all of their audio to be Shockwave Audio, in case viewers had RealAudio and didn't want to get Shockwave. So on the page, viewers could choose between RealAudio and Shockwave Audio. Macromedia felt that their sound quality was better than RealAudio's and wanted people to compare. The team felt that while most people had RealAudio, they might not have the latest version of Shockwave with Shockwave Audio. Using both was the ideal solution. And they made the movie small – the file is a streamlined 44K.*

Ikonic spent the last month performing quality control. Problems were everywhere. Microsoft's new ActiveX plug-ins were crashing the RealAudio slide shows, and the slide shows were crashing Windows 3.0 machines. Ikonic programmers worked for weeks integrating Microsoft's alpha versions of ActiveX. Ikonic's and Virgin's teams tweaked graphics and HTML, trying to optimize the site for most browsers. Ikonic installed RealAudio's beta software onto UNIX and Windows NT servers linked to dozens of test machines, testing the technical differences between the different platforms.

* The Megahertz feature has since been updated to take advantage of advances in technology, including RealMedia and RealVideo.

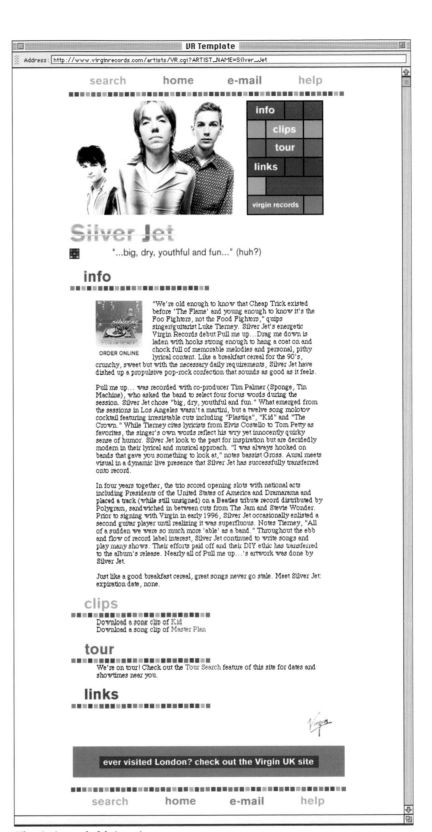

Silver Jet is proud of their section.

The artist-search page allows fans to access both new and favorite artists' sections quickly.

As Microsoft's marketing people watched the site take shape, they invited Virgin and Ikonic to showcase their work at Microsoft's worldwide launch of IE 3.0. Ikonic committed even more resources to the site, optimizing the ActiveX and adding IE 3.0 features.

With the extra help, things seemed to be under control for the Microsoft debut party. Ikonic FTP'd the site to Virgin's Los Angeles-based Internet service provider and tested the final features. In the last few days, no one stayed later than 7pm – an improvement over previous past-midnight code jams. There were the usual last-minute changes, like updates to news sections. And then the ISP's server went down just before Bill Gates was to look at the site on stage.

Success

In the end, the site worked. Ikonic and Virgin demonstrated the site successfully at San Francisco's new Yerba Buena Center. They viewed the site using both the ISP and Ikonic servers – the audio on one,

everything else on another.

Both at the demonstration and afterward, Virgin and Ikonic received excellent feedback. Bill Gates and others surfed the site, chatting with Tom and Cynthia. After the launch, the fans' responses continue to be very positive. The artists, too, are happy with their sections.

One final question remains: the site is getting the traffic and good reviews, as well as selling albums online, but can Virgin break a new artist on the web site? Tom thinks it's possible. After all, artists featured on the home page get 40% of the overall traffic on the site. Relative unknowns like Silver Jet are getting thousands of visitors once their name appears in the vibrant home-page grid. The site provides a place to hear clips of music and read tour dates – information sometimes not available at retail stores.

Virgin believes their site is a good investment. It's a powerful marketing venue that speaks the language of Virgin's customers. It provides an additional marketing venue. Whenever an artist has a product or event to promote, the site serves as a relatively inexpensive tool to aid in the promotion. Web pages are now budgeted by the product managers, who decide what portion of the marketing budget goes to print advertising, other media advertising, and web promotion. All artists get a template page when they release a new album. Says Cynthia, "The decision whether to beef up pages and have a mini-site for that artist comes from a committee of multi-media-department members and the artist's product manager. Additional pages are budgeted by the product managers once we determine if the artist is web-friendly and would

Ikonic, Inc.

Ikonic, Inc. (www.ikonic.com) builds businesses on the Web. For 12 years, the company has been a leading provider of strategy, design, and implementation services that meet specific brand and financial goals for global clients. Ikonic has partnered with clients such as Virgin Records, News Corporation, Time Warner, Microsoft, American Express, General Motors of Canada, Matthew Bender & Company, and Prudential Investments from its offices in San Francisco and New York. The company has won many prestigious awards, including those from *I.D. Magazine*, the International Interactive Media Festival, the New York Festivals Multimedia Competition, the Internet Professional Publishers Association (IPPA), *NewMedia* Magazine, and the Interactive Services Association (ISA).

2 Harrison St., top floor, San Francisco, CA 94105 415-908-8000

benefit from having more than a template page."

Plans for the future include making the site a resource for hard-to-find music. Virgin plans to use the site as a way to stimulate the sales of hard-to-find catalog pieces like score albums and other eclectic music.

Virgin and Ikonic reached their goal. The design is clean, easy to navigate, easy to update, and was delivered on time and within budget. The site earned awards from ID magazine, a CINDY, and was a CLIO finalist. Ikonic's Robert May says, "Like most masterpieces, there's a lot of sweat under the paint. Mega-sites like Virgin's are a great example of the collaborative spirit of dozens of talented partners." Tom maintains the site himself but contracts out the more ambitious projects, like new RealAudio slide shows. Moreover, it's about the artists, not the label, and the resulting attention from the fans

Ultimately, it's about selling records – fans can order albums online.

Cynthia Sexton	*Vice President of Multimedia*
Tom Dolan	*Co-Creative Director, Designer*
	Senior Art Director
D. Thom Bissett	*Lead Designer*
Al Wong, Michael Moroney	*Producer*
Robin Raj	*Co-Creative Director*
Sara Ortloff	*Design Director*
Gretchen Anderson	*Production Management*
Sharilyn Neidhardt	*Interface Designer*
Doug Muise	*Graphic Designer*
Jon Thompson	*Senior Media Production Engineer*
Tim McCoy, Pam Miklaski,	
Sasha Panasik, Maureen Agius	*HTML production*
Cameron Reid	*Perl programming*
Lars Nyman	*ActiveX Developer*

proves they were on the right track. Cynthia says, "Our goal is to make sure we expose as many people as possible to the music our artists produce and turn people on to artists they may not otherwise have heard. Ultimately, it's about selling records." And it's about building successful relationships – team members from Ikonic and Virgin continue to collaborate on projects.

RREEF Welcome

Address: http://www.rreef.com/

ЯREEF

contact
subscribe
resources

news items

RREEF Research
Wylie's new map is now available. See his forecast for continued economic expansion.

Senior Housing
RREEF has hired Kevin Cardin as the Portfolio Manager of RREEF's Senior Housing Group.

Designed by Verso

Welcome

BROKER shows what we buy, sell, and lease

CONSULTANT delivers valuable resources to the consultant community

INVESTOR gives our clients secure access to timely investment information

PRODUCTS helps identify the right investment for you

PROCESS tells you who we are and how we work

wylie's map
job growth and economic activity

Purpose of the site

The RREEF Funds built a web site as another of their personalized services to their clients.

The players

Christina Cheney
Mary Tesluk
Todd Fahrner
Mike Young
John Shields
Wayne Pryor

Launch date

January 31, 1997

When RREEF's Mike Young thought of selecting web developers, he thought about what he'd read in *Creating Killer Web Sites.*

Focus what you will learn

How Verso overcame problems caused by late assets and technology difficulties to build this sophisticated site.

HE WANTED A third-generation web site for his company, so he went to the source, David Siegel and Studio Verso. In David's office, Mike presented the situation. A full-service real estate investment advisor, The RREEF Funds, had few regularly published materials, one company logo, no current glossy brochures, and no branding standards. They had about 150 clients, most of whom weren't online. Some of them didn't even have computers but still were interested in becoming involved in the new technologies. Since customer service is an important aspect of RREEF's business, the company was willing to support their clients'

installation and training on web-optimized computers.

In some ways, the situation was ideal. For once, Studio Verso wouldn't have to argue about why the client brochures wouldn't work online. They could relax a little about making the site accessible to everyone and could design for a select few. The challenge would be to have the client agree on a corporate look, to decide what the content would be, and to deliver it.

RREEF's goal was to launch a sleek, visually sophisticated site at their annual client conference as another example of their personalized service. Mike explained, "It's a chance to get a large number of

RREEF's Four Quadrants

RREEF's four site quadrants.

clients together and show them something we consider a state-of-the-art delivery channel for information." RREEF did not believe that even the slickest web site would inspire anyone to invest millions of dollars with them. The company did believe that well delivered information would demonstrate the extra service the company provided and would give them a competitive edge.

David realized that overall, RREEF was looking for quality. In that first meeting, he said to Mike, "You're going to be a problem." Before Mike could walk out, he continued, "Because you have good taste, and good taste is expensive. But the site will reflect your good taste, and people will be able to tell the difference." Mike settled back in his chair. After what he'd heard from other web developers, this philosophy sounded just fine to him.

Sold on methodology

Before beginning the search to hire a web developer, RREEF put together an in-house web-development team to determine what benefit, if any, a

site would have for RREEF and its clients. Three men from different departments, each reporting his findings to different partners in the firm, brought their perspectives to the table. Wayne Pryor represented Information Technology, John Shields was from Client Relations, and Mike Young was from Research.

The three sat around a conference table, brainstorming things to put in the site. Ideally, the site would be useful to RREEF as well as its clients. It could have different levels of access, with the latest real-estate investment data served up by a database. They came up with four conceptual quadrants: public/external for the general public, private/external for clients and consultants, public/internal for RREEF employees, and private/internal for individual RREEF employees. Mike, Wayne, and John each presented the idea to his respective partner. Once each partner approved it, Mike, Wayne, and John began interviewing web developers.

They weren't impressed. Wayne says, "We interviewed several design groups. Their general approach was, 'Okay, what do you want? We could do that for 75 bucks a page, as many pages as you need. They didn't ask, 'What is your business? What are you trying to accomplish? What's your focus? Who are your customers?' We were asked all those questions in our initial design meetings with Verso." When the RREEF team (or the "Three Amigos" as they would come to be called) met with Verso, they were impressed by Verso's process model. Mike, Wayne, and John looked at a sample project site and saw how all of their decisions, emails, agendas, schedules, and creative work would be posted on the site for access at any time. Wayne says, "The fact that we were dealing with people who had a project-management methodology in place made a huge difference, because we knew that these were people who'd been through this before, they knew where the pitfalls were, and they'd developed a system for getting from start to finish without a lot of problems." Since

The project site kept both the clients and Verso on track.
See Part II, chapter 6, for more on project sites.

RREEF had so little formal marketing material, it made sense to go with a team that put so much emphasis on the strategy phase. RREEF and Verso signed a contract to proceed and started planning in earnest.

Planning the web site

Verso likes to plan its web sites with the end user in mind, but the Three Amigos insisted they shouldn't worry too much about their customers. RREEF customers, Mike argued, are generally new to or unfamiliar with the Internet. He said, "We're taking a supply-side approach. We're going to build it, we're going to drive the whole process from our years of experience in delivering timely information about investments, we're going to get them excited about coming here – and then they'll come." However, Verso felt strongly that they shouldn't skip their usual step of sending questionnaires to potential visitors to the site, and sent questionnaires to the three key audiences for RREEF's information: investors, consultants, and brokers. From these questionnaires, Verso determined such factors as how the customers would interact with the site, what information they'd use on a site, and even whether they preferred information in text or graphical form.

On October 16, 1996, Verso's producer Christina Cheney, design technologist Todd Fahrner, and creative director Gino Lee spent six hours with the RREEF team, discussing RREEF's business and competitive environment, marketing strategy, and goals for the site. To meet the conference deadline of January 31, they narrowed the scope of the site from four quadrants to one. While RREEF was willing to allocate

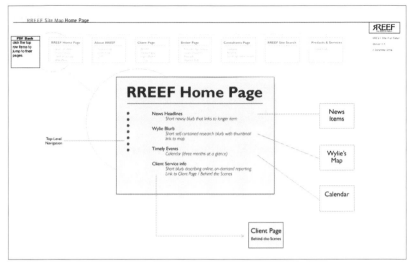

Above: After the strategy phase is complete, Verso creates a structure for the site. Below: Clients can access documents like questionnaires or the technical spec from the project site.

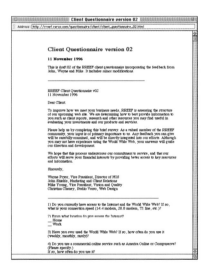

resources to buy its customers software if necessary and to teach them to use the site, they wanted to handhold as little as possible – the design had to emphasize ease of use and ease of access to information. It also had to convey honesty and intimacy and appear solid and stable.

Todd used information about the customers and the desired functionality to write the technical spec. He found building a site for such a targeted audience to be unusual. "Either no one would see it anyway, so it didn't matter if it was a little

steep technically, or there would be tech support and suggestions from RREEF that would do a good job with the site using the latest technology. We felt free to use almost whatever we wanted. For example, the site didn't have to work well in Netscape 2.0 or with low-end hardware." While eventually the site would be database-driven, the tech spec said for now the site would be designed and built "with greater emphasis on fixed content, look-and-feel, and user interface than on easy database administration or complex interactivity."

After getting the questionnaire responses back and discussing the responses with RREEF, Christina wrote several specific documents. The first of these was a User Models document, which listed their descriptions of the target users for the site, a site diagram showing the hierarchy of information of the site, and a final estimate. Next she created a 15-page Requirements and Goals document, listing in detail marketing goals for each quadrant of the site and graphic look-and-feel goals and suggesting the staff RREEF would need to maintain the site. She prioritized the goals into a 10-page document, listing specific objectives. They were now ready to begin design – and the RREEF team was very eager to see their company's new look.

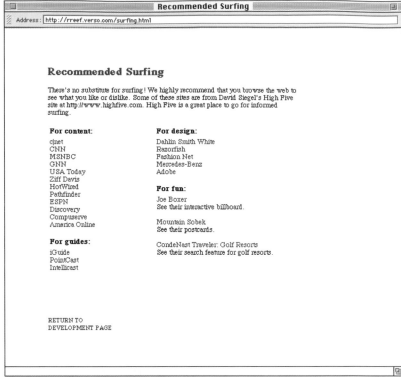

Recommended Surfing

There's no substitute for surfing! We highly recommend that you browse the web to see what you like or dislike. Some of these sites are from David Siegel's High Five site at http://www.highfive.com. High Five is a great place to go for informed surfing.

For content:
cjnet
CNN
MSNBC
GNN
USA Today
Ziff Davis
HotWired
Pathfinder
ESPN
Discovery
Compuserve
America Online

For guides:
iGuide
PointCast
Intellicast

For design:
Dahlin Smith White
Razorfish
Fashion Net
Mercedes-Benz
Adobe

For fun:
Joe Boxer
See their interactive billboard.

Mountain Sobek
See their postcards.

CondeNast Traveler: Golf Resorts
See their search feature for golf resorts.

RETURN TO
DEVELOPMENT PAGE

Verso encouraged RREEF to get familiar with the Web.

All RREEF had was a black-and-white logo.

Cool, edgy, and financial?

Design Director Mary Tesluk has years of experience in information design and converting information into usable models, but she'd rarely had this much freedom in working with a corporate client. Since RREEF had no existing look to refer to, she would be free to explore any avenues she liked.

Verso began the design phase by asking the Three Amigos to review some suggested business web sites in related fields. Their comments helped Mary get some sense of what they liked. They said they wanted

something "eye-catching and out of the ordinary," but she says, "It seems in this business a lot of people say that, but in reality, this is a major investment firm. They're fairly conservative, and they're not going to be able to carry it off."

Before the creative review meeting, Verso posted thumbnails of the designs on the project site. The Three Amigos could view each of the 12 designs and have time to think about them before the creative review meeting. While the designs varied in colors and presentation, conceptually they were very similar, with the home page set up as an educational page to explain the site and sections.

Mike, John, and Wayne's comments ranged from critiquing the color choice to moving navigation elements around and were more positive toward the more classical designs. Mary says, "They started to see the reality of 'cool' and 'edgy' mixed with

RREEF and RREEF's clients." Some clients may have been overwhelmed with so many choices, especially without having any design frame of reference, but the RREEF team was well balanced. If one of them got stuck on a detail, the other two drew him back to the big picture.

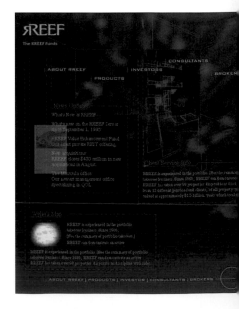

From their responses to all of the designs, Mary incorporated their comments into a new design that blended some elements from two designs they liked most. She likes the result they went with. "It's different from typical web sites in that it's not 'button-y.' It's really educational. It sets up a nice vocabulary for the rest of the site. It pushes information and uses typography as a tool to explain the information." RREEF was happy to use words instead of icons and pictures that have become so commonplace on web sites. Mary came up with complementary designs for the deeper levels of the site, as well as posting the RREEF palette and type specs on the project site for future

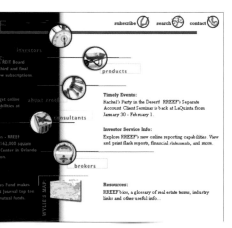

All of Mary's designs used the home page as an educational page that explained the site and its sections.

reference. But before production could begin, they had to address the question of content.

Late-asset disease

The RREEF project was beginning to suffer from a common ailment – late and fragmentary content from the client. The site map had provided categories, but once they got into specifics, content didn't fit into the design. Verso had wanted to see specific content to ensure the site would accommodate it. RREEF wanted to see templates and felt they could format their content to fit into each template.

Since they'd had to design the site without seeing specific content, Verso found that some assumptions they'd made were now proving false. Verso had anticipated three levels to the site: a home page and primary navigation element, a secondary level of navigation specific to each of the five section heads, and a tertiary level with the content. But as content came in, organization demanded a fourth level, which had been overlooked in the original plan. The additions stretched the range of the secondary navigation element.

Wayne feels that Verso should have taken the lead on making RREEF conform to the design. He says, "Verso was saying give us all of your content, so we can finish the design. And we were saying, 'Let's just get it up as we go.' We made design decisions on the fly." But making decisions on the fly meant dealing with far more clean-up and

production work than anticipated. A great deal of content arrived in long, inconsistent tabular format that took some grueling all-night grooming to bring into shape. Christina found herself pitching in to edit the tables in HTML. The production team was plagued by stylistic inconsistencies.

Verso has since added a content development program to their design phase to minimize such surprises during the production phase. Both Verso and RREEF acknowledge they approached the issue from different

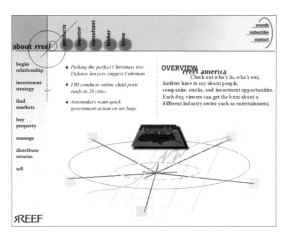

perspectives. Wayne says, "It would have been all right with us if you had said 'You know, we know what the heck we're doing and you should do it this way.' We would have said, 'Thank you very much, we'll do it your way.' As much as you might think that we had an attachment to our content, we really didn't. We expected Verso to set the style and design standards for us." Verso hadn't anticipated how RREEF's inexperience in submitting material for an interactive medium would be a factor in getting the content produced.

Todd created a system to streamline production of the hundreds of headers.

The Domino effect

The design phase wasn't ending, yet Todd needed to make sure pages were coded consistently as assets trickled in. Todd wanted to automate the system as much as possible. While Mary's design presented most of the content in text, not images, more than 300 graphical headers had to be rendered, cropped, and positioned consistently in the text.

To accommodate ongoing edits and additions, the first move was to get it into a flexible source format.

Todd created a 300-page Quark XPress document. Each page was the final size of the heading, with the text positioned so that no tables or other hacks were necessary to position them in the HTML flow. He defined style sheets in Quark to format the header variants. Once styled, he exported all the pages in EPS format using an AppleScript, converted the EPS documents to high-quality PICT images with Adobe ScreenReady, and then "let DeBabelizer loose on them to optimize and spit them out as GIFS with a consistent naming scheme.

The whole path from Quark to final GIFS took about four minutes as a batch," says Todd. The system allowed global style changes and text edits, with no risk of manual errors creeping in.

Todd ran into a subtle bug that forced a re-thinking of the basic frameset and the associated art-work. While revisiting the frameset, he identified some issues with the use of images in navigation. The initial design had proposed a graphical secondary navigation element, but Todd felt this bar needed to be HTML text to load more quickly, especially since this element would need to change more often than they had anticipated (before the content's organizational depth became clear). Late in the production phase, he and Mary settled on a final design direction and exerted it throughout the site.

While Todd's systems were helping remedy the late content problems, they didn't help with serious server difficulties. In the early stages of the project, Wayne discussed server platforms with Verso. Based on those discussions, RREEF decided to employ Lotus' new Domino server to leverage their in-house Lotus Notes expertise as well as prepare for content management, workflow, and database connectivity. It was agreed that the Domino platform would be a transitional phase for RREEF until other standards-based technologies matured. Neither Verso nor RREEF were prepared for the incompatibilities between the development environment and the proposed production environment.

When Verso transferred the development site onto RREEF's server, they discovered that Domino was ill-suited to serve non-Notes-based material.

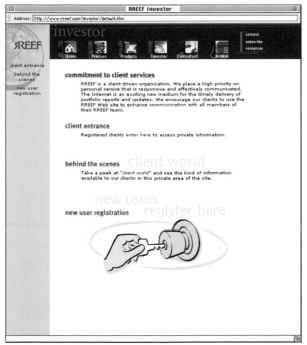

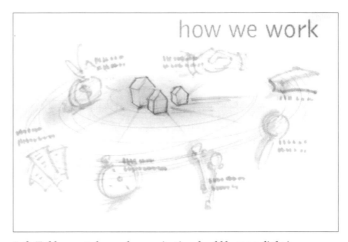

Left: Todd suggested secondary navigation should be HTML links in the left-hand frame. Above: Illustrations for the site evolved from rough sketches to finished graphics.

After several unsuccessful attempts, the service hosting the site put it on a different machine. Verso soon discovered the new machine didn't support password-protected directories, because it was running Windows NT 3.5.1 with an earlier version of the Microsoft Internet Information Server. The CGI scripts weren't working on this machine, either.

Todd and his team had to redirect any sensitive pages or pages using scripts to the Verso server until the site could be transferred. Says Todd, "At one point we had the site spread across three servers – they have two boxes over there. Whenever anything changed, there were lots of opportunities for things to break." Todd spent a lot of time making sure that links

Production specification for www.rreef.com

This document describes the structure, coding conventions, and production processes employed in the construction of www.rreef.com, providing templates, scripts, palettes, and other raw materials. It is intended to assist future site administrators and content managers in maintaining, extending, and improving the site. This document is straight (unstyled) HTML for the sake of maximum utility. The major divisions are linked here:

1. Directory structure and nomenclature
   a. Top level
   b. Middle level
   c. Bottom level
2. HTML coding tools, conventions & templates
   a. Comments on top level files
   b. Commented source of (mid-level) frameset template
   c. Commented source of (bottom-level) content frame template
   d. Commented source of secondary navigation template
3. Graphics specification and production processes
   a. Heds
   b. Postcards
   c. Maps, Charts, and Illustrations
   d. Thumbnails
   e. Miscellaneous

Directory structure and nomenclature

Linked below are screen shots representing the RREEF site's directory structure and file naming conventions, with comments. There are three levels of hierarchy: a top, a middle, and a bottom, paralleling the three levels of organization in the site's user interface, (global nav, local nav, content).

Top level:

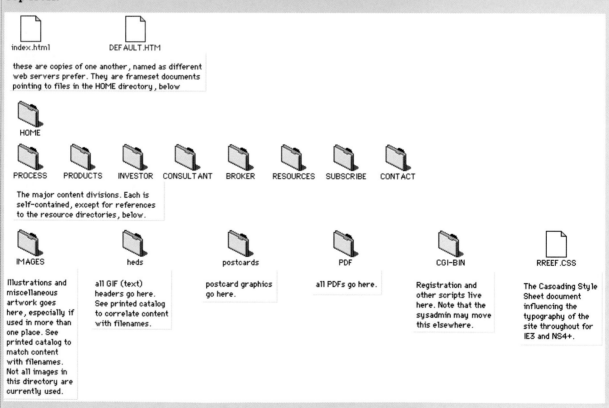

Todd created a detailed document explaining how the site had been created and how to maintain it.

still worked whenever they'd make a change, a tedious process. Eventually, RREEF's hosting service got a new server.

Todd feels strongly that Verso should have made a prototype site for RREEF as a technical proof-of-concept. At the end of the design period, the production team should have made and tested "a little microcosm of the site to stress-test the navigation scheme and final format choices, even if with dummy content." He feels this skeletal version of the site would have shown the problems with the design before the critical production period began. Unfortunately, revising the design at that stage meant reformatting some of the graphics and much of the HTML. In the future, Todd says, "The design phase isn't over until the prototype says the design works."

Wowing the investment community

The site went up on January 31, 1997, in time for the client meeting. Their head of marketing, Steve Steppe, Partner in Charge, Client Relations, demonstrated the site to the clients with no problems. Mike, Wayne, and John were happy. Most important of all, their clients were impressed.

Verso and RREEF continued to work together to iron out server difficulties. RREEF had hired a hosting service, and while Todd wrote a detailed document explaining how to maintain the site consistently, it still took lots of communication to get the site fully operational without help from Verso.

Verso is proud of the site as one that fulfilled its strategic, marketing, and communications goals. It has become a viable and award-winning

VERSO

Gino Lee	*Creative Director*
Christina Cheney	*Producer*
Mary Tesluk	*Design Director*
Todd Fahrner	*Design Technologist*
David D. Cullinan	*Production Manager*
Brian Dame	*Production*
Robert Frank	*Illustrator*

RREEF

Mike Young	*Vice President and Director of Quantitative Research Information Technology*
Wayne Pryor	*Vice President*
John Shields	*Manager, Client Relations*

Seated (from left): Mary Tesluk, Wayne Pryor, John Shields. Standing: Mike Young, Todd Fahrner, Christina Cheney, David Siegel.

channel for delivering information – RREEF was the first real estate investment manager site to get a five-star review from PikeNet, a web site that covers the commercial real estate market and reviews related sites. Prominent industry pundit Peter Pike wrote, "RREEF has created one of the very best commercial real estate sites that you'll find. It's graphically attractive and packed with information that addresses the needs of three distinctive communities – investors, consultants, and brokers. Don't miss it." The Three Amigos were delighted. Now they really had a high quality communications medium for extending the company's client services.

As part of its company tradition, Verso gave RREEF a traditional letterpress lead bar to commemorate the launch.

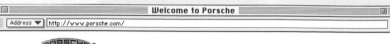

Welcome to Porsche

Address ▼ | http://www.porsche.com/

PORSCHE®
Official Web Site

Best when viewed
at this width with

NETSCAPE
Now!

Our thanks to the IPPA
for recognizing this
site with their Award
for Design Excellence
And to David Siegel,
for the prestigious
High Five Award.

Where does a Porsche come from? The obvious reply, of course, is it's from Germany, from places like Weissach and Zuffenhausen. But the place we're talking about doesn't exist on a map. It exists in the minds of those who know this: Porsche. There is no substitute. Come with us to that place. Just click on the sign.

©1996 Porsche Cars North America, Inc.
Created by The Designory, inc. Produced and hosted by Genex Interactive

Purpose of the site

This site was created as a "toe-in-the-water" site to test the medium, see the visitors' response, and then possibly expand the site.

How the developer was chosen

"Keeper of the flame" for the Porsche brand for more than 10 years, The Designory was already familiar with Porsche and its design standards.

The players

Chip McCarthy
David Glaze
Lannon Tanchum
Walter Schild

Launch date

April 16, 1996

Chip McCarthy was a little anxious.

How The Designory adapted its 25 years of process from the print model to project manage their first web site.

HE'D BEEN INVITED to Reno to meet with the heads of Porsche's many departments and brainstorm ideas for their web site. In his capacity as art director at Porsche's design firm The Designory, Chip was supposed to use his knowledge of the Web to guide the meeting; to know whether ideas were plausible, too expensive, or not good for the Web. He felt his performance at this meeting might decide whether his company, The Designory, got the contract to design Porsche's site.

The Designory has been what they call "keeper of the flame" for the Porsche brand in North America for more than 10 years, working primarily on Porsche's automotive brochures. A few months earlier, The Designory's Interactive Group had offered to make a presentation to Porsche about their capabilities and to give an overview of new media in general. The Designory created a full-blown presentation, covering topics from the state of interactive multimedia to the future of the Web, concluding with specific ideas for a Porsche site.

Chip, the interactive group's creative director David Glaze, and The Designory's executive creative director Lannon Tanchum saw this presentation as an opportunity to present Porsche material as it might apply to the Web, carefully integrating the brand, visual images, position in the marketplace, and current

What sets a Porsche apart from every other car in the world? The obvious answer is performance. Porsche cars, after all, have been held in the highest esteem by generations of drivers who value performance above all. But that's only part of the answer. What truly distinguishes a Porsche from everything else is passion. The passion for excellence.

It can be seen in Porsche No.1, the first of the new sports cars introduced in 1948 by Professor Ferdinand Porsche and his son Ferry Porsche. Today, it is a passion pursued by the designers and engineers who cherish the philosophy laid forth long ago by Professor Porsche: "To change is easy, to improve is hard."

It is a passion often lost in the demand for things made en masse. Yet from your first encounter with one, you'll see it's something that can still be found in a Porsche: that sense of what is possible when a car is crafted on a human scale.

Most car companies today are ruled by committee. The cars they produce reflect the compromises of conflicting agendas. Not so with the cars of Porsche. Each design change has evolved from Professor Porsche's uncompromising edict of continuous improvement. Each new idea has proven itself in the hands of the world's most demanding drivers on the world's most demanding racetracks. And each new model has been crafted by the skilled hands of workers whose length of employment can often be measured in decades.

Porsche heritage

Porsche craftsmen

Porsche drivers

home   people   driving   creating   Porsche

From product information to the company founders, the site thoroughly covers all aspects of Porsche.

advertising with the new medium. They wanted to show the client, not just describe, the interactive group's capabilities by presenting on-screen comps of possible layouts for the Porsche site. They explained their philosophy: "We believe the Web is about communication. We believe you should go to a communications firm, not just a technology firm, to put a web site together." Porsche nodded and took notes but went home to Reno without making any firm plans.

Months passed as Porsche sounded out their options for web developers. Porsche's ad agency gave a

There's a road Porsche engineers drive every day, twice a day. Yet they never find it dull. It's a narrow country lane that leads to and from Weissach, Germany, home of Porsche's Development Center. With its uneven pavement, its dips and bends, the road to Weissach has become an unofficial test track. When the local government planned to improve the road, Porsche engineers helped the authorities see that such a change might not be an improvement after all. You see, to Porsche engineers, the focus of creating something new has always been to create something better. And in doing so, they make sure going to work never gets boring.

Design philosophy

Milestones

home   people   driving   creating   Porsche

presentation. Two-person start-ups proposing to do the site overnight for $500 competed with university professors offering to have their class assemble the site as a project and professional teams saying the site would cost half a million dollars. The proposals were so wildly divergent, Porsche had to take its time deciding which would be best for them and what they wanted.

Now, at this brainstorming session in Reno, Chip had a chance to

distinguish his group from the others. He walked into the conference room to find 15 department heads already started on their wish lists. Glancing at his watch, he confirmed he wasn't late — they'd just been eager. Joel Ewanick, Porsche Cars North America's General Marketing Manager, rose to introduce him. "Here's Chip McCarthy from The Designory," he

announced to the group. "They're the ones who are doing our web site."

Chip realized not only had The Designory been awarded the contract, but also that this brainstorming session was the site's kick-off meeting. He was as eager as the Porsche department heads to begin work. "Okay!" he said. "Let's get started."

Branding a web site

This site was all about branding. Porsche wasn't interested in selling cars online or creating an online community of Porsche owners — at least not yet. They certainly wanted to provide some information about their cars for those interested in Porsche, but mostly it was about communicating and furthering the mystique of Porsche. Porsche wanted a "toe-in-the-water" site, to test the medium without too much expense,

model lineup

driving

The 911 Family

Carrera The 911 concept in its purest and most elemental form. Available as a coupe or cabriolet.

Targa It's the best of both worlds. A large glass panel retracts at the touch of a button.

Carrera 4 Combines the response of the Carrera with the stability and traction of full-time all-wheel drive.

Carrera 4S The all-wheel-drive concept blended with the brakes, tires, suspension and aggressive styling of the Turbo.

Turbo The ultimate expression of the 911 concept. Over 400 horsepower from twin turbocharging.

Boxster The purity of a classic roadster with the performance of modern technology.

home   people   driving   creating   Porsche

see the response, and then expand the site once they had a sense of what visitors wanted. It had to have direct access to information and be easy to navigate.

Porsche also wanted to make sure that anyone could access the site and see it as it was intended, no matter what browser people were using. The clients felt that just as a Porsche car is technologically sound, so should the site present no technological problems. While Chip and David were designing the site, they contracted out the production to Genex Interactive. Their partner at Genex, Walter Schild, knew that a

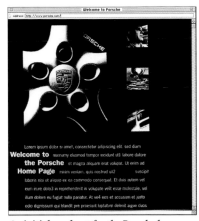

An initial mock-up for the Porsche home page.

site that worked in every browser would challenge him and the programmers. He knew he'd have to consult on the page layouts to make sure they could be done as intended.

In their original presentation, The Designory had suggested three main sections for the site: the passion of people, the passion of creating, and the passion of driving. These categories, combined with the list of ideas from Porsche's department heads, served as guidelines for brainstorming site content. From 10 years of experience with the Porsche

brand, The Designory already had a good sense of the Porsche assets they might repurpose for the site. After all, one of the reasons The Designory first formed an interactive group was its feeling it was in a unique position to develop sites – with 25 years of experience at creating and organizing masses of client information into well designed print presentations, the company knew it could organize assets into well designed web sites.

Once they had a site map, they sent it over to Genex Interactive to make sure their ideas were workable and to consult on navigation. The Designory wanted to have all of the section icons at the top of every page and highlight which section the user was currently in. This could present problems for some browsers, especially AOL. Genex got to work testing ideas and workarounds while The Designory focused on the design.

Gestaltungsnormenvergnugen: the joy of design standards

Porsche has spent years developing distinctive, global graphic standards, so The Designory had to adapt these standards to the Web judiciously. Chip and David wanted to be certain they were consistent in their web design. Porsche's parent company in Germany had established the straightforward, clean look and use of flat colors, all of which adapted well to the web site. Also in keeping with the standards, Chip and David kept a lot of white space on the pages, both for an open look and to keep the copy in easy-to-read chunks. David and Chip chose to use drop shadows behind type and vignette some

images to give them a soft edge – while not commonly used in Porsche's print design, they felt these treatments gave the pages a more dimensional quality. They chose

The 911 brochure uses lots of white space for a straightforward, clean look.

white backgrounds, both for consistency with Porsche's graphic standards and because black type on a white background was easier to read.

As The Designory's relationship with Porsche has grown over the years, The Designory has developed an in-house team familiar with

The final design used white space and stamp-sized photos for consistency with Porsche's design standards.

Porsche's look and feel, including a copywriter who works on Porsche's print materials and a product specialist who knows the product line intimately. Chip and David pulled in the copywriter, Rich Conklin, to help them develop a conversational tone for the site. Because the largest percentage of web users are American, The Designory chose an American voice for the copy, which is consistent with Porsche Cars North America's advertising and collateral materials. "The German tone is much more matter-of-fact, with a cooler, drier feel to it," says David. After all, it was a toe-in-the-water site. They could test the American tone and globalize the copy later if the client requested.

Chip and David learned quickly what was and wasn't possible in HTML. Chip says, "David and I would throw together comps, and we would do some screen grabs and send them over to Genex. We made a lot of phone calls asking if we could run type around a picture, things like that." Once they established the overall look, this give-and-take process on layout became more streamlined.

Chip mocked up the designs for the main pages and all possible variations of sub-pages and printed the designs from Quark for presentation to Porsche's Joel Ewanick, with whom they had worked on previous projects. "There was a level of trust on his part," says David. In the review, Joel had a suggestion: the addition of a fourth section, the Passion of Porsche. It would encompass all their corporate information, like press releases. Other than that, he approved the look. Now all The Designory had to do was finish some pages and get them to Genex for production.

Refining the process

The Designory needed to track which assets were missing from Porsche, what sections had gone to Genex for production, the status of corrections on those pages, proof rounds, client reviews and corrections, and all the assorted details that go along with making web sites. While it wasn't The Designory's first interactive project, the company was still refining the adaptation of its 25-year-old print project-management processes to the interactive division. When asked about the tracking system he used, Chip jokes, "I had a very sophisticated system in my head ... I kept various lists, desperately trying to keep all the balls in the air at one time." To help with organization, Chip and David divided their production into increments, so they could send sections of the site to Genex. It seemed every section they'd send would be 90-95% done, leaving one or two more items to track down.

Chip found The Designory's "checkers" system for tracking modifications worked well for the Web. Chip explains, "If I made a change to the cover page, I would print that page out and staple it on top of the old cover page. And so we had stacks and stacks of papers. I'd run all of these through proofreading. They would come back with red marks on them, and I'd make these changes and print them out and staple them on top of the red marks, and give them back to proofreading to double-check the changes." Keeping the checkers up-to-date can be a time-consuming process, however. In later projects, The Designory hired a producer, Jason Deal, to assist with traffic, leaving the designers free to concentrate on creative work.

The Designory

Founded in Long Beach, California, in 1970, The Designory, inc. (www.designory.com) is a firm of integrated marketing communications designers. The Designory approaches interactive projects from a standpoint of integration, to help ensure that the customer is always greeted with a consistent product and brand image. This demands a focus on architecture, graphics, and navigation design as essential elements of content. Together with affiliate Pinkhaus in Miami and additional resources in New York, The Designory and Pinkhaus are one of the largest independent design firms in the United States.

211 East Ocean Blvd., Suite 100, Long Beach, California 90802-4809 Contact: Lannon Tanchum, 562-432-5707, lannon.tanchum@designory.com

From left: Lannon Tanchum, Chip McCarthy , David Glaze of The Designory, and Walter Schild from Genex Interactive.

While they had many assets in-house, they still needed others from Porsche, like Motorsports information. But that content had to come from Germany, and there was no one at Porsche who had time to weed through their extensive material to decide what should go up. Chip says, "They were doing much less racing

Located in the Heritage section of the site, these photos are of great interest to Porsche fans.

that year than in previous years. Porsche wasn't sure which stories they wanted to tell, and we wound up without any Motorsports information when the site went live." Assets in the u.s. were more readily available. Chip spent an afternoon in Reno going through the Porsche library of stills and footage to get additional materials. He says, "We knew we needed more images but we weren't sure what would work until I could actually see the assets, select some, and bring them back to The Designory for review."

At first, they sent hard copies of Quark files, designed to look like web pages, to Porsche to be approved by their marketing and legal departments. As the site progressed, Porsche began referring to the project site Genex had built. This project site had different levels of

Genex Interactive (www.genexmedia.com) produces interactive CD ROMs, web sites, and kiosk programs. The company offers full-service production capabilities, including project concepting, design, programming, production, and hosting. Genex also provides technical support, marketing and sales support, customer service, and assistance in online product sales. Genex works in partnership with leading advertising agencies and design firms to extend clients' existing marketing programs, projects, and brands into the competitive and growing new-media arena. Its specialty is helping to create and implement corporate strategies, build effective and scaleable web sites, and incorporate existing outreach and marketing programs.

10003 Washington Blvd., Los Angeles, CA 90232 310-845-9500 info@genex.com

access, with one level for The Designory to approve and one for Porsche to see. Walter describes the project site as a tool that enabled Porsche to view work in progress. "We gave Porsche a password, so they could enter the project site from any location in the world. We were able to discuss concerns by phone, working together to find solutions quickly."

The launch date was approaching rapidly, and The Designory had to finalize every page and send it to Genex. They'd fallen a little behind schedule and would rely on Genex to make up the time. Genex had about two weeks to get everything working in every browser – perfectly.

A site for all browsers

The Designory and Genex are about a 20-minute drive from each other. Chip and David became very familiar with the road. Genex's project manager would call and tell them to take a look at a page on the staging server, saying their design hadn't worked for all browsers and here was a revised layout. Sometimes, this revised layout wasn't acceptable. Chip and David would drive over and work with Genex to find alternatives. Chip says, "I would stand over somebody's shoulder, and we would work though the process together. It was more efficient, and we got to our final project quicker."

Walter explains, "We put up almost 100 pages of content that were produced in about two weeks, so there was a lot going on. There were issues about things that couldn't be done a certain way. The Designory was very particular about how copy broke and how images were aligned. We did a lot of tests, like different ways of doing soft-edged headlines." Another challenge was compressing full-screen,

Genex managed to compress these gorgeous, full-color photos to less than 40K.

full-color photographs to less than 40K, the upper-limit the team had set. Genex ended up modifying some custom software to enhance file compression with less pixelation and noise. Although this software proved useful, The Designory still needed to review each photo to determine how much dithering and noise was acceptable.

The Genex team started staying in the office until three and four in the morning, getting everything to work right. Netscape and IE upgraded their browsers mid-project, which caused more trouble. When Walter remembers the situation, he still sounds frustrated about it: "If you had a carriage return inside a cell of the table, in Netscape 1.1 it was fine, but in Netscape 2.0 it entered a black line underneath the table. It was fine in Netscape 1.0 and America Online, but Netscape 2.0 came out and it looked terrible. We had to change 60 pages. Netscape 2.0 introduced client-side image mapping, which is a nice way to speed up the time it takes to request another page, so we had to go in and add that to all the pages." The AOL browser was causing its own problems. Determined to make their site take advantage of new features as well as make sure it worked flawlessly, Genex tested and retested all of their pages.

The Final Product

The week before the site launch, Genex went into overdrive, testing the site on every possible platform and browser once again. A reporter from *Forbes* joined the Porsche clients and The Designory team at Genex, pushed a button to turn the server on for the launch, and got to see the first live log-ons, which arrived within seconds of launch – even though Porsche had done no advance promotion. The launch went smoothly, and Porsche was happy.

One decision they had made, not putting an email address for Porsche on the site, immediately began haunting Walter. "Everyone wants to email Porsche, but Porsche doesn't have the staff to reply to this email. But visitors to the site have lots of questions, because they're fanatics about the cars. People see Genex's name and email their questions – and Genex has a policy of replying to every email. Ninety percent of the time we can't answer the question. 'I'm looking for a 911 Porsche, do you have a source for a used one you can recommend?' So we send back, 'Try your local dealer. In your area, there are these three dealers.' You try to make it useful." But he believes there should be some other mechanism in place to deal with the email, perhaps via a bulletin board on the site.

The Designory continues to generate interest in the site by doing non-traditional promotions online. Their January promotion for the Boxster increased traffic to the site from 125,000 pages served in September to nearly 900,000 in January, and traffic has remained consistently high since. The site has won numerous awards, including the High Five and IPPA, and has been recognized by *Communication Arts* magazine. The toe-in-the-water site has proven a successful vehicle for reflecting the excellence of Porsche,

and Porsche is committed to expanding the site.

For the people involved, the most rewarding aspect was completing a large project quickly with only a small, dedicated team. Chip says, "It was a very small team of people and we were able to pull it off." But while he is proud of the accomplishment, he acknowledges that one more member of the team would have helped – The Designory has since hired Jason Deal as its web-site producer, who helps keep all the balls in the air at the same time.

PORSCHE

Joel Ewanick	*General Manager Marketing, Porsche Cars North America*
Kevin Nicholls	*Porsche Great Britain*
Dr. Loris Casadei	*Porsche Italia*

THE DESIGNORY

Lannon Tanchum	*Executive Creative Director*
David Glaze	*Creative Director*
Chip McCarthy	*Art Director*
Rich Conklin	*Copywriter*
Peggy McCabe	*Account Executive*
Alan Rifkin	*Proofreader*
Jason Deal	*Producer*
Chad Weiss	*Copywriter*
Brian Kennedy	*Product Specialist*

CONSULTING

Wes Haynes	*Creative Director*
Steve Davis	*Art Director*
Tina Viramontes	*Project Coordinator*
Lisa Dimitrov	*Computer Production*

GENEX INTERACTIVE

Reilly Cheung
Elizabeth Morse
Ray Odell
Walter Schild

Purpose of the site

Evantide created The Hamptons as a demonstration site both to help clients understand the Web and to show off their design and technical talent.

The players

Lizi Obolensky
Anders Brownworth

Launch date

September 11, 1995

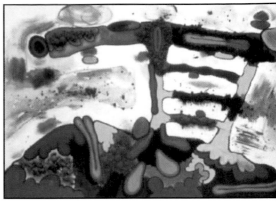

The site features paintings like this one,
Integrated Painting 5 by Carroll Dunham.
Courtesy of Sonnabend Gallery, New York.

Lizi Obolensky and Anders Brownworth had made this same pitch eleven times.

Chapter 14

www.thehamptons.com

Focus

what you will learn

How this two-person partnership convinced their community to invest in the Web, and in the process, built a successful business.

THE HAMPTONS was perfect for a showcase site, Lizi explained. It was a beautiful area. Playground of the rich and fabulous, the site could be targeted toward an affluent clientele. The wonderful art collections of the museum and galleries would add depth to the site, whereas sections about Hamptons events, like the Hampton Classic Horse Show, would help draw people to the area. Lizi and Anders ended their presentation by suggesting this company get on board, too, by paying Evantide Graphical to build a site for them.

The company executive leaned back in his chair, nodding. "Tell me," he said. "What is this ... World Wide Web?" He pronounced the words as

if he'd never said them before.

Anders and Lizi took a deep breath and tried to explain the concept again, this time concentrating on the basics. The CEO looked interested but blank. Lizi needed something to show him – not just a web site, but a destination web site. She couldn't explain it in words. And until the directors of the organizations and institutions understood what The Hamptons online could be, they certainly weren't going to pay to be included. They didn't understand how it would benefit them, either.

Lizi and Anders decided it was time for a new approach. They would build the Hamptons site without any paying clients. After it was built, they

The Hampton Classic Horse Show group was web savvy from the start.

would have a demo to show. In the meantime, they'd have to put together a new proposition for the Hamptons community, one offering something for nothing to get content for the demo site. It was a gamble – Lizi would keep her day job and try to do her side of the work at night. Anders would live off his credit cards in hopes of making money later. And the deadline would be determined by his credit limit.

A new proposal

Armed with her new proposal, Lizi made another round of sales calls in the community. Besides offering to build sections of The Hamptons site for each organization, Evantide Graphical would host their sites-within-the-site for free for one year. After the year was up, the organization could choose to pay for hosting or to take their section down. She chose high-profile institutions, the pillars of the community, to approach with the new deal, calculating that if they agreed, the new site would attract the attention of these institutions' business-owning boards and members – who might become

paying customers once the site was up. She adds, "They also have exceptional collections of private art, so it seemed like they would fit into place."

The new proposal went over much better with the directors of each organization. While still no clearer on the Web, they understood the concept of getting something for nothing. Lizi says, "The Hampton Classic Horse Show group was the only one who had any Internet savvy at that point. The others had sort of heard of it, and they weren't quite sure what to do with it." As organizations like the Parrish Museum and Guild Hall of East Hampton signed on, Lizi and Anders saw that their new idea was working.

Not every institution was an easy sell. While trying to get the Designer Showhouse project, a benefit for the Rogers Memorial Library where

prestigious architects and interior designers work together to create Hamptons dream homes, Lizi ran into bureaucratic troubles as the institution went through a succession of directors. She'd get approval from one, try to make a follow-up phone call, and find not only a new director, but a new assistant as well. The new assistants had to understand the project before granting Lizi an appointment to explain the Internet to the new director. "I had to approach people several times just to get in the door and then finally get to the person who could do something about it," she says.

Once each director approved the project and agreed to let Lizi and Anders use their content, it was another obstacle to actually collect assets. Since the organizations weren't paying to have their sections built, they had no incentive to meet deadlines or to assign someone within the organization to help Lizi. She found herself driving around the island, trying to convince people to give her photographs and copy that

Guild Hall enriches the site with its extensive art collection.

she and Anders could use. Some of the materials weren't high quality enough to scan – the library in particular gave her photographs they couldn't use. "I had to get copyrights from all of the photographers and get in touch with all of the designers, and get people to send me the photographs because the library provided really poor-quality prints." Finally, she had to write the copy that appeared on each page herself. Since the demo site, with its seven community pillars, was rapidly approaching 800 pages of content, she knew that she and Anders were in for some long nights.

Designers and architects from all over the world can study the breathtaking rooms of the Designer Showhouse.

The home stretch

Meanwhile, Anders had spent two weeks getting a new server up to speed – the site would be hosted through Internet Computing, his former company, and Internet Computing had just replaced their Sun machines with Pentium boxes. Once the site had a place to live, he could focus on design and navigation issues. The site had to capture the character of The Hamptons – affluent yet rustic, it was a place where celebrities signed big deals over breakfast at the

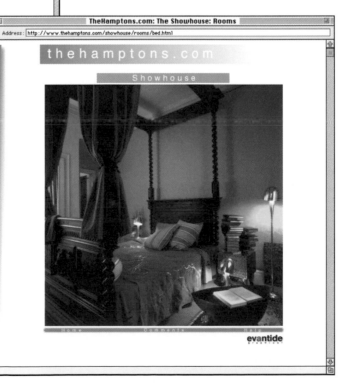

1. Visitors choose a section from the main table of contents page.

clicks deeper into the section, another blue bar appears, giving the name of that subsection. But that's the limit – two bars. Any more than that would make the page cluttered, according to Anders. The trouble is when the user then clicks deeper into the site. "There are some sections where it's not very definitive how deep you are in the site with just two GIF bars at the top," muses Anders. "I might rethink that."

Once Anders had decided on the navigation and look and feel, Lizi could help him produce the hundreds of images they had to keep track of, scan, clean up, and compress. They didn't want to make their mark by debuting with accidentally colorized or altered works of art, either. Their scanner had a bad habit of turning blues to blacks, requiring painstaking color correction. Lizi recalls, "The trickiest part was when the museum would give us dirty slides and we weren't sure which part was a

3. When visitors move deeper into the section, a second navigation bar shows the path they've taken.

Candy Kitchen and where gorgeous landscape and prestigious events merged. He chose white for the background and a soothing light blue for the header and navigation elements. Anders believes his design reflects The Hamptons: "It's uncluttered, open, airy, like beaches with their empty expanses of space." A clean, sans-serif, all lower-case typeface contributes to the classic, understated look. Postage-stamp size photos lure the user into the site with a glimpse of the area's natural beauty.

The site's navigation challenged Anders. The home page presents each sector in a blue bar. As the viewer goes into each site, its name appears in a blue bar at the top of the page. When the user

Jackson Pollock and which part was a smudge." Abstract art posed its own difficulties, as Lizi swallowed her pride and called curators to ask which way was supposed to be up.

Anders chose the technology he used on the site carefully, creating scripts to make production more efficient. "We experimented with some Java stuff, but it never went live. You have to watch out and make sure everything you put up belongs there, rather than because it is the newest and flashiest thing," he says. He wrote scripts so that headers and footers could update on every page automatically.

2. The table of contents page takes visitors to that section's "home page."

It had been nearly three months, and the team was getting frazzled. Lizi was staying up until four a.m. learning HTML to help Anders and then going to her full-time day job. Anders was working 24-32 hours at a stretch, hoping to beat his credit limit. Sometimes they'd surf over to rival destination sites to see what the competition was doing. Anders says, "We'd cringe for a bit, then come back to The Hamptons and say, 'Ah ...'" But while it seemed to take forever, eventually the site was ready to launch.

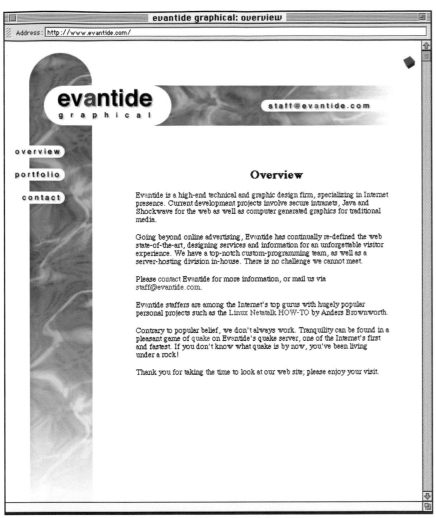

The Hamptons site helped Evantide Graphical launch their now successful design business.

Evantide's capabilities and philosophies. Then they ask for information on the client's company, so they can get an understanding of the company's objectives. Anders says, "If you had a business that wouldn't lend itself to the Web, we would tell you quite frankly if it didn't. Some things aren't so great handled on a web site."

If Anders and Lizi think the company is a good candidate for a site, they meet and discuss more of what the company hopes to accomplish. They try to build a mental picture of the site and its scope before talking price. "A lot of people try to force you into ballpark prices, and you can't give them accurate estimates without knowing how

Lizi Obolensky,
Anders Brownworth.

The post-debut difference

There was no confetti, no launch party – The Hamptons launch went off quietly and as planned. Winning the High Five six weeks later surprised and delighted Anders and Lizi. The site rapidly picked up additional awards, like Microsoft Network's pick on New Year's Day and AOL's Blue Plate Special in their Web Diner. They had only hoped to have a wonderful demo site for potential clients, but it seemed their site was much more than a demo.

Almost immediately, Evantide Graphical was approached by paying clients – a big relief to Anders and his credit-card company. Some wanted to appear on The Hamptons site, and others just wanted Evantide to produce their corporate sites. One of their first sites was for Capital Growth Mutual (CGM), which handles realty and fixed-income growth funds. CGM gets 15-20 contacts per day through its site, and eight to 10 of those contacts turn into leads.

They've got enough business that Lizi quit her day job and devoted her energy to Evantide Graphical full time, Anders paid off his credit cards, and they could afford to refuse clients. Now, when prospective clients call them, their first step is to send the client a PR kit that explains

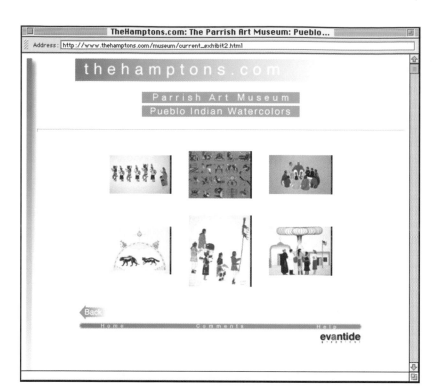

Visitors can view several works from the Parrish Art Museum's collection at once and then click to enlarge those that engage their interest.

much time you'll spend on the project," Anders says. They think about the size of the project and how it will integrate into the company's current marketing campaign before giving an estimate. Their clients have ranged from Marquette de Bary, the oldest discount brokerage firm in New York, to Panther Martin Fishing Lures for Harrison-Hoge Industries, and the team consults for Dow Jones on a regular basis. The Jewish Museum has asked Evantide to submit a bid for their upcoming web project.

TheHamptons.com

But while Evantide is pleased to see the corporate web-site production side of their business flourish, they are most proud of the success of the site that made it happen. Lizi and Anders watched like proud parents as new members joined the Parrish Museum after seeing the site online. A mention in the online newsletter about Roy Lichtenstein generated email requests for purchases, some from as far away as Germany and Sweden. Art posters promoted online attracted orders for the asking price of $200, giving Lizi an idea. The site could expand to have a Main Street section, a shopping area for the high-end products and souvenir items sold by Hamptons merchants. One of the first local products to be promoted is the Shelter Island Runabout, a powerboat with an asking price of $300,000, built by Peter Needham of Coecles Harbor Marine and singer-songwriter Billy Joel, a Hamptons local.

In addition to the Marketplace, the team has been working with the

Native American residents of the community to add a feature on their culture as another pillar of the site. Evantide wants to add to the current site content to make it more powerful and more substantial than it already is. The site currently consists of 1500 handwritten pages, and Lizi has volunteers wanting to write even more. The team is determined to continue to keep the site's content updated and use it as a community springboard for both established and upcoming writers, artists, and merchants.

The community has embraced the site with enthusiasm. Last summer, the library hosted a gala Internet affair at $200 per ticket, complete with big white tents, orchestras, good food, and giant TVs capturing the party live. With the cooperation and sponsorship of Toshiba for joint promotion, Evantide brought in five Macs and hooked them up to some of the TV sets, so that while some TVs captured the dance floor and conversations among the guests, some showed off the site. The Hampton Classic Horse Show selected The Hamptons as an official web site for their 1996 event. More importantly, many of the pillar sites, like Guild Hall, the Parrish Art Museum, Group for the South Fork, and the World Affairs Council, have added the site's URL on stationery, business cards, and collateral materials. To Lizi's relief, she is no longer driving around the island persuading people to give her content. They are coming to her and asking nicely if Evantide will take on their project. And she doesn't have to explain what the World Wide Web is anymore.

From top: Lizi and Anders show off TheHamptons.com at a $200-per-ticket, gala Internet affair.

Center: Televisions provided both live coverage of the party and The Hamptons site.

Bottom: The World Affairs Council helps promote the site on its stationery and promotional materials.

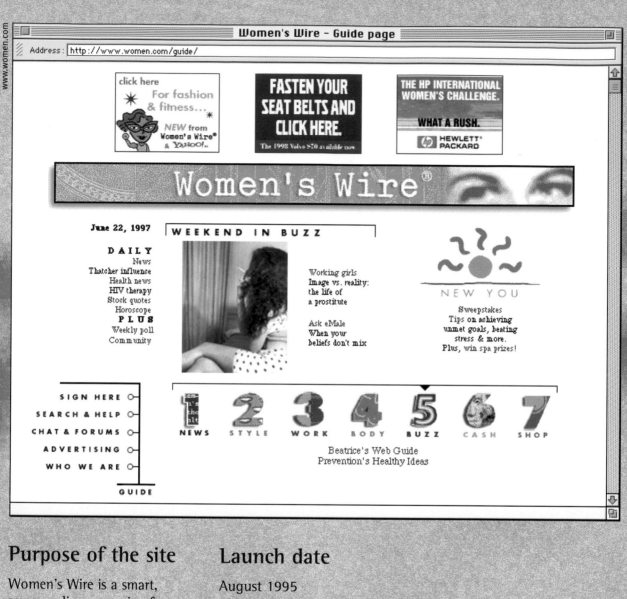

Purpose of the site

Women's Wire is a smart, savvy, online magazine for women. Revenue is primarily advertising driven.

Launch date

August 1995

Redesign launch date

June 1996

pullquote

"You've got a serious movie-going habit...

While redesigning this magazine site to make room for more content and advertisers, Women's Wire made sure they stayed true to the elements that made their site a success

After just eight months of operation, Women's Wire faced a problem they were happy to have – they had too much content and nowhere to put it.

Chapter 15

www.women.com

Focus

what you will learn

How Women's Wire's in-house designers approached the redesign of their successful online magazine with an eye toward pleasing both their audience and their advertisers.

As Vice President of product development at Wire Networks, Inc. Ellen Pack puts it, "We were bustin' at the seams with content." An even better problem was their need for more space for advertisers.

According to their mission statement, Women's Wire provides a place for women around the world to connect with each other. Besides offering live chat and discussion forums, Women's Wire provides extensive, smart coverage of topics ranging from news and health to fashion and work. They've successfully positioned themselves as the leading web site for independent, intelligent women – no "how to catch a husband" articles here. Editor in Chief Laurie Kretchmar explains their editorial position: "We're not about telling you what to do. We hand you information that we hope helps you make good decisions."

During their first eight months on the Web, Women's Wire's approach paid off with loyal visitors and advertising dollars. They were ready to expand the content on career, fashion, health and fitness, and more, but the existing design only allowed for a finite number of features. As editors juggled the content, everyone knew the redesign was coming soon. Ellen Pack points out, "We're not a company that does a million other things and had to design a web site. Building web sites is what we do."

The challenge would be to redesign the site in a manner true to the formula that had made Women's Wire a success to its readers and advertisers.

Marketing is your friend

While gaining room for content was the redesign's primary goal, the redesign had to serve both advertisers and the audience better. Women's Wire's marketing department presented ideas for how the redesign could meet this objective. Since Women's Wire makes most of its revenue from advertising, the site needed to provide more space for ads. Marketing suggested making the site "flat" rather than "deep" would encourage visitors to click to new pages instead of scrolling – and new ads could be placed at the top of each new page. They specified how many advertisements needed to fit on each page and how large they had to be.

"Marketing is your friend," explains Ellen. "Not just because ad sales are so important, but because they help us know more about the demographics of our visitors. They know who our audience is and what they're interested in." Marketing brought in survey results to help reinforce the message Women's Wire had so successfully sold to its readers. "We wanted to keep some of the elements that best represented our site, in this case the logo and the eyes. We wanted to be careful to build on what we had done and not start with a completely blank slate, because we'd built up significant loyalty," says Ellen.

Creating content channels

The product-development department formed a redesign team, with members from editorial, art, and production. They reviewed the content they had, noted which subjects were popular, and which areas they wanted to expand. The

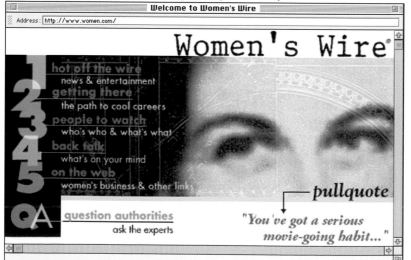

The "body" section covers more than health and fitness.

content seemed to fit best into seven categories, which they named with quick, snappy soundbites: News, Style, Work, Body, Buzz (an entertainment section), Cash, and Shop. They chose the names carefully to allow for a wide range of content within each section. For example, Body expands to cover health, fitness, nutrition, skin care, and even relationships.

The old design had used yellow, chunky numbers to point at the content. Some at Women's Wire felt the numbers were limiting and that they should use the redesign as an opportunity to change to icons. They argued they could make an icon more evocative of News than the number one. But others resisted switching to icons, feeling they were overused and hard to do well. Plus, keeping the numbers would be in keeping with marketing's suggestion that they keep some elements from the old design, so as not to alienate existing readers.

Ellen felt numbers weren't limiting at all, but that instead they could act

The prior design aligned five features alongside the yellow, chunky numbers.

as a channel in the same way people associate numbers with television stations. Regular visitors would know to tune in to channel three for work content, two for style, and seven for shopping. New visitors would be able to navigate based on the headings that accompanied each number. She felt icons were more limiting – for example, if they used a dress for their style section, visitors might not know to go there for beauty tips as well. She admits some of it is just personal preference. "The big chunky numbers sort of remind me of Sesame Street. There's something comforting about them."

Art director Lourdes Livingston worked on the numbers design to find a solution to please both camps. While she produced the concepts for the redesign, she had plenty of input from the team to help her along. Says Ellen, "The team worked very closely together. We were in each other's offices all the time looking at things." Lourdes would show an idea to the team, incorporate feedback, and have a revised idea the next day. The solution to the numbers versus icons debate was to give each number an almost icon-like design treatment. Instead of having all the numbers look alike as in the previous design, Lourdes gave each number a distinctive background, ranging from the lipsticked mouths of Style to the money green of Cash. Each number had a different personality to complement the different nature of that channel's content.

Navigation and flexibility

The new design had to be flexible. Women's Wire had learned a lesson from the existing design's lack of expandability. Some channels would

Women's Wire kept the numbers but gave them a more icon-like appeal.

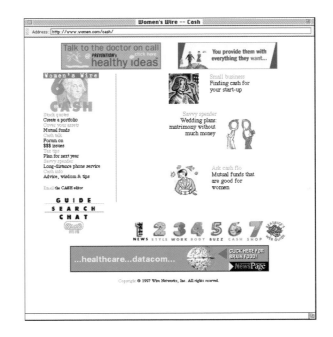

The main pages for the different sections show the variety and amount of content Women's Wire puts up in each category.

The guide page acts as a table of contents and also provides more room for ads.

have more content than others at the start, and the design had to allow for this uneven content as well as provide room for growth. Also, while they planned for some features and departments to update daily and others weekly, they didn't want to be limited by the design if one of the weeklies should go daily.

The site needed some sort of menu or table-of-contents page to list the content for the reader. The team wanted to be sure visitors had easy access to past features, and that features and departments retained high visibility for some days after their launch. This table of contents page would showcase certain articles, rotating out features and promoting new ones, thereby adding a dynamic quality to the site – when visitors come back to the site the next day, new features await them. One idea was to list each piece of content under the channel name, so that visitors could simply scroll through the list of articles for content of interest to them.

But having this long list on the home page seemed to clutter it unnecessarily. Not only did it leave less room to promote that day's features, it left no room for branding – the elements that would establish the site as being Women's Wire. Ellen says, "We decided to design it so the top section of the screen, which is basically what's visible on someone's browser, highlighted what's fresh today. But if you're someone who wants easy access to your favorite item, you'd scroll down for the full table of contents." Since the table of contents isn't visible from a standard screen, some visitors may not even know it's there. "And that's fine," says Ellen. "That's always the question – how much do people scroll? But there's no way of knowing that." To brand the site, the team decided to use a splash page to set the tone and mood – but the site encourages visitors to bookmark the guide page, not the splash page.

Now the problem of getting visitors to the content was solved, but how would visitors get back? The number navigation bar would appear on each of the channels' main pages, thus giving the reader the ability to click between sections quickly. The content pages themselves contain HTML links back to the guide page, a search page, and to the chats and forums. Women's Wire felt it was important to provide readers with a quick way to hop around the site.

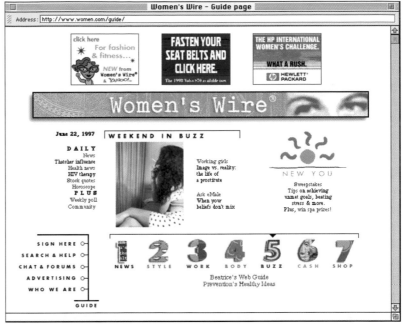

The splash page sets the tone and mood of the site, leaving more space on the guide page.

Working with advertisers

Levi's approached Women's Wire and asked for ideas on how they could sponsor a section of the site more actively, to be part of the experience. Levi's felt their target market of young and college-age women was on the Web, and they felt more active sponsorship was a good way to reach them. They hoped Women's Wire could come up with a section of the site for them to sponsor that would appeal to their target market. Ellen Pack says, "And the cool thing about Levi's is they said, 'By the way, it doesn't have to be about fashion, and it doesn't have to be about jeans.' That gave us an open door that's pretty rare and refreshing."

Excited to collaborate with an advertiser who really wanted to work with them to connect with the audience, Women's Wire gathered information on Levi's goals, products, and markets. They agreed to come up with a proposal and put a small team of editors together to create it. "Everything here is very team oriented," says Ellen. "Even when there's just one person leading the charge, there's constant feedback. 'Did you think of this? Can I show you this?'" After brainstorming, the team decided that in Women's Wire's experience, the number-one topic on the minds of young women is career. "They've told us this in surveys, we know it from our site, they talk about their careers, they ask for career advice," says Ellen. Led by Editor in Chief Laurie

Women's Wire worked with Levi's to develop this section of the site, called "Getting There."

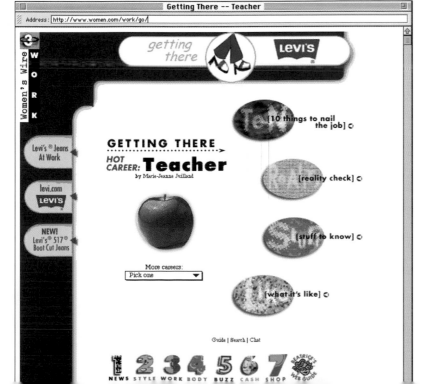

Kretchmar, the team recommended Women's Wire put together the ultimate guide for choosing and getting started in a career – sponsored by Levi's. It would be called Getting There.

"It'll be the career services office on your college campus that you *wish* you'd had," Women's Wire presented to Levi's. "The one that told you what these real careers are like and how people get them and talks to real women in their 20s, women who are doing the jobs you want." Levi's liked the idea – it worked well with their marketing campaign and positioning, and they liked that it had such great appeal to their target market. Moreover, the site would be far from static. Besides frequently updated content, the site would get a new look every quarter. Women's Wire agreed to update the section with new careers and a new look quarterly, concurrent with Levi's seasonal marketing campaign changes.

Serving your audience

The real test of Women's Wire's redesign would come when their readers saw it. Women's Wire was concerned from the beginning about their reader's reaction and tried to anticipate their needs. Ellen describes their average reader as 34, professional, highly educated, and having a high income. Fifty percent of their readers are married. "I think the hardest thing on the Web in general is knowing who your audience is, understanding who that audience is, and then serving that audience. And I think you serve them both through editorial as well as design – how easy you make it to navigate, how you present your information.

"When you go to a site, you immediately pick up a lot of stuff from how it looks as well as the content. Just like the real world, when you're walking around and you might – I mean, none of us do this – but you *might* judge somebody by what they're wearing. You judge a web site by how young does this look, does this talk to me, is it friendly, sophisticated."

When the redesign was nearing completion, marketing brought in a 20-person focus group. Each participant browsed the site and filled out a questionnaire, answering questions like "Was this content easy to find? What did this icon make you think about?" The focus group's positive response reassured Women's Wire

that their redesign was on the right track.

Looking ahead: another redesign?

The site's growth has corresponded to growth in Women's Wire's staff. Since the redesign, they've grown from having two to six editors and from two to seven salespeople. Women's Wire has also added two new sites, Beatrice's Web Guide (www.bguide.com) and Prevention's Healthy Ideas (www.healthy-ideas.com), with the goal of becoming a network of sites. Advertisers can buy ad packages for all three sites.

Beatrice's Web Guide and Prevention's Healthy Ideas make up two more sites in the network of sites the team is building.

Women's Wire has noticed significantly higher traffic to the site since the redesign. Ellen attributes the higher traffic in part to the different subject areas. "Our style channel has a big following. And I don't think it's the same following – not that there's not any overlap, but I don't think the same people go to our cash channel." She thinks each channel acts as a specialty magazine. "You can tell through the chats and forums. You can really see different personalities on the different channels, so I think they attract different kinds of people."

But while the redesign has been successful both expanding their content and their business, Women's Wire already senses another redesign on the horizon. Their design needs to reflect that Women's Wire is part of a network of sites produced by Wire Networks, Inc. Plus, already they have more content areas that don't seem to fit, like a new home and garden channel. Once again, they are bustin' at the seams with content. Keep watching Women's Wire to see what's sure to be an innovative and successful solution.

The team

Ellen Pack	*Vice President Product Development*
Laurie Kretchmar	*Editor In Chief*
Lourdes Livingston	*Art Director*
John Hoag	*Web Director*
Paige Manzo	*Producer*
Sarah Stillpass	*Producer*
Katharine Mieszkowski	*Sr. Editor*
Tam Putnam	*Sr. Editor*
Barb Moffatt	*Associate Editor*
Margo Carn	*Assistant Editor*
Deborah Russell	*Copy Editor*

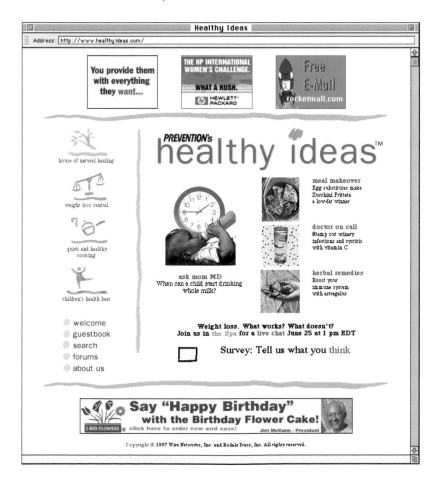

marketing ···⟶

functional ···⟶ ···⟶

creative ···⟶ ···⟶

administrative ···⟶

expansion

contraction

pre-production ···⟶ ···⟶

production

communication

validation ···⟶ ···⟶

strategy

marketing

design

creative

production

engineering

delivery

mainte-nance

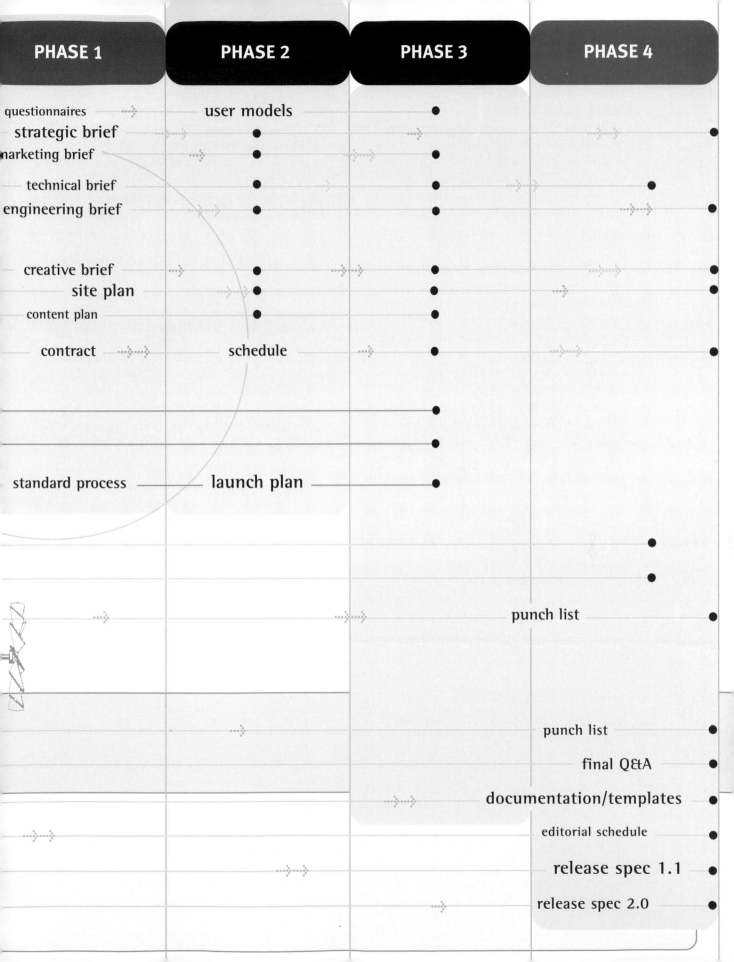

PHASE 1	PHASE 2	PHASE 3	PHASE 4
questionnaires	user models	●	
strategic brief	●		●
marketing brief	●	●	
technical brief	●	●	●
engineering brief	●	●	●
creative brief	●	●	●
site plan	●	●	●
content plan	●	●	
contract	schedule	●	●
		●	
		●	
standard process	launch plan	●	
			●
			●
		punch list	●
		punch list	●
		final Q&A	●
		documentation/templates	●
		editorial schedule	●
		release spec 1.1	●
		release spec 2.0	●

INTRODUCTION TO PART II

The web is a bullet train. Just a couple of years ago, nobody had the word "web" on his or her business card. I have a handful of friends I haven't even seen since the Web took off, and they live just a few blocks away. Yet I "talk" regularly with people in Australia and France, and I often introduce people using just my keyboard.

Private threads of "conversation" seem to form the undercurrent of intra-company communication, with no formal mention in meetings or at lunches. People surf during their lunch hour with a mouse in one hand and a sandwich in the other. People work in teams from home, hotel rooms, inside customer organizations. Conversations take place among 20 people at once, often for months, leading to single-day "summit meetings," where everyone is prepared and people can get right into deciding the substantive issues face-to-face. On Mondays, someone in my company sends out an "announce" message to all computer screens rather than yelling, "Come on downstairs, it's time for the meeting!" What has happened to talking around the water cooler? What has happened to communication?

Communication has gone online. If you can't type, you are email-challenged. The intranet is replacing the interoffice envelope. Paper resumés will soon be artifacts. People in my office routinely send URLs to everyone in the company, pointing out things we shouldn't miss, whether they are the latest installment at www.starwars.com or an article on new internet ventures at www.herring.com. This isn't something to do after hours – this is *required surfing*, something designers are expected to do as part of their work in a small web-design and consulting group.

I've had the opportunity to watch several web-development projects and talk to many of the people who work on the Web. One thing is consistent: most projects are 10% ideas, 20% implementing them, and 70% communication. Although the forms of communication are new, the basic ingredients of project management are timeless.

In contrast to the first half of this book, this section documents the Studio Verso process and philosophy of web project management. There are three caveats I want you to be aware of as you read:

Caveat 1: Use common sense. This book is filled with tips, pointers, and lists of things to do. You can't use all of them on one project. I have outlined many of the steps I think are necessary for running a large project, which leads to discussions on many topics that should not concern you if your project is small. Take from this book and others. Add your own ideas. Do it your way, not mine.

Caveat 2: Everything is a work in progress. Much of what I've written in this book I didn't know a year ago. Most of the specific techniques apply to the tools we have today. If this book were a web site, it would be different every day.

Caveat 3: Not everything goes wrong. This book is necessarily filled with warnings and tales of near-death experiences, but they won't all happen to every project. Most projects go fairly smoothly. This book is meant to help you see problems before they happen, not to scare you into a state of paralysis.

Finally, don't forget to visit the book site for more resources to help you implement the secrets you'll learn in the coming chapters. (Join our online producers' discussion by sending a message with the subject "subscribe" to **majordomo@secretsites.com**.)

Part II

"Wouldn't it be great if your pay was related to how you work?

Or if you could pick the jobs you wanted to work on?

Or if you could be in control of your own future?"

– Cameron Foote, *The Business Side of Creativity*

"The last 29 days of the month are always the hardest."

– Nikola Tesla

The web-design revolution parallels the desktop-publishing revolution of ten years ago.

IN THE MID-EIGHTIES, the number of people calling themselves graphic designers in the U.S. went from about 50,000 practicing professionals to about 500,000 "desktop publishers." Most of these new "designers" had little previous design training. They bought computers and laser printers and started designing brochures, menus, price lists, notices, newspaper ads, and so on. Many did not make as much money as they made when they worked for someone else, but they enjoyed working at home for themselves. Their hours were longer and their benefits worse.

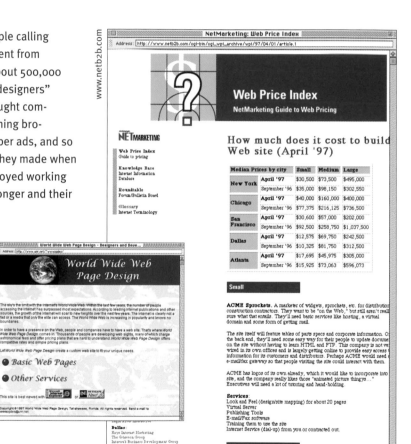

Most web "designers" are not design professionals.

Web design prices in 1997.

When the supply of designers floods a market – as it did in desktop publishing and is in web design – the middle of the market mostly goes away. Clients who want the best seek out established, professional firms, while clients who are less discerning tend to put savings ahead of quality.

This happened to me in the type market. I designed typefaces that became so popular, unscrupulous vendors started renaming and putting them on CD ROMS with thousands of fonts for a few dollars. Desktop publishers, faced with a choice of forty dollars or more for one font versus virtually free, chose the free fonts. Only the discerning graphic designers were willing to pay the previously acceptable prices for fonts. As the middle of the market disappeared, I did what almost every other typeface designer has done in the last few years: I opened a web-design business. I found myself taking meetings with prospective clients.

Clients

Clients are the lifeblood of any design practice. They are businesses or individuals who want web sites built. They must find someone to take them through the process of designing and crafting a site that meets their needs. In most cases, they are prepared to maintain and support their site once it's built.

Clients can be either producers or decisionmakers. A producer, or team leader, is in charge of having the site built but is not the primary decisionmaker. A team leader is often a mid-level marketing manager – someone who has dealt with graphic designers to make brochures, annual reports, and so on. Her main role is to facilitate the con-tractor relationships and build consensus. A decision-maker can be a principal, director, or vice-president, who also plays the role of the team leader.

These two types of clients differ mostly in the size of their projects. The process of working with clients is the same, whether they own the local pet shelter or they work in corporate headquarters.

Who's who on the client side

The team leader (or *project manager* or *producer*) is responsible for overseeing the project and the relationships with contractors. On a small team, this person can also be the key decisionmaker. The team leader is in charge of communication within the client organization.

Decisionmakers can come from anywhere in the organization. The more there are, the longer a process will take. The more informed they are, the smoother the project will go.

Webmasters are often members of the client staff. Webmasters make the hosting decisions that govern the day-to-day running and maintenance of the site.

Contentmasters come from anywhere in the organization. A contentmaster is responsible for a particular set of assets on the site.

Contributors are writers, photographers, artists, graphic designers, and others who add to the content.

Contractors

Four kinds of contractors work on web sites: proprietors, partnerships, boutiques, and agencies. Each group can handle a certain range of jobs.

A significant percentage of web-development contracts end in disputes or threatened litigation.

I wrote this book to help lay a foundation for better client-contractor relationships. Because it's a never-ending learning process, we strive to communicate better and improve our practices daily. Join our discussion online by sending an email to majordomo@secretsites.com with the words "subscribe producer" in either the subject or body fields of the message. Come join us!

www.los.com

Proprietors are usually a single person, but a pro-prietorship can include up to about eight people. The average proprietor is an individual with a technical background who has built a site or two and now wants to create sites for money. Most proprietors dislike marketing and shy away from the administrative aspects of running a business.

Partnerships are serious about making sites for a living. A partnership usually forms around people with creative, technical, and business skills. Most partnerships in web development are strongest in technical skills, they vary in their creative skills, and their business skills are, on average, below average.

www.p39.com

Small partnerships can make good money. If they develop a good reputation, partners will be able to do larger and larger projects. When they try to make the jump to boutiques, many partnerships fall into the chasm of unprofitability (I'll elaborate on this in a later chapter).

Boutiques are proprietorships or partnerships capable of growing beyond 10 people. They have producers, general managers, and administrative and sales staff. Their portfolios can include a small number of technical sites or a larger number of well designed sites.

Small boutiques usually number from 7 to 14 people; enough to require an office manager. Many small boutiques are financed on revenues, which means they have difficult months in between growth spurts.

Large boutiques have from 14 to about 30 people. At this size, they have constant pressure to keep new work coming in. They usually have two or three large jobs in house at all times. They will be smaller  if they focus on design, larger if they focus on technology. They usually have a source of outside funding.

Agencies are multidisciplinary. They typically have print and CD ROM design groups; larger ones have direct-mail and video/TV production units. Many are ad agencies with new web divisions. Many agencies  outsource web work to boutiques and partnerships.

Agencies want account work, rather than single projects. They look for large companies with multiple web-related services (ad campaigns, hosting, renewed content, and so on) and try to do everything for those clients. Agencies have dedicated sales people who are skilled at making presentations and responding to RFPS (requests for proposals). They usually have high minimum-dollar requirements for new client work.

Who's who on the contractor side

An executive producer is the person with ultimate responsibility for the project on the contractor side. If the producer is not doing his job, the client asks the executive producer to take care of the problem. The owner of the developer company is typically the executive producer on every job her firm produces.

An account manager works as an advocate for the client, making sure the contractor serves the client's interests, while also trying to figure out what other work the group could do for the client in the future. He is in charge of the pre- and post-project relationship with the client.

A technical consultant helps the design staff work within the perimeters of the presentation medium. It may be a person from the production staff, skilled in HTML, animation, web protocols, databases, and so forth. In larger firms, this person is usually a research specialist who consults on every job throughout the process.

A production specialist helps bring web sites to life using HTML, client-side scripts, Java, animation, and so forth. In small firms, everyone works on production. Groups of more than eight or so people usually have at least one production specialist.

A production manager oversees, documents, and continues to improve the process of production. This person manages the production staff and schedules resources.

A creative director determines the vision for the site. She writes the creative brief and coaches the design staff during the process of exploration. She and the producer decide what to show the client.

A system administrator makes sure the machines and the network are running well. He handles software updates and security issues, sets permissions, resets permissions, makes custom tools, and invents new ways of keeping everyone happy.

A designer conceptualizes solutions to problems, makes comps and models, and prepares presentations. This person may make general decisions on design directions or may be very specialized, like someone who designs navigation systems or user-interface design.

> "The producer is the person who ultimately takes responsibility for the project and makes sure the production team is empowered and informed."
>
> — Kirsteen Barton, Ikonic, Inc.

A producer (or *project manager* or *line producer*) is responsible for the day-to-day activity and for managing the budget and the schedule. Ideally, the producer facilitates the process of getting the site built. The producer is responsible for everything that goes on the work site (see Chapter 6).

Creative staff includes writers, web strategists, game designers, user-interface designers, and so on. This is often a mix of in-house talent and outside subcontractors.

An office manager handles the administrative duties. An office manager lets the contractor team work on the project without having to worry about contracts, billing, paying bills and staff, messaging, and so on.

Engineering

When I say engineering, I mean databases and underlying functionality that goes beyond simple scripts, rollovers, user-interfaces, and other cosmetic programming. Many chapters that follow have special engineering sections that relate specifically to groups doing database design and construction.

Who's who in engineering

The architect designs the overall strategy (*schema*) that maps the database to the task at hand.

A project manager is responsible for the delivery of the programs and documentation within the spec and on time.

Developers/programmers write most of the code to implement the schema. *Server-side developers* work on middleware, connecting HTML documents to databases and other systems. *Client-side developers* add functionality to the browser by writing Java applications and scripts.

Technical writers are responsible for internal and external (client) documentation.

The business cycle

The typical service-business cycle finds the contractor working hard for clients while fielding a few calls for more work, then a period where the new work hasn't come in

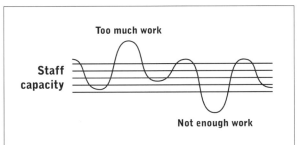

The project cycle: one deep trough and you're out of the game.

Pro bono sites let you exercise your design muscles to benefit the community.

yet, then more work, and so on. As busy as web designers are these days, this cycle still holds true. A larger group cycles between profitability and breaking even, while smaller groups cycle between profitability and poverty, as they make the following types of web sites.

Pro bono sites are those that a firm designs without charging the client. Many groups make sites for friends and non-profits, exercising their design skills while doing a service for the community. Some have created resources to give away at their own site, attracting visitors and having fun with their own content ideas. By giving to people in cyberspace, you will attract attention and build the goodwill every small firm needs.

Mike Nuttall on Clients

Clients generally want two things.

First, they want safety. They want projects done professionally and on time. They don't necessarily think about winning design awards. They think about what happens if the contractor can't deliver.

Second, they want stability. They are looking for a partner. They don't want to have to find a new vendor for each project. The more reliable and consistent you are, the more they will want to keep working with you.

Mike Nuttall is a principal of IDEO, a 350-person product design consultancy headquartered in Palo Alto, California [www.ideo.com].

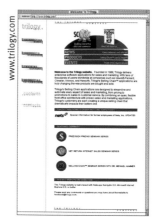
www.trilogy.com

Business-to-business sites can range from "quick and dirty" marketing brochures to interactive commerce applications. Commercial sites are quickly becoming mission critical, which means companies expect to see a profitable return on their investment. These sites are becoming strategic assets companies can use to build relationships with both existing and prospective customers.

Retail/commerce sites are feature-driven. Functionality often drives the process. If a commerce site is growing, it is getting feedback. It should be changing constantly, accommodating visitor requests.

www.irs.ustreas.gov.com/prod/cover.html

Consumer sites range from the local pet-store site to an automobile manufacturer, insurance company, or government site. They can be extravagant productions driven by ad agencies and multimillion-dollar budgets. They may want to emphasize community or their dealer network or provide editorial content to encourage brand loyalty. Consumer sites involve original content creation, provide value for customers, and are among the most stressful projects.

Vanity sites are small, promotional sites or exhibits for a company, individual, or organization. They may be up temporarily, with frequent changes during a short period, or they may be small and static, giving out information. For example, film sites are usually up for only a few months.

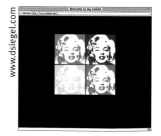
www.dsiegel.com

Periodicals range from academic papers and newsweeklies to consumer dailies. Designing periodicals requires design for unknown content. Contractors must emphasize template design and ease of maintenance over fancy one-off pages.

Entertainment sites are typically advertising based. There are many forms of entertainment sites, from magazines to movie-promotion to puzzles and games, mysteries, comics, serial soap operas, and much more. They typically have a fast editorial pace and an anxious set of regular visitors demanding even more content.

Intranets are among the fastest-growing segment of the market. Information-technology groups design and create intranets, often with little consultation on usability or presentation. While they budget well for functionality and online resources (like 401(k) plans and benefits applications), these departments most often do not hire outside designers or user-interface experts.

The bottom line

Informal research shows that most boutiques and agencies have yet to be profitable. They have to keep investing in new people, tools, and techniques. Many are able to bill only 50% of their available hours. As the industry matures, we will see low-end proprietors making a reasonable living, partnerships with particular skills and good portfolios charging enough to make a profit, and the agencies coalescing into larger companies with more stable income models.

Design and creative businesses don't go public, and they are rarely purchased. When they are purchased, the multiple is usually one to two times revenue. You must put 100% effort into every job, and most of the company's assets leave the building to go home every night. There's an upper limit on how much you can charge, and the chances of losing money in any month are fairly good. The upside in design is that you run a business with 10% profits after taxes, you get to do exciting, creative projects in a well designed environment, you expense most of your meals and travel, and you work for yourself.

If you thrive on being your own boss, handling clients, self-promotion, constant change, and the ups and downs of the business cycle, you'll love it. There's a small chance you'll be bought by a larger company, but in most cases, the reward behind the rush of small web-design services is pride of ownership. If you work better when someone gives you a deadline and takes care of the business details, you may want to join a boutique or agency.

Starting a business on the Web is an exciting ride. Balancing fun, excitement, and the stability (or should I say insanity?) of constant change makes it one of the most outstanding entrepreneurial opportunities of our time.

Secret Weapon Number One

Market segmentation

There are a lot of people coming into the business now – small one- and two-person shops that increase the client's choices. Making it depends on how savvy and focused you are. Make sure you offer value to clients. Know your goals and go after the clients you want.

– Jonathan Nelson, CEO of Organic Online

An interview with Jonathan Nelson, CEO of Organic Online

David Siegel: Jonathan, you have more than 60 people in one of the largest integrated web design and engineering companies in the country. What makes your culture unique?

Jonathan Nelson: We do a lot of community and nonprofit work. It doesn't pay the bills, but we really enjoy the chance to push ourselves in new directions and do something for others. Everyone at Organic, down to the receptionist, gets equity. I think it's important to share the wealth we create with all employees. We don't have much employee turnover. We have fantastic benefits and pay above-average salaries. Everyone works very hard, and it feels like family. We are dedicated to our own continued education and preserving our culture of challenge, leading-edge work, and fun.

DS What about your process of site development?

JN I can tell you we are constantly working on it. First, we are highly integrated. We have people who specialize in media placement, content, strategy, production, databases, commerce, work flow, etc. They're all in one big room, and there's a high degree of crossfertilization.

Handoff from one group to another is quite smooth. Our process is mature and quite systematic. We've formalized the 80% of the things we do that are similar from project to project, which gives us a better chance to innovate on the things that are unique about each project. We have actively gone to filmmakers, magazine producers, and even academics who specialize in organizational behavior to constantly compare and refine our process against other possible models. Right now we have two outside consultants looking with us at our process and helping us make it even more efficient. All our department heads have a mandate to manage well and improve the processes in their departments. This research isn't billable, but it saves us money in the long run.

DS What advice would you give to companies coming into the market today?

JN There are a lot of people coming into the business now – small one- and two-person shops that increase the client's choices. Making it depends on how savvy and focused you are. Know your goals and go after the clients you want. Make sure you offer value to clients. It's harder to just wing it. These days, you have to be more specialized or more generalized, and the clients are more discerning.

Because this is a new form of business, some of the ad agencies get it, and some don't. It's not business as usual for them, which gives opportunities for new shops to spring up and help clients in these online areas. I'd say that advertising agencies, in general, don't have the rigorous engineering and documentation in their culture that would let them compete with companies like ours.

DS What does it feel like when a project goes well?

JN Our projects usually go well, because we're careful about choosing whom we work with. We look for good chemistry first: if it isn't going to be fun to work with someone, what's the point? Having fun and enjoying the company of our clients is important. We often stay friends with our clients long after the site is finished.

DS How do you know when a project isn't working out?

JN When it doesn't work out, you know it. Relationships with clients are just like personal relationships: you have to keep working at them, but if you're not meant to be together, it's obvious to everyone.

Chapter 2

The value of design

"Let's say you are a manufacturer.
Your advertising isn't working
and your sales are going down.

And everything depends on it.
Your future depends on it,
your family depends on it,
other peoples' families depend on it.
And you walk into this office
and talk to me,
and you sit in that chair.

Now, what do you want out of me?
Fine writing?
Do you want
masterpieces?
Do you want
glowing things
that can be framed by
copywriters?

Or do you want to see the
goddamned sales curve
stop moving down
and start moving up?"

– Rosser Reeves, *Reality in Advertising*, 1961

Design is a formalized field of study, just like architecture.

FORTUNE 500 COMPANIES spend millions building and maintaining their corporate identities. Why should your identity be different on the Web? Why do so many sites look like they were designed by engineering or MIS departments, or by high school students? The more you do it, the more you learn the basic principles, or foundations, on which to build an appropriate web site. The design process, as I hope to show, is one of taking clear steps toward well-defined goals.

The value proposition

A successful site sits at the intersection of four strategic values and four tactical values. Although many sites reflect some of these values, a winning site has all eight values in measured proportion.

Strategic values are important in the long run. *Branding* not only identifies your company, but it also lets visitors know they're on your site. When sites look alike, it's hard to tell where you are. *Impact/news value* gives people

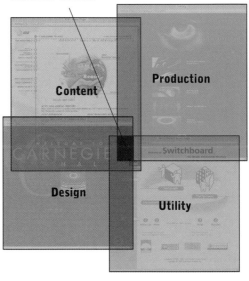

Nexus of tactical values

Content · Production · Switchboard · Design · Utility

something to talk about. If your site always has something fresh and newsworthy, you will constantly attract new visitors. *Audience/community values* are a reflection of a site's ability to satisfy the target audience. *Competitive values* are features that keep you ahead of the competition. If your competition counters with something more attractive to your customer group, you'll have to fire back, escalating the feature wars.

Tactical values are immediately apparent. *Design value* means that a designer with a sense of design and concern for the visitor has translated the goals into a visual experience. *Content value* means that editors and contributors have prepared content for display on the Web. *Production value* means that the person doing the HTML and graphics work knows and understands the principles behind third-generation site design (see *Creating Killer Web Sites*, by David Siegel). *Utility value* means people can do things on your site (buy, sell, fill out forms) – that it responds quickly, solves problems, and all the links work.

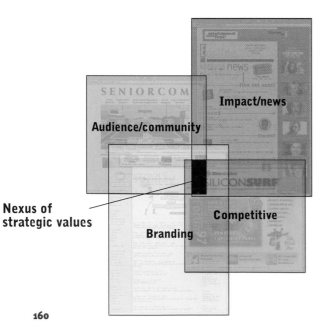

Nexus of strategic values

Impact/news · Audience/community · Competitive · Branding

The four phases of design

I divide the process of web design into four distinct phases. (Part I of this book describes a variety of approaches to the web-design process.) This summary introduces the phases, which later chapters will cover in more detail.

Phase One – Strategy. Get information and listen. Get to know the client's business, who their users are, and what they want. Work on having the ideas that will drive the project forward. By the end of this phase, you have a schedule and a set of deliverables.

TIP

For more information on the value of good design, contact the Corporate Design Foundation (www.cdf.org) and ask for their insightful e-zine, @Issue.

Phase Two – Design. Work out the "look and feel" of the prospective site. Consult with the client on developing structure and navigation, style, and technical components. Create design models, get approval, then hand the models over for production.

Phase Three – Production. Although the production team is involved all along, it's now time to build the site. Production people take the models and turn them into HTML. They pour the client's copy and content into a database and templates or into straight HTML.

Phase Four – Delivery. Work out the kinks, set up the beta site for viewing and testing, make final changes, and add final content. Move the site to the target server. The team works to launch the site. After a successful launch, planned maintenance and updates begin.

The value of good design

I can't guarantee that by spending a hundred – or five hundred thousand – dollars on a web site the client will get a profitable return on the investment. If the client has a bad idea for a product, any amount spent on a web site will be money thrown away. The two basic reasons to build a web site are to save money and to make money.

Clients can save money. Many companies have reduced product-support costs significantly by putting frequently

asked questions on their web site. Delivery services let people track packages themselves. Annual reports are printed in smaller quantities. Catalogs are now available with new information instantly. Cisco Systems, one of the leading Internet hardware manufacturers, sells over $6M in equipment *per day* at its web site, saving over $500M/year in order costs. How can you use the Web to save money?

A government webmaster once told me, "It's easy for you to say how we should build these web sites to serve people, but if we ask for the money, we'll get turned down. We don't have the money to build fancy web sites." I replied: "How much did you spend on photocopiers last year? How much on envelopes and postage? How much on phone centers? The money you need to build web sites is being spent all around you."

Every phone center in the country is ripe for at least partial migration to the Web. Every mail room should think about shipping bits down the wire rather than paper in envelopes. Every time you fill out a form, envision

What does your web site do? Utility is perhaps the most important tactical value.

someone on the other end, keying the information into a database. Why not enter the information directly into a database yourself? Direct capture of information and feedback is one of the major advantages of the Web. A fully functional web site may be a complicated project, but it will pay off.

Ease-of-use is part of good design. If customers can't find answers to frequently asked questions, they will call instead. As web sites become more functional, they blur the lines between documents and applications. Information designers and user-interface designers can add a lot to the quality and usefulness of a site, directly affecting the financial bottom line.

Clients can make money. Whether you're selling books, concert tickets, investment advice, or software, the Web can be a profitable method of distribution. Catalogs and retailers are doing good business. Specialty malls (like www.weddingusa.com) attract lots of customers. The Sharper Image gets an average of $160 per sale at their web site (and the cost of processing the order is significantly lower than using the 800 number).

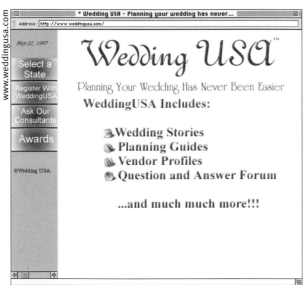

Specialty malls of all kinds are doing well on the Web.

The Web offers convenience and low price through *disintermediation* – the removal of middlemen. Travel agencies are already on the Web. Writers and designers work long-distance for clients they never meet face-to-face. Banks, brokers, and government agencies are meeting customer needs online. This is the real world of the Web. The money isn't only in web-industry tools and banner advertising. The money is in replacing expensive procedures like photo finishing with online enhancements like printing a poster of your family from a digital photo. The opportunities are limited only by our imagination.

Very few entertainment sites make money directly from advertising. Be careful if your business plan includes significant revenues from advertising. While advertising is always nice, if you're counting on it, you should be a search engine.

What price quality?

How much does a web site cost? It's difficult to get an accurate sense. According to NETMarketing's Web Price

Index, small 20-page sites have a median cost of $26k. A medium-sized site, with about 100 pages, password-protected directories and a search engine, costs $102k. A large site with all the new technologies cost on median $596k. These findings, based on bid requests from 21 web developers in late January, "suggest that site-building pricing tends to be all over the place," according to www.cyberatlas.com. "For example, bids for a large site ranged from a rock-bottom $15k to a heart-stopping $2.8m."

So how does a client decide how much time, effort, and money to spend on a web site? I can't offer any guarantees of success, but I can break the problem down into what we know and what we don't know.

Design certainties

Design is one of the table legs that holds up a good site. Many sites today are awfully tilted because that leg is shorter than the others. As the Web matures, design becomes a hotter topic at site-planning meetings.

Design is more important when you have competition. If you have the only taxi stand on the Web, you might be able to get away with a first-generation site. If your competitors start offering the same products and same service at similar prices, you'll have to differentiate. The three ways to differentiate are design, functionality, and content. All three work together to help build a brand, a community, and a buzz about your site.

> "Business-to-business commerce is the killer application of the Internet."
>
> – Peter Solvik, CIO, Cisco Systems

There isn't a one-to-one relationship between quality and success. With ad agencies charging millions of dollars for sites, and with thousands of people willing to make sites for $10 per page, it's hard to know where the value is. Are the expensive ones indistinguishable from the cheap sites?

There is a serious difference in quality, and I'd like to say that the 100 most-visited sites are well designed. But they aren't. Many of them aren't even well engineered. As web traffic increases and competition heats up, sites will have to improve.

It's easy to confuse a beautiful site with an appropriate site. I'd love to say that if you make a beautiful site, people will flock to it. Unfortunately, this isn't true either. While design is a differentiator, so is functionality. If another site lets people do more, you might be stuck with a pretty site that sits there gathering cyberdust.

If the audience loves and uses it, it's a success. Serve your core audience and make them ecstatic users. Make sites deep before making them wide. In most cases, design will play a role, but it may just be a supporting one. Always look to improve on a success!

Not to design is to design. Because your first-generation site is doing well doesn't mean a redesign won't be worth the effort. For starters, any popular site will attract competition. Second, a certain number of people will be frustrated by some aspect of your site, especially if it's grown considerably. Testing the existing site against design alternatives with real users will probably uncover surprising weaknesses in the current design.

If the client's server is slow, visitors will blame the graphics. If the client has a rich third-generation site with images optimized to fly down the wire, but the server, or provider, or the Internet pipeline between the server and the regional hub is overloaded, surfers will blame the graphics. The more robust a hosting service is, the better a site will perform, and fewer people will be irritated trying to get the content.

A few people are turned off by graphically rich sites. Fortunately, they are a small, vocal but not particularly lucrative group, so you can mostly ignore them. On the other hand, some visitors need an up-to-date text-only version to get value out of your site – plan on providing one.

Owning a copy of Adobe PageMill or NetObjects Fusion, or "knowing HTML," doesn't make you a designer. It's a lot easier to teach a print designer how to create web pages than it is to teach an HTML jockey how to use type, colors, images, metaphor, and theme. A client who pays a lot of money for a web site is paying for experience – in design, in project management, in engineering, and in creativity.

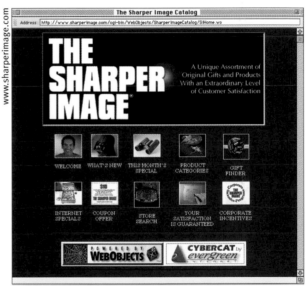

Design is more important when you have competition. Sites must continually maintain a fresh, yet familiar look.

Many advertising agencies put brochureware on the Web. In general, the most progressive sites are being designed by a new wave of multimedia and web-design houses – not the ad agencies and their "new media" groups. One advertising person told me that there aren't any awards on the Web that people in ad agencies want, while there are plenty of awards for print, TV, and radio advertising.

The Web has a strange effect on designers. When people finish a site, they are always proud of it, no matter how ugly it is. Weeks later, they realize just how bad their work is, but it's always hard to see at the time, often because they are proud of their technical accomplishments. Even

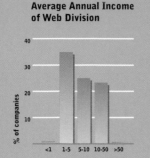

Average Annual Income of Web Division

% of companies (vertical axis: 40, 30, 20, 10)

US$ in tens of thousands (<1, 1-5, 5-10, 10-50, >50)

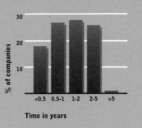

Web Division in Operation

% of companies (vertical axis: 30, 20, 10)

Time in years (<0.5, 0.5-1, 1-2, 2-5, >5)

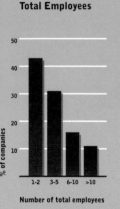

Total Employees

% of companies (vertical axis: 50, 40, 30, 20, 10)

Number of total employees (1-2, 3-5, 6-10, >10)

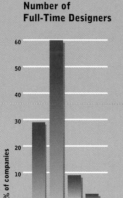

Number of Full-Time Designers

% of companies (vertical axis: 60, 50, 40, 30, 20, 10)

Number of designers (0, 1-2, 3-5, >5)

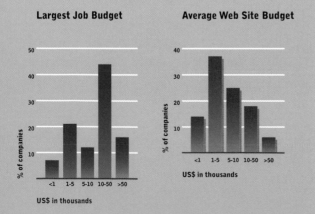

Largest Job Budget

% of companies (vertical axis: 50, 40, 30, 20, 10)

US$ in thousands (<1, 1-5, 5-10, 10-50, >50)

Average Web Site Budget

% of companies (vertical axis: 40, 30, 20, 10)

US$ in thousands (<1, 1-5, 5-10, 10-50, >50)

good designers can fall into the common traps of adding horizontal rules and bullets to sites, or adding huge background images that give visitors problems. My first site was full of horizontal rules, and I was proud of them.

Image is important. Look at consumer catalogs and other media. Some companies pride themselves on having low prices, others focus on service, while many try to create an enticing atmosphere. Image on the Web is as important as price and functionality, but not more important.

Web design costs more than brochure design. Brochures and annual reports may be fairly inexpensive to design, but then you must print them, and that's where they get expensive – not to mention hard to change. Don't make the mistake of using brochure design as your guide to setting the budget for a web project.

Maintenance costs more than expected. A high-quality site is expensive. Maintaining design and content standards through the life-cycle of the site is also expensive. Because most clients don't budget enough for maintenance, sites tend to change remarkably – often for the worse – within months after launch.

Design uncertainties

We can't answer certain questions until after the site has launched. Here are a few questions to keep in mind as you go through the four-phase process.

How will people react? We can test and verify, but we don't know what will happen until we launch the site. Testing ideas on groups of existing and potential customers during development helps reduce the risk. A small early win helps pave the way to a larger endeavor.

How will the Web change? Technology, not design, drives the Web. We know it will change, but in which direction? What will happen to HTML? Will web sites be programmed in Java, skipping HTML all together? No one can guarantee a web site will last five years. Neither do you want it to be out of date the day you launch. Talk with technical people as well as designers to determine what they think will affect your target user group and how the site should respond to those changes.

Is it important to have a database behind your site? A small site that's well conceived and designed can be as effective as a site with half a million dollars' worth of engineering. Only by making lists of features and their expected benefits and talking with people who know the Web can we determine the level of functionality a site needs.

Will people buy? The return-on-investment question is probably the biggest unknown. While it's possible to attract a lot of visitors to your site, and to please them, that is no guarantee of success. People often remember television commercials, but not the product or even brand. You need luck, good timing, and a longer break-in period than you might expect to generate the critical mass of customers that will put your site into the black.

Solving the business problem

Online producers often meet with clients who haven't defined the business objectives of a site. In first consultations with clients, I tend to look at the entire marketing problem, trying to save the most money or serve the most profitable groups of customers first. If the Web is involved, we discuss ways to use it effectively.

Training. I once met with a group that spends $40M on training every year. They wanted to use a combination of videotapes, in-person training, paper, and web resources to do a better job for less money. While they weren't looking for a web site yet, they were trying to determine the right combination of the three methodologies, so they could budget for the web site. They were probably spending $10M a year in a way that was already cost-effective, $20M in ways that could be improved, and another $10M inefficiently. I suggested they try to find which aspects these were, and treat them as follows:

$10M Efficient	Little or no change in the first 2 years.
$10M Waste	Identify immediately and eliminate the need or the sources of waste, with or without the Web.
$20M Needs improvement	Combine programs that would benefit from different solutions. Start with the group where you can save the most money.

The Web can't solve all your problems. If Fed-Exing videotapes costs $100K less than a fancy, unproven video-streaming technology, consider getting the job done rather than using all the newest bells and whistles.

Skiing. Another client group wanted to knit together all their ski resorts' web sites. They wanted a super-site, where people could learn about all their resort offerings. Plus, they had a new system to track the number of vertical feet skied during the day and throughout the season. They wanted to give prizes online to those who'd skied the most.

In our initial consultation, I learned that day-skiers contributed approximately 80% of their business profits. The average skier came to their resorts between one and two weekends a season. "So," I said, "what would happen if we could get a majority of the local day skiers to come back for one more weekend per season?"

They said, "Can a web site do that?"

"Absolutely not," I replied. "Furthermore, some 19-year-old with plenty of time on his hands is always going to win your most-vertical-feet contest. Do you make more money on 19-year-olds or on families?"

"Families, of course," they replied.

So I suggested they give prizes to teenagers for skiing a lot of vertical feet, but that they mostly use the system to track the number of weekends people came and reward

Secret Weapon Number Two

Solving the business problem

Most web-site producers meet with clients who haven't defined the business objectives of a site. In initial consultations with clients, I tend to look at the entire marketing problem, trying to save the most money or serve the most profitable groups of customers first. If the Web is involved, we discuss ways to use it effectively.

A television commercial directed by Ridley Scott will probably cost about $4M more than the same commercial without him behind the camera. Yet that commercial may get more results. If it will cost $40M to air the commercial over four months, the $4M may be a reasonable expense. Quantify your expectations, make lists of features and benefits, measure results, and look at various scenarios before deciding on a budget.

Ridley Scott's "1984" commercial was well worth the expensive production values.

them on their third weekend of the year – then make it really special to come for the fourth weekend. This helped them focus on turning good customers into great ones.

The next step was to work on a total marketing plan for families and see how to reinforce it on the Web. Then they could go after travelers and weekday skiers – who are served by travel agents, event coordinators, and conference planners. These services are already online, so I suggested they partner with these sites to provide packages to their clientele, rather than putting a lot of money into one big branded site. I suggested they set up a modest, informational site for their resorts and put their energy into "kiosks" at travel and conference sites.

These examples illustrate that clients need to address overall marketing goals before budgeting their sites. Once you know what the goals are, quantify how much you'd be willing to spend to accomplish different numbers and levels of goals.

How much do web sites cost?

Clients consistently underestimate the costs of building a web site. Two of the determining factors that drive costs are scope and special features. *Scope* refers to the *size of the project* – not the size of the web site.

I'll give some guidelines, but note that they change with location, market, time, and the price of pixels in Pittsburgh. These are for high-quality solutions from experienced teams.

In three weeks you can build a fast ten-page site. It won't have much functionality, but it can serve the purpose. Using a tool like NetObjects Fusion, you can quickly build and launch a medium-size site that will be presentable and informative. A three-week project usually involves a team the person responsible for content, a designer, and a production person. A three-person team will charge from $15K to $30K for such a site, depending on quality and original content.

A larger team may be able to accomplish a miracle in three weeks. Expect to pay between $20K and $60K for a sophisticated rush project. As tools get better, designers will be able to add functionality to these projects without significantly increasing costs.

In four to five weeks you can do a three-week project with a week or two of planning, which might cost an extra $5K to $25K. You can turn a fast three-week project into a site that will last considerably longer.

In two months you can do a small jewel of a site or a more automated site with less design. Assuming content problems don't hold up the launch, this is a reasonable period for a small or large team to plan and execute a fairly straightforward site, including photo shoots, animation, sound, and some back-end scripting. Projects like this can range from $40K to $180K.

In three to four months you can plan, design, build, and launch a medium-size site properly. It may include some back-end capabilities and maybe even a custom commerce solution. You can create alternate scripts for different browsers and perhaps an alternate version for visitors using WebTV. It will have various areas with their own editorial schedules or functionality. It will have a branding plan, a content plan, and a public-relations plan. It will probably have custom scripts running behind the scenes, and it may have animation, plug-ins, and innovative ways of attracting visitors to the site. These sites run from $30K (two people) to $700K (core team of 10 people plus specialists). Strategy for such a project may include commissioning market-research studies. Prices can be reasonable. Paying $2.5K for a market study of buying behavior of online shoppers might be well worth the expense.

In four to eight months you can build a large-scale system that includes a commerce application and a custom database. If the three-month project results in a house, the 6-month project results in an office building or a shopping mall. These projects have strategy, engineering, editorial, and design teams working together to build something big and new. Innovation is part of a project this size – the team will invariably be doing *something* that has never been done before. Such projects range from $150K to over $2M.

Hosting and maintenance during the first year of ownership range from 50% to 150% of the cost of creating the site. Anyone who budgets less than 50% will have a static site, unless the project has cost millions of dollars to build. Mid-size web-based magazines, like Women's Wire (www.women.com), have two dozen full-time employees and several freelance contributors. The 50 most-visited sites on the Web almost all have over 80 people on staff.

Special features can quickly drive up the price of a site. They divide into roughly two camps: expensive functionality and expensive content.

Expensive functionality usually involves programmers and databases. Real-time credit card verification will cost a few hundred thousand more than doing it on a delay.

Expensive content usually involves paying for a known brand. Getting Francis Ford Coppola to contribute a monthly column to your film-theory site will add quite a bit to the cost. Getting Sofia Coppola to contribute a column to your fashion site will cost less, but it will still cost more than if you had a staff writer do it. Similarly, you won't be able to put Spiderman on your site without permission, and permission will cost money.

Engineering services usually involve databases. A product like Allaire's Cold Fusion or Claris Filemaker Pro may serve your publishing needs with few hassles, or you may need to license an industrial-strength database, hire programmers, and implement a content-management system. General guidelines: if you have a heavily trafficked site and need to serve HTML dynamically, combined with fresh content entered into the database daily, you will spend $100K to do it badly and $200K to $1.5M to do it well. These are general guidelines, but the relational database license alone will cost between $30K and $150K.

What's next?

There is value in design, and there is value in process. Communication, strategy, and just being there day-to-day don't go onto a web site, but they make the difference between a success and a ho-hum presence on the Web. While a producer often doesn't leave a visible mark on a web site, no winning web site is without a winning producer working with a winning team. The producer is the first person on a project and the last to leave. The producer enjoys reading email comments from visitors and seeing that the client company is happy in its new home on the Web. With this goal in mind, we are ready for a detailed look at the process, from getting the client to launching and maintaining the site.

"I'm not bad,
I'm just
drawn
that way."

– Jessica Rabbit, in "Who Framed Roger Rabbit?"

Chapter 3 Partnering (for clients)

You need a web site, and you know when it has to launch. All you have to do is find a group of expert web designers to get the job done.

YOU'RE A CLIENT. You're looking for people who can do the job. People you can trust. The goal of a search is not to design a web site or gather ideas, it's to find the right group so you can find solutions together. It's important to see this as a two-step process:

Step 1: Narrow the field to a small number of candidates, any one of whom could do the job.

Step 2: Choose one of the candidates and agree on a budget and schedule that works for everyone.

This chapter discusses several ways of going through both steps from different perspectives. *Opposing forces* try to maximize their own gain, while *joining forces* is a new paradigm for long-term partnership. I begin by discussing some of the methods used in other practices, then I'll describe a disastrous scenario I hope you'll find humorous and perhaps a bit instructive. I'll finish the chapter with a method that is easier on everyone. The method I recommend puts more responsibility on clients, not only in the process of selection, but in the process of working with the group you choose. I assume you can locate a number of possibly qualified groups – simply by eliminating all the obviously unqualified ones – and there our adventure starts.

Partnering (for clients)

Creative people have been providing services for thousands of years. Traditional methods of finding a contractor put the client and designer on opposite sides of the table, each trying to get the best deal. While some of these methods are helpful, many of these approaches get in the way of setting up a good relationship.

Traditional approaches

Before you choose any creative group, you must have a good feeling for their work and their style. The amount of time you spend choosing is often proportional to the size of the job. Different situations require different methods of finding a qualified group to work with.

Word of mouth. Possibly the number-one way people find an architect, a lawyer, an accountant, or any service is to ask people they trust. This tried-and-true method often results in a single phone call that both initiates and closes the sales process. Indeed, any decent web designer who attends a large party will usually be asked for her business card several times. In most cases, recommendations are a big factor in the decision, but the client still needs to see that the people are right and that the portfolio shows they can do the kind of work the client envisions. Recommendations by several trusted associates can easily compensate for less actual information about the service provider (sometimes to the project's detriment).

The pitch. Ad agencies must pitch to survive. They put together a team to win a prospective account, mock up ads, shoot videos, prepare graphics, and rehearse their story. On the chosen day, they hope to win the client with their creative examples and dynamic presentation style. Agencies are fiercely competitive, because if they win, they win big. An account will often stay with an agency for years, providing a steady stream of income until the client decides it's time for a review.

The competition. Commercial architects sometimes participate in competitions. Often, the developer pays the architect, who doesn't make any profit from the conceptual work or model-making but will profit if he wins the competition and the job. Occasionally, the client will pay several architectural firms a small amount. This doesn't cover the costs of competing, but it does convey the client's commitment to getting ideas from qualified firms.

It can take months to prepare for a competition. Architecture firms can only afford to compete if they can stand the expenses involved. But firms agree that the rewards more than compensate for the risk.

The web site you seek – indeed, the right solution to any problem – is a natural by-product of the right relationship with the right people.

The interview. If you want a house built, you interview architects. You check with the owners of the houses they've designed, compare notes, and rank them according to your own criteria. Then you go to the top firm on the list and talk price. If they can do the job within your budget, you sign an agreement to begin work. You trust the architect to take you through the process of designing a house *together*, and the architect's personal impressions have a strong influence on your relationship. You want to go through the process with someone who makes you feel comfortable. In the end, a combination of personality, track record, and recommendations guides your decision.

Which method is best? It depends on how much money your account represents to the firm and what kind of relationship you're looking for. If you're looking for a house on the Web – not a skyscraper or a city that needs a full-time set of planners – you may want to interview and get to know a couple of groups.

How much are groups willing to spend to get the account? They will usually spend up to two percent of the total amount they expect to get from the client – five percent if they are going all out. Groups without full-time salespeople may *want* to put more energy into getting your business but find they don't have time. Others who have time might not be qualified to do the work.

A surprisingly large number of projects end in conflict, or worse, disaster. Many of these partnerships should not have been made in the first place. Clients are often in a hurry to put up a web site, which puts them in an even bigger hurry to find a group to build one. Panic and tight schedules are behind the increasing use of RFPs.

The request for proposal (RFP)

A typical RFP is a 20-30 page document describing the scope of a company's "future online presence." This document lists all the departments of the company and categories of products and services, and usually includes words like "chat area" and "feedback form." It includes a project schedule, a list of deliverables, and protocols for submission. Clients usually send them after contacting a group and having them sign a nondisclosure form. Busy groups get one to three RFPs a week.

Clients often use RFPs to *qualify* groups. Some clients send RFPs as a filter, to narrow the field to a few groups, whom they can then visit in person. They expect the RFP will help them find the group of finalists from which to choose. Some companies send 20 RFPs out, just on the off chance that they will get three or four interesting responses. These are called *shotgun RFPs*. Ask many good design firms, and they'll tell you they won't respond to an RFP without some kind of prior conversation.

Are clients really getting the results they want? I think the reason so many web-development contracts end in tears is that most of these joint ventures never should have taken place.

When are RFPs appropriate? RFPs are really designed to choose one firm among several firms that you'd be happy doing business with. In established industries, there's a good reason for RFPs. At any particular time, one vendor will have more good people, more desire for the job, more up-to-date equipment, or some other advantage over other vendors. In these cases, sending RFPs to three or four vendors to bid on large-scale projects may be appropriate. It may also be inappropriate – in many cases, it is more useful to invite them for a pitch or go to their site for a visit.

When small-shop web designers open packages with RFPs from big companies, they think they have a real shot at getting the work. Why else would a company send them the RFP? Judging by the number of RFPs I've seen in the last year, I'd say the chances of having a good partnership with a company that sends an RFP with a deadline with no prior contact are less than 1%.

Misusing the RFP process

A few companies are used to sending RFPs to ad agencies. They send them to web shops because that's the way they usually find vendors. These clients misuse the RFP process by sending RFPs when they:

Use the RFP process as a starting point to finding a group.

Haven't narrowed the choices to four or fewer qualified groups.

Have an RFP form and don't want to put much effort into finding a group.

Have basically selected a group but need a few other bids to make sure they are covered.

Think they know what they want and are looking for a group to execute it.

Are told they have to secure a certain number of bids.

Include a list of features they want priced out.

Are looking for the best free ideas.

Are looking for the lowest bidder.

Have a deadline and think there is no quicker way to do it.

Have a small job that can be done in less than two months.

Most companies aren't using RFPs properly. Reliance on RFPs wastes time and money and gets the two groups off to an adversarial start. The following story illustrates what can go wrong with the RFP process. While you probably don't know anyone who'd do any of these things, it isn't as far-fetched as it sounds.

Partnering (for clients)

1 Opposing forces

2 Astro Cabs

3 Joining forces

Astro is a made-up, dummy company with a futuristic service. But their document contains all the classic earmarks of an inappropriate RFP. Astro is a fictitious name, not to be confused with any existing trademarks or companies.

Round 1 – The Astro RFP

The Astro Team Leader took a meeting with the Big Astro Cheese, who was head of the Astro Steering Committee for Online Marketing. The Team Leader knew he needed to find a group to implement the site for their new service – CabMan. They brainstormed. They ordered the best-selling books on web design from Amazon.com. The Team Leader spent four weeks writing the RFP, refining all their ideas for what a good web site should be. The Team Leader hoped to get some clever ideas and find a low bidder to implement these ideas in time for their press event, which was now coming up in three months. He was willing to pay $35,000 for the project, but he thought it would be best if he didn't say anything about the budget. He did a Yahoo! search and decided to send the RFP to two dozen design firms.

```
Astro Cabs Request for Proposal


  REMINDER: YOU ARE UNDER NONDISCLOSURE

  Astro Cabs is the nation's oldest cab
  company, dating back 150 years, when it
  gave rides to generals of the Confederacy.
  Our motto, "Giving You the Ride of Your
  Life," traces back to those early days.
  Astro Cabs provides safe service through
  urban battlegrounds, risking other peo-
  ple's lives to get you where you need to
  go (or within walking distance).

    To celebrate our 150 years of quality,
  Astro Cabs will announce a new service.
  *CabMan* provides customers with their
  own personal cellular cab, driven by robot
  technology. Through an 800-number or a
  special cellular signal ring, the sub-
  scriber makes a request and CabMan arrives
  within 5 minutes. CabMan then transports
  its owner to any destination (some have
```

```
  inflatable pontoons), and drives away
  before the door can close. Bills are sent
  monthly, based on global-positioning
  coordinate deltas.

    To promote this new service, and Astro
  Cabs' traditional cab service, we are
  conducting an RFP review. Over the next
  few weeks, we will review responses and
  select a design firm to produce the Astro
  Cabs web site. We will be looking for the
  highest level of design and technical
  expertise exhibited by the contractors.


  The goals of the new Astro Cabs web
  site:

  1. Highlight and feature CabMan, a
     revolutionary new service offered by
     Astro Cabs.
```

2. Promote Astro Cabs as a reliable cab service available in major cities.

3. Use cutting-edge Internet technologies such as QTVR, VRML, and Shockwave – CabMan is a revolutionary service and we want the site to prove it!

4. Provide potential customers with useful cab-related history, information, tips and tricks, trivia, and FAQs.

5. Provide a sign-up form for obtaining insurance.

6. Spotlight the various CabMan features and models. Include engine simulations and robot "personality" profiles.

7. Provide a Java-based chat room for Astro customers to talk to us.

8. Build a database of potential customers (one-to-one marketing).

9. Create an electronic subscription system (e-commerce plus security).

Content

Astro Cabs has a great deal of printed material that can be used. To the winning team, we will dispatch a messenger to your firm with samples of our Press Information (PI), News Clippings (NC), Brochures, CD-ROMs, Press Kit (PK), Q & A, and Other Promotional Materials (OPM). Astro has designed an extensive site map, which we will fax separately upon request.

Design Considerations

1. Create a navigation system that reinforces the ease of using Astro Cabs or CabMan and provides organized access to the web site. Use of Java rollovers is preferred.

2. Design graphics that are both historical and futuristic to represent Astro Cabs great past and introduce its exciting future. Use of graphics database is preferred.

3. Since CabMan is a new service, introducing the brand should be the most important part of the web site. Advertising the company in an attractive way to potential Astro and CabMan customers will be the most crucial part of building a successful web site.

We expect at least three ideas sketched out and presented in your response. Be prepared to explain why your ideas are the winning ones. Your response must include a detailed description of all tasks involved in completing this project, with costs included for each major step involved. Please include detailed descriptions of all team members, with backgrounds and driving records if possible.

The web site is scheduled to launch in three months. You have one week to reply. We are looking forward to hearing your ideas.

Sincerely,

Astro Cabs

The RFPs went out. Most of the boutiques that received it didn't have time to respond. A few called and asked the Team Leader to come to their offices and discuss the project, but the Astro Team Leader knew it would be more competitive if he waited for the responses. No one asked for the site map.

A week later, the Astro Team Leader went to the mailbox and found nothing. What was wrong with these firms? He sent an email message to all the firms giving them a ten-day extension. Just to be safe, he sent the RFP to a dozen smaller firms he found through Yahoo! as well.

On the second date, the Team Leader had ten responses! The RFP process had worked. Five were beautifully designed. They were from graphic-design firms eager to get into the Web. They all said they didn't know much about Java, but most had someone who knew Director, so they were sure they could do it. Their fees ranged from $5k to $60k.

Three responses came from web firms with some experience. They were short, didn't have too many ideas, but the prices were remarkably similar. Based on the assumptions of the RFP, they would charge $78k, $72.5k, and $86k, but all said they would approach the site differently from what was requested in the RFP. This ruled them out right away. The Team Leader was also disappointed that none of these bids came with pictures or examples of how to design the site.

Two responses were Word documents from groups that knew about JavaScript and ActiveX controls. They had received the RFPS from friends. They could do all kinds of fun rollovers for the Astro site. They would make the site come alive with lots of colors and amazing sounds. They could do 3-D VRML demos of cabs in action. For the next version, they could do the entire site in Java. They had enthusiasm and could make the most cutting-edge sites

If you already know what you want, don't hire a web-design contractor. Hire an employee.

on the Web. This was what the Project Manager had wanted! Unfortunately, the group he liked best had bid $94k, and the one he didn't really like that much was $16k. The group he liked had only been working together for three months and was halfway through a "big job for a secret client." The less expensive group was still working on their own site – they hadn't done any actual client work yet. They were ready to start. Certain things in the low-bid group's response bothered him, especially the fact that their programmers were still in high school and had exams coming up.

Round 2 – Try again

There was only one thing to do: rewrite the RFP and send it out again. This time, the Team Leader was more specific about what he wanted. He drew pictures of all the pages and told them the budget up front: $25,000. He included the four-page site map. He also said there would be a $10k bonus to the firm that submitted the best proposal. He requested that the responses be sent within one week.

Again, the three busy firms invited him to come to their office to discuss the project, but he was too wise for that. Two of the graphic-design groups sent in their new proposals, which looked just like the old proposals,

except that the prices over $25k were lower, and those under $25k had now come up to $24.5k.

Seven new proposals came in. They were enthusiastic, and they all had prices between $22k and $24k. The Team Leader's boss asked if he had chosen a group to do the new site yet. He said yes. He was going to go with the graphic-design group that had the nice stationery (good branding skills!) and the best price ($24.2k), and he would ask the more expensive programming group to work on the animations for a reduced rate.

Because they wanted the Astro name on their client list, both groups agreed to work for him. The Astro Team Leader said he would be the producer and would also write all the content for the site. They had four weeks left. Plenty of time to build the site.

The press event came and the Astro Team Leader had nothing to show. The site would not be ready for the big launch. It would take another two weeks, he said, as he left the meeting with the Big Astro Cheese.

Two months later, the Astro site still had not launched. The Team Leader had gone off to join a cult. The Big Cheese had taken on the project, but the contractor had quit. The service was six months delayed in launching anyway, but their site budget was spent. The Big Cheese got an offer from a company that was about to go public, so he left. That was when the new Team Leader walked into my office.

How can you get a good bid without sending an RFP? The answer is simple: *don't try to get a good bid.* If you choose the right group, that group will work with you and your budget. If you focus on getting the right price, your chances of ending up with the right group are slim, and your chances of wasting money are great. Furthermore, anyone who gives you the price you're looking for knows you will end up paying more in change orders later. RFPs are less helpful when your goal is to find a group to help you define your needs and become your strategic partner, especially when so many vendors have little experience in what you're trying to do.

The right answer
The wrong problem

In joining forces, the client becomes a responsible party to the process, an active partner who's willing to help, even when selecting among several groups. An active search means walking around and sitting on the same side of the table as the contractor, looking at the relationship, rather than the price.

Round 3 – The active search

The new Team Leader, Carla, was on time for her appointment. I gave her a tour of our offices and introduced her to everyone in the company. I had seen the original RFP and had responded by inviting them to visit, but I hadn't heard from them until Carla called and asked for an appointment. Carla was eager to explain how things had changed.

She said that although they had lost all the money on the first contract, the new launch of the service was going to be critical to the success of the company. Because the product still had a few bugs to work out with the global navigation system, she had four months until the new product launch. She had been hired to take on the project and deliver the new site.

TIP

Tell a design firm what your budget is! They must qualify any potential client, so make it easier by giving them a range up front and explaining how much you'd be willing to pay. If the design firm is asking questions about the "scope" of your project, they're trying to uncover your budget. Why not get the relationship off to a good start and tell them?

After discussing public transportation and the inevitable frustrations associated with human cab drivers, I asked, "Who will make the decisions?" She replied, "We have a task force of three people: two from the steering committee and me. We will make all the decisions, and I will be responsible for communicating our decisions." I then asked, "How much have you budgeted?" She said, "We're not sure. The overall ad budget for the launch is pretty big, but we don't know how to decide how much should go into the web site. We need to know how much bang we can get for our buck."

After a few more questions, I asked, "How many other groups are you talking to?" After doing some serious surfing, she had chosen five. She said, "I found sites that attracted me, then I used Alta Vista to learn who designed

Beware the web site you ask for – you might get it.

them. I found a list of designers at www.highfive.com, and these were very interesting. After looking around on my own, I was amazed at the number of design firms with cool sites of their own, but their portfolio sites aren't nearly as good."

I said, "I'll give you some references from our previous clients. I'd like you to call them. Then I'll ask you to do some homework. Is that okay?" "What kind of homework?" she asked. "It's a questionnaire that will give us the information we need to give you a good idea of how we will approach the problem. If you'll spend time answering the questions, we'll do our best to give you a picture of what's possible." She seemed interested. "Can I give it to the other groups and ask them to respond to it too?" she asked. I said, "Certainly, but go visit them and see how they work. They're all good firms."

The project profiler

This is our current project profiler. You'll find one on the book site, and it may be slightly different. We're always changing it as we learn how to help clients communicate with us. Use the general outline as a starting point and design something that works best for your situation. Different projects may require different kinds of feedback.

The project profiler

I. BACKGROUND AND GOALS

Company

Please provide corporate and industry descriptions, including competitors, along with a brief critique of their sites. Include contact information and a description of the group who will be working on the project. Who are the decisionmakers, who else would be contracting, who's responsible for what, and what human resources you have for various stages of the process.

Project

What is the mission statement or summary of your project?

What are the basic goals of this project? (e.g., branding/identity reinforcement, improved access to information, direct sales, corporate communication, etc.)

What outcome will make this project successful? How will you measure success?

What are your schedule requirements?

What is the budget for this project? Is there an acceptable budget range, depending on the level and comprehensiveness of services provided? Please explain.

Describe any work that has been done toward designing/redesigning a new web site.

Will the web site reinforce an existing branding or marketing strategy? How?

Discuss any identity/branding assets (logos, other artwork, and fonts) or issues.

Rank the following, in order of importance:

   A web strategy that fits with our corporate strategy

   A web strategy that fits with our marketing strategy

   Repurposing existing content

   Creating a community of dedicated visitors

   Quality execution (graphics, writing, navigation, etc.)

   Time to market

   Ease of maintenance

   Doing better than our competition on the Web

   People bookmark the site because they get so much out of it regularly

   Staying within the budget

   Sending the message that we know the Web and use it appropriately

II. AUDIENCE, CONTENT, AND FUNCTIONALITY

Audience

What types of visitors do you want to attract?

What are your goals for each type of visitor?

What are the products/services involved?

What are your goals for these products/services?

Content

Where will content come from? Will it be new, repurposed, or both?

How often will you add new content?

Who will update the content?

Functionality

What functional requirements do you believe to be necessary? (e.g., download areas, database-driven webpages, commerce, catalog, applications, etc.)

Who will update these functionalities?

Are there extraordinary security issues?

Are there other technical issues or limitations?

Have you budgeted for hosting and maintenance of the site? If so, what is your budget?

Who will maintain the site contents?

How will the site be served/hosted?

What types of legacy systems/databases are in place?

What is your long-term plan for the site?

III. THE FIELD TRIP

This part of the profile is very important. The more work you put into it the more your project will benefit. Find the three highest quality sites (more is better) on the Web that relate to your project in the following categories:

   Branding in a similar situation to yours (new company, new brand, established brand, etc.)

   Appeal to same target group of customers

   Whether or not you would build the site if you were in a different industry

   Colors, look-and-feel, user interface, layout

   Size of site

   Size of project

   Publishing model (frequency, novelty of content, etc.)

   Attracting new people to the site (newsworthiness, giveaways, impact, etc.)

   Your competitors' sites

   Quality of content

   Quality of graphics

   Functionality (things sites do for people)

   Community, special features, responsiveness, other categories important to your project

   Overall favorite sites (for whatever reasons)

Note: you'll find an interactive version of the project profiler at www.secretsites.com. It comes loaded with several suggested URLS for more directed surfing.

Round 4 – The mid-profiler call

A week later, the phone rang while I was eating a veggie burrito. "Carla?" I said. "How did you know it was me?" she asked, puzzled. "Lucky guess. Don't tell me, you're working on your profile, and it's taking longer than you thought." "Well," she sighed, "the profiler is serious work!" "Yes," I replied, "but it's important to anyone who designs your site. You'll need to do it anyway, and doing it up front will help you find a group that understands what you need. You're not only saving money, you're saving time in the long run." Carla was still surfing. She said, "I think the most valuable part really is the surfing around, looking

said we'd have to spend more time together to be more specific, but if she could handle the range, we could offer her more choices within that range.

The following week, Carla brought her two task-force members to our office. After calling a few references, they had eliminated two firms. Now it was down to three. They wanted to talk site features, but we kept steering them toward the overall marketing plan and the place the web site would have in it. We were eager to work with their advertising agency, because we felt that in this case, the launch should be coordinated.

It's in your best interest to evaluate firms by meeting at the contractor's office. You'll pick up clues about working with them, and you can watch them in their environment. You can see what their priorities are and where they spend their money. They will be more relaxed than if they have their sales hats on.

for things we like and don't like. I'm amazed at what people are doing out there. But I want you to do something *different*, not just copy things we like from other sites and put them together."

I answered, "That's right. The field trip is just a starting point. It helps us get to know you, so we can both see if we want to work together. It helps us give you some ballpark prices and talk about the *process* you'll go through. It has only a little to do with actually designing your site – to do *that*, we have to go talk to your customers – but it has everything to do with our relationship. Do you want us to design a site for your steering committee or for the people who will sign up to buy your service?"

Round 5 – The budget

We received Carla's completed profile with a request for a response within a week. We worked on it, adding our thoughts about Astro's marketing opportunity to our standard response document that explained our approach. We outlined what we thought was the minimum site they needed to launch to achieve their goals. We stated how that could be done in the most inexpensive way, and then in a way that promised more payoffs as the site grew. We outlined an even more ambitious approach, how much more it might cost, and what it would achieve. We gave her ballpark figures for the different approaches. We

Round 6 – The final choice

Carla and her team were professionals – people you like to work with. She asked me what advice I had for choosing a firm among the remaining three. I said, "Did you call my references?" She said "No, I figured they were going to say good things about you." I said, "Call my references and ask them hard questions. No project goes perfectly. If you work with us, Christina will be your producer. Do some checking on Christina, because the week before your launch, you'll have to trust that your site is in good hands."

"That's not the problem," she said. "The problem is that I've found three firms. After meeting with everyone, I think they'd do something different, but I'd enjoy working with all of them. I don't know how to decide." I said, "I'm sure you'll get a quality site from any of us. Why don't you use the selection matrix and let the numbers decide?"

"The selection matrix?" she asked. "It will give you an objective way to decide. I would be happy to work with you, but I want you to choose our firm knowing we're the best fit. Call our references, and call me personally if you need more information. And Carla, may I suggest one more thing?" "Sure," she said. "Make sure to have fun working with the group you choose. If you're having fun, it will show on the web site."

So ends the story of Carla and Astro Cabs' search for a design firm. I won't tell you which firm they picked, but if you should see them later in this book, you might be able to figure it out.

The selection matrix

Before choosing a design firm, decide what your criteria will be. Get their reference phone numbers. Surf their site and visit their portfolio sites. Use the method below to give your finalists a total numerical score. When you find a winner, sign a memorandum of engagement (see Chapter 5) and get started.

The selection matrix really tries to answer two questions: "Can they do it?" and "How much do they want to do it?" Start with the following weighting scheme for choosing a vendor in most web-design projects (higher numbers are better). Adjust the weighting and add/delete categories to suit your project. Build the matrix by putting the company names across the top of a grid and the following questions down the side. (This scheme, for example, emphasizes design skills and reliability over technical back-end database expertise.)

Weight	Criteria
0-5	Quality of their own site
0-20	Quality of each portfolio site (that relates to yours)
0-30	Referrals from people you trust (one each, up to three)
15	For each site similar (in design, production, or functionality) to the one you want built
0-50	For each of their past clients who report on their project-management skills
0-30	Demonstration of ability to write the strategic documents for your project
0-40	Overall design skills
0-30	Overall technical skills
0-40	Demonstration of a clear methodology
40	They will assign a producer to your project who does *not* do any technical work
0-50	Quality of their client project site(s)
0-20	Ability to subcontract specialty work (photography, programming, sound, etc.)
0-30	Ability to design web sites with both legacy and future browsers in mind
0-40	Ability and energy to help solve your business problem
0-10	Ability to help bring traffic to your new web site
-20	They *cannot* write Perl or other server-side scripts in-house
1-30	Can write JavaScript, ActiveX controls, Shockwave animations, Flash, rollovers, etc.
0-30	Principals are accomplished designers in other media
0-30	Their overall enthusiasm for your project
0-50	Personal chemistry, overall feel of wanting to work with them

CLIENTS ARE ENTITLED TO:

1. Good estimates

2. Honest, constant communication

3. A written contract

4. Immediate notification of delays, problems, and extra expenses

5. Pay only for work authorized

6. Audit hours if paying by the hour

7. See the project as it develops

8. Reasonable turnaround and response

9. Reasonable security and privacy precautions

10. Deliverables that work as described in the contract

11. Own all appropriate rights to the site

Note that criteria like *size of group* and *availability* are not on this list. They are *dealbreakers*. I won't list all possible dealbreakers here, although it may be helpful for you to list your own. When you discover a dealbreaker, cross that group off your list and save them for another project.

Certain other things are not on the list: amount of press they've generated, whether they've written best-selling books on web design or project management, whether they have a charismatic president, location, years in business, and so on. These things are irrelevant in choosing a design firm.

Susan Rockrise
on matchmaking

Susan Rockrise is the worldwide creative director responsible for brand consistency in print/electronic media at Intel. She gives agency-relationship training to both clients (often product managers) and their certified contractors. She spoke with me about *matchmaking* – the art of finding the right creative group for a project.

David Siegel: Why do you need to certify creative groups?

Susan Rockrise: We don't have time to start over every time we need creative work. When I started, there were more than 900 agencies certified as "vendors." Now it's down to about 50 agencies worldwide. The work gets better as we continue to work with them.

DS How do you find new firms to certify, say, for web development?

SR I go talk to other clients and developers and just listen to what's going on. I call real people. I surf the Web to find sites that grab me and find the source of that design.

DS Once you've identified the potential candidates, how do you choose a vendor?

SR I never call an agency a vendor. Vendors sell nuts and bolts. Agencies are problem-solvers. Agencies are strategic assets. We buy brains, not arms and legs.

  We start with a *communications brief*, a document that tells them about us, our marketing objectives, and our goals for the project. It includes a section on how to work with us. We expect them to take this brief seriously.

DS How many groups do you approach?

SR I send the brief to three certified groups I think would get excited about the project. *It's unfair to ask more than three prequalified agencies to bid on your project.* It takes at least a day's worth of effort to prepare a response. Normally, we ask for a one-week turnaround response, and it is not to contain any free creative work.

DS Then what?

SR After a week, they typically send a thorough response. Many agencies don't even follow up to see if we've received their response. They should do that, and they should make sure we know they are excited about the project. Rapport with the agency is a huge part of the decision. We read the responses and decide which agencies to call back for presentations. We often pay their expenses if we think it's important to bring them in.

DS Do you go with the low bidder?

SR Depending on the quality of their response – and chemistry – we often call the *high* bidder and ask them how we could work with them to get the expenses more in line with what we'd like to spend. We also give objective feedback to the groups we didn't choose. Saying, "We didn't like it," isn't good enough.

DS Do you have any tips for clients?

SR These are my ten steps for agency management:

1. Create strategic documents that give the right information.
2. Interface with purchasing.
3. Use an agency-evaluation matrix to ensure objectivity.
4. Discuss schedule, expectations, and realistic time frames.
5. Train them in corporate identity standards.
6. Manage based on strategy and goals, not implementation or "micromanagement."
7. Follow through to be sure they are paid as soon as possible.
8. Conduct post mortems to improve the relationship and process.
9. Thank them for awesome work; provide feedback for any disappointments.
10. Treat them as strategic assets. Continue to build long-term agency relationships.

"You got to know when to hold 'em,
know when to fold 'em,
know when to walk away,
and know when to run."

– Kenny Rogers, "The Gambler"

Chapter 4

Partnering (for contractors)

Chapter 4 Partnering (for contractors)

Converting prospects into happy clients is more than just being good at what you do. It's being good at sales.

Chapter guide

Partnering (for contractors)

TO BE GOOD AT SALES, you must master the art of reading between the lines. For many small firms, it's the difference between doing what you want and doing whatever comes in the door. A sales and marketing plan will keep quality clients coming in and the production department producing web sites. Your ability to get good work and avoid train wrecks will determine the success of your business.

1 Setting up

2 Responding

3 Logistics

Sales don't happen by accident. Making sales is a process, just like everything else. Small companies have to sell themselves, but if you want to grow, you'll want to hire a pro.

The sales chain

The sales process for web designers is similar to that in other creative services. Once you've identified a client you'd like to work with, take deliberate steps toward them. First impressions count. Think of the sales process as building a chain, starting on each side and building toward the middle. Each link is important. You must attach them in the right order, and the chain won't hold until the last link is in the center. From the contractor's point of view, the sales chain has the following links:

Client link #1	Learn of a potential client's interest
Contractor link #1	Qualify a client
Client link #2	Get information from the contractor (preferably a site profile)
Contractor link #2	Respond appropriately – so they can envision working with you
Client link #3	Get the client to come to your office
Contractor link #3	Focus on the relationship while narrowing the business parameters
Final link	Close the deal

I will address each link throughout this chapter.

The salesperson

Whether you're one person, a partnership, or a small boutique, there are times when you must put on your sales hat and round up clients. I'd like to make two points in this section, 1: You need a salesperson. 2: You need one sales/marketing/PR/sales-support person for every 10-20 people in your company.

You need a salesperson. No matter how big your firm, you have to dedicate a certain amount of time to talking with prospects, selling your services, writing marketing literature, updating your web site, and so on. The great thing about not having a salesperson is that when you need a janitor or an HTML hacker, the salesperson takes off his sales hat and gets back to work. The downside is that you don't always have your next job when you need it. Even a small office should try to hook up with a professional. You can probably find someone who could work 10-20 hours a week and help you with new business development while you make web sites. Doing it yourself is not a

CONTRACTORS ARE ENTITLED TO:

1. Know what the budget range is up front

2. A completed project profile

3. A written contract

4. Have their time valued – client delays cost contractors money

5. 25-50% of the bid/estimate up front

6. Prompt payment

7. Manage the process without being micromanaged

8. Make up for their mistakes

9. Be paid for consultative work or ideas

10. Be told when they are out of the running for a job

11. Retain all appropriate rights to assets created for the site

Contractors' bill of rights

Client link #1

Learn of a potential client's interest

With hundreds of new sites going online every day, people are asking themselves how they can have a new or better web site. You win an award or get into a magazine, and the calls come in. Most web developers have no shortage of calls and email inquiries.

You can often tell by the tone of the contact whether a company sounds like a good prospect. When I received the following (unaltered) email message, I knew this was a group I'd like to work with.

```
Dear Mr. Siegel,

My company, the SWA Group, is an interna-
tionally recognized consulting firm spe-
cializing in landscape architecture and
urban design. We are considering hiring
someone to help us design our company's
web page and I would like to suggest you
as a candidate to our selection committee
(which would, incidentally, include me).
It is my belief that our web page must
reflect our company's reputation for high
quality, innovation and trend-setting
design, and these values seem to be
compatible with yours.

If you are interested, please contact
me by email, or you can call me at the
telephone listed below. Thanks for your
attention.

    Bob Jacob
    The SWA Group
```

Contractor link #1

Qualify the prospect

You don't need a lot of information, but you must determine whether the client meets your internal criteria for taking new work. Learn how big the job is, when it starts and finishes, and what the budget is. Try to understand their decisionmaking process. A client who values your time will tell you how big the project is.

As soon as you determine that the client meets your criteria, send them an informative brochure in the mail. Clients like to see something on paper.

good model for growth. Remember, you're going up against firms with people whose full-time job is to respond to RFPs.

On the other hand, if you're 1-4 people, you do great work, and you don't expect to grow, you can get along with one person handling sales part time, *as long as that person has some sales talent*. It shouldn't be the producer. Handling clients isn't the same as handling prospects. A good seminar or some good books on sales techniques will probably be worth the expense.

You need one sales/marketing person for every 10-20 people. Any company larger than four people should have at least one half-time sales and marketing person. My rule would be one full-time sales/marketing person for every 10-20 people, depending on how aggressive you want to be. It's important to see sales as the method for getting the jobs you want, rather than the jobs that come in the door. If you want to grow, get the best salesperson you can't afford and make a deal with her.

Few firms spend less than 10% of their human capital on sales activities. Once a firm reaches 40 people, it may be able to do with fewer salespeople, but marketing, PR, and other promotional activities will come close to the 10% rule. If your plan is to work for ad agencies exclusively, you can take advantage of their staff. This rule is meant as a starting point, not an absolute requirement.

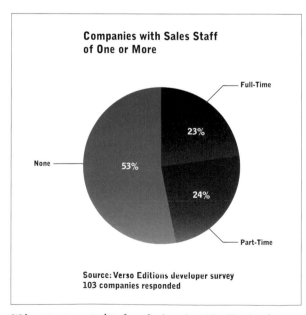

Companies with Sales Staff of One or More

Full-Time 23%
Part-Time 24%
None 53%

Source: Verso Editions developer survey
103 companies responded

Web contractors get a lot of new business inquiries. Turning them into clients you want is a different matter.

If the site costs more than $10k, it's appropriate to address the prospect's particular situation in writing, or at least in a substantive meeting. Responding to a profile is more effective than responding to an RFP.

Responding to profiles

A project profile is just one step toward forming a good relationship with clients. If you've had good meetings and phone conversations, a profile will help you talk more specifically about their project. When you have a complete profile, you should have enough information to give them an idea how their site will develop and attach ballpark prices. The document you send back should have boiler-plate material and a specific response section, blended so the client can't tell which is which.

Boilerplate material should describe your process. Start with client testimonials. Include a summary of your philosophy and focus. Because there are so many site designers, consider targeting a limited number of industries or market segments. Build your portfolio deep, rather than wide, so your marketing materials can address a specific audience. Ideally, this brochure should go deeper into your methods and strategic advantages than your web site, so you give potential customers a detailed look at what it's like to work with you.

Specific response material should address the client's business, site strategy, and site-implementation issues. If you have no chance of meeting with the clients before they make a cut, address their project as well as you can. Draw a few pictures (verbally or visually) that show what their site could achieve. Focus more on satisfying customer needs and achieving big goals than on using specific technologies. Get them to imagine the experience of going through the site. Spend time outlining the difference between the low-budget solution, the middle solution, and the high-ticket (for example, database-driven) solution. Give them ballpark prices for each solution to show them what you can do and for how much. It also tells them you're willing to work with their budget.

If you think you can get them to come in, write your response with that goal in mind. There's an element of risk, but your chances of winning go up dramatically if you can get them to call and schedule a visit. Clients should be willing to come if you can show a distinct competitive advantage.

Make it look professional. Use wire binding and good cover stock. While I'd rather send clients to a password-protected web site or a PDF (electronic document), they like to have something they can hold in their hands and read at their leisure. Paper tends to get passed around at meetings, find its way from desk to desk, and generally stay around longer than a quick look at a web site. Both are important.

Responding to RFPs

When you get an RFP without any prior contact, you can interpret it in one of three ways – **1:** this is what we usually do, **2:** this is a cry for help, or **3:** we are a big account, we know who the qualified groups are; if you want our business, you'll have to play by our rules.

> "Prepare for meetings by learning about your client. Find opportunities to convince clients that you understand their business situation better than they anticipated you would. Be knowledgeable, insightful, and perceptive of their constraints. Couch your understanding in an explanation of your process, getting them to see the final product coming to life. Without doing a lot of extra creative work, spend time in meetings working with them, so they come to value your input. Then you can start charging for the meetings."
>
> **– Mike Nuttall, principal, IDEO**

Mike Nuttall on Partnering

"Responding to an RFP will involve creating an informed, thorough response. Just as an RFP is uniquely tailored for each project, so should the proposal. It should also include rough site schematics, creative, strategic and technical objectives, key scheduling information (a detailed schedule may not be needed at this early stage), scope of services, level of technical enhancements, fees, exclusions, etc. Both parties should walk through the proposal together, to clarify and confirm the outlined information so that the client can make an informed selection."

Emily Ruth Cohen is a graphic design business consultant who specializes in writing estimates, proposals, contracts, and business correspondence.

do the job quickly. Make it professional and enthusiastic, knowledgeable and experienced. Give them 10 good reasons to choose you over the competition. Then hope for the best.

The alternative is to try to talk them out of it. In that case, treat the RFP as a cry for help.

The Astro Cabs RFP is a cry for help. Either you're in a position to make the team leader a hero, or this is a company you want to stay away from. Try to build a relationship. Call the team leader and talk about the RFP. Try to establish some rapport. Every minute you spend talking is another small link in the chain. The RFP is not the solution to his problem. Ask questions that point out weak spots in his plan and show how you can make him look like a winner. Get him to explore some other options. If he resists, try to get to a decisionmaker and go around him. If he's receptive to your comments (you've really thought about his business problem), you have a great selling opportunity. If he's stuck on the RFP, let them go.

One way out would be to offer to work together on a requirements document so that at least he'd have Phase One and could proceed from there. Would he be open to that? Would he be willing to fill out a project profile?

A large RFP. If the job is big enough, and you have spoken to the team leader to know who the other players are (or at least how many), *and you really want the client*, then it's time to play creatively by the rules. It's important to decide how much time you're willing to spend. If you're going to do it, do it well. Spend 30 hours on one RFP rather than ten

Business as usual. If you get an RFP out of the blue, consider your firm to be one of 20. Many purchasing systems require several bids. It could be a formality. If they don't contact you within a few days, it's a bad sign. It could be that they've worked hard to define needs, set goals, and assess the audience, but if they haven't called, they are just looking for "cost-effective" execution.

"27% of all insured architects reported a claim against them in 1993. Why do so many relationships, presumably originally founded on trust and faith, deteriorate into legal squabbles? An extensive review of decided cases [suggests] that poor communication, particularly during programming and the estimation of projected costs, lies at the heart of many disputes."

– Robert C. Greenstreet, contributor, *The Fountainheadache.*

The exception here, of course, is if you're already pre-qualified to work with them. In that case, it may be business as usual, *and you may want the business*.

If you want to respond to an execution-oriented RFP, remember that they are looking for a price and that they will compare your price with others, even if they are different enough that they shouldn't be compared. You can state your assumptions up front – and you should – but they will still make unfair comparisons. To win, you'll have to impress them with your ideas and your ability to

hours on three. Here are some suggestions. Many of them will help in responding to a profile as well.

Chemistry. Bonding is important, sooner the better. You need to "click" with the team leader as soon as possible, because you want to stack the deck in your favor, and you'll need to do it little by little.

The proposal you send back is valuable only insofar as it reinforces an existing relationship. If you don't have one, you'll need to start one soon, because a so-so proposal and an existing relationship will almost always beat a superior proposal and no relationship.

Are you their friend? People like to hire their friends. Do you have *any* connections to this person? Do you have anything in common? If they mention any little thing you can pick up on, see if you can find a link there and establish a common interest or social group. How willing are they to exchange small talk at the beginning of the conversation? How well can you steer it to explore possible connections?

Restate their problem. Articulate their business situation succinctly. The proposals put your written marketing materials into action on their project. It's more important to restate their problem than give them any answers. The answer isn't the product. The RFP is just another link in the chain.

Don't solve the problem. Deep down, subconsciously, they don't want you to solve the problem in the RFP. They want to find that one document in the pile that makes them say "Here. This is it. This is the group." If you have a good feeling for what they *really* want, give them reasons to believe you've already got the solution, but they'll have to engage you to get it. Do this subtly.

Ask for clarification. It's easier to write an RFP with a long list of web-site features than it is to state the overall business problem. Asking for clarification shows that you're thinking about their problem. It also gets you spending time on the phone with the team leader. Ask about certain things that *aren't* in the RFP. Ask for more details. Ask questions that start with "What if..." or "Let's suppose..." Try to get some insight into what they haven't thought about and use that to increase the value of your discussions.

Stack the deck in your favor. If you can get them to rewrite the RFP in a way that "makes it stronger" in their eyes but also happens to play to your strength, you're off to a good start. Tell them you have to know more about the assumptions and get them to help you with the assumptions you should make. If they're not familiar with your assumptions when they receive the document, they're likely to gloss over them and misunderstand your proposal.

Glow with excitement. Think of the last time you hired someone to do something. Doesn't it make a difference if the person really enjoys the challenge? This is what they want to see. While it doesn't qualify you to do the job, a

---

Client link #2
Get information from the client

This will either come from an RFP or a project profile. In most cases, the information will be incomplete. In the worst case, they have everything already designed, with elaborate color printouts and site maps. In the best case, they know their customers and they have lots of questions about what would be appropriate on the Web. Ask for more information if you need it. For instance, if they're having trouble with the profiler, bring them in for a guided field trip around the Web, asking them questions about which sites they like and why. Try to understand their decisionmaking process.

Contractor link #2
Get them to envision working with you

In your response, draw a picture of the partnership. Make connections to things they know. Speak their language. Put a custom cover on your response. Make sure they know you're available to meet and talk with them. Go to their office and give a small seminar on web strategy. Put together a list of things to do and things to avoid during their project. Read books on their industry. Be creative in working with them at this stage. Make it enjoyable for them to contact you.

---

lack of enthusiasm can easily disqualify you from making it to the next round. Respond with passion!

It's only a small part of a longer process. Use the RFP to get to the next stage. If you can write well, your proposal is another chance to "spend time with them" in a different way – make it count!

Give price ranges. If you give a fixed price for a certain amount of work, they will want that same amount of work for a lower price. Relate the price to *value*, not deliverables. We might be twice as expensive, but we provide four times the value. If you must give a figure, give three. Give a low-end solution, a likely solution, and a high-end price. That way, the client will understand they probably won't get the high-end site from you at your mid-level price.

Don't sit back and wait for the phone to ring. After you deliver the RFP, keep the process alive. Follow-up is every bit as important as the RFP. Expect to take the next step with them – assume it in all your conversations. If you've bonded, they will find it hard to say goodbye.

The pitch

At some point, you may find yourself in a client's conference room with about half an hour between you and a knowing smile of approval as the team leader thanks you and escorts you out, saying he'll be in touch *real* soon. Clients expect you to be in the communication business. They expect you to wow them and make them feel secure, to embrace them and give it your own special touch, to pound your shoe on the table because you care so much. They are looking for that special edge you have over the competition. It isn't self-confidence, it isn't a rehearsed show, and it isn't even that you've read all the books on pitching and selling. Give them that one overriding factor that makes you the horse to bet on, and reinforce it with five other reasons that you're better than all the rest.

Partnering (for contractors)

1 Setting up
2 Responding
3 Logistics

Before moving on, there are a few more details to cover. You'll need to decide how to charge, and you'll need to spot a disaster waiting to happen. No matter how good the relationship is, you have to be able to say no when it's best for your company.

To bid or not to bid

Whether you bid or charge by the hour really isn't important. Anyone who works on a fixed bid will tell you that the change orders make up for it, so you're essentially working by the hour anyway. The key to preventing sticker shock is good estimating.

The fixed price. I imagine that over 90% of contracts in web development are fixed-price, for any size project. Clients like fixed bids. Many require them. Besides, the serious money is in bidding jobs, the way ad agencies do. Not only are you guaranteed a certain amount of money, but also the client agrees to pay for any extra changes. All you have to do is work efficiently.

Time and materials. If the client decisionmakers trust you, they will benefit from paying on a time-and-materials basis. Because no one can determine how much work the creative process will involve, the bid process will either leave a design firm with extra cash at the end or with lower margins than they find acceptable. If the client group thinks they paid too much, they might not want to repeat that experience. If the creative group has to "eat" their profits, there will be a strain on the relationship. In many cases, working by the hour is appropriate.

For such contracts, a *not to exceed* amount keeps an upper bound on the cost. This works if a contractor stays within the amount and if the amount set is reasonable. When new developments occur that threaten to increase the cost, the contractor should present options, one of which should always stay within the original budget. If there's a reason to exceed the budget, a flexible client will be able to make a decision. Many clients cannot get more money, so don't assume this is a possibility when you sign.

Every time you meet or call someone on the client team is a chance to get to know them better and a chance for them to remember your name and your work.

Estimating

Be precise about estimates, not just for your clients but for your business. The best way to provide an accurate estimate is to know how your business and team operates. The technology of new media is constantly changing, but you can still track the work required for every deliverable and every phase. Start by keeping a record of hours and tasks completed. The more detail, the better. If you can identify how long and what kind of talent each task takes, you can estimate the cost, and you can explain the reason for the cost. The more line items the client team sees on an estimate, the more confident they feel about the estimate and your ability to deliver.

Get together with the project team members and ask each one to estimate how long it will take to complete each task. Identify potential problems and predict the resources you'll have to reserve in case one comes up. Include subcontractors and miscellaneous expenses for materials, travel, and so on. Be sure to inform the client about different rates for overtime or rush jobs.

Make internal estimates as accurate as possible. Never add contingencies to internal numbers, because you need to check your actual against your projected numbers when the project is over. Be as accurate as possible and keep improving your estimating skills. Then add a contingency reserve to the total that covers unexpected expenses. A common practice is to *pad* the estimate by 20-30% to allow for additional costs. If you pad by less than 20%, the project had better be quite straightforward, and if you add more than 30%, it is because there is too much uncertainty in the outcome.

When you are done with the numbers, determine whether the client will go into sticker shock. Depending on the client and the job, you may want to adjust the number. *Don't do it.* Revisit your internal numbers and see how you can make it work. Trying to give them the number you want will cut into your profits and could lead to an unprofitable job. Don't undermine your estimating process. If you find you're always adjusting the same way, fix the underlying estimates, not the final adjustment.

It's common practice not to show any padding of numbers to the client. But if a client knows you have a built-in cushion, he may want to try to negotiate down. If you can see he's trying to eliminate your pad, offer to save him money by doing the job on a time-and-materials basis. The pad compensates you for the risk of providing a fixed bid. It is a legitimate business practice, the price he pays for the satisfaction of a fixed fee.

Know when to hold 'em

The ideal client trusts you, yet is taking a chance on working with you. You aren't a long-time friend or reliable vendor, and the client is thinking of ways this project can go wrong. The best relationship is a goal-driven, trusting relationship in which the contractor must continually

Client link #3
Get the client to come to your office

If the client team won't come to your office, it's a bad sign. They need to see your working environment and feel the enthusiasm. It's important for them to invest the time and energy to understand whom they're dealing with. One ad agency has a big wall outside their conference room where new clients paint their names, graffiti-style, to help embed them further into the contractor's culture. Without this link, your producer will have to spend a lot of time at their location so they feel comfortable working with you as a member of their team.

Contractor link #3
Narrow the business parameters

Narrowing the business parameters can take three months or three hours. You need to 1: Understand the business problem, 2: Come up with a web strategy that fits the business strategy, and 3: Explain how you'll implement the web strategy in phases, and 4: Tell them how much it costs and why. The time it takes to forge this link depends on how big the project is. The client must be clear about the goals, and you must be clear about your estimates of time and materials to achieve the goals in different ways. Give clients a set of choices so they can find a solution that fits their budget.

Estimate Template

Task	Hourly Rate	PM	Strategy	Design	Consult	Production	Total hours	cost
Project Management	$7							
Strategy	$16							
Design	$16							
Consultation	$22							
Production	$11					hours		
PHASE 1: Strategy								
Strategic and Creative briefs.		2	2	2	2	2	10	$20
Technical baseline established.		5	5	5	5	5	25	$50
Site structure established.		6	6	6	6	6	30	$60
Project Management		21	21	21	21	21	105	$210
Phase Totals		34	34	34	34	34	170	$340
PHASE 2: Design								
Initial design studies/concepting.		2	2	2	2	2	10	$20
Final design direction developed.		5	5	5	5	5	25	$50
Design implementation.		3	3	3	3	3	15	$30
Project management		6	6	6	6	6	30	$60
Phase Totals		16	16	16	16	16	80	$160
PHASE 3: Production								
Development and HTML		2	2	2	2	2	10	$20
Alpha		1	1	1	1	1	5	$10
Beta		3	3	3	3	3	15	$30
QA		6	6	6	6	6	30	$60
Project management		6	6	6	6	6	30	$60
Phase Totals		18	18	18	18	18	90	$180
PHASE 4: Launch								
Final site.		2	2	2	2	2	10	$20
Documentation.		1	1	1	1	1	5	$10
Project management		5	5	5	5	5	25	$50
Phase Totals		8	8	8	8	8	40	$80
PROJECT TOTALS: Total:								$760

Spend time developing good estimating templates and practices.

The final link

Close the deal

Forging this link takes that one, skilled strike with the hammer – and the chain is in place. Miss the strike, and the chain falls apart. Strike too soon, and the link won't hold. The longer you are in the consulting business, the more you appreciate the saying: it's not over until the ink is dry (plus three days to make sure they haven't changed their mind).

No web designer is the ultimate salesperson. We're not natural closers. A client can get away at the last minute, and it's not your fault. When it's time to get them to sign, *put yourself in their shoes*. The better you can see it from their perspective, the better you can understand what it will take to choose you over others. They will make the same choice you would make in the same situation.

Always be closing

It's better to be busy with too much work than to get caught in a lull. A shortage of clients can really hurt a small business. For every outdated commercial web site, you'll find someone in the company trying to make it better. Often, they just don't know how. Pick up the phone and see what you can do.

Remember, market research shows that:

48% of all salespeople give up after the initial sales call

25% more give up after the second call

12% more give up after the third call

5% more give up after the fourth call

10% make the fifth call

80% of all sales are made after the fifth sales contact

Source: Murray Gray, Blueprint Technology

---

assess the work and report back to the client to make sure expectations are being met.

In general, clients with smaller jobs tend to be more difficult than those with larger jobs. Larger jobs are not only more profitable, they are easier to manage because the client gives you more responsibility.

Smaller projects, generally, are those in which:

there's less profit

the client tends to think he can do it himself faster

the client wants to make every decision

the client wants to be intimately involved in the creative process

the client always wants a little something extra

the client doesn't know the difference between a contractor and an employee

Bigger projects, generally, are those in which:

the focus is on the big picture

the focus is on results

the client is interested in quality

the client is aware of production costs

the client wants to look good within the company

Know when to fold 'em

Problem projects come in several different flavors. Hard and fast rules aren't appropriate, because your specialty may be taking all the jobs no one else wants, or your business model may be quite different from mine. Here are a few observations that might serve as a guide.

Startups. Working for startups can be exhilarating. It can be a source of great satisfaction, and it can also be your worst nightmare. Startups have three main problems: tight schedules, big egos, and small budgets. They want you to build their site for the excitement factor. Count yourself lucky if you can work with a startup to make a great site for them on time and on budget and still be friends at the end.

The demo. A client comes to you and says, "Our engineers got something together, and we have to give a demo in three weeks. Can you make it look good so we can get our financing? We can do the job right later." See how enticing this sounds? This is one of the most difficult kinds of jobs, because it looks reasonable from all points of view, yet it

Secret Weapon Number Three

When to say no

If a client doesn't meet all your criteria, ask yourself if it's worth making an exception. Because big jobs are better than small ones, it might be better to turn down the little ones in favor of going after the big ones (provided you don't go after jobs that are too big).

1. Have an informative web site that differentiates you from the competition.

2. Have a brochure with testimonials and information about how you work with clients.

3. Be a person they want to do business with. Make sure they know you are professional and capable.

4. It's a two-way street. Make sure you want to do business with them.

5. Learn about their business proposition.

6. Direct them to your previous customers who are ecstatic about your work.

7. Don't go below your minimum unless you have to or want to.

8. Make sure they are seriously considering you and at most three other shops before giving project-specific information or a bid.

9. Estimate well.

10. "I don't care if I don't like it, and I don't care if you don't like it. What I want to know is whether your customer loves it or not."

11. If they are ready to sign, don't leave without a memorandum of engagement (see Chapter 5, Setup).

often leads to a failed relationship. You can easily be blamed for the "disaster demo" when they don't get their funding, the demo doesn't work, or someone doesn't like it.

If you make their demo look great and they get funding, there'll be no reason to revisit the underlying visual principles of information flow and user orientation. The demo becomes the product. Only when it gets into the hands of users will you be let go for making them look bad. The longer a demo exists (and there are some Top Fifty sites that are basically monster demos), the longer the corporate culture buys into it, and the harder it is to convince them to do it right.

If they need something in three weeks, make a canned demo, not a web site, and put together a separate technology demo.

Damaged clients. Anyone who has already spent his first budget for a web site and has had bad results is *damaged*. A lot of things can go wrong, technically, but it's usually poor project management that leads to a meltdown. Damaged clients are burned, gun-shy, late, often out of money, and upset. The only way to work with them is if they'll get the money you need to do it right. Otherwise, wish them luck. Learn whether any groups have gone before you, and if so, how much has been spent.

The quick fix. A company may have waited too long or put up a site that doesn't work. They're looking for someone to come in and apply a bandage. Once the bleeding is stopped, they say, they'll be able to judge whether they want to continue working with you. This is how they can test you out to see if they want to take the next step and work on strategy for the long term.

The intermediary. This guy calls you. He has this big client, and he's decided you are going to be the lucky firm to do the web site. All he wants is his cut and you'll be able to

"A group from an existing client wanted a bid to update their site. We had to bid against another company, even though we were already working for them. We submitted a formal response. I knew the competition hadn't submitted a bid yet, so I asked what happened to our competition. They said that the other firm hadn't prepared anything, but instead had asked, 'What did Organic bid?' The client, who knew us well, said, 'We're not telling.' So the guy at this other agency said, 'Well, I don't have a bid together, so I'll bid zero.' So the client called me back and said, 'We have a weird situation – they bid zero. They are willing to do the job for free. We have to consider that.' We were a fairly small company at the time. I said, 'Okay, I bid negative $1. Invoice me.' And they did. They invoiced me, and we paid a dollar to do the job. In the end, we did very well, because there were so many change orders and additions that we made more than the original bid and kept the client."

NOTE: Organic doesn't *usually* pay clients to do their web sites.

I could do this myself if I only had time. Clients are using you as a pen if they start showing you all their sketches and ideas for where the buttons go. Any client who wants to use you as a pen is a client to run away from.

They want so-and-so to work on it. Some clients want to know who will be assigned to a project. Some clients even put a clause in the contract entitling them to *approve* who works on the project! This is one of those big warning signs that says you are far from a trusting relationship. The president (or partners) of a professional group is responsible for all work that goes out of the shop. It is her responsibility to see that it is done properly, to spec, and to the client's satisfaction. There aren't many circumstances in which a client should expect that a particular creative person will do a particular job. If a client has a problem with any member of a design team, the client should ask the owner to address the problem. The client is contracting with the firm, not the firm's employees or subcontractors.

Logo wars. Clients will come to you with logos that don't work on screen. They will want you to "fix" them so they look good on the Web. Since you're the site designer, you have nowhere to go but down. If you do a good job, they will wonder why you charged so much money. If you don't do a good job, you're to blame. Logos are sacred cows. Do them properly or leave them alone.

put this company on your client list, but everything has to go through him. If he's a true one-man producer, that's one thing, but they are rare. More likely, he's a *middleman*. Offer to pay this person a finder's fee when the client signs a deal and pays you directly. If he doesn't go for it, be prepared for a rough ride. A middleman is in it for his cut.

It's a surprise. A few clients want to surprise their bosses by doing something really great, just in time. Unfortunately, bosses hate surprises, even pleasant ones, because they have no idea what will be behind the curtain at show time. If you don't have regularly scheduled presentations with top-level decisionmakers, you run the risk of a *reset* — having to start over — and that's the number one way to waste money.

Follow up

If the client calls to say you didn't get the business, be gracious. Ask questions to try to improve your process. If you ask about checking back to see if they might need anything else, they will say yes. Rather than asking about future jobs, wish them luck and bow out. You can always call back later.

If you don't hear from a client, call back. It's important to understand what their decisionmaking process was and why they chose another group. Clients will be straightforward and informative during these calls. Don't argue, because they've already made their decision. If you've worked hard to get their business, they feel they owe you at least an explanation. It is always a valuable experience.

"Given the opportunity,
the institutional client –
represented by the building committee –
will have its way totally,
bullying and badgering the architect
until it gets a building that
responds perfectly to the budget
and program,
no matter how ugly or poorly detailed
the building might be.
This is the proverbial camel,
a horse designed by committee."

– Roger K. Lewis, architect, *The Fountainheadache*

You've found a dance partner.
It's time to negotiate the business terms
and get to work.

THIS CHAPTER BRIEFLY DESCRIBES everything you'll
need to start the project. Call it *Phase Zero* – the setup.
Too many projects skip this phase because it seems like
a handshake is good enough and everything will go well.
Anyone who's been through the experience more than a
few times understands the value of being clear on exactly
what will happen, who will do it, and how much it will cost.
This chapter has three parts, **1:** Formalities, **2:** The fair
deal, and **3:** Team building. The fair deal is by far the most
important, and it is for clients as well as contractors.

Once you've agreed to work together, the following formalities will help get the project off to a good start.

Show me the money

Although clients would prefer to pay *after* they see the work, most groups won't get started without some payment up front. Given the fickle nature of projects on the Web, this is a reasonable precaution. Unfortunately, clients do not usually enclose a check with the signed contract. Small companies can usually cut a check within a week. If you can get your first check from a big company inside of two weeks, you're doing well.

I ask the client team leader to help us get the first check under the fastest possible circumstances as we begin work on the job. Then we ask them to pay on their normal 30-day schedule. Many large companies can't pay in 30 days, even if they say they can. Many contractors have deep scars from working with large corporations. The bigger the company, the longer they take to pay.

So let me put it this way: *a client who will work hard to get us paid as quickly as possible, walking checks through the payment process and making sure that if the contract says we get it on Friday, it comes on Friday, will get extra special treatment when it's time for favors.* A client who knows the ways of the accounts payable department is a client I'm happy to work for again.

Legalities

I would love to write a whole book on legalities. There are too many details to cover here, but I want to address the basic documents you'll need. I've provided some of these documents at the book site for you to use, but the important thing is that you understand why and how to use these legal tools.

The nondisclosure agreement. If you haven't signed a nondisclosure agreement by now, you should at least offer one to your client. The NDA is a sign of trust – it obliges you to keep important information secret, so your client can feel more comfortable telling you about upcoming plans and events. If the client's competition learns something valuable, and the client can show you were the source of the leak, you can be held liable for damages.

A good NDA will also bind your contractors and immediate family, making you responsible for their actions. You should give necessary information to people you can trust, and your client should trust you to make those decisions. Don't sign an NDA that restricts your rights to share information with subcontractors. (There is a useful NDA on the book site waiting for you.)

Noncompetition. In some industries, you cannot work for two similar clients at once. Advertising agencies in the U.S., for example, don't work for two competing car manufacturers, airlines, computer makers, and so on. The clients wouldn't stand for it. In Japan, however, ad agencies routinely split into separate groups to handle competing clients, and the clients don't seem to mind.

If a client wants an exclusive contract, weigh the pros and cons of entering into that kind of relationship. To what degree are you really limiting new business? To what degree can you harm them by taking a related, but not directly competitive client? Look at the agreement they

---

TIP Clients: Once you've chosen a design firm, immediately call the firms you haven't selected. You will do them a big favor by telling them you've decided to go somewhere else as soon as possible, so they can make other decisions affecting their business.

---

want you to sign. Is it worth it? If you are giving up a possible business opportunity by signing, you should either **1:** ask for more money to make it exclusive, **2:** limit the noncompetition term (which can extend for many months after the contract is over), or **3:** be more specific about the kinds of competitors you agree not to work with.

If possible, sign non-exclusive contracts and use your own ethical standards to guide your decisions. After all, if you do something to harm a client's competitive advantage, you won't be generating much goodwill for your firm.

The memorandum of engagement. I often start work on a handshake agreement, rather than a contract, but I always put that handshake agreement in writing. A memorandum of engagement is a commitment on both sides to begin work while negotiating the details of the contract in earnest. It's a short document whose main goal is to establish penalties for pulling out between now and the time I sign a contract. It is a commitment to pay for work performed. It can take the place of a purchase order, but when dealing with large companies, you should get a PO as soon as possible. It isn't air tight, but as long as you're working on a contract, it should suffice.

Copyrights. The person who creates a work owns it. If you write or draw something original, or if you photograph something, you automatically own the rights to the distribution of that work. There are a few exceptions, like **1:** if you are an employee of a firm and you create the work on company time, then the company owns the rights; **2:** if you photograph someone, you may need a release (or permission) from that person to sell the rights to its use; **3:** if you photograph something copyrighted, you probably don't have the right to reproduce and distribute that photograph commercially.

Facts and ideas are not copyrightable. If you put brilliant ideas on the Web, anyone can take or use them. Only the

expression – the physical, tangible rendering – of an idea is protectable. The copyright law also protects those who create parodies of well known works, as long as the creator has altered the message so as to create his own work.

Trade dress and look-and-feel issues will be interesting areas of legal development. If a site designer knowingly takes advantage of another site's colors and visual themes, trying to create a confusingly similar service that might fool the average person into thinking he is doing business with a well known entity, that designer (or his client) will probably be held liable for damages. Such a suit hasn't occurred yet, but it's best to avoid any possible confusion.

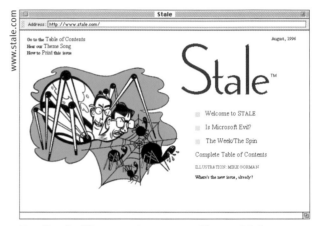

Parodies of well known works are protected by copyright law.

Links are considered to be informational, not artistic expression. You can always link to anyone else's site without asking permission. But if a webmaster asks you to remove a link, you have the responsibility to do so. If you refuse repeatedly to remove a link from your site to someone else's site, that person would be justified in suing you.

Transfer of rights. I would need an entire book to describe all the complicated legal issues of rights as they affect web developers. Here I want to make four important points.

Clients are entitled to all rights necessary for the Web. The developer should, as part of the contract, sign over all rights to the materials developed for the site. This includes text, HTML, images, sounds, and so on. It is very important that the developer have these rights to assign. The developer should obtain specific written permission from any subcontractors assigning the rights to their work to the developer. The developer should have signed employment contracts with all employees saying their work is

Secret Weapon Number Four

The Memorandum of Engagement

Always carry a blank MOE to meetings, in case a potential client turns into a new client sooner than expected. Failure to sign an MOE is a sign that you are rushing into the project. (Get a simple one at the book site and carry it with you wherever you go.)

"made for hire" and all rights go to the firm. The developer should pay for and receive rights to use stock photography, clip art, and fonts on the Web. These rights should be tran-sferable to the developer's clients.

Developers are entitled to retain certain rights. If a developer builds a site, he will likely make images at a resolution of 72 dots per inch. I would say the client is entitled to all on-screen rights (video, Web, CD ROM, and so on), and that the developer retains the rights to all print reproduction above 72 DPI. The developer should retain the rights to those images at higher resolutions. Clients should expect to pay extra for a certain image that, say, would go into a printed brochure. The contract can state that such images will be produced and licensed at industry-standard rates for printed media. Clients may use "screen shots" of all 72-DPI images, but they aren't allowed to resample the images and reproduce them as "artwork" for a brochure. The reason is simple: clients often do this, and it looks terrible. The same goes for online logos, photographs, and other representations.

Don't put someone else's work on a web site without permission. That's what links are for. I've had to send cease-and-desist letters to people who take my writing and images and put them on their web sites. The concept of "fair use" is not only complicated, it's changing as new uses of the Web challenge it. It's best to be on the safe side and not take anything from any source that isn't in the public domain. In general, works over 75 years old are in the public domain. Most photos taken by U.S. Government photographers are in the public domain. Unprotected

In a typical web-design contract, the designer should retain the rights to all images for uses other than on-screen. Clients should expect to pay extra to apply these images to a printed work, like this brochure.

If you try to confuse people by taking advantage of a known brand, you can be held liable for damages. Note: this is a fictional example. The xpedia URL is owned by someone whose site looks nothing like this. This doctored image is used as an example only.

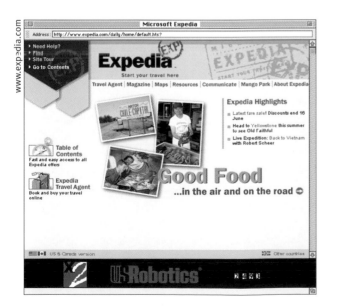

works that were created before 1978 are in the public domain, but they're hard to verify. When in doubt, do without.

HTML copyrights are not important. I think HTML copyrights will end up being unenforceable, but it shouldn't matter. What matters is the content of the page as it looks when viewed through a browser. That should be copyrighted. You shouldn't feel bad about copying other people's source HTML, especially "snippets" of code you find here and there. This goes for JavaScript and other client-side scripts.

Several good resources on these issues are on the Web, and there are some excellent books. Please see the book site and give us some feedback on what questions you have concerning cyber rights.

The contract. I hope it's clear by now that you need a written contract. Because lawyers are expensive, people like to draw up their own. This works until you need something that isn't covered. If you're planning to build web sites for a living, I suggest starting with a book on the subject (see the book-site bookstore for recommendations), writing your own, and taking it to a lawyer for review.

A contract specifies the nature and scope of work to be done, assignment of rights, conditions of payment, what can go wrong, and what happens if it does. Contracts should address concerns I'll specify in later sections of the book, like what happens if a client doesn't deliver content on schedule.

Clients may require you to sign their contract. In that case, you should pay a lawyer to review it with you and charge the client for this time elsewhere, as part of the cost of doing business with them. **I do not, under any circumstances, recommend signing a client's contract without a lawyer's review.**

Some day, someone will put a good contract on the Web that all developers can use (let us know if this interests you), and then we will all be able to use that contract, one that puts a fair deal on paper and gives both sides the rights they deserve.

Setup

1 Formalities

2 The fair deal

3 Team building

In looking for a win-win situation, we must first understand how clients and contractors get themselves into no-win situations. Then we can explore a new approach, one that works for both parties.

The client dilemma

The fact that clients send RFPs isn't really the problem. If more RFPs looked like project profiles, contractors would be able to give clients better information. But RFPs come loaded with site maps and site features, and that's when contractors have a hard time understanding what clients really want. The following example illustrates the typical exchange that puts clients and contractors in hot water. This should be familiar territory to most developers who've had problems with clients in the past.

THE CLIENT DILEMMA

act 1, scene 1

Contractor's office, mid-afternoon. A client walks in, asks for a meeting, and is escorted to a makeshift conference table. The house music is turned down so they can talk. After initial formalities, they get down to business.

CLIENT: We'd like a web site. We don't want brochureware. We want it to be a theme park for our customers, with all kinds of cool things for them to do.

CONTRACTOR: Great. Let's get started.

Client: Hold on! We need to know how much it will cost first.

CONTRACTOR: How should I know? We haven't

spec'ed it yet. Let's spec it together, then we can work out a price.

CLIENT: That won't work. We need to approve the budget ahead of time.

CONTRACTOR: You want a price for a mid-sized theme park in one language, with attractions for visitors of all ages?

CLIENT: Yes.

CONTRACTOR: Well, I'll tell you what. I don't have enough information. You spec it, I'll give you a price. The more details you give us, the better we can give you a price.

CLIENT: How much detail do you need?

CONTRACTOR: How should I know? More is better.

act 1, scene 2

The following week. Contractor stops playing networked video games long enough to meet with client.

CLIENT: Here's our new spec. We've worked really hard on it. Tell us how much it will cost.

CONTRACTOR: Let's see, it says here you want your customers to enjoy the community aspects of the site. Does that mean you want a database? Do you want to serve pages dynamically, or do you want it static?

CLIENT: How should we know? We just want a lively community.

CONTRACTOR: Will you have moderators and licensed content?

CLIENT: Do we need moderators and licensed content?

CONTRACTOR: How should I know? I haven't talked to your customers.

act 1, scene 3

The following week. Client stops in on his way to a trade show.

CLIENT: Okay, we've got it all dialed in. We know exactly what we want.

CONTRACTOR: Great. Let's see, you're going to implement a Java-based community center?

CLIENT: No. *You're* going to implement a Java-based community center.

CONTRACTOR: How much do you want to spend on that?

CLIENT: I have no idea. Listen, can't you just bid this thing so we can compare you against the other groups? We'll figure out the exact features later.

CONTRACTOR: You want me to bid it, but you're not sure you want it built.

CLIENT: Right.

CONTRACTOR: We'll figure it out later.

CLIENT: Right.

CONTRACTOR: But for now, you want some numbers, so you can put something in your budget.

CLIENT: Right.

CONTRACTOR: So you can change it later.

CLIENT: Right.

CONTRACTOR: Will your budget change later?

CLIENT: No.

CONTRACTOR: What if we can figure out how to do something even more appropriate for less money than your feature set would require?

CLIENT: We'd want to save the money, obviously.

CONTRACTOR: Obviously. How soon do you want this built?

CLIENT: It needs to be ready in six weeks.

CONTRACTOR: When do you need a response?

CLIENT: By the end of the week.

CONTRACTOR: How much do you want to spend?

CLIENT: If we told you that, we wouldn't be able to compare you against the other groups.

act 2, scene 1

The bid has been sent off to the client. The contractor is busy working on his own web site. During this entire act, the contractor sits, working silently, with headphones on. The music of Velocity Girl can be heard coming out of the headphones at full volume.

act 3, scene 1

Contractor's office, mid-morning. A new client walks in, asks for a meeting, and is escorted to a makeshift conference table. After initial formalities, they get down to business.

NEW CLIENT: We'd like a web site. We don't want brochureware. We want it to be a personal interior decorator for our customers, where they tell the site about their house and it gives them all kinds of great suggestions for how they can redecorate.

CONTRACTOR: Great. Let's get started.

The curtain closes.

END

Verso Editions web-developer survey

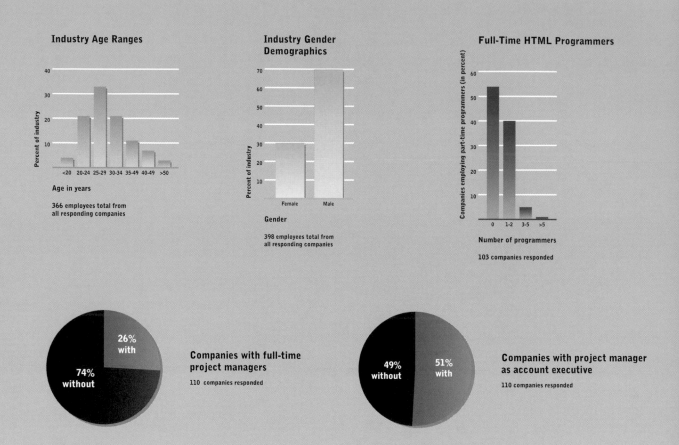

Industry Age Ranges

Percent of industry

40

30

20

10

<20 20-24 25-29 30-34 35-49 40-49 >50

Age in years

366 employees total from
all responding companies

Industry Gender Demographics

Percent of industry

70

60

50

40

30

20

10

Female Male

Gender

398 employees total from
all responding companies

Full-Time HTML Programmers

Companies employing part-time programmers (in percent)

60

50

40

30

20

10

0 1-2 3-5 >5

Number of programmers

103 companies responded

26%
with

74%
without

Companies with full-time project managers

110 companies responded

49%
without

51%
with

Companies with project manager as account executive

110 companies responded

What's wrong with this picture? Who's at fault here? The contractor, obviously. He made his mistake early, when he said "If you can spec it, I can bid it." While this is true, it forces the client to retreat and come up with a number of features for his site, beginning the downward spiral of trying to put a price on something that isn't defined, and trying to define something that isn't worth pricing.

The two-stage project

When a project has too many unknowns to bid properly, a contractor should propose doing the first strategic phase as a separate project. This 2-6 week exploration leads to a set of goals, deliverables, and an estimate the client can use – even take to other groups. This approach gives the two parties a chance to work together and define the project, while working within the budget to scope and price the final deliverables.

Stage One consists of the normal Phase One, outlined later in this book. Once the client has used the project profile, interviews, and the selection matrix to choose a group, she engages that group to conduct a definition phase. The contractor group writes several documents that define the problem and work on possible solutions. They select a set of solutions they think will be within the budget, and they price them out, adjusting as necessary to stay within the budget (or to justify an increase in the budget).

Clients who haven't done this before often want a deal on this phase, because it is exploratory and may lead to a larger contract, but this is a false economy. Because it's among the most important work a contractor does, and if the client is free to take it to the competition to bid, the contractor has a right to charge a premium for this initial stage. Strategic work takes more thinking than design work and should command a higher rate.

The contractor can either bid this stage or do it by the hour. Both are common. If the client and contractor have worked together before, the hourly approach saves money. Some contractors require a minimum payment, which might exceed the work done in Phase One and assumes the continuation of the project subject to the negotiation of the second bid. If the client wants the freedom to take the results of this phase to other contractors, the client cannot also reserve the contractor's team in case she decides to have the contractor do the work. If a third party shows up and wants to pay for work, the contractor should have the right to start this new job as soon as the first phase is over. One possible compromise is that if this happens, the contractor agrees to give the client the right to sign up for the rest of the project – a right of first refusal.

Stage Two. With the bid in hand, the client can now set the budget and decide how she wants it implemented. If she has been happy with the first stage, she signs a contract to receive the web site on the date specified. This involves Phases Two through Four, as outlined in chapters to follow. If she thinks it would be good to get another bid, she goes back to the companies she narrowed down earlier and asks them if they'd like to bid on producing the site as it has been specified.

The fair deal

A fair deal is one both companies would willingly repeat: the same amount of work for the same amount of money. The contract you sign should try to put the two-phase process on paper, so there is no one-sidedness.

Probably the most common strain on the client-contractor relationship is the inaccurate estimate. As you can imagine, clients don't like to be told $x and billed $3x. The two-stage project starts with a budget range, rather than a fixed amount. This lets the contractor team work more creatively in Phase One, while giving them the responsibility of selling the merits of their good ideas. After discussing possible deliverables and prices, both sides can see what will be done and what it will cost.

Bigger projects require more flexibility. In new-media development, you're always breaking new ground and inventing new ways to accomplish new tricks. No matter how careful the estimate, the client/contractor team may make decisions based on new information. If the client and contractor have set the deliverables and price together,

the contractor will be more invested in the initial bid and will try hard to keep the project in the range specified.

Once a client and contractor decide to work together, by definition they both want the best outcome for the client. The fair deal gives the client the best site for the money while giving the contractor a reasonable profit. I believe the fair deal comes from separating Phase One from the rest of the project. There are many ways to do it. This is the general appraoch I recommend:

1. The client signs up to have a complete site designed, developed, and shipped. The contract breaks the project into two stages, with a chance for the client to bail if the contractor cannot satisfy in Stage One. The client supplies an initial budget in the form of a range, rather than an exact number.

2. Agree on an estimate for Phase One.

3. The contractor works on an hourly basis during Phase One, typically at full normal rate and possibly higher for special strategic services.

4. At the end of Phase One, the contractor delivers several options that give the client a choice of deliverables within the range of the budget. Make estimates tight but not perfectly precise. The group works together to choose the solution that should deliver the most results for the money.

5. Mutually decide on the deliverables, schedule, and milestones.

6. Negotiate an acceptable fixed-bid price.

7. Sign an agreement amending the contract to include the fixed bid for the agreed-upon deliverables. This should cover any contingencies and how to handle them

8. Proceed with the contract, making changes as necessary.

Whether you use a fixed bid or time-and-materials, the key factor in controlling costs is to separate Phase One from the rest of the job.

There is a shelf of books on team building at your local online bookstore. The entire team assembled for a web project – developer, client, and sub-contractors – forms a group of people who in most cases haven't worked together before. Knowing everyone's role will help pave the way to a successful project.

Team strategies

When it comes to web development, contractors are always scrambling for the talent to implement something new, something exciting, something that's never been done before. It's impossible to have all the right people lined up to work on each project as it comes in the door. The principals on both sides of the contract must balance resources carefully, according to the needs of the project and the availability of talent. There are two basic kinds of team structures: the assembly line and the project group. Small shops must choose one or the other, while boutiques and agencies may choose either or both.

The assembly line, perfected by Henry Ford, saves money and increases consistency in the product. A similar approach to web design isn't nearly as boring, and it can be a good way to use available talent. The producer – or at least an account executive – must stay with the project through all phases but may be the only person common to all phases of the project.

The project group is what I call "building Volvos," because of the famous factory in Sweden where a team assembles a car from start to finish, then goes back and builds another one. Partnerships often take this approach, with different people wearing different hats as project moves through its phases. In some cases, they will need to hire a special subcontractor to write a script or set up a new server – someone they can't afford to have on staff at all times. Project groups are stimulating and increase the level of commitment to the finished product. They encourage closer bonds between client and contractor, increase communication, and lessen the chance of surprises.

The core team, perhaps the best solution, combines the strengths of both approaches. In an agency, where several people will be assigned to one account as it moves through the shop, there is usually a core team, including the producer, who stays with the project from beginning to end, using specialists as the need arises. The art director and technical analyst will follow the project, as will a strategy or marketing person. In this model, the core team dons different hats as they implement their own ideas, handing the more technical or repetitive work off to the production department as necessary. This is the way most larger shops do it, combining the assembly line and the project group into a team that can focus on the client's needs and see the project through to the end.

Ideal teams

In discussing ideal teams, I often use the term *design cylinder*. A design cylinder is a billable team that can work on one job at a time. If you look at a design agency as an engine, a small one will have only one cylinder, but with about every 6-10 people, you add another cylinder. It's important to visualize the cylinders firing alternately rather than simultaneously. If you have two large projects on the same timing track, you will need more people to service the projects than if they are staggered. This staggering helps smooth out the highs and lows of the business cycle. It lets you keep people working continuously without burning them out.

Scaling your business is a matter of adding cylinders. You can have one large and one small cylinder, for example, and you're probably better off with two large

Staffing Up

# of Employees	1	2	3	4	5	6	7	8	9	10	11	12	13	14	15	16	17	18	
Production																			Team
Production manager																			
Programmer																			
Scriptor																			
System administrator																			
Design lead																			
Designer																			
Technical analyst																			
Producer																			
Sales																			Staff
Marketing																			
Office manager																			

Units: ■ = one quarter of a full-time employee

# of Simultaneous Jobs	1	2	3	4	5	6	7	8	9	10	11	12	13	14	15	16	17	18
Small	1	1	1	1		1	1	1	1	1			1					1
Medium					1	1	1				1	1	1		2		2	2
Large							or 1	1	1	1	1	1	1	2	1	2	1	1
Very Large											or 1	or 1	or 1		or 1	or 1	or 1	or 2

cylinders than four small ones. To increase the size of a cylinder, offer more services, like PR or media purchasing, strategic consulting, database engineering, and so on. Another way of saying this is to keep your ratio of billable to non-billable people as high as possible, while going after ever larger projects.

Beware of no-man's land. I think in many cases, there is a no-man's land between 10 and 15 people – the size of a small boutique or large partnership. In this range, you must have a complete support system (office manager, system administrator, sales/marketing), but only one billable design cylinder. The troughs in the business cycle are deep for a 12-person company with only one core billable group. Even if the sales person keeps jobs flowing, profitability will be a challenge at best. It's best to have one cylinder firing lean and mean (7-10 people) or jump to two as soon as possible. Whatever your business, determine the 1.5 cylinder size and avoid it.

Proposed ideal staff requirements for different sized groups. Note: this is biased toward a design and strategy group, not an engineering concern. They are meant only as guidelines – your mileage may vary. Does not include outside contractors.

You think you've got problems

Jim Waldron

Jim Waldron is a freelance producer who often works with ad agencies and others on award-winning web sites. His story of working with the Swedish Post Office on a big project highlights the kind of trouble producers can get themselves into and still come out alive.

"Posten is the name of the postal service in Sweden. Unlike the USPS, Posten is fairly efficient, but it's still a 200 year-old company hot to improve its image and bottom line through the Web. I was working with a New York-based advertising agency with Swedish roots. In 1995, we had completed exactly one web site and two demos. After an impassioned pitch, we won the job to produce the Posten site that would link all of Sweden together, with hundreds of communities of interest, shops, and secure financial transactions. Cool idea, pretty large undertaking – the equivalent of a Swedish 'America Online.'

Problem one: we were in New York, 5000 miles from the client. Problem two: Posten business culture works on the group decisionmaking method. Problem three: everyone in Sweden is polite, making sure to let everyone have and discuss his point of view. Problem four: Posten likes to hire consultants to decide which consultants to hire. Problem five: seven months to rollout. Problem six: no one was designated as the King. Problem seven: I only know the Swedish words for "fish, customer service, and kiss-kiss honey."

As the project evolved from one to three major sites, and the consultants began hiring consultants to redesign the interface, system architecture, and payment mechanisms, the staffing for the project swelled to over 200 people on two continents and four countries. Even the hosting servers were moved to a remote location away from the development team, due to some government wrangling about jobs in rural areas.

A few weeks before rollout, one of the late-coming technical consultants changed the root directories of one of the community servers without informing anyone. Over 50 programmers in Stockholm and across the sea were excluded from access to critical files without which they could not continue working, delaying significant features of the site. Needless to say, I learned a few four-letter words in Swedish that week.

Seven months later, we rolled out a very expensive, partially functional, content-weak, disorganized, and difficult-to-navigate site. Despite its flaws, the site is now one year old and continues to draw upwards of 30,000 visitors each day. Small miracles can occur in cyberspace."

"Miracles
sometimes occur,
but one has to
work terribly hard
for them."

– Chaim Weizmann

Chapter 6

The project site

Chapter 6 The project site

Everyone should know how
to make and use a project site.
It's one of the fundamental
communication breakthroughs
of our time.

The project site

THE YEAR IS 1995. My client team is located in Boston, Santa Clara, Los Angeles, and on airplanes in between. We have no way to keep track of things using email alone. We have decisions to make long-distance, and we have to be sure we're looking at the same thing. I decide to build a special web site that essentially functioned as a "war room" online. Everything is in one place, carefully numbered, and arranged chronologically as the project moves along.

A growing percentage of web-design groups now use project sites. Many companies are discovering the benefits of using a web site to house all the information for a project. It's a new form of communication combining email and Lotus Notes-style capabilities with the ease of use of the Web. Developers all over are coming up with new ways of improving this basic idea: run your project on the Web.

A *project site* is a client-contractor communication center. In web jargon, the project site is an *extranet* – a password-protected site designated for only those involved in a project. A hand-made project site is a primitive but useful form of *groupware*. Use it well and your project stays organized and on track.

Note: this chapter discusses the project site as it relates to the four-phase process described in the following chapters. For best effect, skim this chapter first, then read it again after digesting the material in chapters 7-10.

The project site

This section describes the project site in detail and shows several examples of project sites.

The producer's tool

Harry S. Truman said: "Whenever you have an efficient government, you have a dictatorship." In the Verso project-management method, our producer is the benevolent czar of the project. Because the producer is responsible for the deliverables, her method of getting the job done is to use other people. She *must* be the conduit through which work flows from the contractor organization to the client organization. During peak periods, a producer can spend an hour a day updating the project site. It must be tight, well written, and tailored to the specific project.

The average project either gains or loses at least one team member before it's finished. Imagine being assigned to a new team and having to track down everything that's happened – email, faxes, telephone conversations, interviews – it could take weeks. A few hours at the project site will thoroughly brief a new team member. Project sites take a few extra person-days to put up and maintain, but they pay for themselves in added productivity.

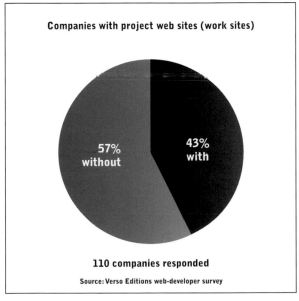

Companies with project web sites (work sites)

57% without

43% with

110 companies responded

Source: Verso Editions web-developer survey

More and more developers are using project sites to communicate with their clients.

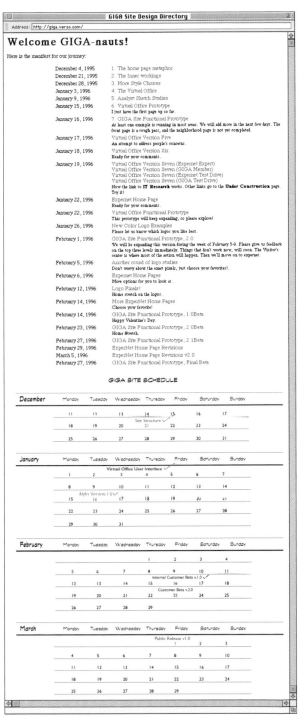

My first project site.

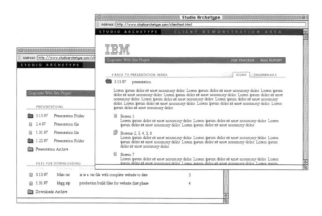

Different groups have developed their own way of presenting project sites.

Our thanks to Studio Archetype (www.studioarchetype.com), Atomic Vision (www.atomicvision.com), and Indigo Group (www.indigogroup.com) for their generous preparation and release of project-site pages.

Project sites are already in use around the world. This one is courtesy of Petr Van Blokland in Holland.

A project site supports *asynchronous communication* – communication between parties at different times, through a common messaging medium. Message boards, voicemail, and email are forms of asynchronous communication. Email can be a very effective tool when used in conjunction with a project site.

Any project can benefit

More than 300,000 businesses in the United States now have access to the Internet. Anyone working on a collaborative project should consider using a project site to communicate with members of the team. You don't need to do web design to benefit from a project site.

Architects can use a project site to show the evolution of a house, from initial sketches and blueprints to final virtual models and photos of actual construction. Imagine seeing a VRML (3-D) mock-up of a building on the Web for clients, saving money in modelmaking and shipping. Some day, the city planning department may accept plans submitted as the URL of a project site.

Engineers need to make drawings, schematics, plans, and diagrams – and the inevitable revisions. As teams become distributed and people work from home and satellite offices, project sites will help keep everything together.

Design and creative directors can make good use of a project site, even if they aren't in the business of building web sites. They can use it to track a project, get approvals, discuss possibilities, and deliver final artwork.

Photographers can forget about CD ROMs. If they have a special area of their site for each project, they can show everything right on the Web. Using JPEG compression and thumbnails, photographers can put up an edit and go over it with a creative director right from a location on assignment.

Ad agencies can put entire presentations on the Web at the last minute, even as the account representative is on the way to the meeting. By making presentations on the Web, clients and agencies can have multiparty conference calls and make asynchronous decisions easily.

Event coordinators can run their projects online, saving client visits and countless faxes. Imagine a wedding co-ordinator who puts all her projects on the Web. Clients can check in anytime, add to or update lists, preview the work of prospective vendors, and approve the budget. A project site is the perfect way to coordinate events like this.

The anatomy of a project site

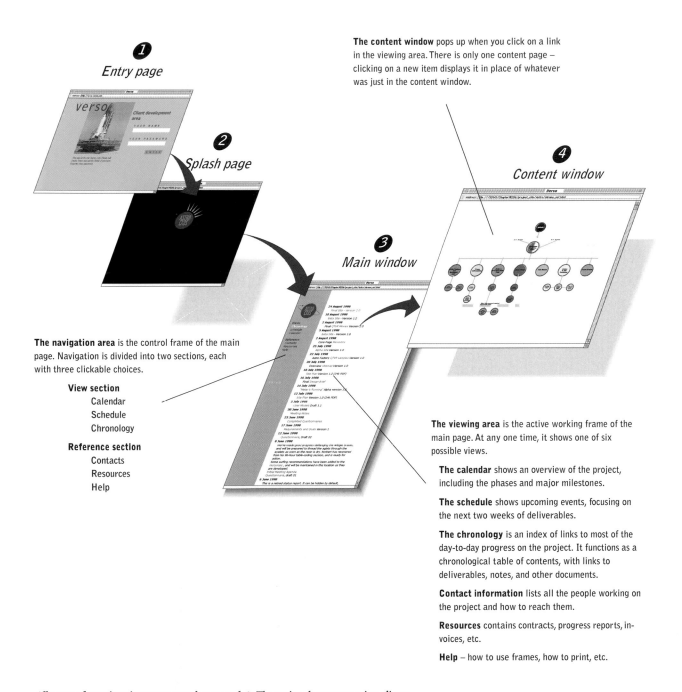

① *Entry page*

② *Splash page*

③ *Main window*

④ *Content window*

The content window pops up when you click on a link in the viewing area. There is only one content page – clicking on a new item displays it in place of whatever was just in the content window.

The navigation area is the control frame of the main page. Navigation is divided into two sections, each with three clickable choices.

View section
> Calendar
> Schedule
> Chronology

Reference section
> Contacts
> Resources
> Help

The viewing area is the active working frame of the main page. At any one time, it shows one of six possible views.

The calendar shows an overview of the project, including the phases and major milestones.

The schedule shows upcoming events, focusing on the next two weeks of deliverables.

The chronology is an index of links to most of the day-to-day progress on the project. It functions as a chronological table of contents, with links to deliverables, notes, and other documents.

Contact information lists all the people working on the project and how to reach them.

Resources contains contracts, progress reports, invoices, etc.

Help – how to use frames, how to print, etc.

All pages of a project site are password-protected. 1: The optional entry page gives clients a way in from the contractor's site. 2: The splash page welcomes visitors with the proper password and serves as an index into multiple projects. Clients click through this page to reach… 3: The main window, which serves as the control and displays some of the content. 4: The content window pops up to view side-by-side or on top of the main window, depending on the size of the viewer's screen. In this case, it shows a site map.

Access to the project site

A sophisticated project site has four levels of access. You restrict access through the use of passwords. A webmaster, rather than the producer, is typically in charge of passwords and security.

Testers are people who answer questionnaires and review the site. Testers should have an area where they can log in, answer questions, and give comments. They should not be able to see the rest of the project site.

Subs include outside illustrators, writers, contributors, and consultants. They may have restricted access, but they usually get the same privileges as the rest of the team. If they are not allowed to see the development, they may have a special page where they can submit their work.

Team includes inside contributors for both client and contractor. This includes subcontractors vital to the project. The team has access to everything but financial and legal information.

Key members of the project include the producer, officers of the developer's company, the client team leader, and the client's decisionmakers. They should be able to view the contract and financial updates on the site at all times. This area should require a special password to enter.

The project site

1 A new form of communication

2 How to make a project site

3 How to run a project site

4 How to extend the project site

It's not hard to make a project site. You can write HTML from scratch, start with the templates we provide, or start with a program like NetObjects Fusion. At Verso, our project site has evolved to the model you see here. Feel free to modify it to suit your own needs.

Make your own project site

There's no need to start from scratch. We've built a project site for you, and it's available on the book site. The first few pages of a project site are mostly for branding purposes, but they add a nice touch to the first-time visitor's experience.

The entry page is located on your company's site. It's helpful in case anyone forgets the URL of his project site. It's certainly not necessary, but it tells prospective clients there's something interesting behind the door.

A splash screen not only impresses clients the first time they see it, but it gives them a source of pride in working with us as they show it to others.

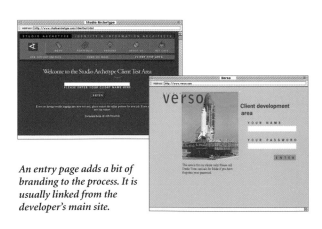

An entry page adds a bit of branding to the process. It is usually linked from the developer's main site.

A fast splash screen looks professional and impresses newcomers. Regulars can always bookmark the interior pages.

Two windows

The site consists of two windows: the main window and the content window. The *main window* serves as the controller for the site and is always meant to be open. The *content window* pops up to display reports, diagrams, and other content.

The main window is a *frameset* that contains two frames: the left frame contains the persistent *navigation area* and the right frame contains

the *viewing area*. The viewing area defaults to showing the *chronology*, the most important view of the project. You can add a top frame that gives a title to the page and adds your own branding, but we've found that it takes up valuable content space.

Instead, we put our name at the top of the window (the document title) and we add a link to our site at the bottom of the navigation.

Using frames, the material on the left doesn't scroll away. However, if the visitor wants to print the right half of the page, he has to know how to open that file in a new window. Remember the golden rule of using frames: never provide a through-frame link. Always link to a new window that pops up, to avoid navigation problems. (See *Creating Killer Web Sites* for more on frames.)

If your clients are really non-frame-aware, you can build the whole site without frames. It's not that hard to do, but it leads to more out-and-back trips. I prefer to use the frame-based version whenever possible.

The navigation area has two sections: the view section and the reference section. The *view section* is the nucleus of the project site. It contains all the time-based views of the project: the calendar, the schedule, and the chronology. The *reference section* contains the assets of the project: the resources, contacts, and a help page.

Opening a link in a new window allows the user to print the document. Simply use the right mouse button (Windows) or hold the mouse button down (Mac) to pop up a brand new window. Use this to compare two documents side-by-side or for easy printing.

We've gone a step further in providing a visual cue in the navigation area to reflect the state of the most recent choice. When you click on "help," for instance, the "help" link changes color – in this case, to white, matching the background of the document. This isn't done with any special scripting, it's done by brute force: switching to an entirely new frameset each time. You can use either text or images to get this effect. You could use a scripting language to switch the colors, but that can cause problems on certain systems. While this solution is admittedly inelegant, it never fails. This should be of no concern to the producer, however, since once it's set up there's no need to recode or maintain these pages.

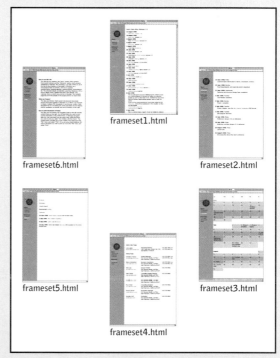

frameset1.html

frameset2.html

frameset3.html

frameset4.html

frameset5.html

frameset6.html

One frameset is actually six, allowing you to provide visual feedback of the area you're viewing.

Note: We use two side-by-side frames because so many clients have 14'' monitors. We prefer to maximize vertical real estate and put the navigation on the side. Alternatively, you can put a thin horizontal navigation frame on top.

Astro Cabs Project Calendar

	S	M	T	W	T	F	S
		1 June	2	3	4	5	6
	7	8	9	10	11	12	13
	14	15	16	17	18	19	20
	21	22	23	24	25	26	27
	28	29	30	1 July	2	3	4
	5	6	7	8	9	10	11
	12	13	14	15	16	17	18
	19	20	21	22	23	24	25
	26	27	28	29	30	31	1 Aug
	2	3	4	5	6	7	8
	9	10	11	12	13	14	15
	16	17	18	19	20	21	22
	23	24	25	26	27	28	29
	30	31					

Phases
- 1
- 2
- 3
- 4

Callouts:
- Strategy Session
- Questionnaires Due
- All Phase 1 documents due
- Design Review
- Content Freeze
- Beta Site
- Site Walkthrough
- Launch Date

The calendar shows the project from a bird's eye point of view. Building calendars strictly from HTML (using colored table cells, as shown at right) results in an uneven look. I recommend producing calendars in Photoshop, labeling key dates, and shipping it as a single GIF file.

The schedule typically has more detail in the upcoming two weeks. Make sure to keep it up to date.

The content window is where you put most of the reports, diagrams, discussions, and deliverables of the project. Anything you want to present goes into this same window, driven by the lists in the navigation area. If you are looking at Report A, then you go back to the chronology and click on Site map C, the new item (Site map C) appears in the content window, replacing the old item (Report A). Think of the navigation area as the controller for the viewing area and the viewing area as the controller for the content window.

Because you can put anything from a notice to an entire web site into the content window, you may set up your own links inside documents. You can also link to adjacent documents. When the user wants to see something else, she simply goes to the main window and selects from there.

The calendar

The calendar is the high-level view of the project. It isn't a day-to-day tool. It gives the big picture of the project, showing how much time it spans and where you are in it. Show the phases and the important milestones, any holidays or non-work periods, and the final deadline. The calendar should reflect any changes in the delivery date or major events, but you won't have to update it often.

After several experiments, we've found it's best to make the calendar a single large GIF image. To make sure everything is viewable at once, the only way you can be sure it will be seen properly is to freeze it in a single image. Use Photoshop's layers to make it easy to update and make a new GIF whenever you need to show a change to the calendar.

The schedule

The schedule is the secondary-level view of the project, showing only what is coming up. It focuses the team on impending deadlines. It's not meant to be a comprehensive chronology, but rather an overview of coming dates, phases, deliverables, and milestones. It highlights the next two to four weeks. The producer should regularly send the schedule to all team members as an email and modify this file to reflect new changes.

The chronology

The chronology is the main body of the project site and the final level of detail, showing daily – sometimes hourly –

updates to the project. It presents the developments you want to share with the client. It is an index of headlines and associated descriptive text. Add a new item to the chronology every time you have something to show or discuss. Most firms prefer to use a reverse-chronological list to show the most recent additions at the top. We've taken this one step further and added the latest project news to the top of the page, so everyone can keep up with recent developments. Past days are summarized in a short few sentences below each link. (See the chronology illustration on page 217).

(See the chronology illustration on page 217).

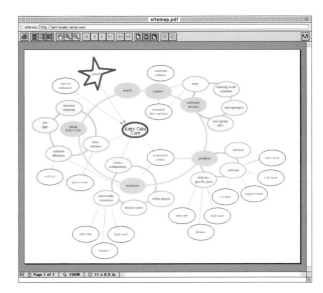

TIP

To write all content into a single window, you'll need to add a *target designator* to your HTML links. This works in both Microsoft and Netscape browsers – see the code at the book site (and see "Frame Magic" in *Creating Killer Web Sites*) for details.

A chronology will have many entries during periods of peak activity. You might see nothing happen for a week or so, but then you might see two or three entries per day as things heat up. Put the following kinds of things into the chronology. (An item with an asterisk (*) should also be distributed by email as a follow-up.)

Meeting agendas.* If you put meeting agendas on the site, you'll be able to compare them against meeting minutes, which helps you gauge the effectiveness of your meetings. Although you'll send the same information by email, putting it on the site gives people a chance to go over the agenda before the meeting.

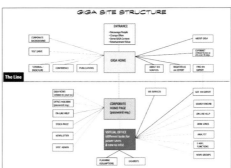

Meeting minutes.* Discussion is important, but what people take away from a meeting is more important. The producer takes notes during a meeting, follows the conversation, and keeps the discussion on topic. The producer should distribute task lists later. It's especially important to document decisions. Because revising decisions can easily invalidate the work that has been done, the producer keeps a clear record of all decisions on the site.

Site maps come in several varieties. They differ in complexity, functionality, and ease of manufacture. If you're trying to convey simple relationships, you can sketch things by hand, scan them, and put them on the site. The next step might be to use a program like Photoshop. However, you'll get more flexibility from a draw program

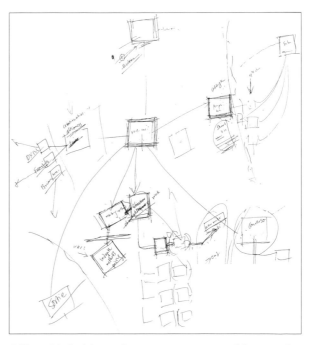

Different kinds of sites: an image map, a PDF prepared for processing in PageMaker, and a scanned drawing.

like Illustrator or a layout program like PageMaker. To present these documents, convert them to PDFs and include them on the project site. The image-map method of diagramming is effective, because you can build in hot spots that let the visitor "drill down" through the various thumbnails to see representative pages from the site (more on image maps in the "file format" section, later in this chapter).

Project sites
Christina Cheney on

"The creative aspect of building and maintaining a project site is developing a logical organization, good terminology, and implementing some interactivity. As I became more experienced with the site as a communication tool, I began to implement more features, like email threads, PDF presentations, and interactive forms. There is a continual process of improvement to meet client needs, like multiple levels of passwords for clients, outside contractors, and the internal team. Everyone on the client and the Verso teams participates in improving the project site because it is such a valuable tool."

– Christina Cheney, producer, Studio Verso

Project sites don't have to be gorgeous. Use a program like PageMill to make a simple one.

Other diagrams. You may want to show any number of other diagrams. I like to show any illustrations I think will be helpful.

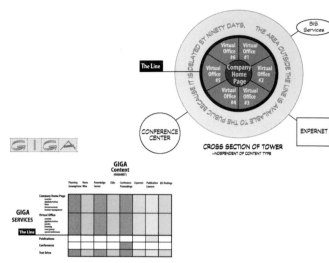

Another strength of a project site is its ability to present visual materials.

Visual explorations. I like to explore variations on a document in one direction at a time. Put each visual exploration up as its own entry in the chronology. (See Chapter 8 for more on iterative design.)

Presentations for your client. Visual designers can support clients by making presentations the client can then take to meetings. She may need special graphics, charts, and diagrams. Although most clients know how to use a

Put letters next to variants of the same thing for easy reference.

presentation program, putting the presentation on the Web and in the language of the site itself will go a long way toward making her look good. Besides, you'll know the presentation includes the most current versions of everything.

Beta tests. You can put your work-in-progress on the site and invite people to run through it. Set up a special test-page directory with links to only those items you want testers to see. Even if you make just a small change to a beta site, do not put it back up over the old one. Give it a new number (e.g., beta 2.4) and a new link.

The contact page

The first item in the reference section is the contact page. Contact information should be up front and comprehensive, including email addresses that pop up to open an email window. Put the producer's name and telephone number at the top of the contact page for easy access.

Because the contact page displays in a separate frame, some people will not know how to print it. A short training session or a visit to the help page should explain how to open the framed page in a new window. Of course, you can also periodically email contact information. Knowing it's always available on the project site may even reduce the need for printing.

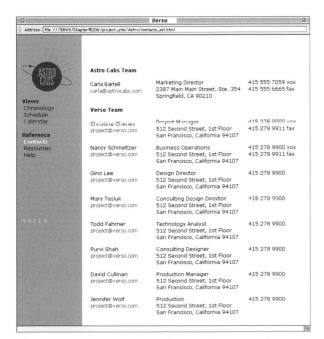

A contact page should have "mailto" pop-ups for easy email access to team members.

The resources page

Resources hold any timeless material you want to make available to the client or team. This page is an index, similar to the chronology, and the items themselves appear in the content window. If you have an important resource, like the contract or progress reports, you might want to add a link one level up, in the navigation area.

Contracts should go onto the project site. Because most projects end up differently than you planned, add any significant change to the contract in the form of an addendum.

Progress reports form an executive summary of the project's weekly progress. Imagine that the chronology has weekly progress reports. Because of the number of items there, it may be difficult to scroll down looking for them (though you could color them differently if you like). We've found it helpful to keep a page of links to these documents, so the client can find them easily.

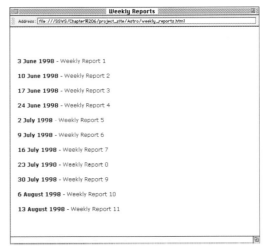

Provide links to regular or important progress reports. The actual documents appear in the content window.

Invoices. Keep a running invoice of hours spent, money charged, and amounts paid on the site. It should be available only to the client team leader and upper management. With the information on the project site, the bill will come as no surprise. This is especially true of fixed-bid projects, because they invariably have change orders. To see the cumulative results of change orders, show the running total. This information can go into the weekly reports the producer puts on the site.

Pre-existing content. It may be helpful to scan documents, brochures, color schemes, logos, and other assets that

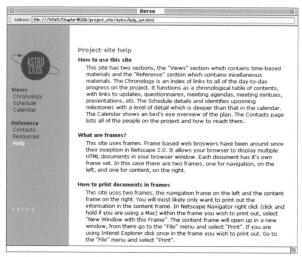

The help page is mostly for people who aren't used to frames, PDFs, etc.

people will want to refer to. Only do it if it pertains to the web project.

Other content. You may generate diagrams or get statements from people that you want to put here for everyone to see. Anything that doesn't go into the chronology goes here.

The help page

Never assume your closest contacts are the only ones using the site. A key decisionmaker may want to show the site to a close associate – now you have two potential novices surfing the site unaided. It must be intuitive and clear, but you should also provide help to get them out of any traps. For instance, using frames makes printing difficult; provide instructions on printing frames up front, as well as other helpful hints.

A project site is a serious undertaking. It requires dedication, know-how, and the right tools to keep it working. This section addresses some of the details involved in keeping your project site productive.

Dave's rules

A project site is a tool. We've designed the one you see in this chapter for easy maintenance. Here are some rules I've found that help make the project site more effective.

Live on the site. A project site is only as good as the information on it. The more time you spend working on it, the more familiar you'll be with it. When something important goes up, remind everyone to see it. Look at the log files, so you can see who is using the site and who isn't.

Only the producer can update the project site. Everyone else has read-only access to the project site. The producer makes all the changes. This ownership helps reinforce the producer as the driver of the process.

The project site is not a free-for-all discussion. It is a one-to-many discussion with the producer at the center. If people could express their views in a forum-style

conversation, politics and the hierarchy of people's places on

the totem pole would make it hard for everyone to speak freely. The producer moves things forward by having one conversation with everyone via the project site.

Never revise the chronology. You can add items or change deadlines, but never delete or modify a document you have put on the site, even if it is a project timeline. The chronology records the entire history of the project. For example, if you make a spelling change to a site, duplicate the site and include it as a new entry.

Write well, concisely, and consistently. Make it as easy as possible to get through the project site. The shorter your messages, the better. Edit everything, including email messages, to make them readable.

Enforce strict version control by numbering and dating everything. If you are on the phone with the client, you want to be sure you are looking at the same image at the same time. If you number everything, you have a reference to confirm that you are on the same page. (See "version control," below.)

Put up only what you want the client to see. A project site is for client-contractor communication. Do not put up internal discussions or intermediate versions unless they are important to the client. Normally, you'll be communicating with your internal team via email, phone, and meetings. If necessary, make a separate project site for internal use.

Archive assets off-line. Save sketches, photocopies, memos, emails, and internal communication in a separate file. Not all of it has to go onto the project site.

Annotate and update the schedule as necessary. Always keep the latest schedule available at the top of the site and archive old schedules. As you set dates for new deliverables, keep the schedule in tune with what is just up ahead. The upcoming two weeks of a project may have more detail and command more attention than any other part. Use colors and concise notes to project short-term and long-term objectives clearly.

Make sure all decisionmakers bookmark the project site. The more they know about the project, the better your chances of getting approval. Send them email when new developments occur on the site.

Version control

Number everything you put on the site consistently. Because the site shows progression over time, visitors will see the same things over again, often with only small details changing from one day to the next. I use the following scheme to number my presentations:

    Release
    Item description
    Version
    Variation

Release, as discussed in chapters that follow, designates what goes into the first set of deliverables. Releases allow you to put into a future release what you can't finish by the coming deadline.

Description. In a complicated project, a release will have many components. You may want a descriptor for each component as part of the numbering scheme. You could use a descriptor scheme like this:

    SiteMap
    Questionnaire
    FunctionalSpec
    Budget
    Graphic
    Navigation

Note: Do *not* abbreviate these descriptions with cryptic acronyms, like SM, QU, etc. Make it clear – spell it out.

Version tracks the development of a feature you want to refine. For example, version 1 may be the core page, version 2 may be the core page plus one second-level page, and so on. Or version 1 may be the green version or the big version. You iterate within a version, adding variation designators to each iteration. Sometimes a version will have many changes, other times only a few.

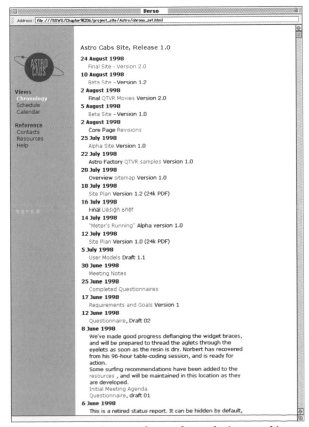

Create your own version-control system by numbering everything properly.

For a given project, I might come up with a version plan ahead of time. For example, I might say "First, we'll work on the overall metaphor (version 1.x), then we'll look at which background images to use (2.x), then we'll do logo placement (3.x), color studies (4.x), typeface choices (5.x), navigation (6.x), and then we'll see where to go from there."

Use decimals for intra-version explorations. If you're working on a particular feature, you might make a set of images and present them to the client. That set will be version 1.1. The client likes some of them, but it's not conclusive. So you work some more and present version 1.2. Several iterations later, version 1.13 is a winner, and you can move on to the next version. (Note that these are not decimal numbers. Version 1.13 – pronounced "one point thirteen" – is eleven iterations away from 1.2.)

Variations are items you want to compare within a version. Because you'll often put these on the same page, I prefer a letter designator to a number. In the example above, version 1.1 may have had six variations, version 1.9 may have had four (1.9a, 1.9b, 1.9c, 1.9d), and version 1.13 may have had only two (1.13a and 1.13b). *Note: You don't need a variation letter if you have no alternates.*

A particular graphic, then, might be:

Release 1 Graphic Version 3.2b

Or, alternatively,

R1graphicV3.2b

You can use these designators to name your files as well. You could call that file "R1.1V2.1," but you may want to use more descriptive file names.

Each graphic, each site map, and each version of a web site or logo or budget should have its own unique identifier, and that identifier should go into the HTML title of the page to display at the top of the screen. That way, when you are on the telephone, you can make sure you are both looking at the exact same page.

Note: There is no phase designator – phases are part of the process, not the deliverables. Increment version numbers without regard to phases.

File formats

A project site should be a visual experience. To make images for your web site, you need to choose the appropriate file formats. The more you know about building web sites, the easier it will be to build one by hand and incorporate the images. If you are unfamiliar with web-page techniques, find a person or a program to automate this for you.

TIP Know your client's hardware and software setup. If some people in the company use an old browser, you may have to "detune" your site to accommodate their needs.

Raster formats. Although designers prefer to work in programs like Photoshop, you don't want to put a Photoshop file onto the Web. Instead, compress the file, using a file format like GIF or PNG. Everything I'm going to talk about here refers to comps, site maps, and other images that contribute to the *project*, not the final production version of the site. When you get into production, you'll have to make the images for your site much more carefully.

When making images to put on the project site, you must know the connection speed or modem speed with which your client will connect. If your client connects at 28.8kbps or lower, take care to reduce the color depth* of your images. If the client has an ISDN or T1 connection, you can ship larger images. For an average project, I make sample web pages about 700 pixels wide by 1200 tall and 6-7 bits deep. These files usually compress to around 60K to 80K – good enough for development work.

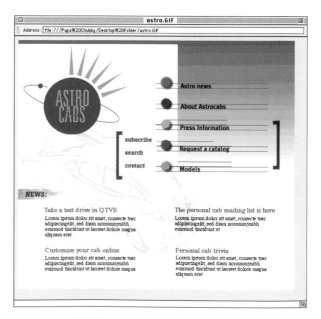

An HTML model. This entire page is one GIF image.

You must also consider the amount of memory (RAM) the client has. If the client has very little memory (I mean on his *computer*!), you must beware of image inflation.* If your client has 16 megabytes of RAM or less, try to keep your image sizes down – not the compressed file sizes, but the actual image dimensions.

HTML. Many of your documents will be in HTML. You can hand-code HTML the way most developers do, or you can use a visual editor like NetObjects Fusion. Another option for documents like contracts is to use your word processor's ability to "save as HTML."

PDFS. At Verso, we use Adobe PDF to make our local desktop files web-ready. GIF or PNG compression will work for many images, but we often lay out pages and presentations using combinations of text and images. This is where the PDF format comes in handy.

We often use PageMaker to lay out a series of page designs. We "print" a multi-page document to a file and put that file on the Web in seconds. Sometimes, we add navigational or "hot link" elements to a PDF, linking items to other pages. This requires a separate program called Acrobat Exchange to create hot-spots on PDF documents. This can be an even faster way to build flexible project sites, although the process is roughly the equivalent of using an image-mapping program.

You can make a PDF of a budget you've built in a spreadsheet. Simply "print" the spreadsheet using the PDF driver, and the spreadsheet file is ready for the Web.

Todd Fahrner on PDFs

"Making PDFs is as easy as printing. After you install Acrobat 3.0 or later, all applications will include 'print to PDF' in their printing options.

"After you 'print,' a PDF will appear on your desktop or in a folder. You can open the PDF with Acrobat Exchange and add annotations, like web or internal hyperlinks, 'sticky notes,' movies, web-ready forms, and so on. You can then put the PDF on the web, email it, or keep it as 'digital hardcopy' for your records.

"If your document is printed, and you can't get at the source file to prepare a PDF, scan the document and use Acrobat Capture to convert it to PDF. Unlike a normal scanned graphic, the resulting PDF can be very small on disk, and most text will be fully searchable."

– Todd Fahrner, design technologist, Studio Verso

Thumbnails. It's useful to show many variations on one page for easy comparison, but showing them full-size would take too long to load. It often helps to make thumbnails of concepts and sketches, allowing visitors to "drill through" to see the larger image or document.

PDF Distiller can turn a PageMaker document into a presentation.

Thumbnails give people more choices and make for faster browsing.

* See Chapter 3 of *Creating Killer Web Sites* for a detailed explanation of these concepts.

Image maps. Image maps are effective because the visitor can click on areas of a diagram to see expanded views or more detail. You can use image maps to present many kinds of diagrams, especially site diagrams.

There are many ways to make a diagram like this. You can draw on paper and scan the drawing. You can use special diagramming software. You can use a vector-based drawing program, like Adobe Illustrator. You can use PageMaker, Photoshop, or even a Java-based program like Randomnoise's Coda. To make an image map, you'll have to export your image as a large GIF or PNG image and then use a special program (like ImageMapper or Mapthis!) to actually make the image map.

Maintaining image-mapped diagrams is laborious. For that reason, we usually try to get by with PDFs first.

How to add to the project site

The producer sets up and maintains the site, either by hand-coding HTML or through a WYSIWYG editor like NetObjects Fusion. In either case, the producer should be set up to write files to the server. Fortunately, new tools make this task easier than it used to be.

Uploading via FTP. If the producer is using a web server, she will either use a separate FTP program or one built into her editor. In either case, she must have access to the proper directory on the server. Because access to servers involves UNIX commands and permissions, I won't try to explain how it's all done here. Take my word for it: when this stuff works, it's great, and when it doesn't, you need a professional, not me.

Image maps are effective but take more time to make and maintain.

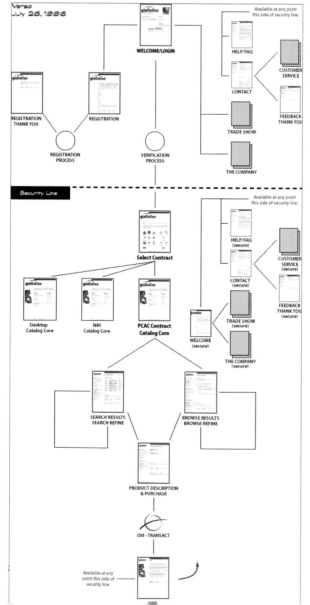

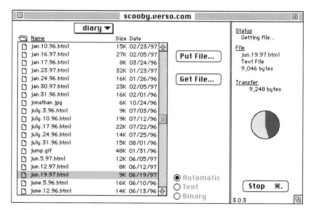

Uploading an update via FTP.

Uploading an update via NFS is convenient and intuitive.

Uploading via NFS. If you have a direct connection to your server, you can use an NFS program to create a folder on your computer. It's more direct than FTP, and it accomplishes the same thing. To upload to the site, drop new files into the folder, and they will go onto the site.

Serving from the desktop. It's easy to serve entire web sites and all your local files right from your own machine. Several free server programs can put your designated files and folders on the Web, where you can get at them from anywhere. Using personal web-server software, you can protect files and folders, make them available to the surfing public, and move files over the Internet as easily as you move them on your local network.

Unlike some of the more powerful software designed for dedicated servers, personal web servers are easy to set up and administer, and they don't demand much of your system's resources. Details vary among the half dozen or so personal web servers (they come bundled with browsers and operating systems these days), but the general idea is that you open the program and specify a directory on your machine as the *root* (top level) of your web site. Anything you put in that folder becomes available on the Web. This is quicker than copying files

to a remote server, where file structure, permissions, and version-control issues can be confusing. Personal web servers usually log traffic, which you can monitor to confirm that the right people are visiting. You can even set up CGI scripts with some personal web servers, as well as FTP, news (NNTP), and other services.

If you have more than one computer in your immediate work area, personal web servers can facilitate quick cross-machine site development and testing. With FTP services enabled, they can even replace other file-sharing software. This is particularly useful in a cross-platform environment. Finally, personal web servers can help you keep your work in sync at home and in the office – use your browser from home to "surf" the files and folders of your office computer.

Secret Weapon Number Five

The project site

The project site is our "killer app." It is not only the best way to work with clients, it's a great way to get clients. Showing prospective clients your meticulously maintained project site shows your degree of professionalism.

Christina Cheney on

"Email is not only an essential communication tool, it is also a convenient way to track and view progress. Organize incoming email according to your process. I often rename the subject field of a message before storing it, so it clearly describes the contents. I keep every email message, except the most trivial.

I often post running email threads (discussions) to the project site as they progress. I edit as necessary to keep things readable."

– Christina Cheney, producer, Studio Verso

	Label	Who	Date	K	Subject
		Jordan	Wednesday	2	Action – write cellular cab white paper
		Lisa	Wednesday	2	Clarify – When is the next meeting
		Kayla	Wednesday	2	Response – Danny should write the white paper
		Daryn	Thursday	2	Question – where can we get taxi stats
		Nathan	Thursday	2	Response – cellular white paper will be ready by Tuesday
		Daryn	Thursday	2	Question – Astro cabs logo for brochures
		Gary	Thursday	2	Idea – Ask people to contribute content, start with Lisa
		Danny	Friday	2	Response – Astro cabs logo
		Nathan	Friday	2	Request for discussion – Astro cabs launch plan – conference call
		Jordan	Monday	2	Help requested – Need content for family page
		Daryn	Monday	2	Help offered – I can write for the site. Can I help?
		Nathan	Monday	2	Clarify – Which sections use stats?

Using your own set of keywords for a project helps the producer sort messages.

The project site

Project sites are quite young. New tools and ideas will extend the project site's capabilities. This section points to other developments and possibilities for improving the basic project site.

Subcontractors

It is tempting to think of the project site as a place where *everything* happens. But if you are working with a subcontractor – say, an illustrator – you don't want her uploading roughs and comps to the general project site without your permission. Instead, set up a private sub-project site, so you can look at her work and send the URL on to others who need to see it. Alternatively, you can set up a "receiving dock" (a page where contractors can upload their latest graphics and text). Using a personal web server, those assets land in a folder on your desktop.

Interactive Groupware

Several companies now offer software that lets you inter-act with team members in various ways. Producers are experimenting with new technologies to improve commu-nication. *Groupware* is the catch-all term for these tech-nologies. The two kinds of groupware are synchronous and asynchronous. Using synchronous groupware, everyone is present at his/her computer at the same time – the Internet extension of the conference call.

Video conferencing. Videoconferencing via the Web has been around longer than you might think. It started at Cornell University with a program called CU-SeeMe that quickly became a hit in the academic world. The images were small, black-and-white, jerky, and blurry, with no sound. But now, thanks to the efforts of thousands of engineers and tons of venture capital, new systems are hitting the market that deliver medium-sized, 256-color, fluttery, blurry images with marginally acceptable sound.

Many factors conspire to keep videoconferencing a few generations away from being truly satisfying. Video requires a quantum leap in bandwidth – only experimental and expensive systems carry it reliably today. Until the protocols and technologies improve, video images on the Web will be diced, if not dicey.

Whiteboards. A *virtual whiteboard* is software that lets you share cursor movements among distributed teams. For instance, if you're looking at a diagram of a circuit board

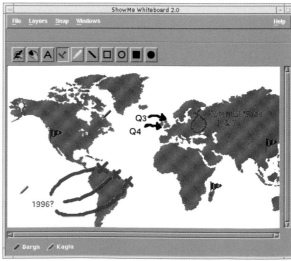

CU-SeeMe: the first videoconferencing system on the Web.

Groupware allows people to interact simultaneously via the Internet.

with thousands of tiny lines, you can control a yellow cursor, while your counterpart controls a red one. Using cursors, you can talk about specific lines and points on the image. With an *overlay*, you can make chalk-talk-style diagrams and use gestures to illustrate your thoughts.

Virtual tourguides. Remote-control software will let a producer take control of the client's screen and "drive" while giving the client a hands-free virtual tour of the site. One such program, Virtual Places by AOL, lets you design your own people icons (called avatars) and lets you even design your own bus. People then "get in" the bus and can make comments via on-screen thought bubbles as the bus driver gives a tour. While it is cool to do this on screen, you can also do it by telephone, making sure you are both at the same URL simultaneously.

Some groupware lets you give a guided tour of the Web, with others "riding along" on your virtual bus.

Project-management software

Traditional project-management software focuses on resource allocation. The project site is a tool for *communication*, and it is going to get better. Some advanced developers have already constructed template-based solutions on top of existing content-management systems. At Verso, we now use CGI scripts to connect our project sites to a small database that helps collate answers to questionnaires and other feedback.

What is the future of the project site? The custom solutions will get more custom and more elaborate. They will also take more time and cost more money. We know that start-up companies are working on new solutions that will give us even more power with less programming. When the first wave of web-based project-management tools hits the market, we will be the first to try them. I hope the hand-coding methods described in this chapter will be obsolete by late 1998.

Within the next few years, new extranet tools will help producers build and run project sites. Java-based appli-cations will make all the capabilities described in this chapter look like grade-school exercises. *See the book site for more exciting developments in project-management software.*

Use your imagination

It's important to remember that the project site, email, and videoconferencing are great, but there's no substitute for a handwritten note or buying lunch for the team. Sometimes, Fed-Exing hard copy really is the answer. I've found it helpful to print project resources, cut them out, and tape them to team members' monitors for handy reference. I call people to tell them to look at the project site. As you work with project sites, you'll find more and more things you can do with them, but don't expect them to make you a good communicator (or a good espresso).

Use your imagination to see how you can improve on the concept and make it work for your situation.

Client Team	Phases and Actions	Project Management	Design Staff	Technical Staff
	Phase 1: Strategy and tactics			
	Project Tools	•		
•	Contract	•		
•	Schedule	•		
•	Questionnaires	•		
	User Models	•	•	
	Goals & Requirements			
•	Strategic Brief	•	•	
	Creative Brief	•	•	
	Technical Brief	•	•	•
•	Basic Content Plan	•	•	
	Site Map	•	•	•
	Engineering Specification	•	•	•
	Final Schedule	•	•	
	Final Estimate	•		
	Phase 2: Creative development			
•	Content Identification	•	•	
•	Content Schedule	•		
•	Content Development	•	•	
•	Editing and Preperation	•		
	Initial Design Studies (concepting / branding)	•	•	
	Comps (look and feel / navigation / UI)	•	•	•
		•		
	Prototypes (final direction)	•	•	•
	Working Model (implementation)	•	•	
	Phase 3: Technical development			
	Production	•	•	•
	Engineering	•	•	•
	Alpha	•	•	•
	Internal QA	•	•	•
	Beta 1, 2	•	•	•
	Internal QA	•	•	•
	Final Internal Site	•	•	•
	Phase 4: Delivery			
•	Content Freeze	•		
•	External Staging	•	•	•
•	External QA	•	•	•
•	Site Measurement	•	•	•
	Documentation/Templates	•	•	•
	Preflight Check	•	•	•
•	Launch	•		•
	Strategy Assessment	•	•	
•	Maintenance	•	•	•

The following four chapters cover the four phases of the Verso project-management system shown in this diagram.

"The important thing
about our relationship with clients
is that I spend as much of my time
on education
as I do on anything else...
How do you effectively communicate?

You spend a lot of time with people
and you look
at a lot of buildings with them.

Sometimes when we attempt
to educate clients and have
explained an issue several times,
they say,
'Hartman, that's bullshit!'
Maybe it is.
And we have to rethink it."

– George Hartman, architect, in *The Fountainheadache*

Chapter 7

Phase One – Strategy and tactics

No one wants brochureware, yet clients often begin by asking designers to put their printed material onto their web site and add some animated buttons.

Strategy and tactics

Chapter guide

IF YOU START WITH BROCHURES, there's a good chance you'll end up with brochureware.

How do you avoid putting brochureware on the Web? What should a web site try to accomplish? Will it be worth the effort? If the client and contractor work as a team to define the problem together, the strategy that results will be more appropriate for the Web and less like brochureware. Designers must look at the business problems first, so they can put the web effort in context. Then they work with the client to decide which of several alternative choices will, when implemented, lead to a successful web site.

This chapter describes the research and documents that pave the way for a successful site. If the strategy isn't right, all the tactical values won't matter. If the documents don't convey the strategy, the team will be inefficient. It's not as bad as it seems – few projects need every single document described in this chapter, and many of the documents are one-pagers.

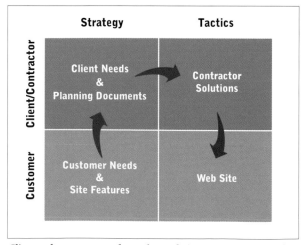

Client and contractor work together to design a strategy that works for the client, and a site that works for the customers.

Planning saves money

For a typical project, clients can expect to pay about 20% of the price for strategy and 25-30% for project management. The strategy and tactics phase should take one to six weeks. Almost half of the work does not go into the site but into a comprehensive set of documents the customer won't see. Why not just skip all that documentation and get into exploring design alternatives?

Clients are not used to paying for strategy. In many creative endeavors, the strategic phase is missing entirely. When it's time to make an annual report or another set of brochures or to redesign the product, the client usually knows what she wants. Many contractors are willing to skip the planning phase and get right into design. Because designing for the Web requires new thinking, the strategy phase is actually the most important part of the project. It doesn't matter how much the client likes it if the customers don't find it compelling.

Designers don't exactly embrace this process, either. If you follow the guidelines of this chapter, you'll see there are a lot of documents to write. Contractors don't think of themselves as writers. The last thing they want to do is put together a book of written documents, with proper grammar, spelling, and formatting. Yet without these documents, the project is much more likely to run into trouble.

Enter the producer. Producers should feel comfortable writing all these documents. Because writing is difficult under any circumstances, the producer should concentrate on keeping all documents as short and clear as possible. Good editing skills are as important as good writing skills.

Small design groups should consider adding a freelance producer to the team.

A set of planning documents is the blueprint for a successful web site. In Phase One, the producer and client

> "Strategic planning gives you a roadmap for reaching your business goals. It allows you to plan not only where you are going, but how you will get there. Strategic planning should take into account a company's current situation, market conditions, and business objectives. That means finding out what a company's many constituents – including customers, the press, analysts, and Wall Street – think about that company, its products, and the markets it serves. Armed with this information, you can make more informed decisions about what your company needs to do to reach its business goals."
>
> – Andy Cunningham, CEO, Cunningham Communications

send out questionnaires to customers and prospects, do market research, evaluate the results, and set the goals for the project. The designer constructs user models to represent the site audience, then writes the overall strategic, technical, and content plans that will guide the project through the next three phases.

This chapter is broken into two main sections: strategy and tactics. You could give each its own phase and create a five-phase process, but I've chosen to keep them together as Phase One.

Strategy and tactics

1 Strategic planning

2 Tactical planning

During the first part of the phase, see how the web strategy fits into the overall business strategy, then refine the web strategy to include overall site goals, design goals, branding, user-interface, and technical goals.

Marketing strategy

A good web strategy fits in with the overall business strategy. It's usually best to start with a focused, service-oriented site and keep expanding from there. If you define the audience as "all teenagers" or "all people surfing from noon to 1pm," you will have to launch something the size of clnet to be successful. Here are some hypothetical examples to show the process in action.

Custom windows. Suppose your client sells made-to-order windows for houses. The first question to ask is "Would you like to support your dealer network, or would you like to take orders from customers directly?" If the answer is "Both," then it's time to talk to customers. If customers surfing the Web are much happier ordering online than being connected to a salesperson, you should focus on a site that satisfies serious do-it-yourselfers. It may turn out that these people weren't ordering through your normal sales channel, so you're expanding the customer base – a win for everyone.

Insurance. Suppose you sell insurance or a high-end service. Your biggest accounts may be too important to leave to a web site. Target your top-twenty customers and make sure they are cared for with personal contact on a regular basis. If a special private web site (also known as an extranet) enhances your relationship, do something special for these customers. If, for example, 50 of these top customers don't have web connections, you may want to buy them PCs and set them up, with the home page set to their extranet site. This is building customer loyalty.

> "A little research showed
>   that visitors coming to one of our
>   memorabilia sites
>   from a search engine like Excite
>   spend an average of twelve cents,
>   whereas a visitor coming from
> a movie fan-club site generates
> seventy-five cents in online revenues.
>   We spend a lot more on advertising
>   at fan-club sites
>   than we do at Excite."
>
> **– John Wells, CEO of Netstores, Inc.**

Your next 2000 customers are ripe for receiving outstanding service on the Web. From questionnaires, you find that customers can't get in touch with an agent when they want, and they'd like to track their account information online. Instead of increasing staff, create a web site that serves these 2000 customers. Before trying to bring in new business, establish an online service that works overtime for these 2000 people.

After it is working, you'll find it easy to get new customers by pointing to your existing satisfied customer base. By not going for the beginners first, you can reduce costs and increase profits early. Make sites deep before making them wide. Make them work before making them big.

> "We sent out questionnaires to learn
> what people wanted from the IRS site.
> They didn't want to order forms
>   or learn how to contact the IRS.
> They wanted as little contact
>   with the government as possible.
>   They wanted to
>   file their taxes online and
> get refund checks."
>
> **– Greg Woods, National Performance Review,**
> **Office of the Vice President**

A local weekly newsletter. Suppose you want to create an online directory of local art and entertainment events. I don't recommend "putting up your stuff" and hoping for enough traffic from search engines to sell banner ads. Instead, look at the competition to see if they have any kind of edge into the local market, then break the surfing audience into groups:

> Nonlocal surfers
> Locals looking for something to do
> Event planners
> Local parents
> Local kids
> Event promoters/booking agencies
> Local press
> Travelers
> Locals not looking for something to do

Event planners are probably the most profitable group, because if they link to your site, you'll get many more visits. The local press also gives the site quite a bit of leverage. Consumerwise, "locals looking for something to do" is your most important category. On the other hand, "locals not looking for something to do" is probably the best group to convert into "locals looking for something to do," so they are next. Knowing that people ages 14-24 most often go to movies, we decide to focus on locals

24-40 who go to bars and enjoy jazz, rock, and other live shows. Looking for a minimum-effort first release, we break the visitors into consumer groups and referral groups:

	Consumer	Referral
Release 1.0	locals 24-40 looking for something to do	local press event planners
Release 2.0	locals 24-40 not looking for something to do	travelers

If you can do well with the Release 1.0 groups, the site will prosper. Write a document that describes what it would take to satisfy these three groups, then plan to expand the site as you learn more about what customers want.

Customer profiles

Geoff Moore, in his excellent book on consumer marketing, *Crossing the Chasm,* explains the purpose of creating customer profiles:

"Markets are impersonal, abstract things... they do not elicit the cooperation of one's intuitive faculties... We need something that feels a lot more like real people. However, since we do not have real live customers as yet, we are just going to have to make them up. Target-customer characterization is a formal process for making up these images.

"The idea is to create as many characterizations as possible, one for each different type of customer and application for the product... Using the scenarios as a guide, rate the compelling reason to buy at each customer-application intersection... Apply traditional market research techniques to evaluating each of these candidate market segments. Use the market research to impose a final priority order on the candidate segments, producing a hot-target list."

Customer profiles are one of our secret weapons in site design. Always make profiles, even if you don't think you have time. I know three ways to get customer profiles:

Get them from real customers
Make them up carefully
Make them up quickly

Real-world profiles. To create real-world profiles, listen to the marketing department and listen to any customers you can find. Marketing departments typically know a lot about their customers and can help find groups of people to

profile. The other approach is to send out questionnaires. At Studio Verso, we write and send out questionnaires for almost every job. We sometimes call a market-research firm and ask how we can work together to profile the customers for the site.

In writing questionnaires, we often create three versions: one for the people in our client's company, one for our client's select customers, and one for prospective customers. We get approval on the questionnaires and send them out. This lets us get to work on other planning documents while waiting for the questionnaires to come back.

Questionnaires to **potential customers** should put the site in context of all the other sites vying for their attention. What would it take to get you to come to a new site? What would you like to be able to do that you can't today? What would it take to get you to spend time at the site?

In a questionnaire sent to **dedicated existing customers**, ask for suggestions. They are often willing to spend time elaborating on their needs and wishes. Focus on specific problems and solutions. In particular, find the mission-critical issues that are best served by a web site and how customers would like to access those services. What is the site doing now that it could do better? What are the three most important things you would like the site to do?

Secret Weapon Number Six

Strategy

That a web-design group goes through a strategy phase, or better, becomes known for the quality of their strategic work – is a differentiating factor. Any design group whose producers work on strategy and solving the client's business problem is going to look attractive to clients who take the Web seriously.

Earl Sasser is the guru of customer service. His books and articles are must-reads, not only for web designers but for most of their clients. He publishes occasionally in the *Harvard Business Review* (reprints are available from HBR at their web site). Look for these publications:

Heskett, J., Schlesinger, L., and Sasser, W. E. *The Service Profit Chain.* New York: Free Press, 1997.

Jones, T. O., and Sasser, W. E., Jr. "Why Satisfied Customers Defect." *Harvard Business Review* (November-December, 1995).

Reichheld, F., and Sasser, W. E., Jr. "Zero Defections: Quality Comes to Services." *Harvard Business Review* (September-October, 1990).

Sending questionnaires to **people within the client company** gives them a voice and keeps them involved. Try to determine hot buttons and concerns. Yes, there will be political battles, but it's important to get everyone involved in the process from the start. You can get great information from customer-service representatives and others in contact with customers daily.

In reporting on the results of the questionnaires, summarize answers that can be quantified with charts and tables. Put cogent individual comments into the document. Draw conclusions and see if the client agrees. From the categories of people you've contacted, draw your customer profiles and rank the customer groups by criteria that let you decide who the first customers will be.

Make them up carefully. Following Geoff Moore's advice and using techniques developed at ad agencies, we often throw ourselves into the world of a small group of representative customers. We create fictional people who fit into the categories we're aiming for. We make up names for them: Zack, Esther, Jimena, Bobby, etc. For a prototypical customer, we establish age, day-to-day routines, amount of time spent reading, leisure time, budgetary

constraints, favorite television shows, etc. Then we get magazines the person might buy and surround ourselves with those images. We cut up a dozen magazines and put the ads and articles all over our office walls. Each person gets a name and a wall of magazine images and articles. We make these people as real as possible, discussing where they like to eat, what kinds of friends they have, etc.

Illustrations by Philippe Augy

Bobby
Age: fifteen
Lives: Modesto, CA
Occupation: High school student
Family: working parents, one sister.
Enjoys: sports, friends, debate
Media: 2 magazines, 1 hour of television, 1 hour surfing, no books.

Jimena
Age: 30
Lives: Brooklyn, NY
Occupation: Wife
Family: husband, 7-yr-old daughter.
Enjoys: food, health, collects kachina dolls
Media: 6 magazines, 1 hour of television, .25 hour surfing, reads one novel a week.

Esther
Age: 58
Lives: Sedona, AZ
Occupation: Widow
Family: 2 sons
Enjoys: food, fitness, playing bridge online.
Media: 3 magazines, .75 hour of television, .5 hour surfing, reads one novel and one nonfiction book a week.

Zack
Age: 39
Lives: Chicago, IL
Occupation: Salesman
Family: Divorced, 3-yr-old daughter.
Enjoys: sports, betting, investing, camping
Media: 2 finance magazines, 1 paper, .3 hour surfing

Profiling four made-up people helps you visualize the customers. Illustrations by Phillipe Augy.

Now think of Zack surfing the Web. What are Zack's surfing choices? Where does he go first? What has he bookmarked? How does he use bookmarks? What does he tell his friends to see? What holds his interest? What makes him impatient? How can Zack have his needs met on the site?

Make them up quickly. For whatever reason – usually limited time – your client might want to "skip Phase One as much as possible." In an accelerated Phase One, the client must assume responsibility for shortcutting the normal procedure. Insist that the client provide the customer profiles. Send a handful of questionnaires and ask the client to fill one out for each fictional visitor, specifying demographics, psychographics, technographics, etc. Have the client sign off and take responsibility for this "research."

The strategic brief

Once you have generated some good ideas, know who the users are, and have looked at the original goals, you can write the real mission statement for the site. The strategic brief covers:

Mission statement
Marketing goals
Competitive analysis
User requirements
Branding strategy
Measurements of success

A mission statement is usually one or two sentences that drives the project, reminding everyone what the key issues are. A good mission statement helps keep the team focused. (As an exercise, see if you can articulate the mission statements for each of the sites in the first half of this book.)

Marketing goals describe the overall objectives that the owners of the site would like the site to achieve. The goals for it should be divided into sections, by priority. The goals for a relatively modest site that advertises a garden center, for example, might be:

RELEASE 1.0

1. Get people excited about plants!
   - perennials, annuals, trees, shrubs, herbs, orchids, seasonals, etc.
   - do something that catches the attention of the press

2. Offer products for sale by mail, but don't spend too much
   - specials, seeds, tools, work clothes, etc.

3. Give information for care and feeding of all major plant groups
   - low-cost post-sale support

4. Give company and "what's different about us" information

5. Tell people how to get to the center

6. Advertise local events, workshops, and sponsorships

7. Collect addresses from locals to send them email or paper newsletter

RELEASE 2.0

1. Encourage an enthusiastic community of gardeners to participate and contribute

2. If things are going well, automate the catalog and order process with a database and consider adding a local database of gardeners and services

This is a goals document. It has no feature list, existing content, or deliverables. It lists goals, ranked in order of priorities. A more complicated goals document, like that for the RREEF site, discusses the goals in detail by customer group.

Secret Weapon Number Seven

Customer profiles

At Studio Verso, creating customer profiles is one of the most valuable tools in our toolkit.

It gives us a small number of people to satisfy.

If you had only four people coming to your site, and losing one of them meant a 25% reduction in traffic, what would you be willing to do to keep them all coming back?

Competitive analysis. This doesn't have to be a long document, but it should accurately describe what you know about the particular industry on the Web. If possible, it should contain some idea of what the competition is planning to launch in the next six months. This document summarizes what is working and what is not working for the client's customer groups at various sites.

User requirements. Once you have completed the user models, you can then "ask" each hypothetical user what he/she wants to get out of the site. List both *requirements* (a particular visitor has a very slow modem and hates to wait more than 20 seconds for a page to load) and a *wish list* (someone wants to be able to chat with others who visit the site).

The branding strategy. Brands represent more than the use of symbols, fonts, color combinations, and navigation bars. Think of a web site as part of a larger branding strategy in a broader theater of communications, where competing brands contend for mind – and marketshare. Within a web site, instant gratification and new forms of interaction create branding possibilities that move beyond the static images on magazine pages or billboards, beyond the seductive, moving images of television. Web designers can use the web's functionality to connect to customers with unprecedented intimacy. Think carefully about the role your web site will play, frustrating or delighting customers as part of this larger demand fulfillment system that itself becomes part of the brand experience.

Branding basics

Branding – building a name people recognize – is a challenge. A web branding strategy can be a paragraph or a standards manual. It's important to know which site you are visiting. If you're at the Mustang site, are you also at the Ford site? If you're at news.com, are you also at clnet? Does it make sense to develop a design hierarchy with navigation bars at the top of every page? If so, it must be done carefully. It's possible to "overbrand" and not give people a chance to get at the content.

Established companies should make sure their corporate site doesn't interfere with their product sites, yet it should be easy to get from a product site to the corporate site. Know the elements that form the permanent architecture of the site and those that form the "exhibits" that come and go over time. Translate your company colors to

Overbranding: corporate identity should not force scrolling.

browser-safe colors and enforce the color standards. Be consistent in your use and sizes of type, and make sure the overall navigation scheme is scalable.

Startups need to keep it simple. Don't separate your logo from your name – your logo isn't ready to stand on its own. If you're a web-based company, do all your design at 72 DPI with

Consistent use of color and type is part of branding.

the 216 browser-safe colors before designing your stationery and cards. Don't hire a print-design group to do your online visuals. Find a group who has done online branding and knows the issues.

Measurements of success

How do you know when you've won? When the boss likes it? When you win the High Five Award for excellence in site design? What counts is the impact it has on the customer community. If you've done everything right, but your competition launches an even more ambitious project the week before you do, your minimum requirements for a win just went up. Define ways to measure profitability and the growth of your most profitable customer groups.

Fewer negatives. If you have fewer calls, complaints, questions, requests, or expenses after launching the site, that is a good indication you're headed in the right direction. Reduce actual measurable costs, and you are doing something right.

More positives. Don't count hits, count customers. Count the people using your site, because they are helping you build equity on the Net. Emails are a good sign of participation. Repeat visitors are nice, but credit-card orders are nicer. Impulse buyers buy the "specials" appearing at the top of your pages, and that's something to build on. Use tracking software to see if people are bookmarking your site, how much time they're spending in the site, how many pages they visit, etc.

During Phase One, define exactly what will be on the weekly reports you'll receive after the site launches. Those measurables will help you focus on results as you continue the process.

Functional strategy

Two technical documents serve as the foundation for all the scripting, style sheets, images, HTML, Java, and other technical elements of the site. The technical brief tells us what conditions to meet for the customers to see the site, and the technical spec describes the approach to building and maintaining the site. Many engineering projects suffer from feature creep, which is one of the best ways to make a project late and overbudget.

The technical brief. Most web developers make an attempt to describe the visitors' equipment, so they can build the site appropriately. We want to know how big visitors' screens are, how fast their modems are, how much memory their systems have, how many colors they can see, what plug-ins they have, etc. The technical brief is

A technical baseline document.

Logos are a special case. Few logos survive the transition from paper to Web. Here are a few tips from the trenches of the logo wars.

Logos are expensive. Good logos range from $2K to $10K at the low end, to about $10K to $30K by a regionally known firm with larger accounts. They start at about $40K from nationally known designers and can exceed six months and $100K (that's not a typo).

With a top firm, you get a process that works. They start with a creative brief and do explorations in many directions. Then they use a design grid to explore one or two aspects of the design at a time, methodically narrowing down the choices until one remains. They check it against known marks, registered and unregistered. Then they develop an entire standards program and implementations for paper, screens, laser printers, newspaper, signage, etc. With a few notable exceptions, you tend to get what you pay for.

A perfect logo for an online shopping site.

A good logo on paper, badly executed on the Web.

simply a document that describes the users' capabilities. Also known as "determining visitor technographics," or "establishing a technical baseline," this document comes from actual user data, interviews, questionnaires, or educated guesses.

The functional brief. In deciding what a site should do for visitors, separate functionality from execution. The functional brief describes what the site should do for visitors, now and in the future. Technical constraints influence functional goals; this document describes the tradeoffs involved. For example, you want real-time horoscope readings on your site, but real-time information systems are costly. Start with more general horoscope readings at first, then move to a real-time system after the site is successful.

Examples are very useful. If you see a web site with a certain feature, and you want to use it on your site, show the feature to an engineer and say: "Can we use this to accomplish my idea?" This kind of discussion is always fruitful, because an engineer can explain how a certain feature works and how expensive it is to implement.

Feature creep. Many projects fail due to overambitious functional plans. Web sites can do a lot, but the more you ask for, the more complex the overall system becomes. Build what you need and learn what it takes before scaling it into a massive undertaking. To avoid adding too many desirable features to the site, break it up into the following releases:

Release 0.9	beta test
Release 1.0	official launch
Release 1.1	first set of fixes
Release 2.0	first major addition/revision

A producer sets up these releases at the beginning and makes sure everyone is aware of projected dates. With this nomenclature, the producer can say, "That's a great idea. Let's put it on the list for Release 2.0 and discuss it at the Release 2.0 feature meeting (in six months)."

Strategy and tactics

1 Strategic planning

2 Tactical planning

After the research comes the thinking. To put these strategies in place, write a series of short documents describing your approach. Everything done so far will translate into these working documents, transforming the strategy into a set of blueprints for the site.

Site features

Armed with client profiles and questionnaire results, the producer calls in the creative team. It's time to brainstorm on ideas that will achieve the goals of the site. Look for ways to attract customers, keep them, and serve them.

Attract new visitors. One of the best ways I know to attract people is to give away $100 bills at the site. If you're giving away $50 bills, you'll attract fewer people, but perhaps enough to call it a success. Once we acknowledge that giving away $100 bills is a great attractor, we try to think of a cheaper (yet legal) way to do it. What would be the equivalent for your audience? What feature or content can we provide – usually fresh daily or weekly – that would encourage people to come see what's going on? This question sparks a lively creative discussion: what is the perfect gift we could give to new arrivals? As Rebecca

Farwell of Discovery.com says, "We create feature journalism by way of throwing a good party."

Keep them coming back. Once surfers have shown up, get them to stay. What kinds of enticements encourage people to come back regularly? Regular repeat visitors tend to bookmark sites. So what will make it easier to bookmark rather than type the URL in again? Top-ten lists, awards, a constantly updated map, a cartoon, a joke or word of the day – all of these encourage bookmarks.

Update a bookmark idea regularly. If you change the site every Thursday, are you making sure new visitors know to come back on Thursdays?

Serve the customer. Whether you're serving poetry or stock options, your site must excel at service. Set your service standards high, then brainstorm on how you can

Use any trick in the book to attract people.

Good feature ideas drive many successful web sites.

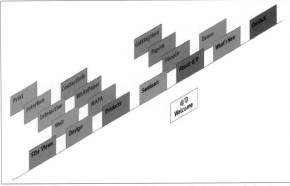

Two kinds of site maps: isometric (above) and plan view (below).

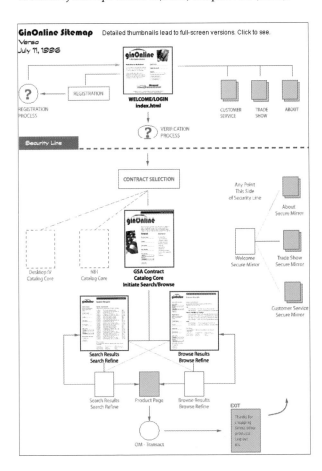

do even more for the customer on the Web. The best way out of the brochureware trap is to serve the customer actively.

Can a web site bake Zack a cake? No. Can a web site take Zack's order for a cake and make sure it gets delivered? Yes. If it's late or the frosting is wrong, that's a chance for a competitor to get Zack's attention. Everything you do for Zack – whether it's on TV, in the local newspaper, on the Web, or part of the delivery – adds up to his impression of the company. If the Web is part of a 110% total satisfaction program, Zack will tell his friends about the cake-order site and the company that made it happen.

It's good practice to prepare a simple document that lists all the site features you thought of and shows the process of narrowing them down. Added to the project site, it helps clients see the features you think should be in Release 1.0, those you think should be saved for Release 2.0, and those silly ideas you thought of but decided (wisely) not to pursue.

Site mapping

A site map is an overhead view of the site showing the route a visitor takes through the site. With all the deliverables specified and the content schedule on track, the contractor goes to work on a site map. If the client has come to the table with a site map, the team should put it aside while getting everything else together. A hastily drawn site map can distort expectations by having a strong influence

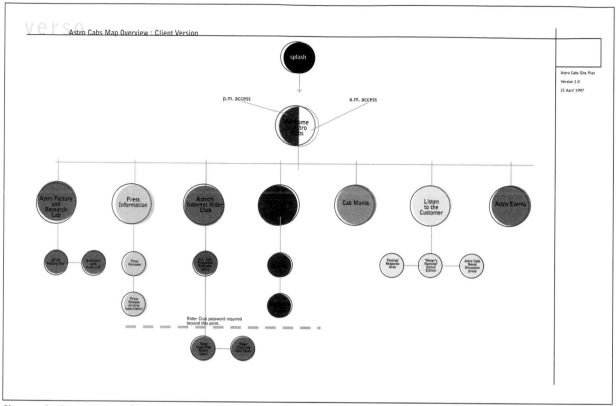

Site mapping is not a matter of using a template and filling in the blanks. Be creative; use the site map as a communication tool.

A creative brief: written in designer language.

on how people think about the site – making it difficult to convince them of a better solution later.

To avoid falling into a trap of second-generation site maps, keep things loose and gradually tighten up the diagram. Start with lots of possible topology sketches, even if the site looks relatively straightforward. Do you want a "guided tour" feature? Will there be a visual map on the site?

The creative brief

The creative brief describes the objectives of the upcoming creative exploration. Although it is an internal communication, from the design or creative director to the team of designers, clients should be encouraged to follow it as it evolves. Even if the creative director is also the art director, who's also the designer, it's a good idea to write and maintain a creative brief.

A creative brief points out visual directions to explore, taking into account all the input from the client and the marketing strategy developed so far. It's very important to spend time with the project profile, learning which sites the client likes and why. It may contain words like evocative, informative, spacious, soothing, moving, personal, etc. It should challenge the designers to do their best work.

Another way to write a creative brief is to write a review of the site. What would a journalist tell her readers? What would a target user tell her friends about the site? These kinds of descriptions can be helpful. The more you involve designers in the first phase, the better they can execute in the second.

A creative brief must also include selection criteria. How will you know the winning design when you see it? Is the design to be scrollable? Does it use colors functionally or decoratively? Does it use red to designate "hot," or clickable, items? What is the visual mood of the site? Does the site convey authority, playfulness, service? Is ordering always one click away? Does it accommodate the four most important user groups?

The content plan

Armed with the site map, the producer divides the project goals into deliverables and dates. Some of the content already exists, some must be modified, and some must be created from scratch. At this point, it's best to be as specific as possible in identifying what the client will be responsible for and what the contractor will generate. Put it all into a written document and make sure everyone knows what she is responsible for. Start lining up resources on the client side – writers, illustrators, contributors.

Technical documentation

Much of the work for a site takes place behind the scenes, behind the design, behind the content. Successful sites require technical expertise not just to implement, but to make sure they won't be obsolete in a few months. The producer and her technical staff must write specifications for the crafting of the HTML (technical spec) and engineering specifications to drive the back-end functionality of the site (engineering spec, functional spec).

Technical specification. The tactical side of the technical baseline is a short document describing the basic approach and technologies used in the markup and layout of the site (not the functionality). Will the pages be made from templates and served from a database? Will it use Cascading Style Sheets? Will it require a plug-in or special control? Will it look its best at thousands of colors and be tolerable at 256 colors, or will it be optimized for low-end systems? Will it be designed using a WYSIWYG layout program or marked-up by hand? Will it use dynamic HTML, layers, channels, push technology? To accommodate the browsers specified in the contract, the site must have certain features that work well in all browsers, but it can have other features that are browser-specific.

> "Content planning is a collaboration between contractor and client. It is possibly the client team leader's most arduous task, because it is difficult to predict the amount of work involved in identifying, collecting, writing, formatting, and editing content. Identify all the content in Phase One, when it can have an effect on the design. The scope and depth of the information will determine the navigation, and the type of content will determine the visual language, tone, and layout of the design."
>
> **– Christina Cheney, producer, Studio Verso**

Christina Cheney on Content planning

Page ID	Page Name	Description	Content Provider	Writer/ Editor	Start Date	Development & Approval Time	Content due to Verso	Date Content Sent	Notes	Page Type	Priority
1	Splash Screen	Content description, graphics, banner ads, animated gif transition with logo and tagline.	Astro Cabs	John Updike	Feb. 10	1 Day	Feb 11	Feb 11	Contact ad agency for changes in tag line.	Dynamic/full screen w/graphic	A
2	Primary Navigation (1) "Astro Factory"	Overview Text	Astro Cabs	John Updike	Feb. 8	5 Days	Feb 13	Feb 13	Update quarterly	static w/header and text	A
3	Secondary Navigation "Research Lab"	New R & D developments	Astro Cabs	Toni Morrison	Feb. 11	4 Days	Feb 15	Feb 15	Requires approval from lead technician	static w/header, text bullet list	A
4	Tertiary Navigation	QTVR Tour	Astro Cabs	Marc Pesce	Feb. 10	11 Days	Feb 21	Feb 22	Late delivery requires increased production time		B

A content plan helps pace your requests and reminds the client to send content.

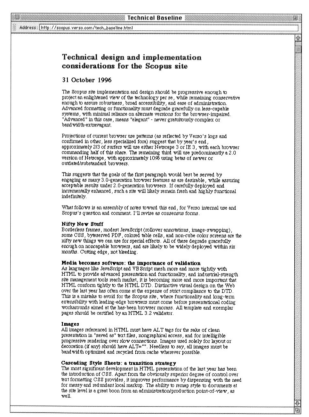

Engineering specification. In a big project, a client will spend perhaps $100K to $200K on design and $300K to $700K on back-end functionality, usually driven by a database. Designers and engineers must cooperate to create a working site. Site designers dream up features, then they ask the engineers whether it's possible to build them. Engineers always answer: "Anything's possible. Just depends how much money and time you have." So begins the negotiation to achieve the most functional bang for the engineering buck. Site designers must strive to balance the customer's experience with the client's budget.

An engineering team usually has an *architect,* who writes an overall document that explains the approach to the site and the technologies she thinks will be useful. Then she works closely with the designers and the client to specify the functionality of the site.

Technical specifications help the team fit the technologies to the task.

The functional specification is a detailed continuation of the functional brief, written in the first half of this phase. The functional spec details the actions of the site but not how those actions are to be accomplished. For instance, a functional spec might state, "When the user enters information, the program sends email confirming the order and takes him to a page that he can print out as a receipt (see sample receipt page)." Write functional specs in plain English and keep them current.

The key to writing good functional specs is to describe only the interaction between the user and the system without getting into details of implementation. As we'll see, it's very important to keep the engineering specifications up to date as the project progresses. The user interface, or front end, won't be integrated with the database, or back end, until just days before launch. Keeping these specs rigorous and updated is the only way the two groups will be able to communicate. The producer and architect should record changes in the master document and keep the team abreast of new developments.

The schedule

Before going to the next phase, the producer makes a master schedule that drives the project to completion. This schedule will have hard dates and more flexible dates. Build in plenty of time to test, review, and approve work. Don't assume clients will approve something within two hours of seeing it. Good scheduling skills come with experience. The more rigorous you are, the better you'll be able to refine your own skills.

Plan to work in small time increments. No matter how big your project is, it can be separated into deliverables of two weeks or less. As projects become more dynamic and spread out, working in teams requires short deliverables to keep everyone enthused and on track. Break the project into small enough pieces so that every week sees tangible progress. Every two weeks, get the whole team to review what's been done. A client should not have to wait four weeks without some sign of progress.

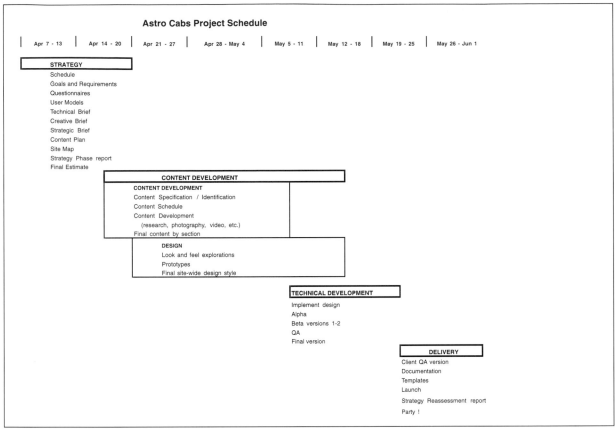

A clear schedule helps everyone see the big picture. This paper version could also appear as a PDF on the project site.

The final meeting

At the end of this phase, the client and contractor should meet to review and approve everything. The client is prepared to provide content, and the contractor team is anxious to begin the design process. If everything is clear, the project moves forward. The approved schedule and estimate should go as an addendum to the final contract.

Assist the team leader in getting final sign-off. The labyrinth of approvals may be filled with many pitfalls. The producer can help by putting together clear presentations at the project site and sending paper documents if it helps. Make clear summaries, presentations, reports – anything that helps the team leader in a meeting where she has to justify how she's spending the money they gave her. Be

sure to allow enough time for review and consideration, so all decisionmakers can give their approval.

In many cases, the two parties will have agreed to complete the project on a bid basis. The contractor prepares a firm bid, subject to approval. The contractor can come prepared and agree to amend the contract, or the contractor and client can work through all their issues and reconvene to review the bid and sign the new contract.

Accurate, consistent estimates increase trust between a contractor and client. Always try to underpromise and overdeliver. Estimate 10% over what is necessary and then come in 10% under the estimate. This will engrave your picture into the client's mind as someone he wants to do business with in the future.

John Katsaros
on strategy

John Katsaros is head of Collaborative Marketing, a strategic planning group that does market research and helps companies take the appropriate approach to establishing a presence on the Web. He frequently matches clients with contractors to build web sites.

David Siegel: How do companies decide how much to budget for their web site?

John Katsaros: If you ask the president of any major company: "Would you want your executives to create a long-term plan for an investment that will span ten years, cost between $10M to $100M, and have a major impact on customer creation, customer retention, and competitiveness?" – the answer would be, "Of course." Yet, ask these same people how much they budget for their web site and they're not sure. Most companies don't plan their web site investment as a resource requirement within their annual budgeting process. Funding for web sites comes during the course of events – new project launches, re-deployment of existing applications and corporate promotion campaigns. Companies don't treat their web sites as a long term strategic investment.

DS Why do corporate web sites look like war zones?

JK Because no one's in charge. In a multi-division company, who controls the web site? Nobody. You can never find the people responsible for poor quality or poor responsiveness of a corporate site. Organizations need a process by which they can quickly and strategically resolve their cross-division site planning and implementation issues. In just a few years, 25% of many marketing groups will be E-marketers. Likewise for other functions. Departments need to reorganize to create E-workers.

DS What can companies do?

JK Take the long-term, high-value approach to being on the Web. Put someone in charge, set a three-year budget plan with a 12-month funding plan. Understand both department and customer needs. Conduct a thorough review of your site relative to your competition's, and keep the differences measurable from quarter to quarter.

Now you can prepare your company's strategic plan. The plan should have five parts, 1: Goals, 2: Key constituencies served (along with a profile of these constituencies), 3: Execution plan, 4: Investment required, and 5: Timing. The more serious you are about providing value, the more your business will benefit.

Chapter 8

Phase Two – Content development and design

"I demand of art,
the role of the challenger...
of play and interplay,
play being
the very
manifestation of
the spirit..."

– Le Corbusier

"Ideas
may also grow
out of the problem itself,
which in turn
becomes
part of the solution."

– Paul Rand

Chapter 8

A clear plan simply sets the stage.
The **heart** of the project centers around the creative people
who bring the project to life.

Content development and design

THE PRODUCER sets everything up so the designers can apply maximum creative value to the site, innovating and brainstorming their way through all the issues outlined so far. Designers use the creative brief to explore the design space and technology needed to realize the design. After a brilliant, convincing presentation on design direction, the client signs off, and the contractor fills out the areas of the site. The designer models web pages using a program like Adobe Photoshop or Adobe PageMaker – making it easier to explore and make adjustments. A brief preproduction phase gets everyone ready for the final production effort.

Design management has always been a challenge. Getting people to love a new logo or visual identity takes more political savvy than design skills. During this phase, the producer runs interference, cheers the team on, contributes to discussions, helps steer the design direction, and then sells the resulting design with total conviction.

BOOKS

By Bob McKim and Jim Adams, co-founders of Stanford's Product Design department:

Jim Adams
*The Care and Feeding of Ideas:
   A Guide to Encouraging Creativity*
Conceptual Blockbusting: A Guide to Better Ideas
*Flying Buttresses, Entropy, and O-Rings: The World of
   an Engineer,* Addison-Wesley Publishing, 1987.

Robert McKim
Experiences in Visual Thinking
*Thinking Visually: A Strategy Manual
   for Problem Solving,* Brooks/Cole Publishing, 1980.

The creative process

In 1982, I took a Stanford class on visual thinking from Bob McKim, one of the pioneers of design education. Bob forced us to have one idea every 30 seconds, sketch it, and move on. He made us keep notebooks with hundreds of ideas. Whenever anyone would say, "Nah, that's stupid," or even, "Hey, that's great!" he'd encourage us to keep sketching. When you ran out of paper, he would say, "Grab another sketchbook." Bob insisted we change our frame of mind when deciding which of the sketches we liked.

He made us have ideas until we were exhausted, then have ten more, then put them aside and come back the next day to rank them and decide which to explore further and which to leave behind.

This chapter looks at the three main parts of the design phase: expansion, contraction, and preproduction. Each has its own section, and its own set of deliverables (remember to skip the engineering section if your project doesn't have back-end functionality).

Content development and design

1 Expansion

2 Contraction

3 Preproduction

During this phase, the creative team explores the possibilities by generating ideas, sketches, and doodles: the more the better. No one writes HTML during this phase. Designers present ideas and visualizations in mock-ups that are easy to modify. Most of this section is meant for designers.

Brainstorming

After internalizing the creative brief and immersing yourself in the culture of the customer, you are ready to design the site. Make lots of thumbnails and sketches, letting ideas take you away from – and the brief take you back to – the central goals of the site. It's time to brainstorm.

Start with the most important page in the site. Work on it until you have at least 15 ideas, five of them promising. When that page starts to gel, work on some of the other pages. Keep exploring, sketching, and having ideas. See what you can do with various effects: server push, streaming audio, dynamic HTML, tags used in a way they haven't been used, etc.

Let your sketchbooks overflow with ideas for entrances, navigational devices, main "driver" images that have impact, and features that can enhance the site. Use collage. Animate a small piece of a larger image. Play with type, layers, textures, emotions. Once you find a strong theme, exploit it and take it as far as you can, then go to another theme and work it until something interesting happens.

In the previous chapter, I mentioned creating a physical environment that reflects that of a particular user. Put on your Zack, Esther, Jimena, or Bobby hat and surf the Web site from his or her point of view. Establish a set of bookmarks that cater to your target user. Surround

yourself with magazines that person would read. Then, in the words of interface designer Alan Cooper: "Consider it magic." What would the site do if it could do absolutely anything? What would make the visitor say, "Wow! I didn't know a web site could do that"?

How do you get ideas? How do you create something different? Something new? Surf the Web. Go to thrift stores, old and used bookstores, cafe bookstores. Visit a museum or an art gallery. Or be by yourself – any of these

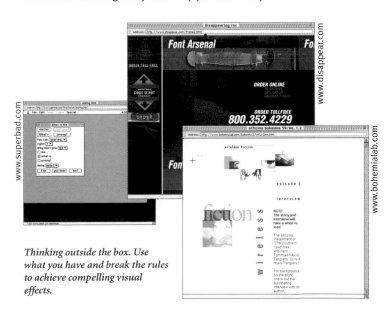

Thinking outside the box. Use what you have and break the rules to achieve compelling visual effects.

could aid the process. Brainstorming doesn't always have a start and finish. You might find yourself at a loss for that beginning point, while at other times, everything might be crystal clear.

When constructing models or brainstorming in Photoshop, take images from other sites, scan magazines, and have plenty of stock photography around. While making comps, you can use anything. You'll have to delete or license any borrowed images to put on the real site when you launch, but for playing around, anything goes. Keep everything in Photoshop or Pagemaker, or some other program that makes modeling web pages easy (mock-up the browser window and all HTML elements).

Brainstorming
Purvi Shah on

"Draw, doodle, think, see, read, refer, flip through things. If you are working on a project for a game company, play games, go to toy stores and comic book stores. Look around and feel what others feel like when they are in that environment. Create that space around you. In whatever state you find yourself, be aware of anything around you, things that confine you and things you can reach for."

Fears
A creative block.
Finding yourself without a starting point.
Inability to generate ideas.
Not having a custom idea for every client.

Tips
Every thought does not have to be a valid, logic-driven one.
Write down every thought that comes to mind.
With the creative brief as a baseline, ask yourself the who, where, when, how, and why questions.
Sketch and draw everything.
Give yourself the space to experience, invent, and excavate.
Look up client guidelines and understand key product-development features.
Look up and research the client's competitors.

– Purvi Shah, designer, Studio Verso

Design language

It is often helpful to create several pages of explorations – not web pages but just visual expressions of a particular feel or look. Play with form and layout without regard to any particular objective. This gives you a chance to try different design "languages," to see which visual elements work together. These creative sessions should not be inhibited by thoughts of "How will I ever do this in HTML?" The artist plays with backgrounds, colors, collage, visual elements, shadows, headline effects, type, and animation to come up with general "rules" for a given look. Once you have chosen a basic look, apply it to various pages of the site.

Explore design language without regard to particular pages. High Five images courtesy of Jon Leong.

Grids

Design students typically spend the first few years of their education studying the foundations of design: layout, typography, illustration, and photography. They spend time learning how to use a grid system to create structure in two dimensions. These days, they learn to master new-media tools, but the basics of design haven't really changed. This book, for example, is laid out using a consistent grid structure, one for the first half (a magazine look) and another for this second half (more of a textbook format).

Web pages are not paper. Good web designers still use grids, but the grids are more flexible than those on paper. You want the page to have structure, but it must accommodate different viewing conditions. Designers must now "think" in HTML and the restrictions of the Web. They shouldn't think about exact markup techniques, but rather what the user's experience will be under varying conditions. Compared to paper, viewing conditions on the Web

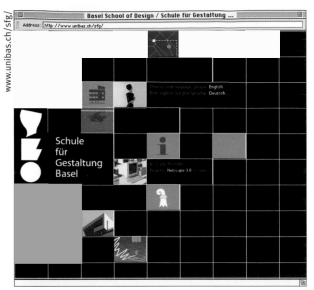

Grids remain one of the designer's secret weapons.

Good navigational systems can be found on the Web. Pick one and modify it to suit your site.

are actually fairly crude. The designer must work to maximize legibility, impact, feedback, responsiveness, and orientation under a wide variety of viewing conditions.

The designer designates different areas of the page to serve different functions. In some cases, the proportions are absolute, in others, the designer thinks in relative terms. What happens if the viewer expands her window? How big is her monitor? As browsers improve, designers will be able to get more design control with added flexibility. Grids will continue to be one of the designer's secret weapons.

TIP | Read *Creativity for Graphic Designers: A Real-World Guide to Idea Generation – From Defining Your Message to Selecting the Best Idea for Your Printed Piece*, by Mark Oldach, North Light Books, 1995.

Navigation

Too often, designers get carried away creating new navigation schemes. They make icons out of everything to help move people around. They want to use animation, lots of colors, rollovers, sound, and other cues to give the navigation that special touch. Take a tip from the sites you admire most: keep it simple. Rotating textured embossed lozenges are out. There are plenty of good paradigms for navigation. Don't try to invent a new one. Instead, adapt an appropriate one for use at your site. People should not be impressed by your navigation. They should simply find it easy to get around your site.

Site designers like to talk about *flow*, or how a person will move around within a web site. On a large project,

develop a flow mock-up – a mock-up of the site in HTML using text only, offering various choices and linking the pages together. In a short time, using a program like NetObjects Fusion, you can build a text-based web site that serves as a point of discussion for moving throughout the site. This is the same as drawing site diagrams, but it is more experiential than visual.

Armed with too many ideas about how to approach the problem, it's time to change hats and decide which ideas will become that successful web site.

During this part of the phase, you must stop being a designer. The producer plays a crucial role as an advocate for the customer. Be a customer first and a client second. All presentations should be in a flexible format.

Astro Cabs Criteria Matrix

	Candidate 1	Candidate 2	Candidate 3
Appeals to target audience (0-20)	18	9	16
Download fast? (0-10)	3	9	5
Work in all browsers? (0-15)	12	11	13
Works on low-end systems? (0-20)	12	9	17
Generates interest in personal cabs? (0-20)	17	16	10
Informative (0-10)	7	6	9
Ease of navigation (0-10)	5	5	7
Encourages exploration (0-15)	11	13	8
Conveys safety, quality (0-15)	3	12	9
Easy to respond by e mail? (0-10)	5	7	5
Total	93	97	100

Astro Cabs Criteria Matrix

	Candidate 1	Candidate 2	Candidate 3
Appeals to target audience (5x)	10	3	8
Download fast? (1x)	3	10	7
Work in all browsers? (5x)	8	6	8
Works on low-end systems? (4x)	5	3	7
Generates interest in personal cabs? (2.5x)	8	8	5
Informative (5x)	6	7	10
Ease of navigation (2x)	9	6	7
Encourages exploration (3x)	6	8	4
Conveys safety, quality, style (1.5x)	1	10	7
Easy to respond by e mail? (2x)	5	7	1
Unweighted Total	61	68	64
Weighted Total	210.5	187	216

There are two ways to set up a weighted criteria matrix. The multiplier method on the right is more flexible.

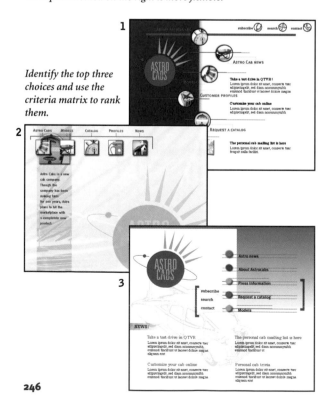

Identify the top three choices and use the criteria matrix to rank them.

Choose the finalists

Once you have between five and fifty possible approaches to your design, it's time to get out the red pen and start slashing. Start by dividing your ideas into three categories, then use a systematic approach to finding your top five choices, and finally, rank them. Your ranked list will guide further iterations.

Three categories. Divide your ideas into three categories: **1**: Stupid ideas, **2**: Favorites, **3**: Alternatives. Leave the stupid ideas alone, reduce the favorites to between five and ten choices, and move the rest into the alternate pile. Next, rank the favorites, using a set of predetermined criteria.

A criteria matrix lists the selection criteria along the top and the various ideas down the left side, so you can see the strengths and weaknesses of each idea. This helps you compare ideas and choose those that complement each other while keeping the feature list as small as possible.

There are two kinds of criteria matrixes: weighted and unweighted. To use a weighted criteria matrix, assign weights (values) to each category, then give each design a score from 1-N for each category (where N signifies the weight) and add them up to determine the winner.

Alternatively, assign multipliers to each catetgory, give all ratings from one to ten, and then multiply the scores by the weights and add up the results. This second method has the advantage of flexibility – you can adjust the weights easily. A multiplier of one is essentially unweighted.

You can either let the matrix make the decision for you, or you can use the results to guide your decision. In either case, your matrix is only as good as your criteria and your weighting scheme.

The finalists. Identify the top five or so choices from the criteria matrix, then choose the final picks. Typically, you'll choose three finalists: your favorite, the wild and daring one, and the more conservative one you're pretty sure they'll like. Now you're ready for the big meeting.

The presentation

It's much better to conduct the presentation meeting in person. If necessary, you can conduct the presentation in a conference call, with all parties looking at the project site simultaneously. Facilitating this meeting requires tact, attention, and determination to make the right decision. Make sure the client feels comfortable with the process you use to recommend and evaluate choices. Make a firm decision and make it clear you'll be going forward down the chosen path.

Most clients want to help make their site as good as it can be. They want to work with a designer who can guide them through the process. Because clients know their market, they can make a project better by helping you understand how their customers will see the various designs. The producer must keep the customer up front and emotion and opinion on the sidelines. This section covers contingencies and general rules for presenting comps to clients.

Boards or on-screen? Boards are printed pages mounted on presentation board. Clients like being able to hand boards around in a meeting. If the people attending the meeting will be wearing suits, you should think about bringing boards or making sure they have a projection monitor that hooks to your laptop. Boards tend to get passed around. They linger. After we've decided to focus on one direction, the boards are still saying, "Look at all the choices you have." Leaving boards with a client may

The creative director should come prepared, preferably with one or two of the design staff to act as backup. The main points to present at this meeting are:

A reiteration of the goals

The site structure

Design language, if appropriate

The core page or most important page (as many versions as you decide to show)

A representative second-level or neighborhood page (one or two alternatives perhaps)

A representative article or feature (makes the project more real)

A first pass at navigation

An outline of a content schedule (gets them thinking about their part)

subject you to charging sales tax (check with your State Board of Equalization), and it may lead the client to believe there are still many choices.

I prefer to make presentations on-screen, usually from the project site, right off the Web (daring, I know). The comps are in RGB colors, not CMYK, so they look more natural on screen. I might bring paper versions to pass around the table, but I'll get them back before I leave.

Only one. Some people, like author Cameron Foote in his book *The Business Side of Creativity,* recommend taking only one design to the client's office. If the client loves it, you've won, and you can move on to refinement. I've done it, and it has worked. I haven't done it enough to see the downside, but you can always show more if the first one doesn't make a big splash.

The big three. Many designers present three choices: one that's modest (a fall-back design), one they are most likely to choose, and one that's more ambitious or that the designer likes personally. Most designers prefer to show three concepts – no more, no fewer. It gives the designer safety and lets the client participate in the process. Clients like to think they have contributed to the design, so while showing one comp may be best for the project, showing three may be best for the client.

"Presenting several concepts to a client, and letting him or her select among them, may seem to be a valid way of offering alternatives. However, offering alternatives confuses many clients. Worse, it often leads them to 'cherry pick' – to select elements from each of the concepts and to combine in a new concept.

"For most assignments the best way to impress clients and enhance your working relationship is to start by selecting one concept as the approach that best addresses their problem. Then be prepared to present and sell it as your recommendation. Only if your concept isn't accepted should you show a second."

– *from* **The Business Side of Creativity**

Frankensteining. Clients like to move elements from one design to another. Sometimes it's okay, but often you have to explain why you can't just keep adding new design elements. If you let them have one little feature they've fallen in love with (it may have been their idea), they'll always check that their little element (sometimes called a *neck bolt*) is there, giving you more room to work on the main part of the design.

On the other hand, if a client wants one third of *this* design, one third of *that*, one third of *the other*, and a *fourth* third from this site they just saw this morning, you have a serious communication problem. If you proceed along these lines, you'll get what kids get when they mix all the paints: mud.

The placebo effect. On rare occasions, you know the person you're presenting to always likes to leave her own mark on a design. In this case, some designers like to add a little something – say, a purple fin sticking right out of the main graphic – to give the decisionmaker a chance to remove it. They expect that the difficult-to-please client will focus on the fin, tell them to lose it, and okay the rest of the design.

"The only problem with this approach," says Larry Shubert of IDEO, "is when they choose the placebo instead of the real thing. Then you have to work extra hard to undo their attachment and get them on the right track."

The candy-store effect. If you show ten good ideas to a client, the client will be impressed. Then you notice they're having a hard time narrowing the choices. Eventually, they choose one design, probably with a splash from another thrown in. No matter how well you refine that design, they will be disappointed. It can't be strong enough to compare with all that creative energy you used to have. They have mistaken the menu for the meal.

The candy-store effect is real. It happens when you work with people who aren't used to making design decisions. Present as few ideas as you can get away with. More is worse, because clients easily get carried away. It undermines the designer's expertise and runs the project in circles. If the client doesn't like something, find out why and fix it. A focus group might make things more quantifiable. Use a decision matrix. Guide the client through a straightforward, logical process of reduction and stop when you're done.

Equipment failures. If it can fail, it will – but not until the last second. At a presentation for the ceo of a Fortune-100 company, we left everything on our web server so he could see it in real time. But their internal network was so slow, the ceo walked out of the meeting, thinking his new web site was going to take ten minutes to load each page. The Web was fine. Our server was fine. Traffic was moderate. Their internal network was under construction, and we looked bad. We should have brought the site on a cd or a laptop as a backup.

The audience

I have found that the number of ideas I want to pitch depends on the decisionmaking team being pitched. I offer these suggestions for presenting to different kinds of decisionmakers.

The candy-store effect: showing too many shiny objects can mesmerize a client.

The Big Cheese. They're hard to please, and they change their minds often. A Big Cheese has to juggle board meetings with press interviews, management crises, and hiring new people, all while trying to make decisions about the design of a web site. The Big Cheese can't delegate this important decision to someone else, yet there's no way she can spend the time required to focus on the process. Big Cheeses put themselves in a difficult situation by having to be the final authority on design as well as everything else.

A Big Cheese can't tell you what she wants, but she'll know what she's looking for when she sees it. When you hear those words, you're in trouble. Suggest she hire an in-house designer to get what she wants. If you *must* work with a Big Cheese, religiously document every decision she makes as you educate her on the design process.

The single rational decisionmaker. Sometimes a startup or a small company will have one person in charge of the development of the site, and that person will have a background in design management or outsourcing. In these situations, you have the freedom of working side-by-side, showing her ideas you'd never show another type of client. She'll be able to eliminate ideas that aren't quite right and focus on the ideas that work.

The even team. The best situation you can have is a small number of balanced decisionmakers. From two to four is best. If they are professional project managers and they rise or fall as a group, you are in luck. If they've been outsourcing annual reports for years and will be cranking them out long after your web site goes up, you have a group of dedicated decisionmakers. It's in their best interest to work together.

You can tell a cohesive team when you see one. The longer they've worked together, the more they've adjusted to individual styles. To these kinds of teams, we often show more ideas.

The uneven team. A small team can be dominated by one person in a position of power. The team's vote is negligible compared to that of one voice. They are there to discuss and offer suggestions, but also to support the decision made by the voice of power. Politics enter heavily into the equation. Treat them as you would a Big Cheese.

The big team. If there are more than five decisionmakers, you're in for a long haul. Without a champion, you will find it difficult to get consensus on anything. If you find yourself among a group of even peers, you might be able

to assert yourself and guide the process, but the more decisionmakers there are, the longer the process will take. If they are willing to vote and move on, you can probably get them to decide fairly rationally. Establish a rule that anyone not present at a meeting loses his vote on those decisions.

Iterative design

The goal for the first presentation is to establish a design *direction,* not the details of implementation. Decide on the big picture, communicate the decisions back to the client, then move into the second level of design elements, and finally, the details. The process can take a few *iterations* (cycles).

Once you establish a general direction, experiment with one line of inquiry at a time. For example, do a color study or a typeface study, or look at different navigational schemes. Look at different ways to separate the company from the products. Animate something and see what its impact is. Holding other variables constant helps make decisions, but you must also orchestrate the evolution of the design as a whole. Once you make a firm decision, add that to the main body of work and go to the next issue.

There's no need to report everything back to the client. Make presentations when you have a number of things to show at once, rather than wearing the client down with a new set of decisions every few days.

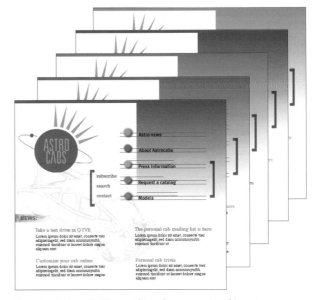

Iterative design – hold everything else constant and iterate on one aspect at a time.

Modular design

Properly designed, each web page will have areas that perform different functions: overall navigation, local navigation, local identity, main stories, teasers, ads, etc. These areas can be broken down into templates that either separate the design from the content or make the content easy to change.

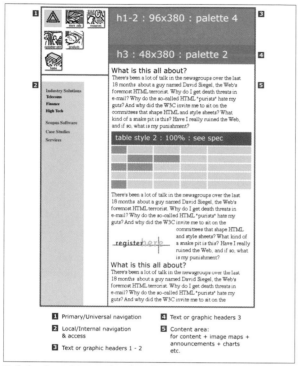

1 Primary/Universal navigation
2 Local/Internal navigation & access
3 Text or graphic headers 1 - 2
4 Text or graphic headers 3
5 Content area:
for content + image maps + announcements + charts etc.

Both database-driven and static web pages tend to be fairly modular. Working with abstract areas helps structure the pages.

Templates separate content and presentation for dynamic delivery.

Most web pages are fairly modular to begin with. Template design requires a deeper understanding of the client's long-term goals and editorial processes than fixed-content design. It is more work to develop a good set of templates than to produce even a large amount of fixed content, because you must generalize the design and production constraints to a larger degree.

If you are developing templates for a site to be published through a database, work with dummy data throughout the design phase. Likewise, the database programmers should work with a dummy front end. The process should continue until each side has finished its work and debugged its half of the final site. Then, at the end, the programmers load a working set of HTML templates into the database and merge them with the content for presentation on the Web.

One template-based site might involve two dozen basic templates, while another of comparable design complexity might involve only three or four basic templates. The difference is in the database's ability to handle complex rules and exceptions. The more sophisticated your database, the fewer templates you'll need, and the more dynamic your pages will be. Work closely with the engineering team to determine the right balance between many or few templates.

Content development

In Phase One, the contractor puts together a list of content for the client to start working on. Traditionally, the client team does nothing about this until they approve the first set of designs. It's the producer's job to get them to own the content schedule and start delivering.

This is the most critical time for content development. If priorities slip and there's too much client energy going into design, site map, features, etc., then it's likely there will be problems in the next phase. Clients must work to stay ahead of the game and leave room for changes.

A full- or half-time writer will be invaluable during Phase One. These people aren't easy to find, and it may take a few tries to get the right person on board. Set up guidelines for writing (style, length, branching opportunities) that help keep the writer focused. Some agencies have writers on staff, most don't. Many clients assume the contractor will hire a writer, and most design firms assume the client will hire one directly. My suggestion is that the client hire the writer, because that person will likely be needed for further updates and maintenance when the designer is less in the loop.

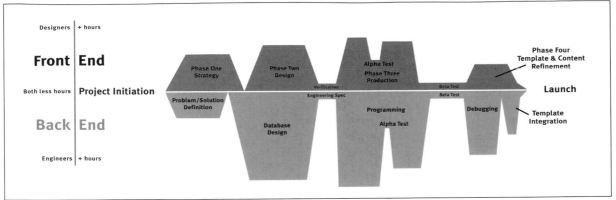

Don't add design templates to databases until the very end. This-time-and effort diagram shows a typical volume of work for both designers (above the line) and engineers (below). The center line depicts people from the two teams working together.

While most design shops are capable of generating images, now is the time to set up photo shoots, get stock photography, or possibly hire an illustrator. Art directors often buy national and local "black books" to browse illustrators' work. Now they can also use the Web. Many illustrators now display their work on the Web; these people are at least a bit more understanding of the limitations of the medium.

System design

While they don't usually make presentations to clients, programmers must also go through a design and creative problem-solving phase. Since most programming behind a web site involves databases, a database architect lays out a schema that establishes **1:** a place for each piece of data to be entered, and **2:** all the relationships between pieces, in response to the functional spec from Phase One. The schema is part of the overall architecture, which describes how the system works. Another layer, called middleware, consists of programs that tie the Web database to the front end (HTML) of the site and to existing databases.

Programmers spend time thinking and preparing, then they get into a frenzy of programming, and in just a few days, a program is born. Before the frenzy, it's best to make sure everyone's on the same track. Whether there is a single programmer or a team led by a software designer, a technical team should write the following documents.

An engineering or implementation spec communicates the design of the program to other engineers. It spells out in detail which functions accomplish which tasks. Properly done, this spec becomes the documentation for the system – the notes that let other developers keep the system up-to-date.

A theory of operation explains the inner workings of the site by abstraction, rather than by explaining the details of implementation. An architect may write a theory-of-operation document to explain how the system works. Large projects often have these documents, because they

In general, make prototypes in a medium that lets you experiment quickly. To design web pages, we use a combination of Photoshop and PageMaker to model HTML. We have a library of pre-made HTML features to simulate the look of a page for presentation purposes.

One reason for this is that Photoshop cannot model type very well. When someone makes a tool designers can use to model their pages, we'll use that instead.

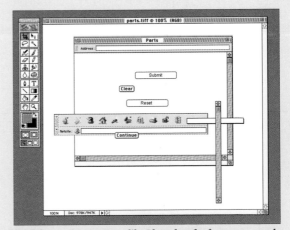

Model HTML in a program like Photoshop for fast turnaround.

Rapid prototyping

help explain the overall concepts to the team. Smaller projects usually don't need them.

A user-interface spec. A user-interface designer breaks the functional spec into a series of screens to experiment with the flow through the system. Properly done, these screens show different users' progression through the site and allow for testing aspects of user behavior. A designer takes a modular, "breadboard" approach, letting user tests and feedback guide the design. As she makes progress with the schematic of the site and the page layouts for each task, the designer updates the user-interface spec and works with visual designers, HTML experts, and back-end programmers to pull it all together.

Content development and design

1 Expansion

2 Contraction

3 Preproduction

Once you've refined the look of your pages, it's time to prepare them for production. This part of Phase Two verifies the design and prepares to hand everything to the production department.

Making it real

Going from a design model to a production model asks the production people to solve too many problems on the fly. Prepare for production by taking a methodical approach, solving most of these problems now, rather than later. The following steps ensure that the site is buildable.

Slicing and dicing: use a grid and precise measurements to accurately break the page into layout areas.

Almost all of the documents you write during preproduction will be internal documents for the benefit of the production team. Put them on the project site if appropriate.

The safety check is an OK from the engineer(s) that the approved visual model is viable. While designers and engineers communicate constantly during the exploration process, make sure you can actually implement the final design. This might involve coding a page or two and seeing how much it weighs (the size of all files on the page, plus the page itself, measured in kilobytes). If you're in the ballpark, you have proof of concept and can move on.

The markup and layout spec is a sketch of the printed pages and how they are to be implemented in HTML and Cascading Style Sheets. It establishes dimensions of the various areas of the pages, the approach to animation, what is background and foreground, typographic specifications, etc. This promotes a discussion between designers and production people on how they will implement the site. It also lets the designers and production group give the client several choices, from easy-to-implement and less expensive to more elaborate and costly. For example, the production team decides what accommodation will be made for different browser and platform variations and whether to make separate templates based on the visitor's browsing software.

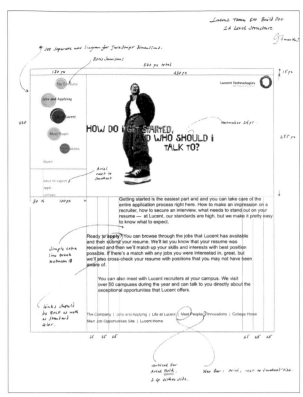

Build the key pages carefully.

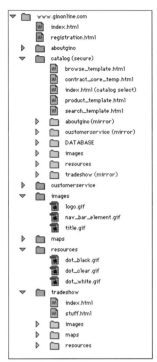

Document where all the files are so everyone on the team can find things.

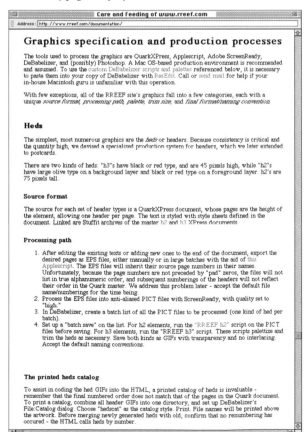

Graphics specification and production processes

The tools used to process the graphics are QuarkXPress, Applescript, Adobe ScreenReady, DeBabelizer, and (possibly) Photoshop. A Mac OS-based production environment is recommended and assumed. To use the custom DeBabelizer scripts and palettes referenced below, it is necessary to paste them into your copy of DeBabelizer with ResEdit. Call or send mail for help if your in-house Macintosh guru is unfamiliar with this operation.

With few exceptions, all of the RREEF site's graphics fall into a few categories, each with a unique *source format, processing path, palette, trim size,* and *final format/naming convention*.

Heds

The simplest, most numerous graphics are the *heds* or headers. Because consistency is critical and the quantity high, we devised a specialized production system for headers, which we later extended to postcards.

There are two kinds of heds: "h3"s have black or red type, and are 45 pixels high, while "h2"s have large olive type on a background layer and black or red type on a foreground layer. h2s are 75 pixels tall.

Source format

The source for each set of header types is a QuarkXPress document, whose pages are the height of the element, allowing one header per page. The text is styled with style sheets defined in the document. Linked are Stuffit archives of the master h2 and h3 XPress documents.

Processing path

1. After editing the existing texts or adding new ones to the end of the document, export the desired pages as EPS files, either manually or in large batches with the aid of this Applescript. The EPS files will inherit their source page numbers in their names. Unfortunately, because the page numbers are not preceded by "pad" zeros, the files will not list in true alphanumeric order, and subsequent numberings of the headers will not reflect their order in the Quark master. We address this problem later - accept the default file name/numberings for the time being.
2. Process the EPS files into anti-aliased PICT files with ScreenReady, with quality set to "high."
3. In DeBabelizer, create a batch list of all the PICT files to be processed (one kind of hed per batch).
4. Set up a "batch save" on the list. For h2 elements, run the "RREEF h2" script on the PICT files before saving. For h3 elements, run the "RREEF h3" script. These scripts palettize and trim the heds as necessary. Save both kinds as GIFs with transparency and no interlacing. Accept the default naming conventions.

The printed heds catalog

To assist in coding the hed GIFs into the HTML, a printed catalog of heds is invaluable - remember that the final numbered order does not match that of the pages in the Quark document. To print a catalog, combine all header GIFs into one directory, and set up DeBabelizer's File:Catalog dialog. Choose "hedscat" as the catalog style. Print. File names will be printed above the artwork. Before merging newly generated heds with old, confirm that no renumbering has occured - the HTML calls heds by number.

Process documentation tells everyone how to "turn the crank" on repetitive work.

There is perhaps no more classic text on programming project management than Fred Brooks' timeless classic: *The Mythical Man-Month*. Written in the days of room-sized computers running Fortran, this book is a must for anyone working with programmers on web sites today.

As Brooks says, "The [written specification] must not only describe everything the user does see, including all interfaces; it must also refrain from describing what the user does not see. That is the implementer's business, and there his design freedom must be unconstrained."

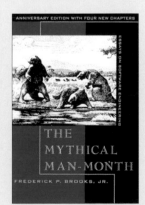

The Mythical Man-Month

Fred Brooks

"If HTML weren't a moving target, the preproduction phase would be less necessary. With
HTML, the materials cost nothing, and spectacular effects can be achieved only with large
quantities of labor. You need to work smart.
The larger the project, the bigger the payoff for
automating repetitive tasks. If other people are
to maintain the structures you build, part of the
deliverables will be a document that tells them
how to maintain the site. Starting this process
early makes it much easier at delivery time."

– Todd Fahrner, design technologist, Studio Verso

The HTML prototypes. In my organization, a design
technologist works with the production manager to
produce the key pages. It's important to document this
process if the client team is to make similar pages on their
own. These prototypes and the following set of documentation can be delivered at the beginning of Phase Three.

This exercise, which can take up to a week, builds the
skeleton for the site. Once the key framesets and pages
are in place – even with dummy content – the production
team can fill out the site. This exercise is different from the
preflight check because when these pages leave the HTML
expert and go into production, they will set in stone the
HTML conventions for almost the entire site. This prototype
should be tested carefully before going into production,
where it will be duplicated many times.

Nomenclature specs. Whoever takes over maintenance
will need to know the file and directory structure of the
site. Determine where you will put and how you will name
the files. Because uppercase and lowercase letters aren't
the same on a server, decide on exact file names and
document your decisions.

Process documentation shows the production department
exactly how to make the site. For example, if there are ten
pages with different, but similar, headers, then the process
describes how to make those headers most efficiently.
Which images are JPEGs and which are GIFs? Is there a common color palette? Do you need any special tools? What
exceptions have to be made for which browsers? This document doesn't have to be long, but it should be thorough,
so a new production person can use it to modify the site.

The launch plan

The site may be a month or more from being finished.
Even though the site is still in design, it's time to flesh out
the launch and media plans. This can be everything from
submitting the site to www.submitit.com (sends your
URL to all the search engines) to a media campaign with
television spots and targeted media buys on the Web and
in magazines. Many small companies send a provocative
postcard to a relevant mailing list. Some web sites have
T-shirts. Some have launch parties. Some get mentioned
on www.suck.com and away they go.

In most cases, the launch plan is not a huge document.
It points out what needs to be in place by when to achieve
maximum launch impact. The schedule should be
conservative enough that other activities don't force the
launch of the site if things are taking longer than expected.

Creative outsourcing

Ideally, a design group has subcontractors available to
become part of the team. Most design firms can't afford
to have photographers, illustrators, writers, and other
specialized talent in house. Yet when the job calls for it,
they must be part of the designer's company. As schedules
become more flexible and employees become more
expensive, contractors become increasingly valuable.

High-end talent tends to be well known and in demand.
First class photographers, talent agencies, illustrators, and
copywriters tend to charge ad-agency prices. A full-day's
professional photo shoot will cost between $5K and $25K.
A single illustration will cost $700, and a great illustration

Many excellent subcontractors have portfolios online.

will cost over $2K. Use high-end subcontractors if you have to get it right the first time. You're paying for experience. If your client's company lives or dies by the site you build, try to convince them to spend more on enhancements like photography or illustration.

Local talent is often excellent and undervalued – whether it's a CGI programmer or a copywriter, local people with experience can be your secret weapon. Find people with high-energy web sites waiting to get noticed. The more you look, the more you'll find a subculture of talent waiting for the right client. You can also put ads at popular sites (see the book site for a list of resources) where you can describe your business and the kinds of talent you're looking for.

Sometimes you can replace live talent with stock solutions. Here are a few tips.

Stock photography. You see a lot of stock photography on the Web. It's great for constructing models and prototypes. If you use stock photography, avoid the images everyone has already seen. Find photographs at a reasonable price – even if you have to scan chromes (transparencies) yourself. You don't need high-definition images. Cheap stock and a Photoshop filter can often give you a unique look. Make sure to pay for a license to any image you use, even if you alter it significantly.

Fonts. I'm a believer in owning a fully licensed, fully stocked font library. Fonts go a long way toward giving a client a special look-and-feel. Several boutique foundries now offer their products exclusively over the Web.

Third-party programming "solutions." Every week there are announcements of new technologies that help you solve your problem by plugging pieces together and having everything work on open standards. There are content-management systems, ready-made databases, customizable templates, configurators, security systems, and more. If something costs $400 but saves you 200 hours of work per year, isn't it worth the expense? On the other hand, you can't beta test every new tool or you'll spend all your time debugging software. Good contractors know whom to call to get the real story on what's hot (and what's still going to be hot in six months). Cultivate relationships with experts and stay on top of new developments.

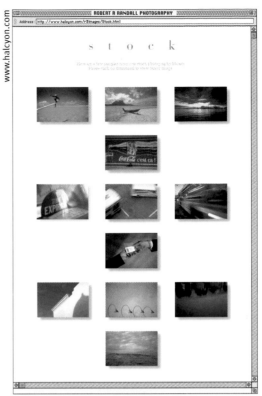
www.halcyon.com

Stock photography is a cost-effective way to add great content.

www.coldfusion.com

New programs offer increased functionality at lower cost.

www.earshotsfx.com

Several web sites now carry stock sounds, including rights for inclusion in web sites.

www.emigre.com

www.fontbureau.com

Pay good money for fonts and enjoy them.

In 1995, The Discovery Channel launched what soon became one of the most popular destinations on the Web, winning many awards for design, including the High Five. Then they changed it.

According to Rebecca Farwell, Executive Director of Discovery Channel Online, "The original grid-

based design was great for experts, but not for new visitors. We learned the hard way that people don't like to go to a new page that often. In many cases, they'd rather scroll. The categories we set up were too cryptic. At the time, it was groundbreaking and well received, but it was inflexible and looked static. They didn't bookmark within the site, and they often didn't reach things that were a few levels down. The old format didn't give us a way to catch the surfers and turn them into settlers.

"We argued over scrolling vs. non-scrolling for what seems like an eternity. It took tons of iterations. We tried everything. The redesign process took much more time than we ever thought. We held focus groups on the new design. All groups except those in San Francisco loved it (they're the advanced users). We knew we'd take some heat from them.

"We launched the scrolling design in December, 1996, and traffic went up 35% immediately. Since then, every month has been a record growth month. The number of minutes the average visitor spends at the site has gone up over 50%. We know people love looking at animals, and this design gives them better access to animals. We're going to build on the scrolling design and give people more to bookmark. There's always something we could be doing better."

Discovery Online's old web site, above, and new design, right.

"How does a project
get to be
a year late?
One day
at a time."

— Fred Brooks, *The Mythical Man-Month*

Chapter 9

Phase Three – Production

In any creative endeavor,
someone must spend long hours
bringing the final product to life.

AT SOME POINT, you must stop generating ideas and start delivering the deliverables.

The goal of Phase Three is to arrive at the main beta test site – the one that everyone thinks is okay – about a week ahead of the actual launch date. Unfortunately, this phase is also the one most prone to problems, because anything done improperly during planning and design is likely to smolder until it becomes a brushfire here in production.

The producer's role

This chapter focuses less on the actual day-to-day processes of production and more on the producer's role as the project barrels toward the completion date.

In web-site production, you create and gather assets, then stitch or glue them together. You build your own tools and discover your own shortcuts. As technology changes, you constantly revamp your tool kit and improve your methods. Phase Three sees three groups – the developer's team, the engineering team, and the client's team – functioning like a well oiled machine. The producer must be in daily contact with the team captains: the production manager, the client team leader, and the chief engineer. The producer's main responsibilities are to facilitate communication among these captains and to keep the project on track by catching problems early.

The production manager is responsible for shipping the beta site. This person can be the producer, a lead developer, or a full-time manager. The production manager's job is to sharpen tools, schedule resources, and control process. The more the production manager can be in touch with the client, the better. The producer's role is not to be a middleman, but to make sure the production manager gets content and change orders as efficiently as possible.

Production managers are in a difficult situation. By the time the project comes into their hands, small problems from earlier phases have become mountainous. A good production manager can see a set-up coming and watches the project during earlier phases to make sure the project is truly ready for production.

The client team leader wants to know things are going smoothly. The one thing worse than bad news is *no news* – any person left to wait a few days will start to imagine the worst. Don't let it happen. Instead, bring the client into the process, focus on her deliverables, and make sure she can

keep her finger on the pulse of the project by email, telephone calls, and the project site.

The chief engineer (or the engineering project manager) is responsible for delivering functionality. A small, efficient team of developers (two to six people) can often accomplish more than a larger group can. Much of the time is spent trying to communicate exactly what the system should do in all cases. Engineers tend to hate meetings, and they don't love to write, but they know the value of a well-written specification. As long as you continue to update the documents from Phase Two, the project will stay on track.

Production

1 **Production**	
2 Communication	*A production manager has a big job. She must make sure things are done right the first time. She must build custom tools, create new processes, and balance schedules. A production manager must deal with any problems that arise.*
3 Validation	

The production process

The production manager keeps her people up to date on the big picture of the project. She should get her group involved in every phase, encouraging them to spend time with the client team. During production, she should have weekly meetings to inform everyone of all local and global changes to the site. The production manager should also discuss everything with the producer, making sure they're both on the same page at all times. A production manager tells the producer of any possible brush fires or delays so they can monitor the situation and decide if/when to tell the client.

Many firms don't have a full-time production manager. They are too small. Yet someone must perform this role. It may be the producer or the HTML person, but someone must be responsible for production and its processes.

When a project has been through preproduction – the key pages are ready for HTML and the content is ready – the production manager calls her group together to assign tasks. First, the production manager hands out a comprehensive *build spec* (a combination of documents from the previous two phases) that documents all the specs and processes for the job, from type specifications and standard header sizes to color palettes. Then she splits the duties into horizontal and vertical tasks.

Horizontal tasks are performed by one person across the entire site. If several areas serve video clips, one person probably will make all of them. The same is true of other specialty items: style sheets, logos, a set of images that should look the same across the site, navigation, scripts, etc.

Vertical tasks give one person ownership of an area of the site. As much as possible, people feel most involved when they can bring an area of the site to life by themselves. Most production people are quite versatile. They learn new programs quickly and like new challenges. Giving them ownership of an area is a good way to keep

Use Equilibrium's DeBabelizer (www.equilibrium.com), rather than Adobe Photoshop, to get accurate browser-safe colors. See "Photoshop Liabilities" in *Creating Killer Web Sites* for details.

TIP

them motivated. Each area owner works with the horizontal contributors to integrate these global features into her HTML. I always start with the central (most difficult) features first and then expand the site, decreasing the likelihood that a given problem will cause a delay.

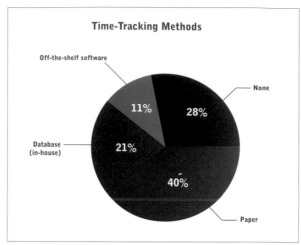

verso

812 SECOND STREET FIRST FLOOR SAN FRANCISCO CALIFORNIA 94107 USA
415 278 9900, 415 278 9911 FAX, info@verso.com

For the Week of 6.7.97 – 6.13.97
Name Jennifer H. Wolf

Time Sheet

Date	Duration	Task	Client	Description
6.9.97	1 hour	ADM	Verso	Staff Meeting
	1 hour	ADM	High Five	Surfing
	1.5 hour	PMG	Verso Editions	Proofing chapters 9-10
	3 hours	PRD	Astro Cabs	HTML, CSS, Image processing
	0.5 hour	TEK	Astro Cabs	CGI Scripting
	1.25 hour	PMG	Astro Cabs	QA
6.10.97	0.5 hour	ADM	Verso	Planning HTML/CSS class with Todd
	1 hour	ADM	Astro Cabs	Reviewing documentation/Focus Group PDFs
	3 hours	PRD	Verso	Learning ?Playing with Flash
	1.5 hours	PMG	High Five	Editing Reviews
	1 hour	ADM	Verso	Email
	1 hour	ADM	High Five	Surfing
6.11.97	1 hour	PRD/ADM	Verso	Production meeting with Sparky
	0.75 hour	ADM	Verso	Database meeting with Eddie
	0.5 hour	ADM	Verso	Misc. Errands
	0.5 hour	TEK	Astro Cabs	Researching Server issues
	5 hours	PRD	Astro Cabs	HTML/Image Processing
6.12.97	2 hours	PRD	Astro Cabs	Animated GIFs
	1.75 hour	TEK	Astro Cabs	Working on JavaScript browser-detect
	0.5 hour	PMG	Astro Cabs	Updating Project Site
	1 hour	ADM	Verso	Process class
	1.5 hours	ADM	Verso	Email
	1 hour	ADM	High Five	Surfing
	0.25 hour	TEK	Verso	Creating new accounts
6.13.97	2 hours	PMG	Verso Editions	Proofing Chapters 3,5
	0.75 hour	PMG	High Five	Conference Call
	0.25 hour	ADM	Verso	Filling out timesheet
Total	35.0			

Time sheets are not just an exercise – the more accurately you fill them out, the better your estimates will be.

Time-Tracking Methods

Off-the-shelf software 11%
None 28%
Database (in-house) 21%
Paper 40%

Time-tracking methods.
Source: Verso Editions web-developer survey

All changes to the site must go through the producer *and* the production manager. Designers aren't allowed to sneak over and ask a production person for a quick change to something. Even if a change is local, it may have global ramifications. The production manager should document all changes as the site progresses. One way is to leave a Word file on the local server that anyone can annotate whenever he makes even a small change. Ideally, the production department would use a database or time/billing/reporting software to log what people do during the day and track specific activities. Keep a set of checklists to use during various phases of a project.

Time tracking

Have all team members take ten minutes each day noting how much time they spend doing various activities. Break billable activities into 15-minute increments. It helps you bill accurately and it helps you refine your estimates and track your margins. Make a form like the one shown and ask people to fill it out twice a day: before lunch and just before leaving. Create categories that make sense to clients and to your internal review process.

If that doesn't work, have each member of the team send email at the end of the day, detailing how much time he spent on various tasks. The producer can send a blank "form" email message every day around 5PM asking people to fill out and return them. Make it part of the producer's job to take everyone's data and enter it into a time-tracking program (or spreadsheet) daily.

Most agencies have an in-house database that does project tracking and resource management. Such systems are not cheap to build or maintain, but the expense is worth it to be able to track a project carefully. The investment pays off in improved processes and estimates.

Asset management

Web production is usually a team effort. One of the most common problems among teams is asset management – the physical tracking of various parts that make up a site. You can divide asset management into two components: *asset libraries* and *version control*.

Asset libraries. Because most computers are now connected via local-area networks (LAN), put master copies of everything on a local server for easy transfer. Asset libraries should contain fonts, images, text, clip-art, programs, files for keeping notes, lists, checklists, and other resources the design and production teams might need.

Version control. If one person is working on a file and another person starts working on a copy of it simultaneously, you have a version problem. Or if you open a file, thinking it's the latest but it isn't, you have a version problem. For many years, version-control programs have been available to people developing software. They function as librarians, requiring each file to be "checked out." This kind of software for multimedia assets is just beginning to show up (see pointers on the book site for relevant vendors).

The folder method of version control

If you don't have a dedicated program, you can still do it the old-fashioned way: using the folder method. The folder method establishes a set of folders on your LAN server that contain all the required assets for the project, including project documentation and notes.

Rules for using a folder-based approach to version control:

1. Set up major deliverables, milestones, test versions, and releases in their own set of folders. Migrate the assets to the new folders as they pass their milestones.

2. Give each area of the site its own folder, and each set of assets within the area its own folder (images, text, animations, etc.).

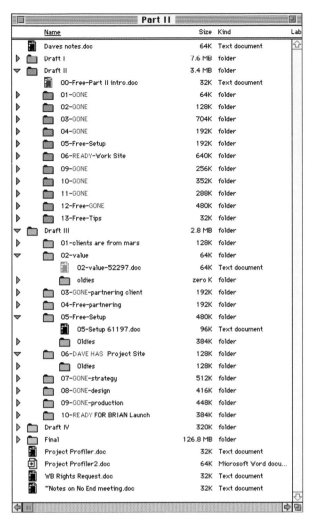

Setting up a folder-based library gives you control over your assets. This one is for the chapters for this book. A name attached to a file means it's "checked out" to that person.

3. Create a folder called "Oldies" within every folder, so the current version is up front, and all earlier versions are sorted by date in the Oldies folder. Treat this folder as a trash can and archive.

4. The folder name designates ownership. Use words like "FREE," "SENT," "READY," "QA-DONE" to indicate status, and names to indicate who is currently the owner of the folder. Anyone may read the contents of the folder, but only the owner may write to it.

5. After a period of heavy work on a file, throw a copy into the Oldies folder and rename the file with the current date. Back up everything nightly.

Automation

It's the contractor's job to save the client money. If a repetitive task comes up, the contractor must decide whether to build a tool or use brute force.

In some cases, you can build a special automated system (consisting of scripts and techniques), so the client can "turn the crank" and add new elements. This allows the client team to create new banners, for instance, when they don't have the expertise to do careful image manipulation.

It might be worth developing or buying a tool (a program, a script, or a system) to make your job easier. Yet it might be unfair to bill the client for the full creation or purchase of the tool. If you can reuse a tool, don't charge for all of its development.

Client-side scripting

Design groups frequently use custom client-side scripts to make their sites come alive. As browsers become more capable, document designers become application/interaction designers. Most of the headaches in web production these days are in cross-platform client-side functionality: *scripting*. Talent aside, it takes a lot of research to write the most current JavaScript, ActiveX, Lingo, or Java. It promises only to become more confusing.

While it's great to have the latest whiz-bang features on your site – many clients walk in the door demanding certain technical features – it's also easy to be cut by the bleeding edge of web technology. Maintaining two sets of code is tricky, if not expensive. Writing rollovers in Java is a virtual invitation to go get a cup of coffee before the site can respond to user input. The playing field changes weekly. What looks like a safe investment can turn out to be an expensive science experiment.

Staffing

Many creative people are not suited to the rigors of production. However, there is another kind of person who has a passion for making things. A good production person takes pride in every piece of every product she builds. A *great* production person also loves the challenge of improving her process, becoming more efficient, improving quality, and finding new ways to stay ahead.

This phase of the project boils down to carpentry: measuring, cutting, fitting, adjusting, testing. Web designers must take pride in their carpentry. People who take a craftsman-like attitude to their products will produce clean code and thorough documentation.

It is better to start people on either the design track or the production track and keep the two sides separate. In a small firm, people do both, and it can be beneficial. Don't ask designers to do production if they are not truly suited to the task.

Scripting — **Jonathan Nelson on**

"For one client, we spent about six weeks building a site. The night before it was to launch, an engineer tried to change one misspelled word that occurred throughout the site. He wrote a UNIX script to do this, but instead of changing the word, his script managed to erase the entire site at midnight. The site was due at 9AM. The staff didn't call me, because they didn't want me to worry. Instead, they called everyone in the company and rebuilt the entire site (hundreds of pages) from a 2-week old backup. I walked in and asked why people were asleep on the floors, but the site launched and it was perfect – well, almost perfect."

– Jonathan Nelson, CEO, Organic Online

If you've bid the project, and the client adds a feature to the shipping set, he has most likely exceeded the scope of the project as described in the contract. It is essential to get an email message from the client acknowledging the change, the increased charge, and the impact on the ship date.

Change orders are common. Don't accept them from someone who doesn't have authority. Keep an eye on the "not to exceed" price specified in the contract. If you're executing a change order every week, you probably missed a step during Phase One.

No longer the facilitator of creative exploration, the producer is an express train, racing to get the beta site up and running. The producer drives the train with clear, constant communication.

Regular communication

Good producers communicate regularly. Predictably. If you have a regular team message, send it at the same time every day. The biggest fear is that of the unknown; regular communications give everyone a sense of stability. If you have meetings, have them regularly. If you have a weekly summary, make sure it's on time and covers everything, including what *hasn't* happened. This measured approach to communication builds trust. Mention something that might become a problem, then report when the problem is solved. This way, you set up a method of addressing difficult subjects in a way the client trusts, giving you a foundation for communicating under difficult circumstances later. Indeed, it's what you *don't* say that the client has bad dreams about.

An expression we use during this phase is "Kill and move on." Put new ideas into Release 2.0 and keep the team focused on the launch date.

Content wrangling

The producer is in charge of delivering the site, and the client is usually in charge of delivering the content. When talking with other designers, I hear the same thing over and over: "Why can't clients get their content in on time?" In most cases, clients don't know exactly what the content should be. They've never done it before, so they have a hard time getting started. **Design firms don't want to hear this, but content problems are *their* responsibility.**

Most of the time, all you have to do is break the process down into small, deliverable chunks, so the client can go after them. Agree on a practical content-development plan, then get the client's permission to remind them to deliver each piece by a certain date. Leave room in the schedule for new developments. Establish a strong paper trail. Ask for content and strict ramifications for late arrival. It must be clear to the client team that a delay in content constitutes a delay in the project. If they're not getting it to you, you haven't set up the right conditions for them to deliver it.

What can the producer do to make the client's job easy? Can the producer locate a good freelance writer who can help? Can the producer set up a weekly content-review meeting to go over what has been done and what still needs more attention?

One thing that will help is to designate someone at the client company to be an editor and someone to be the contentmaster. If possible, the client team leader should not have either of these roles. An *editor* is in charge of the nature and quality of the content. Editors often write, but they also assign, manage, and use outside contractors to generate stories, images, tutorials, etc. It's okay to hire a freelance editor. A *contentmaster*, on the other hand, is in charge of rounding up the content and getting it ready to go on the site. When the client team leader volunteers to be editor and contentmaster, you may be heading for a *showdown*.

The number-one reason for sites launching late is late content arrival. Late content can lead to one of two kinds of showdowns: late, and too late.

The bad hair day

We delivered a model to a client once, and they said they were "extremely disappointed." Everything we had done was wrong, and our relationship was in jeopardy. We decided to keep a low profile and see what they would do next. After a few days, they called and said everything was fine. They were completely pleased with our work. It turned out that the previous two days had been the end of the quarter – the quarterly results hadn't been what they were supposed to be. The next day, the storm was over. The project picked up where it had been a few days earlier. You don't get points for good diplomacy, you get to keep going.

Regular communication

"Projects can go awry for many reasons, but most often it is because of a lack of communication or misunderstanding. The fickle and changing nature of the Web, as well as the complex browser/platform issues, can confuse and frustrate anyone. Sometimes it can be as simple as misunderstanding a term, like template or design spec.

"The producer should speak with the client in person at least twice a week. In every conversation, review what you've completed, what you're working on now, and what's coming up in the schedule. Radio silence is a definite warning sign. Get them involved – discuss their level of satisfaction and comfort with the process. Have the client repeat the action items back to you. If they can clearly express what you've discussed, they've definitely understood you."

– **Christina Cheney, producer, Studio Verso**

Late but not too late. The project is still more or less on track. The client knows the date has slipped because he hasn't supplied the content on time, and the contractor can still juggle resources to finish the site when it comes in. The contractor should recognize that the problem may be one of unreasonably rushing the client or failing to insist on the content as the project proceeds. In this case, make every effort to reschedule and leave enough time to generate the content. If the client has repeatedly failed to deliver, be very clear about what the next steps are. Tell the client that the project is close to being rescheduled. Be direct and firm – one more delay could lead to a reset.

Too late. The contractor doesn't see getting the content anytime soon and must concentrate on getting more work while the client gets content together. This is a reset situation (see below). If the client doesn't want to pay the contractor to sit around waiting for the content, then the client must get back in line when he has the content ready. He can't expect the contractor to jump when it finally comes in.

Problems

An **unforced error** is an issue the contractor should know about or be responsible for. Unforced errors are more likely to grow into problems, because no one likes communicating them. If you've set up a daily communiqué, you will have a way to mention things that may need attention later.

A **forced error** is beyond the control of the contractor. If you're working with another group, or through an intermediary, make it very clear who is responsible for what. Although it is nice to have solidarity among contractors, your allegiance is to the client.

Treat clients exactly as you would want to be treated in the same situation. One possibility is to discuss protocol ahead of time. Ask them what level of detail they want and think about possible scenarios for what can go wrong and ways to handle them.

Resets and meltdowns

In difficult situations, don't react, and don't be provoked. It's not personal. Try to get to the root of the problem. Understand what the client's issues are and address them. Ask them to explain the situation from their point of view.

A **reset** occurs when an error causes a complete halt to the project, a reassessment of the progress and payments so far, and a rejustification for moving forward. A reset almost always results in delays, increased expenses to the client, and a strain on the relationship.

There are no fixed rules for handling resets. They can depend on how much money you owe the client or the client owes you. Be consistent in your messages to the client. Never give a client an absolute deadline without foreclosing on that date. Never promise something by a certain date without being able to deliver. If the client owes you money, take the project site down until further discussion reopens the project. If you owe the client money, do not take the project site down, but come to an agreement before agreeing to return money. If you must return the client's money, do so immediately, no matter what it takes.

A **meltdown** is a complete halt to the relationship. At this point, the project is over. It's time to minimize losses. Let a few days go by to blow off steam; then contact the client in writing. Use fax or letters, rather than email, because it's easier to avoid heated exchanges. Neither group wants the other saying negative things about them; they want to settle and move on. Use a mediator if necessary. Try to settle amicably, on terms that let both sides feel it was unfortunate, but not intentional. Because you can't deduct uncollected debts from your tax bill, turn the account over to Dun and Bradstreet for collection, if necessary.

Six types of errors

CLIENT UNFORCED	CLIENT FORCED
Doesn't deliver content	Changes in personnel force new approach
Doesn't come to meetings or respond	Changes in budget halt work
Can't decide	Changes in product force changes in site
Reverses earlier decisions	Client's competitor launches new site
Decisionmaker sets new priorities	New deadline reprioritizes project
Too many feature demands	Public relations problem comes up, demanding site response
Failure to pay bills halts work	Client team leader removed from project

ENGINEERING UNFORCED	ENGINEERING FORCED
Too many programmers	Problems found in underlying technology
Bad programming	New industry shift causes reevaluation
Bad documentation or communication	Hackers or viruses cause problems
Bad bug tracking	
Too many features, goals too ambitious	

CONTRACTOR UNFORCED	CONTRACTOR FORCED
Distracted by other jobs/potential jobs	Company problems distract or derail project
Hired poor subcontractors	Personal problems distract or derail
Failed to give warning of possible problem	Hackers or viruses cause problems
Failure to back up and archive files	
Burned out, lack of energy	
Sloppy production work leads to many fixes	
In over their heads – cannot pull it off	

Identify and discuss possible problems before they come up.

The production manager prepares to show the product to the world, starting with a small circle of production people, then widening the circle to include the whole contractor team, the client core team, the client company, beta testers, and so on, until the site is ready to launch.

Engineering

If the site has significant back-end functionality, the gating factor on this phase will be software, not HTML. Problems in this phase usually result from overly optimistic engineers or incompatible systems. How you handle problems depends on the engineering group's relationship to the client. There are three kinds of engineering groups: the client's in-house group, the third-party group, and the group within or subcontracted by the contractor.

The third-party group, hired by the client. Everyone reports to the client, and the client must juggle two fishbowls at once, making sure everyone works together and staying in the middle on all decisions. Work with them in the closest possible way, but your allegiance is to the client. If they don't perform, you must be in a position to defend and help your client. Clear documentation will keep you on the client's good side.

The in-house client group. We have worked with a number of clients whose engineering team built the back-end database for the site. It often goes quite smoothly, though it can take longer than expected. When dealing with engineers inside a client organization, you should know that engineers can be your best allies:

They hate politics and can see when you are right, even if others in their company don't. Usually, you can get the straight story from a programmer, which helps you understand the rest of the organization.

They don't understand the principles of visual design and have little appreciation for the work designers do. For some reason, they tend to think they are user-interface aficionados. Once they see the merits of a particular course, they will redesign their software.

The subcontractor group. A small number of design groups have in-house engineering. Most subcontract to outside engineering firms. In this situation, the producer needs a very tight working relationship with the engineering group. The engineering project manager should report directly to the producer. While it's critical to communicate everything in written documents, it's also important to invite the engineering team to as many meetings and demos as possible.

In all cases, the producer must notify the engineering group immediately if the specs for the site change. Because something probably *will* change, a producer will put this kind of notification service in place at the

A client speaks out

A friend of mine, a producer at a large entertainment company, gives us the client's side of the story:

"Developers and production companies need to know that their main client contact *really is doing everything possible* to get content quickly, though it doesn't often appear that way. The department spearheading the Internet project may not have support from all the various content holders. Some groups may not be in favor of the project – maybe they think they should be running the project. These folks could be reluctant to help. You have to tread lightly, not push too hard. Sometimes you run into red tape and have to justify why you need this information and how you're going to display it. Be patient – clients are often doing their best to get you what you need."

– Donna, a producer at a large entertainment company

beginning of the production phase. One of the best ways to make a project late is to discover that the two teams have been working to different specs. This is, in fact, a spectacularly good way to blow up the project just days before launch.

Database testing

The engineering team – working on architecture, schema, middleware, and server-technology issues – needs deadlines to show their progress. The two tests they should pass are the *walk-through* and the *run-through*.

The walk-through (engineering alpha). At some point, the programmers show the first set of subroutines and determine whether several of the core features "sort of work" together. This is something the project manager should see – that the engine is basically working underneath, even though it isn't pretty.

The run-through (engineering beta). Now the programmers show a working version of the system. Assuming the feature set has remained fairly stable, the lead programmer sets a date for a tour of the system, usually with dummy data and not quite everything implemented yet. The interface should be text only, and the topology of the site should be exactly that of the HTML beta test. The only thing that counts is functionality: what can you ask it and what can it tell you? If you can debug the system using a text-only interface that corresponds exactly to the functionality of the beta site, you are on track.

Site testing

No team should work for more than two weeks without a set of deliverables. During production, each team should be responsible for immediate, tangible deliverables that keep them focused on the next leg of the journey. For example, as the team develops pages, they must periodically undergo a *browser-compatibility check* to make sure everything is being done correctly, not just on the development platform but under simulated viewing conditions. Keep checking as you go, moving piecework through the loop and verifying that it is done to spec.

When the top two levels of the site and a few third-level pages are ready, the production team should demonstrate their work. Showing a version of the site lets your team test possibilities. The two major milestones are the alpha and beta tests.

Secret Weapon Number Ten

Treat clients individually

We once worked with a team leader who had a hard time getting us content. We were sending him two email messages a day as we got more behind in the schedule. Finally, he told us that we should call him and ask for one thing at a time. It turned out that he received over a hundred messages a day. When we started calling him in the morning, before he got too busy, he started sending us a steady stream of material that kept the production wheels turning.

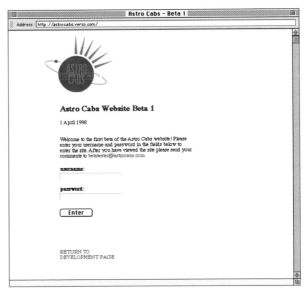

Give testers their own entrance to a beta site. Tell them what you're hoping to learn and how to give feedback.

Alpha test. The alpha test is the first version of the site worth criticizing. The feature set may not be finalized (wording on navigational elements, exact areas of the site to be ready at launch, etc.), and several of the areas aren't ready for prime time, but the site basically works.

At this point, it's worth a meeting with the client to show that the project is on schedule. Ask the client to come in for this meeting. If you have to put it on the project site, be clear about what your objectives are and who should see it. Do not open it for comment to anyone but the core client team.

Beta test. The site takes its maiden voyage on the developer's server with a few of the behind-the-scenes scripts hooked up. This test is mostly one of HTML and navigation. If there is to be a back-end database, it contains only dummy data. There may still be a few unresolved issues, but the development team is anxious for feedback on whether the site is generally working.

Show the beta site to people inside the company, show it to the sales force – but put the feedback in proper perspective. Bring in an eager group of real customers and watch them go through the site. Their feedback is more important than any other. Be diligent in documenting the feedback. When you've compiled the results and decided which changes to make, you have your *punch list*, which is a sign that you're ready to begin Phase Four.

Content is king

In the early 1920s, James Gamble Rogers was asked to design Yale's Sterling Memorial Library, which was to be one of the greatest libraries in the world. It was to hold 3.5-million volumes on 16 levels of climate-controlled stacks. Rogers, a Yale graduate, designed a welded steel frame with a stone façade. The building took four years to construct and became the centerpiece of the campus when it opened in 1931.

Before construction started, Yale threw a party to celebrate completion of the models and drawings for the structure. The great architect was widely acknowledged as having done a superb job, and the models were lovingly fawned over by members of the intelligencia gathered for the occasion. At one point during the party, a young woman came up to Rogers and complimented him on his work.

As the story goes, the woman said something like, "Mr Rogers, you certainly are a magician with stone and steel!" to which Rogers replied, "I'm certainly glad you approve."

"Oh, yes," she exclaimed, "to design such a wonderfully strong tower, one that reaches into the sky and still supports the weight of all those great books!"

She looked around, but Rogers was gone. He had run back to his drawing room. Breathing hard and sweating profusely, he began recalculating the structural reinforcements the tower would need to accommodate the weight of more than three million books.

1. Use consistent nomenclature.

2. Standardize your graphic dimensions into a hierarchy with as few size classes as possible. For instance, big header, subhead, thumbnail, full graphic, etc. Graphic sizes 1 through 5.

3. Determine the optimal palette for images in a class and use that palette on all images in that class. Use DeBabelizer scripts when necessary to assure consistent quality.

4. Use comments in your code to communicate to engineering and content people.

5. Use exactly the same code on different pages to facilitate global search and replace.

6. Strip comments and collapse the HTML (removing carriage returns) for larger pages.

7. Use your tools to the fullest extent possible and upgrade your tool kit regularly.

8. Back up your work every day.

9. Check your work on both browsers and all major platforms.

10. Test, test, and retest – keep shipping versions people can try and give feedback on.

"Real artists ship."

— Steve Jobs

Chapter 10
Phase Four – Launch and maintenance

The beta test has gone well.
People are excited.
The press releases are being written.
All eyes are on the production team.

Launch and maintenance

Chapter guide

AFTER MONTHS OF PREPARATION, it would be an understatement to say the client is anxious for the site to go up. Yet much remains to be done.

Phase Four begins with a punch list and a ship date. The database and the visual elements of the site come together, and the contentmaster adds the content. The developer tests and passes the site before moving it to the final hosting server – possibly behind a firewall. Content flow stops. The final QA team releases the site. After all the aches and pains, the phone calls and the meetings, the site is born. The bad news is that this phase never ends. Sites are like children – sometimes colicky, sometimes precious, a source of pride, and always in need of attention.

This phase is really two phases: the launch of the site on a specific date and the ongoing maintenance of the site for the next several years. It would help, however, if clients saw these two as part of an integrated continuum of service, rather than a date on which they can stop paying the contractor.

1 Launch

In space-shuttle terms, it's time to move the launch vehicle onto the pad, add fuel, step back, and throttle up.

Photo: Nasa

In a typical job, the remaining big task is to get the final content into the site and working on the staging server. Many details still need attention. A punch list might include:

File and page-name fixes
Spelling fixes
Make more banners/headers
Add latest content to all sections
Get CGI scripts running
Update links
Add meta tags
Ensure all images:
    are tagged with dimensions
    conform to color cube
    conform to project color and image
    specs have "ALT" tags
Add copyright and legal disclaimers
Use bold and italic consistently
Specify default:
    background colors
    fonts
    style sheets

The punch list

Staging the site

Typically, the contractor develops the site on her own server – a combination of hardware and software. Clients usually host their own sites or use a commercial hosting service. *Staging a web site* is the process of bringing up the new site on the target machine and preparing to flip the switch. Once it's uploaded, it's ready for final QA and load testing.

This is rarely a smooth process. Before Phase Four begins, meet with the hosting team to go over the delivery protocol. Only a few things can go wrong at this point, and they almost always do.

New server hardware. It's the same software, sitting on a new machine. Transferring the site should be a piece of cake. Wrong. Each machine has its own set of identifying numbers, different amounts of RAM, and probably different drivers. What works on one machine doesn't necessarily work on another. For example, PCs allow spaces and periods in file names, but UNIX machines don't. Because of domain-name propagation delay, it can take up to a week to move to a new server.

New server software. A year-old server is already out of date. Not the machine – the software. It's entirely likely your new site will go up on new server software, or at least a new version. If there's a database or a commercial application running on the site, it will have its own server requirements. Make one change at a time. The more you try to change simultaneously, the more difficult it is to debug.

RAM requirements. Web sites usually need more RAM than they do processor horsepower. Start with 64 megabytes and prepare to double that. A webmaster can help assess your hardware needs.

In the spring of 1996, we moved from Palo Alto to a new office in San Francisco. We got our Internet connection and router set up, then we grabbed the machine and drove it up to the city. During this time, the site was down, and people were frustrated because they couldn't get into our sites. When the server arrived, we had to buy new cables and get the system talking to the new router. It took two days, and the email complaints about our sites built up. We also had to get our new address to propagate throughout the Domain Name System, which took almost a full week. Because we had to install new server software to work with our new router, all our CGI scripts stopped working and weren't fixed for almost a month.

Later, a webmaster told me: "Dave, that's not how you move a server. First, you transfer everything to a temporary server and let the Domain Name System adjust to that new server while keeping your old one running. When the new server becomes dominant, you pull the old one, move it, get everything working, then let the new address propagate through the system."

Security problems. Your server doesn't have a firewall. The target server does. Getting things behind firewalls is not easy. I was once given a password to the Pathfinder site, so I could load my files onto it. Instead of giving me the password, they sent me a little device that displays a new huge number every 30 seconds. It's synchronized with the password-changing program on the Pathfinder server. I tell this story to emphasize how serious some people are about their security – you could run into a few delays getting past the server police.

Legal problems. While preparing to launch an annual report site, we knew we would be cutting the deadline close. We had no time to train anyone how to format the pages properly. We needed to get the quarterly financial data on the server in time to have it go live by 9AM in New York. Because we were under nondisclosure, the client suggested sending us the data the afternoon before by courier. We would spend that night formatting it and putting it on their server. I did not want to have sensitive data in my hands for any length of time. Before the data went public, I didn't want to be part of the chain of secrecy. We decided to have one of our team go to the client's office at 6AM and format it on their computer, which let us get it up by 7AM our time, 10AM EST.

A more common legal problem, of course, is that of rights and notices. Lawyers want a chance to approve everything and make sure proper disclaimers are posted on the site. Make sure you understand any legal requirements in advance.

The gatekeeper. Large companies sometimes have webmasters whose job is to let no content onto their servers unless it is checked, scrubbed, devirused, zipped, unzipped, sanitized, and vaporized. Sometimes it seems their job is to make sure no relevant content reaches the server without properly aging it in large bins, serving it only after it is a week out of date.

Gatekeepers aren't often interested in making your life easier or their lives more complicated. Instead, they have elaborate procedures to make a spelling change. Although they mean well, they are guardians, not facilitators. You may need help from a higher authority in the company. One solution is to host the site somewhere else and get the gatekeeper to put one link on the main site that points to your server. That way, you don't have to bother them again with your content.

Cutting-edge problems. Engineers like to play with the latest, coolest, most untested software. The culture of the Web encourages the commercial use of free software, most of which has plenty of bugs and security holes. Even commercial companies like Netscape have problems with quality control, because they are busy readying the next release. If I listed the cutting-edge problems, the list would already be out of date. Engineers tend to over-promise; put stability and reliability at the top of your list.

Final quality assurance (QA). If possible, the people who built the site should not do their own QA testing. At best, a specialized team of testers with every known browser and system goes through the site and sends you detailed comments. At the very least, have people QA the parts they didn't do. Spelling mistakes are easiest to miss. Make sure an editor reviews the site.

Final approval. You may have to give a presentation at this point. Scheduling a presentation to upper management is probably not appropriate, because you may not be 100%

together at meeting time. You might have other things to do before the site goes live. As we've seen in Part I, few sites are ready an hour before launch. My advice is to get decisionmakers to sign off on the final beta, launch the site, and invite them to see it when things are running smoothly.

Load testing. One of the most vexing thing to webmasters is that peak traffic occurs during the noon hour on the East Coast and then later on the West Coast, with Monday being the biggest day for surfing. That means your server has to handle the Monday lunch hour with ease, then sit around unstressed for the rest of the week. If only we could distribute that load!

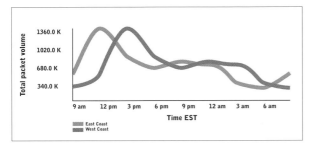

The camel-humps of web traffic: noon on the East Coast and noon on the West Coast.

Instead, we prepare for battle conditions and over-engineer our servers. While it's hard to simulate load conditions, you can try. Ask as many people as possible to test the site at the exact same time on a particular day. You can write or buy a program that will test your site and give you a report on its performance.

Flipping the switch

The server has been staged, tested, load tested, and it's ready for prime time. All you have to do is flip the switch. How do you feel about surprises?

If you have a site that's been up for a long time, you probably have some regular visitors. If you've done your homework, you've brought several of them in during the process of creating the site. One way to ease regular visitors in is to provide a link at the top of the existing page, saying "Here's a sneak preview of our new site!" Then you can watch the traffic for a few days and learn some things. This is actually a "public beta," a good opportunity to get feedback from your regulars before throwing the big switch.

After launching the new site, do the reverse: leave a link on the front page that leads to your old site. This will prevent any mail about how the old site was so much better. Easing the transition will win you points among your regulars until they are used to the new design and can establish roots. Eventually, the old site will wither away, and no one will complain.

Countdowns can help build anticipation for a new site launch.

Working with a PR firm can increase your traffic significantly. You can do PR both online and in traditional print media. I recently saw a "news" item in the *New York Times* Sunday business section "informing" me of IBM's new online annual report. This is not news. This is good PR.

The text-only site

A small group of people will prefer to surf your site with images turned off, even if you're launching an online kaleidoscope shop. They seem bent on discovering visual sites and sending voluminous email about the difficulty of surfing the site.

If you have used "ALT" tags throughout your site, it may be fairly surfable without making a special edition. Otherwise, make a text-only site and keep it up to date. The most common complaint about text-only sites is that the content lags behind the main site.

Documentation

The amount of documentation you deliver for a site is not proportional to the size or complexity of the site. It's proportional to the client's perceived documentation requirements. Most web sites are fairly self-documenting. There are processes you might want to explain, and there might be a few tricks to reveal, but if you turn over the assets to the site and spend a day with the client's technical staff, that should do it.

Some clients require volumes of documentation. If the client is capable of maintaining a site, more documentation is better. A programmer should supply sufficient documentation for a database. You may want to bring in a tech writer to help. A client who wants documentation should expect to pay for it.

Database integration

In some cases, you can wait until Phase Four to integrate the database with the templates. In larger projects, the beta tests during Phase Three require more integration to show the site in action. After debugging the database and getting the HTML ready separately, it's time to integrate them. Put the final set of templates into the database and get it all working. If you are using a content-management system (see "Maintenance contracts"), this integration process may have taken place long ago. If you've planned the templates well, everything will fit together.

When building templates by hand, comment the code so it's very clear to the engineers which features correspond to which code and where the "content holes" are. The final step after getting everything working is to remove or reduce these comments.

I like to make the credits page film-style, using a center gutter, with gray text on a black background.

Send your press releases out just *after* the site launches and you know it's performing. If you know you can get a certain amount of material up on a certain day, you may want to put up a *countdown* – a visible indication of your commitment. A countdown is a great way to build anticipation and get that first group of people to come. It's an invitation to a party. The higher you set expectations, the more you must do to meet them on launch day.

The credits page

It's appropriate to add a link to a page of credits to the front page of the site. If you're doing *pro bono* work, or if you're giving a client a good price, this page should be part of the deal. If you're charging full price, let the client decide. I like to put credits and awards on one page, with the client team listed first.

The most important reason to add this page is to provide a link to the contractor's site. If the client decides not to add this page, you still have the site in your

Secret Weapon Number Twelve

The producer who can handle two projects

"Ideally, every project would be big enough to have a dedicated producer. But with most firms, the producer must master the art of juggling multiple clients and projects. To do this well, a producer's best friend is organization. When things get tight and one of your projects encounters a speed bump, you'll be able to make quick decisions. Experienced producers should be able to handle two fairly large projects at any one time, as long as they don't have simultaneous deadlines."

– Christina Cheney, producer, Studio Verso

portfolio. If someone wants to find out who designed the site, they will find you.

The launch party

Don't forget to have a launch party! The one thing to remember about launch parties is to have them two weeks after the site launches. By then you'll be rested and ready to celebrate. The bugs will be worked out and the site will be running smoothly. Save a few surprises for this event and launch them the day of the party. You will be doing the client a favor, since all the hard work will reflect on her. Who's she going to call when she needs more work?

Launch and maintenance

1 Launch	
2 Maintenance	*The day the site launches, the maintenance phase begins. A smooth transition is a result of good planning and setting expectations properly.*

Hosting

Web designers are often set up to host a small site, but keeping your site up and running is not their core business. Hosting services run from simple *co-location* (they plug in your machine and hook it up to the Internet – you do the rest) to full-service data hotels complete with hardware, software, and content updates. Not surprisingly, you get what you pay for.

Look at it from the hosting perspective. Making a profit hosting sites is difficult. As soon as your employees become knowledgeable, they get offers from companies willing to double their salaries. You need enough bandwidth to handle the peak traffic, yet few clients are willing to pay for it. You need enough redundancy so nobody gets mad at you when the rest of the Internet breaks. The headaches are many, the rewards are few.

Contractors should spend time helping the client find a good hosting situation. Here are a few things to consider.

Multiple carriers. Two of the largest (backbone) carriers of the Internet are MCI and Sprint, both of whom are scrambling to add capacity. A good hosting service hooks to at least two main carriers, giving you redundant access to the Internet. When something happens to the Internet in Denver, a lot of traffic gets rerouted through Dallas. Dallas bogs down, making traffic slow for everyone. Always look for an ISP with plenty of redundancy.

Scalability. Most hosting facilities have found a niche where they make money without giving each client special attention. If your needs grow, their abilities to help you may not. You will become one of their problem sites – a money-loser. They will not be responsive. Offering them more money doesn't help, because they're not set up to meet your growing needs. As your traffic increases, reconsider your hosting options.

Responsiveness. How well does the hosting group understand your needs? Do they offer tracking and good server stats? Can they cache often-visited pages? Can they do load-balancing among machines or give you more short-term bandwidth if your site is chosen as a High Five (or another award) one week, sending thousands of curious visitors to your site? Will the system alert them automatically when something bad happens to your server? Do their people wear beepers? Are they making money off you? If they aren't, you're in trouble.

Find out how they handle emergencies. Make sure they can reboot your machine if it needs rebooting. Be sure that your site won't be dark for three hours before they notice something is wrong.

Security. Like most office buildings, most servers are fairly secure. Webmasters generally use a level of protection that keeps the inquisitive people out. Keeping the bad guys out is much, much harder. If someone really wants your credit-card number, he will get it – one way or another. As with buildings, security is much more a matter of perception and risk than actual hardware and software. In general, more security implies more inconvenience. For most applications, reasonable security precautions take care of 99% of problems.

Backups. Back up your site nightly, so you always have a fallback version. If something goes wrong with your site – the hard disk fails (rare) or parts of it get erased (less rare) – a good hosting service can hot-swap a new version of your site back into place.

Performance-based contracts. Make sure your hosting contract is based on measurable performance parameters of your site. You don't want to pay for bandwidth, you want to pay for the number of people who can be snorkeling around in your site at one time without bumping into each

TIP

Don't measure hits! A *hit* is any file downloaded. If you have a web page with ten images on it, each time a person successfully views that page, your server will register eleven hits: one for each image and one for the HTML file that describes the page. Hits are a meaningless unit of traffic measurement.

other. And you want to pay for attention, in case your server needs it.

Instead, negotiate contracts that pay the hosting service based on accurate reports measuring the responsiveness of your site. Expect to pay more to cover contingencies, but your server won't go down if your power supply fails.

Traffic tracking. Systems for tracking traffic through your site range from free to more than $200K. They all require attention to set up and keep running properly. A tracking system is like an accounting system: once you've collected the data, it's only as good as the reports you ask it for.

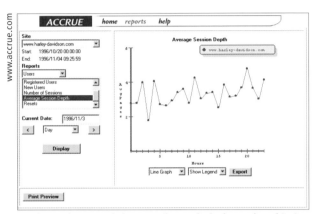

Tracking software can help you understand whether you're achieving your goals or not.

The two things to watch when reviewing your site-traffic logs are the number of visitors coming to your front page and the ratio of visitors continuing through the site. Do most of them get to the second level, but then almost no one goes deeper? That's a sign your home page is doing its job, but your neighborhood pages are weak. Does everyone go right to one specific second-level page? If so, either strengthen that area to serve them better, or strengthen the other areas to attract more visitors, or both.

Maintenance contracts

At meetings among designers, maintenance contracts are a hot topic. Here is the situation:

- Developers are happy to maintain sites if they can make money doing so.
- Clients run out of money when sites are finished and want to do everything in house.
- Web sites look dramatically different just a few short months after launch.

Security is a hot topic among web aficionados, but most web developers don't encounter problems.

Secret Weapon Number Thirteen

Content management versus project management

A web designer uses a project-management system (i.e., a project site) to design and build a client's web site. The client then uses a content-management system to run the site day-to-day, creating content and templates that work with the original design. Both of these tools are rapidly becoming more powerful and more affordable.

Science experiments: some clients are determined to use every trick in the book.

– Designers' portfolios on the Web never link directly back to the client's URL, because designers usually don't want to be associated with changes made to the site since delivery.

Clients have a hard time holding together the overall look-and-feel of a site. They are subject to *button politics* – a situation where people whose content is off the front page wage battles to get their links high up on the first page. They can't resist adding shortcuts and extra icons. There's usually someone at a client's business who "knows HTML," and that person is rarely up to the task of maintaining the production, content, and design values of the site. After a few months, most sites have turned into science experiments.

Designers have a simple solution: kill and move on. They can spend the same amount of time getting a new client and building a new site. Design makes more money than maintenance, and it adds to the client list. Larger ad agencies tend to host and maintain clients' sites under lucrative maintenance contracts, mostly because the clients have no other choice. Smaller groups save a separate version for their portfolio, so they can show it the way they delivered it.

Clients underestimate maintenance. The first year of operation of a web site can cost from one-half to two times as much as the site cost to build. Not to maintain a site is to throw away the money you spent creating it. The two options are to receive on-site training or sign up for a maintenance contract.

On-site training. If a client wants to take ownership of the site, training is more valuable than documentation. For most dynamic (database-driven) sites, clients should expect and contractors should deliver a content-management system. For static sites, clients may need to learn the intricacies of a site's HTML and style sheets. After a day or two of training, the client team should be able to make headers and pages. They should understand the production standards used to build the site. If they can do most of the day-to-day production, they will find it helpful to continue working with the design firm on both the 1.1 and 2.0 releases of the site.

Maintenance contracts are rare. They are usually by the month, with specified amounts of either hours or work to be performed. Sometimes they take the form of a monthly retainer. They are often a package deal: hosting, maintenance, staging and uploading of new content and sometimes even handling email.

Contractors should include standard six-month maintenance contracts as part of an ongoing relationship with the client. Wouldn't it be great if clients asked for this as part of the overall project? An ideal six-month maintenance contract would include these services:

Implement Release 1.1
Train client to do content updates
Help with graphics
Weekly check of site and fix bugs
Weekly server statistics report
Regular site strategy meetings
Develop new releases as needed

Editorial schedule

The *editor* is in charge of the editorial content of a site. The *contentmaster* is in charge of gathering all the content. These two people work closely with *contributors* to keep the flow of content to the site steady. The following guidelines are from Doug Millison, a former Adobe web-site editor who is now a web editorial consultant.

Everything takes twice as long as expected. When working with staff writers and with freelance contributors, I assign a deadline with enough leeway to start over in case the writer misses a deadline. The schedule must also take into consideration all the variables of web page design, the realities of getting all necessary art elements in hand, and producing a finished article.

I work with a calendar that breaks down each editorial element (feature story, interview, profile, news story, press release, etc.) to a series of tasks, and then project deadlines, and assign responsibilities for each task:

– story proposal (Includes a summary paragraph and outline)
– storyboard (the visual elaboration of the outline)
– first draft of text
– second draft (includes graphics, URLS, etc.)
– final copy to designer/HTML markup
– pages proofed, tested, corrected
– final pages posted to the web server

Everything needs rewriting. Writing for the Web is not writing for print. When you see your writing on a web site, the first thing you want to do is rewrite it. You have to take it apart and reassemble it before it looks right. Is there too much clicking or scrolling? Does it encourage people to keep going? Writers cannot take for granted that people

MONTH	COVER	PROFILE	WEEK	REVIEW	FEATURE
FEB 97	JON LEONG	BRAD JOHNSON	12	STUDENT CONTEST	ABOUT THE REDESIGN
			19	BORDER=0	- JEN WOLF
			26	PIONEER ELEC.	
MAR 97	PURVI SHAH	ROGER LOS	5	MUNGO PARK	IDENTITY
			12	PROJECT NZ	- JOE GILLESPIE
			19	FASHION PLANET	
			26	BOHEMIA LAB	
APR 97	CHRISTIAN COSAS	PHOENIX POP (SIMON & BRUCE)	2	SKI DOO	BRANDING
			9	QUIET FOXES	- JOE GILLESPIE
			16	TYPO SPACE	
			23	TBWA /CHIAT/DAY	
MAY 97	CHRIS SCHMITT	SALON	7	REFUGE!	THE PIT -DAVID SIEGEL
			14	JONES & JONES	
			21	VIEW ASKEW	THE PENDULUM -DAVID SIEGEL
			28	ELLIOTT/DICKENS	
JUNE 97	LANCE ARTHUR	AMY FRANCES-CHINI	4	THIS GIRL	FUTURE OF THE WEB
			11	COSMOS MAG /PAVELU	
			18	REVO	- JOE GILLESPIE
			25	4AD	

▓ = WRITTEN   ▓ = CONTACTED   ▓ = NEED TO CONTACT

Plan your content as far in advance as possible.

will read the next paragraph – articles should be short, to the point, and entertaining or provocative.

You can never have too many contingency options. In the magazine and newspaper world, a managing editor always has extra material to substitute when articles do not come in on deadline. An editor should cultivate article submissions from freelancers and should have columnists and feature producers working at least a month in advance. In the event that everybody meets deadlines, an editor has the enviable task of selecting the best.

Content management

In the newspaper business, special systems manage *workflow*. A writer researches a story and submits a draft. The system notifies an editor that the draft has arrived, and the editor puts the draft into the publishing schedule. The editor reviews the piece and calls out opportunities for photos or illustrations. The system then notifies the photographer and illustrator, and they submit their first attempts as the writer makes changes. The system tracks the assets for the project and maintains an audit trail of previous versions and decisions. The writer submits a final draft, it goes for fact checking, credits, and proofreading, then the system helps the layout department add it to the paper.

This is what a content-management system does for a web site. A *content-management system* is a butler that gives site owners a friendly, useable front-end to interacting with the database that drives it. It is a layer of *middleware* between the database and the Web that allows writers, illustrators, designers, editors, and proofreaders to work with their content, not the HTML. Today, these systems are expensive, but they are paving the way for lower-priced solutions in the future.

The basis of a content-management system is the tagging schema. A *tagging schema* associates extra information, called *metadata*, with each piece of content in a site. It "tags" a certain piece of writing as a movie review, a feature story, an ad banner, a sports score, etc. It has the date the information is fresh and when it should be removed from the system. Metadata helps the database determine a given piece of content's role in the larger scheme of the site.

Another example of metadata would be the indexable words for a book. If I were using a content-management system to publish this book, when I first wrote the word "metadata," I would have been able to tag it as an index word. The system would then find all occurrences of the word and build the index automatically. I would simply add a bit of information about how I wanted the index to look, and the system would do the rest.

Release 1.1 spec

After Phase One, you might have some new ideas, and you might have to throw some features overboard to get the site launched. After the site stabilizes, you have time to revisit these features. Release 1.1 should be fixes and items you meant to do but didn't have time. Don't have the

Product Code:
Reg: 46014

Capacity:
Reg: 6,000 cu. in./100 L

Extended Capacity:
7,000 cu. in./117 L

Weight:
Reg: 6 lb. 7 oz./2,920 gm

Material:
500 Denier Cordura Hexstop

Feature 1:
500 Denier Cordura Hexstop Ripstop fabric is structured like a honeycomb for durability.

Feature 2:
Silent zipper pull tabs.

Feature 3:
Dual daisy chains for modular system.

Feature 4:
Occipital Pocket allows for natural head movement.

1.1 meeting until you have some measurable feedback from the site. Decide what goes into Release 1.1 and begin to plan Release 2.0.

Release 2.0 spec

I think of a web year as being somewhere between three and four months. A web year is a concept to show that you have to keep moving. With that in mind, release 2.0 is right around the corner. Maybe it involves a new database or commerce server. Maybe it involves partnering with other sites. Maybe it's a tie-in to your print campaign once the site is doing well. While most companies leave their designers behind and expect to produce Release 2.0 in house, they would benefit from working together.

Plan a second release to keep the customers happy. If the first release is a success, the managers will have more resources to play with. Rather than spreading the site in new directions, look for opportunities to capitalize on your existing market – the visitors to your site who don't participate or buy. Do what you can to convert them into paying customers.

Once you've captured a market, go for new markets. You may want to internationalize your site. If so, do it one market at a time and look for countries where people don't have to pay their phone bills by the minute (not Internet-access charges, local connection charges). Expand into markets that capitalize on the success of your first release.

Contractors with large clients should try to establish a longer-term relationship, working on new releases and new sites for other parts of the business.

Cow creativity

Cow is a 20-person cutting-edge design group in Pasadena, California. Their approach is a bit different from what I've outlined in this book. I spoke with Bryan Dorsey, one of the founders.

David Siegel: What is Cow?

Bryan Dorsey: Cow is an interactive communications company specializing in interface design and interactivity. We don't believe in traditional titles, because we name our people for their core strengths. When working with Cow, you'll find yourself among people with titles like *motive, focus, vision, human, discover, storyteller,* etc.

DS What's so special about what you do?

BD Our strength is in a process we call *Interface Realization.* Interface Realization creates powerful, modular communication tools. We believe in interface systems that focus around one context, something we refer to as one-ness. We also believe in a strong use of classical typography around content that is rationed out in small bites. Cow uses these and other core principles and philosophies to consistently explore new forms of interactive language, unlocking the power of information.

DS Wow. And you don't have producers?

BD We abandoned the idea of "producers" and "project managers" because we truly feel there is no one person who should manage all aspects of what we do. Instead, we have a horizontal structure of management, broken down into four horizontal areas of expertise: strategy, content, design, and technology. Within each area, our projects are managed by the people who know their respective area the best. This empowerment within the Cow culture works very well for us, allowing us to cultivate specialties that can be leveraged across all our clients.

DS Dare I ask about your tools?

BD One of Cow's proprietary tools is called *The Brain.*™ The Brain is used to pre-build entire web sites before they go into production. This tool allows us to test the interface structure and eventually build the entire site (think of it as an engine that creates engines). Our engineers build these custom "smart machines" that build thousands of web elements for every site we do – in about 90 seconds. These elements, layered with JavaScript sounds and animated GIFs, create a superior web product that's faster and 100% cross-platform stable.

We've also created *DummyMaker*™. DummyMaker is a Macromedia Director application used to create dummy graphics (all named and color-coded visually) for entire sites. This is a great tool for cranking out graphics on the fly to feed into The Brain.

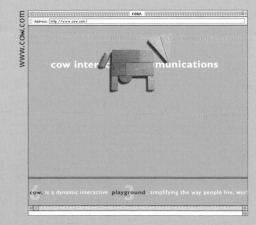

Client Team	Phases and Actions	Project Management	Design Staff	Technical Staff
	Phase 1: Strategy and tactics			
	Project Tools	●		
●	Contract	●		
●	Schedule	●		
●	Questionnaires	●		
	User Models	●	●	
●	Goals & Requirements			
	Strategic Brief	●	●	
	Creative Brief	●	●	
	Technical Brief	●	●	●
●	Basic Content Plan	●	●	
	Site Map	●	●	●
	Engineering Specification	●	●	●
	Final Schedule	●	●	
	Final Estimate	●		
	Phase 2: Creative development			
●	Content Identification	●	●	
●	Content Schedule	●		
●	Content Development	●	●	
●	Editing and Preperation	●	●	
	Initial Design Studies (concepting / branding)	●	●	
	Comps (look and feel / navigation / UI)	●	●	●
		●		
	Prototypes (final direction)	●	●	●
	Working Model (implementation)	●	●	
	Phase 3: Technical development			
	Production	●	●	●
	Engineering	●	●	●
	Alpha	●	●	●
	Internal QA	●	●	●
	Beta 1, 2	●	●	●
	Internal QA	●	●	●
	Final Internal Site	●	●	●
	Phase 4: Delivery			
●	Content Freeze	●		
●	External Staging	●	●	●
●	External QA	●	●	●
●	Site Measurement	●	●	●
	Documentation/Templates	●	●	●
	Preflight Check	●	●	●
●	Launch	●		●
	Strategy Assessment	●	●	
●	Maintenance	●	●	●

"We're on safari to stay."

– The Beach Boys, "Surfin' USA"

No one said building web sites was easy, but it pales in comparison to the challenges of interpersonal communication.

IF YOU COMMUNICATE WELL, you will be successful not only as a producer but also in other endeavors. In this chapter I summarize my thoughts on the process, the relationships, and the relatively new field of online design.

Architecture vs. advertising

More and more, clients are treating web developers as ad agencies – they expect sales pitches, pretty graphics, and snappy copy. While there certainly are web developers who work by the page or crank out banner ads by the dozen, most of us are capable of working with a client to arrive at a custom-tailored solution. We think of ourselves as architects – creative problem solvers who will try to work within a budget to create a company's home on the Web. After the client company moves in, they will have to live there for a reasonable period of time, so they might as well feel it's a good investment.

Like a successful building, a successful web site must be efficient and nice to look at, but it must also be comfy. It should suit the company and its image. It should be a source of pride for the whole company. It should invite people in and give them a place to stay as long as they like. As web developers learn how to help their clients serve their customers, perhaps web sites will become more like sponsored community centers than corporate lobbies.

Results count. You can take the same budget and the same number of hours and build two different sites – one gets measurable results, while the other gets a few looks but no repeat visitors. It's not the designer's job just to take what the client hands over and build a site out of it. Contractors should challenge their clients to offer something unique. They must see the project together, from the same side of the table, as a chance to serve the customer.

The process is more important than the final deliverables. Focus on the process, and you'll get where you want to go. Focus on the deliverables, and you'll end up trying to hit a moving target.

Trade show booth design

If architects have been solving these kinds of problems for thousands of years, another group of people has been doing something perhaps even more directly applicable to web design. Even before there were cities, there were markets – places where traders would meet to see and exchange goods. Trade show booths are similar to web sites, because a trade show – or perhaps an old-fashioned bazaar, or a World's Fair, or a midway – is a good model for the Web. People come wandering by your booth, often with bemused expressions of partial interest, often because they just swerved to avoid a crowd somewhere else, or because someone told them to come pick up the free samples you're handing out. Now you must draw them in and start them on their way from knowing nothing about your company to being dedicated, die-hard fans.

Trade show booths, must be more than just well designed – they must be engineered to hold up under many kinds of stress. Booth designers are the ultimate collaborators, working to help clients attract more customers while making sure the booth packs, ships, and stores economically. If they build a booth that doesn't do its job, they won't get much more work from that client. So they must step back and help their clients focus on what they want to get out of their exhibit and their events.

Web development is like web development

Most ad agencies don't build good web sites, because their cultures support neither the soft sell nor the rocket science necessary to construct a winning site. Web development is different from architecture in that the technology and tools of web development change faster than those of designing and building physical structures. Web development is different from trade show booth design in that the scale of the web is much larger, and the constant need for change is much greater. It isn't like television production, and it isn't like graphic design. It's like web development.

Site design has its own pace, its own set of unwritten rules, and its own way of separating the contractors from the hobbyists. As developers, we take pride in our work, but we must earn the respect of our clients if we are to call ourselves professionals. We can always learn from our clients, and we can always do better. It's one thing to work through a technical problem; it's another to admit your mistakes and take responsibility for difficult clients or projects.

We're human, just as clients are human. We're our own worst enemy. We get lazy. We forget to tell someone when something has changed. We have our bad days. We have our frustrations with the browser companies, the tool makers, the service providers. By our nature, we're not the most patient people in the world.

That is why I wanted to write a book on project management. The most important aspect of any project is the relationship you build through communication. For only when you would work together again under similar circumstances can you say a project is truly successful.

What does the future hold
for web developers and their clients?
A steady stream of surprises.
It is our job to read the
swirling tea leaves to
help our clients predict
what will happen next.

The only school where you can truly learn how to run a small business is the School of Hard Knocks. No one teaches you that clients usually don't know what they want, even if they say they do. Or that a company with a $30K budget will be willing to spend $60K if you can properly explain the benefits. Or that big companies take forever to pay. Or that forced client errors almost always factor into any project. These are things you must learn on your own. Fortunately, several books help shed light on these issues. If you've made it this far, you'll probably be interested in reading a few of them.

The Business Side of Creativity, by Cameron S. Foote, W. W. Norton, 1996.
– An excellent how-to guide for starting your own creative consulting firm, including forms, business plans, and other resources.

5-Phase Project Management: A Practical Planning and Implementation Guide, by Joseph Weiss and Robert Wysocki, Addison Wesley, 1992.
– Short and clear.

The Fountainheadache, by Andy Pressman, John Wiley and Sons, 1995.
– Great stories of architects and their clients.

The Business of Graphic Design: A Sensible Approach, by Ed Gold, Watson-Guptill, 1985.
– Full of practical advice and good tips from well known designers.

The Seven Habits of Highly Effective People, by Steven Covey, Simon & Schuster, 1989.
– Read before every project.

Crossing the Chasm: Marketing and Selling High-Tech Products to Mainstream Customers, by Michael Moore, Harper Collins, 1991.
– Learn to help clients solve their business problems.

Paul Segal – trade show booth designer

Paul Segal, of Segal Design in San Francisco, is a trade show booth designer and producer. His one-man operation is a model for producers who want to work on their own, and his business is remarkably similar to that of many web designers. He designed Apple's modular grid-based show-booth system and has worked for a number of high-profile clients.

David Siegel: How are trade shows different from other media?

Paul Segal: Trade shows are a different world. At a trade show, you'll see 25 guys in suits lined up for half an hour waiting to throw a basketball into a hoop — for a chance to win a t-shirt! You have to get people's attention, give them something, deliver a message, draw them in to learn more about the product. It's a real challenge when there is an overdose of bright lights, sounds, crowds, and models in short skirts handing out cookies at the booth across the aisle. A show booth has to maximize impact during a brief period of very heavy traffic. People who go away saying they'll come back later rarely do.

DS Sounds familiar. Why do companies even go to trade shows?

PS Brochures only go so far. You have to tell a story. A booth offers an experience you can't replicate any other way: touching, feeling, asking questions. You have to try to measure results that can be very incremental and difficult to pin down. Only by looking at the year-long picture can you see what a trade show effort really does for a company.

DS How much does a show booth cost?

PS There's cost to build, and there's cost to run. To design and build a custom booth, costs range from $50 to $100 per square foot and go even higher. But then there's all the labor costs involved in mounting a show. One three-day show can easily cost as much to put on as it does to build the booth. Even fairly small companies can spend half a million dollars per year on their trade show efforts.

DS Who are your clients?

PS Most of my clients are marketing communications people. They are logistics people – they're not used to working at a strategic level. The person responsible for a show booth is often on the bottom of the marketing totem pole. It's a thankless job few people really want to do. They often don't understand the practical aspects of building a booth, and they don't go to the proper lengths to plan and staff it during a show. The people who staff the booth are often those who can put it up and tear it down, or those whose schedule allows attendance.

DS What's the biggest problem you face?

PS Clients with no content. They come in asking for the latest materials or graphics. A few years ago, every exhibit you saw had an inverted cone. Teal was a big cliché. The sheet-metal look was a big cliché. Clients want something that looks cool. They often want booths designed around their business card. In the Eighties, it was maroon and gray. Now it's distressed type and halogen lighting.

I ask, 'What's the message? What message do you want people walking by to get?' Give it to me in ten words or less. People coming by a booth give you about two seconds to get a message across before they go somewhere else.

If you're lucky, you're working with a client who has something to say. For example, a booth often has a theater, where you can present a ten to fifteen minute show. They want elaborate theaters with great acoustics and visibility, but what is the content? What's the show about? They'll put it together later. Where's your producer? What story are you going to tell? What's the beginning, middle, and end? They think, 'We'll build a theater and people will come.' You need to build up, introduce, deliver, and follow-up on your message, or your effort will be a missed opportunity.

A startup once asked me to design a booth for a new high-tech product. It was their first big show. They just wanted their name on the booth – in huge letters. They wanted to establish their brand. I asked them to consider a message that explained what their product did. No one cares about your name. What the heck do you *do*?

DS How do you sell your services?

PS Most of my work comes in over the transom. I don't do much marketing. It's all word of mouth. I'll do three to four proposals (for big projects) a year. If there's a new client I want, I will work hard on a proposal without giving free creative work. Larger companies are profitable because they are interested in maximum impact. But the sales cycle is long. You have to stay with them. You do some smaller projects to get in the door. Everything is based on relationships. Get in and get people to know your name. They hire people they like. I see a lot of RFPs where they've already chosen a vendor, and they just want some other bids to get a lower price out of their favorite vendor. Small shops will respond to you if you're a big client, but I try to figure out what's really going on. I try to get in there and show them my work and establish a relationship early.

The rest of the time, I fill in with three to five quick projects per month, mostly art direction and working with subcontractors. I like to keep moving, do a lot of projects, then take the summers off and travel.

DS Aren't small projects less profitable?

PS Ah, that's interesting: I have small projects worked out. I know exactly how much work it takes to bid a small project and make money. Sometimes the budget is fixed, sometimes it's hourly with a not-to-exceed. It's a good deal for companies to use me as the art director to solve the problem, design the exhibit, and get it done.

I can make the most money when I do a large project and stay under my estimated hours. I make a margin on my subcontractors, who also give me fixed bids.

DS Do you get repeat business?

PS Trade show booths usually hold up, but companies want a new look every few years. I get a lot of repeat business. I also get a lot of referrals. I have friends all over the place.

DS How do you deal with clueless clients?

PS Bad clients require a lot of hand-holding. I have a high tolerance for dumb clients. I tend to stick with them and make it work. I can put up with a lot.

Client management is one of the most important things I do. You just have to make decisions and move on. You have to know who's responsible for the decision. I prefer to show things to the president for a larger project. Presenting to mid-level people is often a problem because they don't own the decision. It's easy to go in circles when there's no clear responsibility on their end.

DS How do you work with their budgets?

PS Booths are more expensive than many clients think. There are a lot of packing and installation details to consider, not to mention shipping and storage costs. Clients do better when the booth comes out of their yearly marketing budget, not the sales budget.

I always try to work within their budgets, but they are usually budgeting to have a booth built, not to get certain results over time. They really don't look hard enough at their return on the investment. Often, they go to trade shows just because their competition is there, and they're expected to show. Some companies attend more than 40 shows a year – in many cases they might do better to put more effort into fewer shows.

You can't budget properly unless you know what a success is. 'Looks cool' is not my definition of a success. It's important to lay out the criteria for success up front. Once I'm involved with a client, I often bill by the hour to get started on strategy and then implement a fixed bid later, when we have the goals set. I often give a range of prices and ideas and let them choose what they want.

DS What is the secret to a successful trade show booth?

PS Theater. Drama. Tell a story that people want to hear. Events really work. It's worth it to do something very well fewer times. Don't just rent a magician in a tux. Create something special. Figure out ways to get people to walk around being billboards. It's not about having cool buttons and t-shirts, it's about people *wanting to wear* the buttons and t-shirts, and telling their friends about what's going on.

Contact Paul Segal at segaldzn@slip.net

AFTERWORD

I wrote this book, in part, to help legitimize site design as a profession. I want people to think of us as architects on the Information Superhighway, not gas-station attendants. I want artists to respect our new visual language and engineers to respect our technical acumen. I want high-school students to dream of becoming professional site designers. I want to see new multidisciplinary programs spring up to challenge the established design curricula, whose tenured proponents have been struck by new media like deer in the headlights of an oncoming 18-wheeler. I want to give web designers their own special awards for solving hard problems.

The good news is that we are already on the way. It's happening, often in the least likely of places. Hobbyists are becoming proprietors, partnerships are forming, clients are turning into contractors, and a few design teachers have figured out how to make web pages before their students did. In contrast to the desktop-publishing revolution, the Web allows people to collaborate from a distance, making a single person sitting at a computer at home with a modem as powerful as any corporation. Those who find their niches and handle their clients well are part of a growing community of online professionals. Associations are springing up. Word of mouth is more effective than ever.

The multidisciplinary demands of the Web favor the creative generalist, a person thought dead as the Seventies dawned and the MBAs took over. Generalists have no problem switching careers. Generalists, not specialists, explore new frontiers. Generalists are leading the online revolution. If you want a great site, find yourself a great generalist – an impresario – someone who can work with you on your business strategy, apply that strategy to the Web, and put a team together to implement that strategy.

Surfing is truly an appropriate metaphor for life on the Web. Those of us who have made surfing our profession know that we must continue to live by our wits. We must deliberately put ourselves out of business every six months; if we don't, someone else will. That is our business plan. The arrival of the Web is the forest fire that removes the old dead wood and allows new seedlings to sprout. We have sprouted, and we must stay flexible to grow. We are not going back to the old days of entrenched middle management and two-year projects. No one is going back.

The communications revolution is a continuous, unpredictable wave of innovation. I find it most thrilling to ride up front, where the wind is deafening and the vibrations are fierce.

Whatever you do,
do it well.

Thank you for visiting
my book.

A

B

ABOUT THIS BOOK

The typefaces used in this book are Meta (designed by Erik Spiekermann) and Rotis (designed by Otl Aicher). The captions are set in Minon italic (designed by Robert Slimbach), and the Secret Weapons are in Monotype Script (designed by FH Steltzer). "The Client Dilemma" (chapter 5) was set in Sabon (designed by Jan Tschichold).

We used Adobe Pagemaker 6.0 on a Macintosh to lay out everything but the cover (for which we used Quark Xpress). We used Adobe Photoshop and Internet Explorer extensively to capture images and convert them from RGB to CMYK (the "Printing inks setup" numbers, for those of you interested, are 24% dot gain, and the gray balance of C: 75%, M: 70%, Y: 80%, K: 70%).

The paper is Champion Influence, 70# soft gloss. The cover is printed in four custom (Pantone) colors and black, with a flat matte protective coating and a spot varnish on top. The cover gets a "double hit" of orange to give the bright, saturated look. The book was printed in Indianapolis, Indiana, by Graphic Arts Center/Shepard Poorman.

You will find links to helpful resources and examples of project sites at the companion site for this book (**www.secretsites.com**), designed and maintained by the Verso Editions team.

ABOUT THE AUTHOR

Since 1995, David Siegel has played a key role in the evolution of design on the Web. He was chosen as a top-100 multimedia producer by Multimedia Producer Magazine and has taught thousands of designers worldwide through his writings, lectures, and award-winning sites. David serves as an advisor to the HTML and STYLE committees of the W3C, the consortium in charge of the further development of standards on the Web. He has consulted for Cisco Systems, the US government, Sony Corporation, and Amazon.com. His design award **www.highfive.com** is in its third year recognizing good design on the Web.

David is the chairman of Studio Verso (**www.verso.com**), a high-end site-design consultancy in San Francisco. Verso has produced web sites for clients like Hewlett Packard, Sony, Klutz Press, StockCenter, Healtheon, Lucent, Navitel, NetObjects, and others. He is also chairman of Vertebrae Technology (**www.vertebrae.com**), a database and applications consulting group that builds back-end systems for web sites, intranets, and extranet projects.

David's previous book, *Creating Killer Web Sites*, was the best-selling book sold on the Web in 1996. His publishing company, Verso Editions, plans to produce many more books on design, tools, business practices, and the phenomenon of the Web. You can learn more about his upcoming books at the web site **www.secretsites.com**.

After receiving his master's degree in digital typography from Stanford University in 1985, he worked at Pixar briefly before going into business for himself. He taught graduate-level computer graphics at Pratt Institute and is active in the theory of story structure in feature films. He is the author of a book on population and environmental issues. David is also known as the designer of several successful typefaces, including Tekton, Graphite, and Eaglefeather. He is a strict vegetarian, consumes no caffeine products, and gives no credibility to the theory that writing causes hair loss in adult white males. Visit his personal web site at **www.dsiegel.com**.

David is a frequent speaker at conferences and seminars worldwide. He may be reached by sending email to **david@secretsites.com**.

```
Date: Wed, 14 Aug 1996 14:55:40 +0100
From: ian
To: david@verso.com
Subject: No sleep last night
```

Hi David,

I just wanted to let you know how excited I am. My copy of Creating
Killer Web Sites arrived yesterday - didn't get a wink of sleep last
night!

Many thanks,
Ian

CREATING KILLER WEB SITE**S**

Site Design

David Siegel

Third-generation web site

A *third-generation site* uses typographic and visual layout principles to
describe a page in two dimensions. Third-generation site designers
carefully specify the position and relationships of all elements on the page,
retaining fine control of the layout. Third-generation sites use metaphor
and visual theme to entice and guide, creating a complete experience for
surfers from the first splash screen to the exit.

Creating Killer Web Sites is the runaway best-seller that has taken the web world by
storm! It has been translated into over six languages and is sold around the world as
the definitive guide to making third-generation sites. It was the best-selling book on
the Web in 1996 and continues to tie the basics of design together with the limitations of HTML. Expressed in the familiar writing style of *Secrets of Successful Web
Sites*, this book shows you the nuts and bolts of design on the Web. It will deepen
your understanding of the material presented in this book.

    Creating Killer Web Sites is available at all online bookstores and most walk-in
bookstores. Watch for the Second Edition coming in the Fall of 1997. See the web site
www.killersites.com for details.

Brought to you by Siegel-Brand Single-pixel GIFs, the GIFs
more web developers use to build their third-generation
web sites. Get yours at **www.killersites.com** now!

The best designed
sites
on the
Web
live at the

www.highfive.com